D1592491

Higher Education

MARIJUANA at the MANSION

CONSTANCE BUMGARNER GEE

First published by Dog Ear Publishing
4010 W. 86th Street, Ste. H
Indianapolis, IN 46268
www.dogearpublishing.net

ISBN: 978-1-4575-1365-7

This book is printed on acid-free paper.

Printed in the United States of America

To my mother,
Marie Bensman Bumgarner Campbell,
in celebration of life
and lessons learned.

And to Gordon,
from whom I have learned much
for better or for worse,
but mostly better.

I am not always good and noble. I am the hero of this story, but I have my off moments.

—P. G. Wodehouse, *Love among the Chickens*

Acknowledgments

IT HAS TAKEN ME THREE YEARS of writing, reflection, discussion, and rewriting to produce this book. Many people have been part of this project at various stages; a few have been with me throughout. I am grateful to you all—or rather, all y'all.

I am most indebted to my editors, Stephanie Covington Armstrong and Ed Huddleston. I also want to thank my friends who read the manuscript during its development, offering encouragement and many useful suggestions: Tom Lunsford, Gren Blackall, Don Welch, Debra Gonzalez, Laura Rose, Claudia Brown, and Cat Rudd. And thank you, Robin Mitchell Joyce and Megan Byrd.

It wasn't easy remaining in Nashville after my pratfall from grace. I am blessed to have friends who stood by me, providing comfort in the form of hugs, home cooking, and sauvignon blanc: Jane Dudley and Dwayne Johnson, Hope and Howard Stringer, Andrew Krichels and Bill Brimm, Mary and Michael Spalding, Elizabeth and Donnie Nichols, Bunny Noel, Reiko Zealear, Celeste Reed and Don Welch, Karen and Kent Cochran, Aleene Jackson and Cowboy Jack Clement, Marshall Chapman and Chris Fletcher, Jennifer Kimball and Bob McDill, Robert Hicks, and Manuel. Special thanks from Rasta and me to Fran Wyner, and to Terita Jones for keeping our doghouse in order and for frequently offering up such pearls as "All money ain't good money."

And to East Nashville, Nashville's very own East Village. The best 'hood in town, where everybody knows your dog's name.

1

Out of the Closet and into the Attic

"VANDERBILT REINS IN LAVISH SPENDING of Star Chancellor," announced the *Wall Street Journal* on 26 September 2006. Five months of journalistic sleuthing, which the star chancellor likened to "a public proctological examination," preceded this front-page exposé in the nation's most respected financial newspaper. But the real dish was the tattling subtitle: "Marijuana at the Mansion." Yes! Marijuana had been smoked in "Braeburn," the Vanderbilt University chancellor's residence, by none other than the wife of the chancellor himself.

The reporters on the beat were bent on digging up dirt on Vanderbilt's highly paid chief executive officer, previously a more modestly paid Ivy League president, whom the "Harvard of the South" had swiped from Brown University. Along with the old news that Vanderbilt had spent $6 million to renovate the chancellor's residence six years earlier, it was reported that the chancellor's entertainment tab at the manse was around $700,000 annually, or $4.2 million over six years. The muckrakers' quandary was that the fundraising payoff had added $1.25 billion to the university's endowment—not a bad return on investment.

Clearly, the story of the chancellor's spending was neither as titillating as front-page news necessitates nor damaging enough for the instigators of the inquiry—a small band of disgruntled trustees and high-level administrators—to pull off their intended coup d'état. A crime more foul, an offering to placate publishers and justify a five-month inquiry, was needed. Other than a steamy sex scandal, what could've been better than a pot-smoking wife?

***

Seven unpleasant months later, the then soon-to-be ex-wife—myself, alas—sat atop the mansion's portico roof, peering down on a lawn party two floors below. I had been ordered to remain out of sight during all Braeburn functions. My husband, Gordon Gee, delivered the demand.

"Stay upstairs or make certain to be out of the house before the guests arrive," Gordon instructed me. "It's the *chancellor's* residence. I'm the chancellor, and you're not."

"Nya nya-nya nya nya," I helpfully punctuated.

I had gone from Vanderbilt's first lady to its first persona non grata in a stunningly short time and a quite remarkable manner. I had been strong-armed into filing for divorce, even as I tried to convince myself that this awful mess would soon be sorted out. Gordon and I would cease this foolishness, reunite, and walk arm in arm into the sunset—me, with an extended middle finger aimed at my detractors. We'd spend the next thirty or forty years referring to this period in our lives as "that truly terrible time," and it would serve as the ultimate reminder of how close we had come to destroying our future together. The added bonus would be a renewed passion for each other and for our marriage. Such was the happily-ever-after scene that looped through my mind. It was the only comfort, other than holding my standard poodle, Lucy, to be found.

Remaining out of sight during events at Braeburn was not as simple as hiding away for a couple of hours now and then. Luncheons, cocktail receptions, and dinner parties large and small were held at the residence four or five days a week. Caterers and event planners scurried around the main floor in preparation several hours before each event and then stayed to tidy up afterward.

Although the command was that I disappear during the event so as not to make the guests feel uncomfortable or further embarrass my husband or the university, I felt the greatest humiliation whenever I encountered the staff, especially the waitstaff. I had always made a point to say hello, ask how they were, and joke with them as we all stood in our places, waiting for the show to begin.

2

They, more than anyone there, knew what it was to be invisible. I could see the pity in their eyes when we would meet in a hallway or stairwell as I skirted the main entertaining areas en route to the kitchen or out the back door with Lucy. The once lively mistress of the manor was now a hollow-eyed specter.

As the weather warmed, I hauled one of the eight front-porch rockers and a side table up the elevator to the third floor, hoisting them through one of my office dormer windows and onto Braeburn's expansive two-story, Corinthian-columned portico roof. That way I could still enjoy being outside while guests were being entertained on the first floor and in the garden. The balustrade that enclosed the portico roof, as well as the rocker's placement to the side and back of the roof, made my makeshift patio difficult to see from the front of the house. It was such a wonderful place to sit, it made me a little sad that I had not thought to use it more often over the previous seven years. It would serve as my short-term refuge before I was tossed from the property altogether. The house manager had already inquired several times about the missing rocker, but neither of the other two people who knew of its whereabouts (Chef Bunny and Housekeeper Nancy) ratted on me. Until I left, "The Case of the Missing Rocker" remained a mystery. Perhaps the chair was residing at one of the fraternity houses?

It was a perfect mid-April evening and a large reception was in progress. I had a bird's-eye view of the event from my perch and watched as guests drove up Braeburn's long, horseshoe-shaped driveway, handed over their cars to the out-of-breath valets, and made their way up the portico staircase. I could hear their enthusiastic chatter and knew my husband was standing at the door greeting everyone with a warm handshake or hug and a hearty, "Welcome! So glad you're here!"

In my mind's eye, I could follow the guests' progress through the house. A smartly dressed Vanderbilt student stationed at a table just inside the grand entry hall gave them their nametags. They lifted a glass of wine or sparkling water from a silver tray proffered by a smiling waiter, or made a beeline for the bar at the end of the hall if they preferred the hard stuff. They wound their way among clusters of friends and acquaintances into the chartreuse-hued drawing room, then into the spacious, light-filled conservatory. Some would remain in the conservatory, but the ones with whom I resonated most would exit the cacophony of the house for the garden. Those guests came back into my view as they emerged onto the garden patio. Bistro tables were sprinkled around the patio and out into the garden, their turquoise tablecloths undulating gently in the warm breeze. I appraised the arrangement of the teak patio furniture that was placed beyond the mosaic-tile fountain, farther out into the garden. *The sofa and chairs ought to be grouped more semicircularly and a little closer together*, I thought.

Nancy brought up a plate of food and a glass of wine, handing them to me through the window. She should have brought the whole bottle, I joked. I could clutch it in one hand as I stumbled down the main staircase, wearing nothing but a soiled silk slip à la Grey Gardens, toward scores of horrified upturned faces—the most satisfyingly horrified being my husband's. She chuckled a little apprehensively, not all that certain I wouldn't do it.

I settled back into the rocker, watched the parade of people, and thought about the utter weirdness of my circumstances. If anyone saw me right now—wineglass in hand, sans makeup or any perceptible attempt at a hairdo, peering morosely through the balustrade bars at the unsuspecting hors d'oeuvres hoovers in the garden below—they really would think I was "the crazy woman locked in the attic." I was living a Hitchcock movie.

***

Two months before, I would have been standing by my husband's side welcoming our guests into the residence. But now my own invitation had been rescinded. It was true that I hadn't succeeded at being the perfect presidential spouse, but it wasn't as if Gordon hadn't been afforded a multitude of early warning signals.

Shortly after we'd announced our engagement—he was then the president of Ohio State University and I was a new assistant professor—we attended a small luncheon at a university board member's home. Two other board members and their wives were there as well. Dessert had been served when one of the guests politely asked me about my area of academic research. I was nervous that the spotlight was aimed at me but tried my best to comply, briefly explaining my interest in public policy related to K–12 (kindergarten through high school) arts education—specifically,

4

federal and state legislation that addressed matters of teacher preparation, course content, and budgeting (or the lack thereof) for art and music instruction in public schools. Our host—a towering, cowboy-hat-and-boots Texan—interrupted me in midsentence to expound on the importance of nonprofit arts organizations and artists to K–12 arts education. His wife was on the Ohio Arts Council and, although she remained silent, I surmised he must have gotten much of his commentary from her.

"We need to bring symphonies and artists into the schools," he declared.

No doubt he expected me to agree wholeheartedly with his assertion. My dissertation research, however, had led me to a completely different conclusion. While in a perfect, mega-funded world it would be wonderful to bring local artists and musicians into schools to augment the study of art and music, the reality is that many school districts barely manage to provide students with the most minimal of arts instruction. There is often little money for art materials and musical instruments or, in many cases, no suitably equipped room for teaching either subject. Any public funding available for K–12 art and music instruction, I firmly believed, needed to directly support the efforts of art and music teachers— those who dedicated their professional lives to teaching day in and day out.

"David, you're wrong about that," I said, with the breezy bluntness of someone more used to academic debate than luncheon conversation with university board members. I proceeded to explain the fallacy of his assumption, not noticing the open mouths of the rest of the party (David's and my fiancé's included) until I was already waist deep in it. Blushing violently with the realization that I had embarrassed Gordon and made the rest of the table squirm, I trailed off with a "but it would be wonderful if there were money enough for that, too."

David recovered himself (I imagine this was the first time anyone had flatly told him he was *wrong*) and roared, "Well, Mr. President, it looks to me like you've got yourself a wildcat!"

Luckily, that broke the tension and everyone laughed as I turned an even deeper crimson. After that incident, Gordon often referred to me as his "waldkatze," but he generally did so with an amused expression that seemed to imply he *liked* that about me.

You would have thought that the wildcat incident would have served as fair warning to us both—him, in terms of the dangers of marrying an outspoken and sometimes brash woman, and me, in that I might have tried harder to "curb" my tongue, as Tommy Smothers smugly advised his brother, Dick. Yet, although forever wayward, my tongue hadn't swaggered too far into the oncoming traffic until we ended up at Vanderbilt University in Nashville, Tennessee.

***

Born and bred in North Carolina, I had happily waved goodbye to the South in my early twenties to move to New York City. I had decided on that course of action at age six, when my aunt Nonie took my mother, my two young cousins, and me to the Top of the Sixes restaurant in the penthouse of 666 Fifth Avenue. Sophisticatedly sipping my Shirley Temple with double cherries while gazing languidly at the cars and people forty floors below, I decided then and there that the city life was for me. By junior high, I had chosen my career path as well, and told anyone who expressed an interest that I was going to be an artist and live in New York.

I found the South of my childhood to be an uncomfortably confining place to live. I had some serious political and gender issues with Dixie that became increasingly conspicuous the older I got. I chafed long and hard at the restraints on personal and social conduct imposed by the traditional expectations of southern womanhood. My family's hardcore political conservatism rubbed a raw place on my hide that, although now scarred over, is still sensitive to the touch.

I cheered when Congress passed the Twenty-Sixth Amendment on 1 July 1971 and, as an eighteen-year-old during the 1972 presidential election, I cast my ballot for George McGovern. Everyone else in my family, paternal and maternal sides included, voted for Nixon. One of my very own parents, whom I won't embarrass by naming, voted for George Wallace in the Democratic primary. (Perhaps this was done in the same spiteful, mess-with-their-minds spirit in which I voted for Rick Santorum in the 2012 Tennessee Republican primary. At least I'd like to think so.)

It isn't that I dislike the South. I am a southerner, and to disparage my homeland feels almost treasonous. I do, however, prefer to admire Dixie from a distance. I like her best when I haven't seen her for a while. For example, I never much cared for grits until I moved to New York. Being from Kansas, my mother didn't make grits, and Daddy preferred flat fries. Most of my grits experience came from my elementary school cafeteria, where it was served not infrequently for lunch. I would let the thin gruel coagulate, then peel it off my plate and waggle it at my tablemates—an antic always good for some shrill screams and giggling. After being in New York for a few months, I became unaccountably desperate to reconnect with the very same southern culture I had been so eager to jettison en route to my new big-city life. Thankfully, I discovered the Pink Teacup, a soul food restaurant in the West Village that I could retreat to for some grits, greens, catfish, and cornbread when the infrequent, but urgent, need arose.

Mine was a romanticized kind of affection, as in "absence makes the heart grow fonder," but not so fond as to want to reenter cohabitation. Long-weekend visits home, once every three or four months, were just right. I heartily resonated with Georgia-born and bred humorist (and Massachusetts transplant) Roy Blount Jr., who sustains a genuine, but not unqualified, fondness for the South. Having moved to the Northeast more than four decades ago, he still hasn't managed to *leave* the South. "I keep needing to get back down there," he writes. "*As long as I can get back out again.*"[1]

I left the South, grew up, found my own way, and learned I could deal with conservative cultural and political annoyances for a few days at a time, during my quick trips home. That was all familiar terrain, but the landscape was a lot different in Nashville. By the time I was hauled back down to Dixie, I'd lived up north as long as I had in the South. I'd left as a middle-class twenty-three-year-old and returned at forty-seven into high-cotton class. I was a card-carrying liberal, feminist free spirit who had to relearn to curtsy and say "yes, ma'am," but, more importantly, to hold my fiercely opinionated tongue. The last part didn't work out so well.

Sitting alone atop the portico roof, I was only just beginning to digest the consequences of my disobedience.

2

An Imperfect Beginning

I WASN'T THE ONLY ONE in my family who had wanted to leave the South. My mother, Marie, had dreamed of an escape almost since the day she set foot in my grandfather Bumgarner's house in the backwoods settlement of Plumtree, North Carolina. My grandmother lived in the slightly larger community of Crossnore, three miles east as the crow flies, but substantially farther over the serpentine dirt and barely paved roads. This arrangement was fine with both my grandparents, who were separated but never divorced. Plumtree and Crossnore are in Avery County, in the Blue Ridge Mountains on the North Carolina–Tennessee border. It is a wildly beautiful but rugged place—a seismic topographical shift for a twenty-year-old Kansan who longed for flat and open. The mountains crowded my mother to the point of claustrophobia, but that wasn't why she wanted to leave the South. She wanted to get away from my father, Clifton, to whom she'd been married for a year. She was a tragic Dorothy, with slippers of pink terrycloth, who would never make it back to Kansas except for an annual visit.

It took her six more years to get up the nerve to buy a one-way train ticket back to Salina. By then, she and my father were living in Raleigh. He had earned his law degree and was the newly appointed chief of the Division of Wildlife Enforcement for the North Carolina Wildlife Resources Commission.

"I was packing my bags to leave your father when I found out I was pregnant with you," she said as we sat at a stop sign in Burlington in her tan Oldsmobile Ninety-Eight, waiting to turn right onto Sellars Mill Road. We were driving to a nearby shopping plaza to purchase some back-to-school supplies at Rose's dime store. I was beginning the eighth grade, presumably old enough to understand her womanly predicament thirteen years earlier. She had wanted to leave him ever since, she added, but was afraid of what he would do to her. She told me that she was also worried about how we would survive financially, but that it had gotten to the point where she was ready to take her chances. She wanted to return to her family in Salina.

"Will you come with me to Kansas?" she asked.

"No!" I stammered. "I don't want to leave my friends or Daddy. Please don't go to Kansas!"

Kansas was so god-awful windy and horizontal; I liked the mountains of North Carolina. I was my daddy's girl that way and many other ways. I knew he could be mean. I knew he was mean to my mother. But he was my daddy and I loved him as much as I feared him.

I'd never much liked Kansas, and I didn't feel especially close to my midwestern relatives. My mother and I spent a week in Salina each summer while Daddy stayed home with our beagle, Smoe, whom my mother had named after the shmoos of Al Capp's *Li'l Abner*. (I was two years old when Shmoo came into my life; I couldn't get my tongue around the "shm," so Shmoo became Smoe.) I felt like an alien among my Kansan 4-H cousins. I couldn't imagine hand-raising a calf only to sell it off for slaughter at an auction. I'd sit silently and wide-eyed at the dinner table, overwhelmed by the boisterous Ping-Pong of sibling smart-mouth among the four of them—Dean Ann, Joyce Ann, Jennifer Ann, and Jeffrey Lynn. (Aunt J. Dean and Uncle Gene just kept at it until they got their boy.)

Nobody talked much at our dinner table in Burlington, but then it was just the three of us. We didn't eat until eight o'clock or later. Daddy insisted on drinking for a few hours before he sat down for supper, and by then, keeping quiet was a wiser course of action than risking setting him off by saying the wrong thing. My father usually picked up a six-pack of Budweiser on his way home from his law office, located across the street from the county courthouse in nearby Graham. He'd drive to a park not far from our house, sit in his Carolina blue Ford Mustang listening to the news or a ball game on the radio, and drink a couple of tallboys. There was a brief window for me to talk with him between his arrival home, when he was in a relatively good mood, and when he checked out with the remainder of the six-pack in front of the television until supper.

***

I craved my father's attention and affection, and when, on intermittent occasions, he gave me both I was in heaven. Every Sunday morning I sat on his knee at the kitchen table while he sipped coffee and read the comics to me. We established that routine when I was two or three, and reluctantly gave it up a decade later when I started feeling a little awkward and moved to my own chair, but pulled it up close to his. We read the Sunday comics together until I left for college.

Daddy made cages to house the birds and baby rabbits that our cats mauled, and we nursed more than a few of the wounded back to life. We raised a baby squirrel that had fallen out of his nest and was found by our Chihuahua-terrier puppy, Bébé. I named him Rutherford Lucius. My mother prepared warm milk for him in my baby doll bottles. We all took turns holding Rutherford in a hand towel, feeding him every few hours for a week until he could begin eating a mashed-nuts-and-milk pabulum, which we fed him from an eyedropper. Soon he was able to eat pecans, and Daddy would crack them open for both Rutherford and me. Those were good evenings, when the entire family sat together in the den—my father and mother, Bébé, our two cats (Tiger and Blackie), Rutherford, and me—with Rutherford perched on my shoulder or on the back of my chair as we both greedily devoured the perfectly halved pecans Daddy deposited in a bowl on the coffee table. When it was time for Rutherford to make a living on his own, Daddy and I drove him to the home of a park ranger who lived at the edge of Umstead State Park, west of Raleigh, and whom my father knew through the Wildlife Resources Commission. The last we heard, Rutherford had left behind his feeding station on the ranger's back deck and had started a family of his own a little deeper in the woods.

When the weather was nice, Daddy and I would take a Sunday afternoon stroll on a large tract of wooded land not far from our house. As we walked (with him carrying a small cooler of beer), he would point to a tree or plant and ask me to identify it. He seemed to know everything. I reveled in his approval when I answered correctly, as I often did.

There was a small lake on the property. A long rope swing with a wooden crossbar hung from the branch of a large oak tree that grew out over the water from atop a high bank. I sat or stood on the crossbar and Daddy would pull it back as far as he could, giving me a good push as I shrieked with delight. It was a thrill to fly out over the water. It was a thrill to be with my daddy, except when it wasn't—but then thrills and fear often go hand in hand.

***

"No," I repeated, eyeing my mother. Even at twelve years of age, I knew the decision was mine to make. If I refused to leave my father, then she wouldn't leave either. A twinge of scorn followed a guilt pang of selfishness, as I made her decision for her.

My mother was a good-lookin' woman, a trim size eight, with her light red hair swept up in an elevated, lacquered French twist. She dressed well and looked smart in her clothes, noticeably different from most of my friends' mothers, who didn't wear suits and kid gloves, and who didn't look like they did sit-ups and waist-bends every morning. She also had a job, as a bank teller. "I want my own money," she often said; "I don't want to have to account to your father for every penny." She was generous with her modest paycheck, spending much of it on nice clothing for me. Mother also liked being out in the world and away from the house. I, more than anyone, understood that. It was unnerving always walking on eggshells, hoping Daddy wouldn't get angry about something and fly into a tirade. But she was also a conscientious homemaker. She kept our mostly beige-toned house sparkling. She fried a good chicken and was renowned for her iron skillet cornbread (no sugar), potato salad (lots of chopped eggs and dill pickles), and chicken tetrazzini (too casseroley for my taste, but a favorite at church dinners).

I called my father "Daddy" until the day he died, but I substituted "Mother" for "Mama" early in high school. I suppose I needed or wanted to distance myself from her. I loved my mother, but I don't remember feeling much joy in her presence. I felt sorry for her. My father belittled and hit her—and she allowed it. He called her "stupid." It made me sick to hear him say that, but I sometimes wondered if he wasn't a little right. I well understood her fear of him, and was beginning to grasp her, and now *our*, dependency. We were solidly middle class, equidistant between wealthy and poor. Yet my father was a lawyer, and there were social cachet and financial security in that. My mother knew what it was to grow up dirt poor during the Great Depression on the plains of Kansas. Her daughter, however, had never wanted for anything material. Her financial security and my own depended on remaining with a man who mistreated her, but who would always provide for us. Marie Bensman had made a deal with the devil when she married Captain Willis Clifton Bumgarner.

***

Marie and Clifton met on a tennis court in Salina in the early autumn of 1945. She was eighteen years of age—a petite but shapely strawberry blond with a sprinkle of freckles across her nose, full lips, and large, light blue eyes. He was twenty-nine and strikingly handsome, with his light brown hair combed back off a high forehead in an effortless Douglas Fairbanks Jr. wave. He was six foot one and blue-eyed, with a straight Roman nose and high cheekbones. She was a former high school cheerleader, buoyant with energy and mischievous humor. He was a World War II veteran, disillusioned with humankind, who had recently filed for divorce, and—as he wrote in his diary soon after he began dating my mother—it was taking "a lot of whiskey to keep going."

Clifton Bumgarner had returned from overseas two years earlier, after a fifteen-month tour of duty in Australia and Papua New Guinea as a pilot in the 19th Bomb Squadron of the 22nd Bombardment Group. The 22nd Bomb Group was the first to be deployed in the Pacific Theater after the bombing of Pearl Harbor, heading out of Langley Field, Virginia, on the morning of 8 December 1941 en route to Muroc Army Air Field in the Mojave Desert. Flying west, my father heard the Congressional Declaration of War on the radio compass set of his B-26 Marauder. The 22nd spent the next two months patrolling the west coast for Japanese submarines while continuing to prepare for combat in the southwest Pacific. On 6 February 1942, they shipped out from San

Francisco to Hickam Field, on the banks of Pearl Harbor. He wrote of leaving behind Kit, his wife of eighteen months, who had followed him to California:

> We had time for a brief but ardent goodbye with our wives on the dock before we boarded the U.S.S. *Grant* and pulled out into the harbor for an idle three days prior to sailing. Through a pair of binoculars, I saw a pathetic Kit standing in silent dejection amid a throng of waving, hysterical women, while a patriotic dockworker rowed passionately behind the ship as we slowly left the wharf.

Kit was two months pregnant and seemed to my father "as a very small child alone in an unfriendly world."

At daybreak on the Ides of March, the 19th Squadron took off from Hickam Field, heading south for Amberley Field, near Brisbane, Australia. A few days after the 22nd converged at Amberley, the group moved north to Townsville, where the 19th was based at Garbutt Field. First Lieutenant Bumgarner saw his first combat on 5 April 1942, when the 22nd attacked the Japanese naval base at Rabaul, in New Britain, north of New Guinea.

My father was wounded on 19 April during his third mission to Rabaul, when a swarm of Zero fighters attacked his fleet of seven planes, and all but him and his wing ship "scattered in panic, running hell-bent for election out of there at full throttle." "A B-26 will not outrun a Zero even at full throttle," he noted, "but [Japanese fighter pilots] have the sensible habit of picking on the last man first, and the last two ships were ours, flying close." A 22-millimeter shell exploded through the cockpit of his plane. "They always go after 'tail-ass Charlie,'" he would say when recounting this war story, pulling his sock down so I could see the ragged shrapnel scar on the outside of his left foot, and the stitched-up incision on top of it where the surgeon had extracted the shell fragment. He spent a month at a hospital in Townsville, and another two months in the U.S. Army hospital outside Brisbane, before being discharged and promoted to the rank of captain. In mid-September, the night before he received orders to rejoin the 19th (then based at Iron Range, Australia), he learned that his son, Wingate, had been born two weeks earlier.

My father continued to run bombing missions for the next four months, witnessing as many fiery deaths among the 22nd crews from worn-out, malfunctioning B-26s as from enemy combatants. He and the rest of his squadron were given two weeks' leave in mid-January 1943 after watching one of their two remaining planes falter and then crash during takeoff, killing eight of the twelve men on board. He described the funeral as being "so impersonal that, even though I tried to listen, I could only wonder which casket held Johnson and which held Seffern and Hatch." He swore, "If I ever fly another one of these worn-out crates at all, it won't be in combat."

He was true to his word: although he flew many more bomber planes, it was never again in combat. He'd lost his nerve, and he was drinking to forget. He wrote:

> I feel restless and completely lost when I am idle and entirely sober. You think too much that way. . . . A certain matter has forced itself upon me endlessly for the past few weeks. That is the fear that I have lost my last ounce of guts. I haven't wanted to admit it even to myself, but feel that, if it is ever to be overcome, I must face it and recognize it.
>
> When I see a B-26 flying by, I dread to watch it for fear that, if I do, it will crash before my eyes. As for flying one of them, I don't think I could bring myself to refuse, but it will be a long time before I can do it without the feeling that my number is up and each flight will end the hard, quick way. I never realized how much courage I did have until I lost it. Looking back it seems that I was either a brave man or a fool. At present, I am certainly not brave—but, definitely, a fool.

His commanding officers saw it, too, and after a few more months of noncombat duty, he was awarded a Purple Heart and a Distinguished Flying Cross and sent back to the States. He returned disgusted with himself, with the war, and with those who direct war from their desks while others fight and are destroyed by it.

How can a war be "won" when it destroys the bodies of its best citizens and warps the minds of the rest? The only victory is the victory of war, itself, over the human race. It is as frustrating as a feud wherein each side forgets its original aim and kills for hate and the love of killing, which, in itself, is unnatural and indicative of diseased minds.

Back stateside, he was assigned to Elgin Field, Florida, to test a new type of B-26. From there, he was moved to various Army Air Corps bases to get "checked off" on flying the B-17, B-24, and B-29 and, ultimately, to serve as an instructor pilot for each of those aircraft.

The first thing he did when he reached California after leaving Australia was to hop on a commercial flight to Norfolk, Virginia. He wanted to get back to Kit (whom he wrote about in his diaries with tender affection) and see his new baby boy. His return took her by surprise and, although she seemed delighted to see him, he found a large framed photograph of one Lieutenant John Bishop on her bureau and Bishop's leather jacket in the hall closet. (There was no photograph of my father on the bureau.) He initially forgave her infidelity. "Knowing human desire for companionship," he wrote, "I resolved to attribute these things to my protracted absence, as I, myself, had taken refuge from loneliness and desire when my wife was on the other side of the world."

Kit followed her husband from base to base, but continued to correspond with Bishop, while flirting openly with other young men. My father retaliated with his own affairs, and the marriage quickly began to unravel. In Tucson, he gave her "the spanking of her life" when he connected a series of events that convinced him she had slept with the man who lived in the apartment next to them. She moved out afterward but returned in a few weeks. Soon they moved to Seattle, where their domestic life leveled out a bit, until "the question of her infidelity again reared its ugly head" and he blackened both her eyes. "That was an incident that I have regretted ever since," he wrote a year later. "It was my first time ever to strike a woman with my fists."

From Seattle, he was transferred to McCook, Nebraska, and then to Great Bend, Kansas. The marriage continued to deteriorate, and as they were preparing to move once again—this time to Smokey Hill Army Air Field in Salina—he told Kit that if she wanted to continue living with him she could, but that as soon as he had completed the required year's residence in Kansas, he would file for divorce. Kit took Wingate and moved to Greenwood, Mississippi, shortly after the divorce papers were filed. Two weeks later, my mother and a male friend joined my aunt Nonie and Clifton Bumgarner, a fellow Nonie had recently begun dating, for a mixed-doubles tennis match.

Marie and Clifton married ten months later, on 16 July 1946. "He was so handsome," my mother told me many years later, by way of explaining her initial attraction to my father. He'd been all over the world, or so it seemed to a young woman of nineteen who had only once set foot outside her hometown of Salina. (She and Nonie had taken the train to Denver between their junior and senior years of high school and gotten summer jobs bartending at Lowry Air Force Base by lying about their ages. She'd "never been around alcohol" and inadvertently mixed water in the first beer she served.) He already had a college degree and planned to return for a graduate or professional degree with the assistance of the GI Bill. She had completed high school, but like most women of the time, didn't think of college as a reasonable possibility. The dashing man in the officer's uniform would take care of her, give her more than she had, and make her more than she was. She knew he had a jealous streak, but wasn't that just part of love? Soon after they were married, he began flying into alcohol-fueled rages, cursing at her and unjustly accusing her of flirting with other men. But it was he, not she, who cheated. A month before their first wedding anniversary, she caught him in an affair. So began a terribly unhappy marriage.

Wingate, or "Win," spent part of each summer with my mother and father until the year before I was born, when Kit remarried and moved, leaving no forwarding address. I have never met my half brother, although I think he might live somewhere in Texas.

My mother described her youthful self as being "full of life and mischief," always telling jokes and laughing. In my memory, she rarely did either. "My mother said he [my father] took away my personality," she said. What Grandma meant, I think, is that he quashed her exuberance and destroyed her self-confidence. And while I have never forgiven my father for how he treated my mother, it has also taken me a very long time to forgive my mother for allowing him to do that to her. As an adolescent, the weakness I saw in her sprouted disdain in my heart for her and all women who subjugate themselves to men.

I didn't realize it at the time, but disdain can be a useful coping strategy for a child. It provides a self-preserving alternative to chronic fear and guilt. Although I often felt disdain for my mother, I sometimes *despised* my father. Yet hating him was like hating myself because it was he, not she, whom I strove to emulate.

"I look just like you, Daddy!" I pointed out when I was four years old, while perched on the bathroom counter watching him shave. I had pushed my bangs off my forehead to study my widow's peak and cowlick, which perfectly mimicked his own. When he sat on the sofa reading the newspaper, I sat next to him perusing my picture book.

Disdain is a dreadful emotion, but it is much more easily sustained than hate—especially hate of the person you most adore. So I looked for everything good in him because I could not bear to hate him for long. I told myself that who he was drunk was not who he really was, and for the most part I still believe that.

***

I grew up very much alone. I was alone in the middle of a war zone, barricaded in my bedroom with my dog and cats. I don't think I would have been able to survive without a warm, furry body to hold on to. To this day, the protection and welfare of animals are important to me above all other social causes.

I learned to entertain myself early on. Before going to kindergarten at age four, I was much more often among adults than with other children. "She's in her own little world," adults would say as I sat in their midst coloring, reading, or arranging and rearranging my treasured collection of miniature plastic farm and jungle animals. My own little world was a safer place than their volatile one.

I don't remember doing many things as a family, as a unit of people who are bonded together as father, mother, and child. I did things with my mother and I did things with my father, but we didn't seem to do much together, in the real sense of the word. I know we saw almost every tourist attraction in the North Carolina mountains during visits to see my grandfather and grandmother. I know we went to the North Carolina and South Carolina beaches, although not as frequently as we traveled to the mountains. I know we made a trip to Washington, D.C., to see the national monuments, but I only remember it through snapshots my mother took of me and my best friend, Cathy, who often joined us on trips or when we went out to dinner. When I think of the three of us spending time together at home, I envision us in the den watching television. Daddy is sitting on the right end of the beige sofa smoking a Pall Mall, with a red-and-white Budweiser tallboy on the side table. My mother sits at the opposite end of the sofa, dividing her attention between the television and a *Reader's Digest*. I'm sprawled out to my daddy's right in the overstuffed, red-upholstered, pivoting rocking chair (the only non-neutral-toned furnishing in our house, other than a royal blue velvet wing chair in the living room). I loved that chair and used it like a piece of indoor playground equipment, bobbing back and forth and swinging side to side—occasionally pushing off with enough force to spin around completely. When Cathy was over we'd sit together in the chair, undoubtedly driving my parents a little crazy with our bouncing, spinning, and giggling.

I met Cathy Joanne Rudd in second grade. I had gone to Burlington Day School for kindergarten and first grade, but I begged my parents to let me transfer to Eastlawn, the public elementary school that all the kids in my neighborhood attended. My parents finally relented, although in hindsight I wish they hadn't. I would have been much better off scholastically had I completed grades two through eight at Burlington Day.

I was the new girl in Mrs. Wicker's second-grade class, having transferred two weeks into the school year. I was also the youngest by several months. My parents enrolled me in kindergarten a year early, because my "twin" cousin, Joyce, and I shared a birthday— we were born five minutes apart on 1 December 1953. At that time the kindergarten enrollment cut-off was 1 September in North

Carolina and 1 December in Kansas. My parents reasoned that, if something should happen to them and I had to live with my aunt and uncle, it would be best if I were in the same grade as Joyce. They were able to skirt state law by enrolling me in private school, although because of my emotional immaturity and diminutive stature, it probably would have been better for all concerned if I'd waited a year. Cathy (now Cat) saw a small, towheaded girl with large, round blue eyes and a pixie haircut standing beside the teacher's desk, anxiously looking around at twice as many faces as there had been in Burlington Day's entire second grade. *I'm going to be her friend*, Cat decided. Green-eyed Cat, then a head taller than I was, slipped her arm through mine as we filed out to the playground for recess. We have been best friends since that day, despite our significant age difference of five months—something of which I have annually reminded her ever since she turned thirty and I was still a youthful twenty-nine.

I was a gregarious instigator; I had to be or I wouldn't have had anyone to play with. I was always going over to the homes of other neighborhood children, knocking on the door, and asking if one of them could "come out and play." Carol, who was one year older and lived directly across the street, always made me come inside and play a few games of cards before she and her younger brother would play with me outside. I dislike cards to this day. I always wanted to be outdoors; maybe that was because of the forever-tense situation inside my own home.

My daddy's drinking was no secret, although my mother and I pretended it was. I was aware that most of my friends' parents would not allow them to spend the night at my house, not that I really wanted them to—Lord knows what might have happened. His drinking embarrassed me; I never knew what condition he would be in. He might be mostly sober and affable, or he might be sloppy drunk, walking around the house in his boxer shorts. Most often he was simply unavailable, sitting by himself in the den reading or watching TV with his tallboy and his cigarette.

Cat was my only friend who spent much time at my house; she knew my daddy and seemed to take it all in stride. Cat's parents, Ruby and Bud, didn't mind her spending the night with me, which was a good thing since we were together two or three nights out of the week. My mother paid Cat's mom to take care of me after school. Cat had two older brothers and a younger sister, and Ruby had never worked outside the home. She was a world-class baker and made the best cakes in the world. Her 1-2-3-4 cake, a cocoa cake with thick caramel icing, was our absolute favorite and sent us ricocheting off the walls. After feeding us sugar, glorious sugar (Ruby's hiccup remedy was a heaping teaspoon of Dixie Crystal), she would banish her "frisky ponies" into the backyard to tear around the racetrack.

***

With the exception of third grade, I was a star pupil throughout elementary school. The truth was that I didn't have to put much effort into my school subjects for two years after transferring to Eastlawn. At Burlington Day School, we learned to print our letters and structure simple sentences in kindergarten; we were taught to write in cursive in first grade. Eastlawn made me return to printing throughout second grade and, in third grade, relearn cursive on a 60-degree slant. (We had been taught to write straight up and down at Burlington Day, where I had taken first place in my class for penmanship.) Adding to the 60-degree-cursive trauma was the very odd behavior of my third-grade teacher, Mrs. Alspaugh. Every morning she would deliver an exasperated treatise to a room full of eight-year-olds about the mineral content of Burlington's city water supply. Her lank, orange-tinted hair was much more manageable with the soft water of her former residence on the South Carolina coast! Tall, bony, and yellowish, Mrs. Alspaugh was sweetly indulgent one minute and hysterically irate the next. (Maybe there was something in the water after all.)

The word *sheesh*, of all things, got me in big trouble with Mrs. Alspaugh. I was probably trying to get a laugh from nearby classmates when I said it, but I really didn't think *sheesh* was such a terrible utterance. After all, Daffy Duck said it all the time. Advancing on me from her desk in two long strides, she exploded: "*What did you say?*" I lamely tried to explain about Daffy, but she didn't buy it. My punishment was to remain inside at recess and write "I will not curse" over and over on the blackboard. (Thanks a lot, Warner Brothers!) Mrs. Alspaugh should have counted her blessings; I knew words a lot worse than "sheesh." My father could cuss like Beelzebub himself.

Mrs. Alspaugh gave me my first and only "unsatisfactory" in elementary school, and she gave it to me on conduct. "Resents authority" was scribbled across the comment section of my report card. All I could think of when I read her comment was: *Doesn't everybody?* My parents had begun to have their own doubts about Mrs. Alspaugh, but they did not sanction disrespect from their daughter toward teachers. They especially didn't like my rather evident lack of contrition about my reported impertinence. That is my first clear memory of an insurrection over a perceived injustice. I didn't voice it, but my rebel heart cried: *Yes, I resent authority— especially tyrannical, whimsical authority! I get plenty of that at home.* The creeping tendrils of my suspicion that a lot of adults were unworthy of respect got a hefty dose of fertilizer that school year. Looking back, though, I wonder if Mrs. Alspaugh wasn't a sort of mad prophet.

I was fortunate to have a wonderful fourth-grade teacher, and to have been placed miraculously into an experimental "accelerated" learning class. Mrs. Aldridge's students did so well and loved her so much that she moved with the entire class into fifth grade. Two stable years with Mrs. Aldridge got me back on track attitudinally and academically—until eighth grade.

While most K–12 teachers deserve a great deal more thanks (and pay) than they get, seventh- and eighth-grade teachers warrant special commendation. I will undoubtedly be reincarnated as a middle-school teacher to pay for the sins of this life. By eighth grade, I had gone from trying to get attention by being a good student to trying to get attention by being a wise guy. My mother's "I'd-be-long-gone-from-your-father-if-it-wasn't-for-you" heart-to-heart at the Sellars Mill Road stop sign probably wasn't the most motivational beginning for a new school year. For whatever reasons, I began to act out my resentment of my father's despotism whenever I thought I could get away with it—which of course was *never* in front of my father. After all, I was angry, not suicidal. Consequently, it fell to my mother and to my more emotionally vulnerable teachers to suffer my budding adolescent backlash.

Mrs. Mosley's French class was fertile ground for rebellion. Mrs. Mosley seemed ancient—a small, brittle woman with white, fluffy hair and wire-rim glasses, probably two or three years short of retirement. She was the looniest teacher I'd had since Mrs. Alspaugh. Whenever she dropped a pencil, a piece of paper, or any-

21

thing else on the floor, she'd bend over the item, with an expression of someone forced to take a big bite of roadkill, and exclaim, "Beriberi, jungle rot, bubonic plague!" Plucking a tissue from the ever-present Kleenex box on her desk, she'd grasp the contaminated object between her pincerlike thumb and forefinger, and deposit it into the trash. Poor Mrs. Mosley probably had a serious obsessive-compulsive disorder, but that was decades before most Americans had heard of such a thing.

Once, when she left the classroom for a few minutes, I stuck a large, dead but intact black fly between her flashcards. The entire class held its breath, watching with enlarged pupils as she picked up the deck of flashcards, gave it a couple of straightening taps on her lecture podium, and flipped through it as a dealer would flex a deck of cards. The half-smashed fly fell out into her hands. She shrieked. Some of the students gasped in horror; others burst out in nervous laughter for a brief second until she leveled her eyes on us and said, with the bone-chilling calm of a psychopath, "Who did this?"

Using our adopted French names, she began with a girl seated at the front, across the room from where I sat staring ashen-faced at the floor.

"Did you do this, Françoise?"

"No, Madame Mosley."

"Jean-Paul, did you do this?"

"No, Madame Mosley."

Down the first row and on to the second and third rows she proceeded, asking each student if he or she was the perpetrator of this heinous crime. Angelique (a.k.a. moi) sat doomed at the third desk on the fourth and last row. (I had selected the name Angelique as a joke, one at which Mrs. Mosley herself had chuckled knowingly. She had moved Jean-Paul and me to opposite sides of the room because we egged each other on.) The end of my life had finally come.

"Angelique, did you do this?"

"Yes, Madame Mosley."

"I will see you after class," she said.

"Why did you do this?" she asked, after what seemed like a very long class on the one hand and a very short one on the other, pointing to a flashcard smeared with the greasy remains of a fat, juicy fly.

"Uhhh . . . c'est drôle? Pardon moi, s'il vous plaît," I managed with a flash of inspiration, pinning my hope for continued life on her love of français.

"Pardon*nez*-moi," she corrected. "When Jean-Paul said he didn't do it, I knew it was you," she added with a flicker of a smile, handing me a note to take to the principal's office.

***

I don't remember having any black classmates until ninth grade, and the only reason that stands out in my memory is because of my shameful run-in with Deborah Martin in science class. It wasn't that we didn't have any black students at Broad Street Junior High; we had a few, but only a few, courtesy of the molasses-slow desegregation policy of the Burlington school board. I never thought to befriend a black student; I was more concerned about avoiding them, especially when they clustered together in the courtyard after lunch looking angry and tough.

I was raised to believe that blacks were inferior to whites, and that most black men were to be feared. I was so steeped in bigotry that I never thought to question those prejudices. My unease around black people was the only sensation that made "them" in general, and Deborah Martin in particular, visible to me. Then again, at fourteen and a survivor in my own right, I was focused mostly on Friday-night dances at the YMCA, my first boyfriend, and having my classmates think I was cool, cute, and *normal*— whatever that was. It was the norm in the midsixties among white southerners to think of blacks as an inferior race. Normalcy was mine in that regard, at least.

In spite of the Supreme Court's 1954 decision in *Brown v. Board of Education*, a lot of southern school districts remained segregated. That was certainly the case in the Burlington city schools and the surrounding Alamance County schools. Although there was an experimental program for gifted black students at Hillcrest Elementary, a predominantly white school near downtown, most black elementary-age students attended B. F. Gunn. White junior high students living on the east side of town (as I did) attended Broad Street. White children living in west Burlington went to Turrentine Junior High. All white students living within the Burlington city limits attended Walter M. Williams High School.

Almost all black students, grades seven through twelve, went to Jordan Sellars Junior-Senior High.

It was the spring of 1968—the year before the racial upheaval that would turn Burlington inside out—and things were heating up. Burlington had a population of around thirty-six thousand, about a quarter of them African American. Alamance County was home to many textile mills, including those of Burlington Industries. Burlington was a mostly blue-collar town, socially conservative and culturally more in step with the early 1950s than the late 1960s—but then that was pretty much the way things were in the South. (I didn't find out about Woodstock until the album came out.) The school board's desegregation plan, carried out by Superintendent Brank Proffitt, was to gradually introduce black students into white schools so that white parents and students could just as gradually get used to the idea. If white Burlington had its way, "gradually" would have translated into "glacially," as in sometime during the next Ice Age.

The South's glacial desegregation plan was accomplished through "freedom of choice," a widespread policy that served to undercut *Brown v. Board of Education* by placing the burden of compliance on students and their parents. It was left up to the individual student to apply for transfer from one school to another. The upshot was that no white students moved to black schools, and very few black students transferred to white schools. So fourteen years after the Supreme Court had ruled that school segregation was unconstitutional, only a handful of black students were enrolled at Broad Street Junior High.

Deborah Martin and I were antagonists on the basketball court during gym class. She was at least a foot taller than I was, and a strong athlete, but like many adolescents whose extremities develop faster than their cerebral motor cortex, more than a little ungainly. By choice or planetary alignment, she and I invariably ended up on opposite teams. I was small and nimble, and could run circles around, and virtually through, the long legs of my opponents. Better yet, when the taller girls encircled me, the referee often either couldn't see or wasn't paying much attention to what I was doing—which was fouling the heck out of any opposing team member who had the ball. That person was often Deborah. I'd just reach out and get the ball out of her hands however I could, and no whistle would blow.

I sat in the second desk of the far left row in science class. My good buddy Ray sat behind me, and Deborah sat behind him. Deborah had a real attitude, but of course so did I. My attitude was: aren't I clever, daring, and entertaining? Hers was more along the lines of: you lookin' at *me*?

I have long forgotten the nature of our argument as we took our seats that day, but I do remember several quick exchanges that hissed back and forth between us just as class was about to begin.

"You better shut up!" she said.

She was right, but I always had to have the last word. Thinking that only Ray could hear me, I whispered, "Nigger."

"*What did you call me?*" Deborah burst out.

She jumped up from her desk, came around to the front of mine, and stood towering over me. At this point, the teacher hurried over to find out what was going on.

Jabbing her finger in my face she bellowed, "She called me a nigger!"

"Did you say that?" the teacher demanded, clearly alarmed by Deborah's threatening stance.

I was shaking in my Bass Weejuns. I knew I had crossed the line. I was going to go down big time for calling someone *that*.

"No," I lied.

"Well, I hope not," the teacher said, looking at me with an expression that clearly said: *Are you an idiot?*

"I'm gonna beat you up!" Deborah snarled at me as she stomped back to her seat.

I made certain to stay out of Deborah and her friends' way for the rest of the school year.

Deborah's threat scared me, but not as much as my own rage and my come-to-Jesus comprehension of where, in a flash, it could lead. That was the only time I ever used that word *at* another person, though it would take some time to rid myself of the bigotry I was raised with. Deborah Martin did me a real service. I stepped back from the edge that year, just as much of Burlington was resolutely marching toward it.

***

In May 1968, the Fourth Circuit District Court ruled that the freedom-of-choice plan of the New Kent County, Virginia, school board could not be accepted as a sufficient desegregation tool—a decision that was upheld by the U.S. Supreme Court. Soon afterward, in *Swann v. Charlotte-Mecklenburg Board of Education*, Judge James McMillan of Charlotte, North Carolina, ruled that crosstown busing was an appropriate means to address racial imbalance among schools. Although the Nixon administration joined the Charlotte school board in fighting the decision, the Supreme Court upheld McMillan's ruling. (President Eisenhower had advocated a "go-slow" approach to school integration, a position to which Nixon adhered.) Even so, it would take another two years and a federal court order for Burlington City Schools to fully integrate.

Jordan Sellars closed at the end of the 1969–1970 school year; until then its high school students were allowed to choose whether or not to transfer to Williams. Only a handful of its best students did. At the same time, Hugh M. Cummings High School was being built in east Burlington and was open to incoming sophomores and juniors for the 1970–1971 school year. Its first graduating class would be in 1972. Cummings was closer to my house than Williams, but because our class—the class of 1971—had begun at Williams, we were allowed to finish there. Thus, my graduating class was the only class to include every high school senior in town—black, white, east, and west. We had six hundred graduating seniors that year—the largest graduating class in the history of Walter Williams. After that, east and west Burlington would be divided once more and, over the years, largely resegregated as the east side of town became increasingly African American and Hispanic.

Many people, both black and white, were unhappy about the pending merger of Jordan Sellars and Walter Williams. Jordan Sellars students would lose a collective identity and many proud traditions. Their marching band was renowned, never failing to steal the show at downtown parades with its rhythmic dance movements, improvisational formations, and funky sound. The Jordan Sellars marching band was a rockin' block-long street party, the pride of Burlington's black community. Exuberant, animated Jordan Sellars and ultra-preppy Walter Williams were polar opposites—and it wouldn't be the Williams students who would be expected to change.

Anger erupted within the black community in May 1969 when the news spread that no black cheerleaders had been elected to the Williams varsity or junior varsity cheerleading squads for the next school year. On 14 May, two carloads of black teenagers came onto the Williams campus, where fights broke out between them and several white students. School was dismissed early that afternoon. The following day, black leaders and students met to draw up a list of demands to be presented to the Williams administration. Their demands included the formation of a black student committee; more black representation in the administration; and the establishment of a investigative board, composed of black administrators, teachers, and students, which would look into all acts of racial violence at Williams and would have the power to expel the guilty.[1]

School officials met with selected students the next morning, Friday, 16 May, to go over the demands. While the meeting was being held at Williams, protest organizers from New York and nearby Greensboro and Chapel Hill incited two hundred Jordan Sellars students to walk out of their classes and march on the Burlington City Schools' Central Administrative Office. The protesters made their way the short distance from Jordan Sellars to the central office, then continued across town to Williams, about two miles southwest. Most of Williams's black students left their classes to join the protesters on the school's expansive front lawn. White parents had been arriving throughout the morning to take their children home, but as the crowd grew larger and more agitated, Williams went into lockdown. I remember my history teacher frantically shoving desks against the classroom door after locking us inside, where we sat for hours half expecting some raging black man to burst in and shoot us.

The protesters left Williams midafternoon to march back to the central office, where about twenty people entered the building, overturned desks, and threw typewriters out the windows. They then moved on to Rauhut Street, the main road through the black section of town, only a few blocks away. Other rioters joined in, throwing bricks and bottles through store windows and at police cars. Two stores were firebombed and gunfire broke out between the police and snipers. Two hundred law enforcement officers and four hundred National Guardsmen finally secured the area in the early-morning hours, and a countywide curfew was ordered.

Then something happened that would mark Burlington forever.

The wooden structure of one of the firebombed stores had burned quickly and was in smoldering ruins when Leon Mebane, a black teenager, slipped out of his house and, along with several friends, went to see what was going on. The police were called to the scene by reports of looting, and the fifteen-year-old Mebane was shot to death. While that much was fairly well established, reports on what actually happened varied considerably.

One version of Mebane's death was that he was caught in the crossfire between police and snipers as he and several other youths came running out the back of the store. Police said Mebane had been looting, but it was later revealed that he had nothing in his hands.[2] A police report stated that, upon their arrival, "two police officers and two agents of the SBI [State Bureau of Investigation] encountered gunfire and observed between 8 and 10 blacks looting the store. The officers ordered the looters to halt, and when they did not they began firing on the blacks, hitting Mebane. He was not inside the store when shot."[3]

According to Zenobia Mebane, Leon's mother, one of the boys with Leon told her that they "were just looking at the burned-out building. There was nothing left to loot."[4] When the police drove up, the other boys told Leon to run, but he refused, saying that he'd done nothing wrong. "Leon stood still; he didn't go nowhere. He held up his hands, and they shot him," she recounted.[5] The coroner's report stated that Mebane suffered seven bullet entry wounds and one exit wound. Zenobia Mebane, who identified her son's body, said that it was "riddled" with shotgun pellets, including a shotgun blast to his neck. "How could anyone be shot so many times if they were running?" she asked.[6]

The Burlington police chief refused to comment on Mebane's death at the time. There was no investigation, and no formal apology or informal condolences were offered to the Mebane family by city officials. Local media quickly turned their gaze elsewhere, dutifully helping to sweep the riot and Mebane's death under the rug—where it has pretty much remained.

Before my recent research into the 1969 Burlington riots, I vaguely remembered that a boy my age had been shot and killed.

The shameful truth is that Leon Mebane's death didn't much register with most of white Burlington, including me. I write about it here because the appalling unfairness of how it was handled is so outrageous to me now. It also adds a deeper dimension to my vivid memories of the riots and to the broader issue of race that loomed menacingly over my high school years. I remember being relieved when the 1968–1969 school year ended. The Summer of Love might have been blooming in San Francisco and on Yasgur's farm, but not east of the Mississippi and south of the Mason-Dixon Line.

***

The influx of black students into my Williams graduating class changed all of us in ways large and small. Ironically, it was the cheerleading squad that led the way. One year earlier, the all-white squad was reciting (with a little pompom wrist action, but otherwise in straight-armed military style): "Our team is red, our team is hot, our team is red hot!" Senior year featured a hip-thrusting extravaganza with the black cheerleaders leading their white sisters in shouting, "UH! Ungawa, we got da powah!" Bug-eyed white fathers watched in horror; white mothers fainted in the bleachers. I began to feel better about the world.

And yes, there was Vietnam—but truthfully, most of us were sick of all the conflict, all the heaviness. We just wanted to have some high school fun. Besides, very few of my friends had any direct relationship with anyone fighting in Vietnam. I was acquainted with one person who served and died in Vietnam, but he was in his midtwenties—which at the time seemed so much older.

I remember a few of my classmates sitting on the front steps of Williams with homemade "Stop the War" signs. I wish I could say otherwise, but I mostly thought they were weird. They also made me feel vaguely guilty—as if I should care about something more important than looking cute and hangin' cool, even as I knew I really didn't care. Hippie fashion was infinitely more interesting to me than war protests. By senior year, we had shed our Pappagallo flats for fringed moccasins, and our man-tailored miniskirts and perfectly matching cable-knit sweaters for tie-dyed T-shirts and bell-bottom blue jeans. During lunch hour, we'd pack into my friend Bill's blue VW van, crank up Led Zeppelin and the Rolling Stones, and pass around a joint. I was so ready to leave Burlington. As an impertinent joke, I asked my homeroom teacher, Mrs. Latta, to sign my senior yearbook. She wrote: "I am really surprised that you want me to write in your annual. Conflict, arguments, excuses, and discussions. Make me a list of those reasons for being late; yours can't be surpassed. But good luck next year."

Next year was East Carolina University in Greenville—three hours east of Burlington, and as far away from home as I could get. I wanted to go to college out of state, but that wasn't an option. North Carolina's excellent in-state tuition rates were a factor, but not the deciding one since my father was willing to pay for me to go to a private college. He simply didn't think that colleges outside the state line were any better than those within it—at least not any that would accept his seventeen-year-old underachieving daughter. I had already made up my mind to study art, and I had a good portfolio thanks to six years of painting lessons. East Carolina was well known in the southeast for its studio art program, and it was far enough away from Burlington to virtually ensure no parental pop-ins. (Unlike the University of North Carolina at Chapel Hill, only half an hour away—not that I had a prayer of being admitted with my just barely B-minus average and ho-hum SAT scores.) The day my mother left me at Umstead Hall on the ECU campus was one of the most exhilarating in my life. To this day, I've never understood why any young person not under financial duress would choose the "real world" over college.

Given my future accidental career as a university professor and first lady, it's a tad embarrassing to admit to being such a sorry student throughout high school and well into college, but there you have it. ECU—or "EZU," as jealous UNC undergrads snootily called it—had a well-deserved party-school reputation. My comrades and I did our best to advance that status during our freshman year, as I quasi-remember. At the end of the first quarter of my sophomore year, however, I made up my mind to put some real effort into my studies. This decision resulted from the earth-shaking revelation that I could flunk a course, a five-credit-hour economics course at that.

My parents had generously sent me to Germany for my sophomore year, 1972–1973. Twenty-eight ECU students and our professors lived in Haus Steineck, a once grand but still handsome four-story residence on a bank of the Rhine, just south of Bonn. The setting was idyllic in every respect, including the picturesque Wein Haus located right next door. We'd walk out the side gate and cross the cobblestone pathway to the Wein Haus, where for the equivalent of $2.50 they would refill an empty bottle with one of several varieties of riesling or a light, sweet pinot noir. (Most of us chose their semisweet, Liebfraumilch-like variety.) Of course, we could always get a bottle of good German beer about any time of the day from the basement "Stübchen" (a small cozy room; in this case, a small, cozy bar with a nice little dance floor where Don Bass and I spent hours perfecting jitterbug gymnastics to "Rock around the Clock," "Boogie Woogie Bugle Boy of Company B," "In the Mood," "Jailhouse Rock," "Burning Love," and on and on). We were allowed to bring beer and wine into our classes, which was a rather popular policy for afternoon lectures. Both classrooms had captivating views of the river, where a bored or semi-inebriated student could watch the passing boats and barges. This was the bonny setting of my academic nadir.

I had applied myself so little for so long and still received low Bs and high Cs, I didn't believe I would ever be given an F—especially since my parents were subsidizing a term abroad for the economics professor and his wife. Apparently, one can indeed earn an F by not showing up for a majority of classes and walking out in the middle of those one does condescend to attend. My father's reaction to the F on my report card (yes, back in the early seventies universities sent grade reports to tuition-paying parents) contributed to my newly found academic motivation: "Get your grades up or get off the dole!" I readily selected the first option.

My year abroad gave me a worldview that became almost as irritating to my father as the F. It was a real eye-opener to read and hear about Vietnam and Watergate from the perspectives of the European media and our young German friends. I proudly posted my absentee ballot for the liberal Democrat George McGovern that November. Over the Christmas and New Year's holidays, all Haus Steineck residents boarded a private bus to Berlin, and then flew on to Moscow and Budapest. My classmates and I became avid supporters of Chancellor Willy Brandt and his Neue Ostpolitik policy of rapprochement between West Germany and East Germany and other Eastern Bloc countries. The experience of entering East Berlin through Checkpoint Charlie and seeing the bombed-out buildings and tons of rubble that still remained almost thirty years after World War II made an indelible impression on me. All Americans should see what the aftermath of a war looks like. I was a very different person by the time I returned home that summer: I was now genuinely interested in national and international politics.

**

My heart's journey was not unlike my academic trajectory—from almost complete lack of interest to keen focus in a flash. I never had a romantic relationship until I fell in love with my painting professor the summer between my junior and senior years of college. I'd had an off-and-on boyfriend in high school, but we were far from serious. I simply wasn't much interested in boys, although I knew I *should* be. Who's going out with whom is supposed to be a riveting high school topic, right? I wanted to have a date to this or that dance or party, but beyond that I didn't much care.

I was the *way* last of my friends to lose her virginity (not until college!). I was also the last to start my period (not until the end of tenth grade, when I was fifteen). I was painfully self-conscious about my body, specifically my small breasts. The British fashion model Twiggy was my saving grace in terms of body image throughout adolescence. I had the same big eyes, and as a high school junior I cropped my hair short like hers. Sure, I looked good in clothes; it was the prospect of being out of them that deflated my sassy, faux self-confidence.

My abdication of virginity during my freshman year of college was entirely premeditated. It had to go—otherwise how would I ever know what all the fuss was about? (It took another two years for the ah-ha of sex to come to me, or me to it.) I liked the guys I was bedding—some I liked quite a bit—but I never had the feeling of wanting to consume and be consumed.

That changed with the gentle, soft-spoken man who had just been hired as a full-time, tenure-track professor and was my new painting instructor. He was ten years older than I was, and he was married, though without children. His eyes were an absorbing, expressive ice blue; he had a good, square jawline and a generous mouth. He was only a couple of inches taller, so when we embraced, we fit together perfectly. And he drew and painted beautifully.

Every weekday morning around seven thirty he came to my house, climbed the stairs to my second-floor bedroom, sat down gently at the edge of my bed, and kissed me awake. Fortunately, my roommate and her boyfriend didn't have any early classes and so remained in her bedroom, but they were well aware of what was going on. My professor and I would hug and smooch for a few stolen moments, after which he would slip back out the unlocked back door and return to the art building, a ten-minute walk away. An hour later, we would meet in my painting studio for coffee and a critique of my previous evening's work. At lunch, we'd slip out for a stroll or, better yet, hole up in one of the very private and comfortable music-listening rooms at the student union.

We made love with every glance and touch, but we never consummated it. I was more than willing, but he was unable to bring himself to betray his wife—whom he also loved—in that final regard.

"It is possible to love two people," he said.

"To be *in* love with two people?" I asked.

"Yes," he said, "and I so love you."

Our chasteness made our romance all the more passionate. We tried to be discreet, but our feelings for each other were written all over our faces and in every gesture. My studio mates were well aware of our affair, as were the art faculty and, no doubt, his wife. He wandered love-struck around the public opening of my senior painting exhibition. My mother remarked afterward, "He couldn't keep his eyes off you." It was true; we were magnetic.

A week before I was to graduate, he said he would leave his wife if we could be together. He'd never said that before, and I knew he was serious. We had taken a drive in my car and were now parked, talking and kissing, on a side street about a half mile from campus.

"What will you do?" I gasped, thrilled yet also alarmed by this new possible reality. "You, *we*, can't stay here."

"I need to stay here," he said. "This is where I have a job. Will you stay with me?"

The air constricted around me in one excruciating convulsion. I envisioned my life forever in Greenville. "But you know I want to go to New York."

"I know," he said, "but I'm asking you to stay here with me, at least for a few years."

An eternity passed, as I comprehended the utter seriousness of the moment. This was one hundred percent for real. If I said yes, he would divorce his wife. Was that what I wanted? I loved him too much to let him take that step, if I weren't absolutely certain. He sat in silence, watching me.

"No," I sobbed suddenly, "I can't. I'm sorry."

He flinched slightly, his blue eyes flooding with longing and loss. He squeezed my hand for the last time and got out of the car. I think he had known what I would say.

***

Although I grieved for years over my inability to commit to him, I knew I did the right thing. I wanted to travel, to live in the greatest city in the world, to have adventures. I would have grown restless, and I may not have been kind to him. I have never loved another man the way I loved him. As much as I loved my husband, I wanted neither to consume nor to be consumed by him. Then again, when it came right down to it, I didn't want that with my professor, either.

3

Liftoff

IT TOOK ME A YEAR and a half—a stint working as receptionist at my friend Nealy's (the former Ray of ninth-grade science class) hair salon in Chapel Hill; a two-month road trip from Burlington, through Mexico, out to Los Angeles; a hosting job at a Mexican restaurant in Marina Del Rey ("Rodriguez, party of four . . ."); and a sculpture class at Otis Art Institute in LA (where I made the ugliest four-foot-tall aluminum thing ever to emerge from its foundry)—but I finally made it to New York. I had been accepted into Otis's MFA program on the merits of my painting portfolio (and in spite of the ungainly aluminum creation), when I got the "thumbs-up" from the prestigious Pratt Institute in Brooklyn. My mother and her friend Nadine flew out to accompany me on the drive back east. We were headed to Las Vegas our first night on the road. Nadine and I were impatient to see the sights and lights, but Mother insisted that we detour to the Hoover Dam "just so we can say we've been there." Although I complained at the time, I must say that I remember the dam much more vividly than Las Vegas. Thus, better for having seen the Hoover Dam, I arrived in New York in early August 1977—a few days before the arrest of David Berkowitz.

"Thank God they got him!" Mother telephoned. Berkowitz, who was charged with the "Son of Sam" series of murders, was twenty-four years old. I remember being struck by the fact that this person, who had terrorized New York City for over a year, was virtually the same age as my friends and I were.

New York was a real mess in the seventies and most of the eighties, and I loved it. Grad school was great—there's nothing quite like being an art student in New York. When I wasn't painting my *Scientific American* conception of light moving through deep space, or stretching hundreds of yards of thin white jersey fabric across Pratt's dance studio in triangular-shaped tunnels (a three-dimensional kinetic exploration of my light-through-deep-space hypothesis), I was frequenting art museums and galleries and participating in raucous debates with my fellow students about whether or not painting was dead. (Long addicted to oil paint's rich hues and buttery sensuality, and to the aromas of turpentine and linseed, I was firmly in the "not" camp.) Whether Pratt's brand-new "new forms" major should more accurately be called "new frauds" was another happy-hour debate special. My stretched-jersey escapades had brought me into closer communion with several of the new-forms majors, so I maintained a moderate stance in the deliberations. There was also jumping up and down in place to the defiant screeching of a punk rock band at the Mudd Club or CBGB to work off whatever subcultural intensity remained at the end of the day.

The Rolling Stones released their *Some Girls* album in the summer of 1978. When the song "Shattered" played, my roommate, Blu, and I would stop whatever we were doing to scream along with Mick: about the crime rate going "up, up, up" and how "tough, tough, tough" we were, living in New York. Blu was from Decatur, Alabama, and was as full of it as I was. Both of us had red hair—hers a natural auburn, mine a henna-assisted carrot—and southern accents. We shared a brownstone apartment in the Carroll Gardens section of Brooklyn and a painting studio at Pratt, so we were together a lot. We fancied ourselves to be a dangerous duo. One spring day we were sashaying across campus when a carload of teenage boys drove by in a beat-up Camaro. "Hey! Ass and no-ass!" one shouted.

We burst out laughing, turning simultaneously to look at our own behinds. There was no question of who was who. "Is mine really that big?" she asked.

"No, you've got a *great* ass," I assured her. "Is mine really that, well, nonexistent?"

"No, it's *adorable*," she confirmed.

Blu and I also shared a work-study job: we chauffeured Pratt Institute president Richardson "Jerry" Pratt Jr., the great-grandson of Pratt Institute founder Charles Pratt. Jerry Pratt was a friendly fellow with a good sense of humor, which was reflected in his "limo" choice—an old Checker Marathon taxicab painted robin's-egg blue. The Blue Goose (named after a seaplane that shuttled passengers around the U.S. Virgin Islands, he explained) was an empowering car to drive—especially if you harbored hostilities toward New York City taxi drivers, which I most definitely did.

Blu and I always had to lie to taxi drivers about where we were going if we wanted to catch a cab from Manhattan to Brooklyn late at night. Cab drivers didn't want to go to the other boroughs because they might not get a return fare. Our scheme was to tell them we were headed somewhere near the Fulton Fish Market and then, once we had four or five dollars on the meter, break it to them that we needed to go "just over the Brooklyn Bridge" to the Heights. Once across the bridge, we would have to coerce them another twenty blocks south to Carroll Gardens. We had, on occasion, been cursed out of a taxicab and abandoned in the dark of no-man's-land Lower Broadway before we could make it over the bridge. That wasn't the only reason I wanted revenge. I had had it in for taxi drivers ever since I first moved to New York and had attempted briefly to drive around the city in a long-ass Pontiac Bonneville with a North Carolina license plate. A young woman nervously navigating an out-of-state, block-long car through the city streets was raw filet mignon to those taxi wolves.

Now, with the Blue Goose and Jerry's gladiatorial spirit, vengeance was mine! A Checker Marathon isn't a car—it's a *tank*. There was a common bond of macho respect among Marathon drivers, even if the one I was driving was blue instead of yellow. As for those other scrap-metal, no-leg-room junkers, it was: *Go ahead—make my day! Mine can run over yours and not even feel it.* There are few things more satisfying than intimidating a New York City cab driver. Jerry usually sat up front, where he served as my combat wingman. If any of our faint-hearted passengers (mostly senior university administrators and trustees) admonished me to *slow down* as we barreled up FDR Drive for a meeting in Midtown, he'd say, "Leave her alone. She's doing great!" "Good move," he'd observe, as I would intrepidly nudge the Goose in front of a glowering cab driver.

Chauffeuring Jerry and other Pratt VIPs around Brooklyn and Manhattan, and occasionally up to a meeting in Connecticut, gave me a valuable glimpse into the concerns of the top dogs at a small college: fundraising, keeping up with or besting the competition, and planning for a weekend upstate or in the Hamptons. As we drove along, Jerry often invited my response to discussions he and our passengers were having about student affairs. I don't know that I still have the capacity to navigate New York traffic and bestow nuanced policy counsel simultaneously.

***

MFA in hand, I hit the streets to find a job as—what else?—a bartender. No nine-to-five for me. I needed the daylight hours to paint and to beg people to look at my paintings; becoming a famous artist required as much. After being turned away repeatedly from upscale restaurants for my complete inexperience in mixology (other than what I'd gleaned about the preparation of birdbath margaritas by watching the bartender at the Marina Del Rey restaurant), I finally secured a position at a West Village lesbian bar called Bonnie and Clyde's. Blu would grudgingly traipse into B&C once or twice a week and submit to a free drink and a public kiss on the lips so that the patrons would not hit on me. One Saturday afternoon my dodge came to an abrupt end when, walking hand in hand with my boyfriend, I ran straight into the B&C bouncer. I flung my boyfriend's hand from mine as if I'd just learned he had Ebola, but it was too late. I had a lot of splainin' to do when I got to work that evening, although B&C's owners kindly allowed me to stay. I was now fair game and, for a time, saw a substantial increase in my tips.

Working the six-to-two shift five days a week was not ideal for much of anything except becoming familiar with New York's after-hours scene. My plan of painting in the mornings and afternoons receded rapidly. At best, I managed to paint for an hour or two in the late afternoon before reporting for bar duty, and on one of my two days off. Every so often I would venture out with my

slide portfolio in an almost always unsuccessful attempt to persuade some bored gallery girl dressed in all black to help me finagle a five-minute meeting with the manager. (Take note,
starry-eyed art undergrads: It's not too late to change your major
to computer technology.) After a year of that routine, it was the
help-wanted ads for me.

My next job was as an account manager at a small advertising
agency, which was followed by a sales position at a technology
consulting firm that placed computer programmers with financial
companies such as Manufacturers Hanover, Merrill Lynch, and
Morgan Stanley. Having an ample expense account to wine and
dine Wall Street junior executives was fun for a while, but I burned
out after a couple of years. Corporate offices weren't my scene. I
missed being around and talking about art.

Jerry Pratt had kept in touch with me, as he had with several
of his former drivers, and knew I was unhappy with the Wall
Street gig. One wintry afternoon in 1983 he called to invite me to
lunch, saying he had something he wanted to discuss. Jerry was
well aware of the almost insurmountable difficulties young artists
encountered in trying to gain a gallery toehold. He'd heard it from
me and countless others. What if Pratt were to rent a small gallery
space in SoHo and stage a few exhibitions of alumni work? It
would be helpful to young alumni and good for Pratt's visibility
in Manhattan, he said. He wanted to know if I'd be interested in
organizing such an effort. I jumped at the opportunity, even
though the proffered salary was less than half of what I was making as a sales rep. I had mounted two shows (to resounding
nonacclaim) when I was tapped to help develop, and then to
direct, a new scholarship program. The Pratt National Talent
Search was a brilliant marketing scheme, and much more successful than our brief foray into the SoHo art scene.

As the retired dean of Pratt's School of Art and Design and a
founder of the National Art Education Association, Charles
Marshall Robertson was asked to help promote the National Talent
Search and provide me entrée to the art education community. He
was also a founding organizer of the Metropolitan Opera Guild,
and for two decades he had kept the same two front-row box seats,
right next to the box reserved for the conductor's guests. Charles
was the first genuine *bon vivant* I ever knew. He was tall and slim,

with a mane of snow-white hair, and always dressed just so. He never slouched. When cocktail hour arrived he ordered "a J&B dry Rob Roy on the rocks with a twist." Charles took the *QEII* ocean liner from New York to Southampton every December to spend two months in London and Edinburgh. He was of proud Scottish Presbyterian ancestry and had a gorgeous paisley shawl collection that he donated to the Montclair Art Museum. (His father's family came from Paisley, Scotland.) Charles introduced me to opera in grand style. We always met for a glass of "ginger ale" (Champagne) in the Belmont Room before the opera, and supped afterward at the nearby Ginger Man.

Did I mention Charles was gay? Well, neither did he, nor did any of the men of his set. They didn't pretend to be straight—none of them were married, as they often are (especially in the South)—but maintained a certain genteel decorum that left room for interpretation depending on the situation and one's comfort level.

Charles and I traveled extensively to state and national art education conferences. We hosted cocktail receptions on behalf of Pratt for the conference organizers and speakers—the political and intellectual leaders of the field. This was a highly effective business strategy in the field of art education. Art educators are not used to getting much attention and are enormously grateful when someone treats them as professionals who are deserving of respect, a glass of wine, and decent hors d'oeuvres. Charles knew everyone, and soon I knew everyone. We also visited hand-selected schools across the country to meet with top high school art teachers and encourage them to encourage their most promising students to apply to the Pratt National Talent Search. The students' art portfolios knocked our socks off.

In 1984, the first year of the program's operation, a faculty jury awarded $250,000 in full and partial four-year tuition scholarships to Pratt's School of Art and Design. One of the five full scholarships was given to Jerold McCain, a young African American man from a poor family in Washington, D.C., and the pride of the Duke Ellington School of the Arts' visual arts program. If we'd had only one scholarship to award, we'd have served it up to Jerold on a silver platter. He was tall, nice looking, and sweet natured. He liked hanging out in my office between classes and chatting with my assistant, Melisa, and my secretary, Mildred. The winter of his sophomore year, we noticed that he was losing weight and always seemed to have a chest cold. "Jerold, you need to take better care of yourself! You need to eat and get more rest!" we'd lecture. He'd often show up at the office around lunch; we'd buy him a sandwich and stand over him while he ate. One morning I received a call from the head of student services informing me that an ambulance had been called to Jerold's dormitory the previous night. He'd been taken to the emergency room at Bellevue Hospital. As soon as Jerold was allowed visitors, Melisa and I went to see him. To our surprise, the nurse handed us face masks. When I asked why we needed masks, she explained they were for Jerold's protection, not ours. Jerold had AIDS. He made it out of the hospital that time, but died a month later, in the spring of 1986. Melisa and I took the train down to D.C. for Jerold's funeral. The shabbiness of the funeral home, and his family's obvious inability to have done anything better for their son, made what Jerold had achieved in his short life all the more remarkable.

Our first entering class of scholarship recipients—Jerold's class—was due to graduate in the spring of 1988. The National Talent Search had been such a wildly successful recruitment tool that by 1988 we were giving out $1.5 million in tuition scholarships to incoming freshmen in art and design, architecture, and engineering. This would be my final year as program director, however. I had decided to pursue a doctorate in art education and favored leaving the city to do so.

Charles was almost as pleased with himself as he was with me over my decision to return for my PhD, but he wanted me to remain in New York. A year earlier, I'd painted the walls of my tiny SoHo apartment a deep forest green. Eleven years of concrete and traffic was enough for me. I was ready to get out of the city and into the woods, and I had my eye on Penn State. Charles kept a pied-à-terre on lower Fifth Avenue but spent much of his time at his home near Doylestown, Pennsylvania.

"State College is just a little over three hours from Doylestown," I reminded him.

"OK," he'd chuckle, "but no farther."

He often telephoned me early in the morning with an idea about this or that. If the phone rang before eight o'clock, I'd answer it, "Yes, Charles."

He'd returned from his annual jaunt to the United Kingdom two weeks earlier, and we'd had supper at the Knickerbocker three or four days before the phone rang that morning in February.

"Yes, Charles," I said.

"This isn't Charles; it's Paul."

Paul was a friend of Charles's. Charles had died of a heart attack the night before at his Bucks County home. Although I didn't move out of the city for several more months, Charles's death stands as the true demarcation of the end of my time in New York. I bought an elegant, black-velvet pillbox hat with a delicate black lace veil to wear to his funeral. Charles would have loved that hat.

***

The first time my father was hospitalized was shortly before Charles died. He had been diagnosed with cirrhosis of the liver in the early 1980s and had stopped drinking for five years. Then he decided, "One beer won't matter." The liver forgives once, but not twice. Within a year of resuming his Budweiser habit, he was in and out of Duke Hospital with bacterial infections and bleeding.

By early March I was flying home just about every other weekend for the latest emergency. Each time he went into Duke, Mother and I thought he wouldn't come out—but he did. And the moment he felt well enough, he'd have a beer. It was maddening. I was so angry that I was almost disappointed when he'd resurrect himself yet again. His final hospitalization came in May.

Cirrhosis is an awful way to go. I wish I could erase from my mind's eye the bloody bruises that covered his body those last days. I wish I could forget the sound of his moans as the nurses tried to find yet another vein to accommodate the round-the-clock delivery of the antibiotics that kept him alive. I wish I could forget the sight of his tissue-thin skin coming off in sheets along with the IV tape, when one vein collapsed and they had to find another one. I'd sit at the foot of his bed squeezing my head between my hands as the nurses worked on him. All I could think was *Please stop! For the love of God, stop!* I wanted him to let go, but he was holding on tight.

One afternoon, the doctor came into the room and asked my mother if she wanted to continue the antibiotic treatment. Mother looked to me to answer.

"What will happen if you stop?" I asked.

"He'll die," the doctor replied, "but either way he can't live much longer."

"Then stop it," I said.

"Yes," Mother agreed.

"Do you want us to put him on life support?" the doctor asked.

"No!" we both answered, appalled at the idea.

"Good," the doctor said. "It's a cruel thing to do to someone so ill."

The doctor had barely left the room when Daddy asked what was going on. We had thought he was unconscious. We had just had this conversation with the doctor about whether to write him off, and he was listening! "I want them to continue the antibiotics," he said. *Oh, dear God!* "Of course, Daddy! Of course, if that's what you want! I'm so sorry!" I ran to the nurses' station to relay his wish. They immediately returned to his bedside to go exploring for another vein. Mother and I wept as he moaned. He was sleeping when we left him around 9:00 p.m. for the drive back to Burlington.

The phone rang just after seven the next morning. Mother was dressed for work, and I was preparing to return to the hospital. We knew immediately what the call was about. Daddy had died that morning. It was a conscious decision on his part, I firmly believe— a last-minute selfless act, to spare us from having to witness more of his suffering.

While there is much about my father's dying that I want to forget, I replay a few frames longingly. The tenderness that passed between us when I clumsily washed his still luxuriously wavy hair is precious to me. It was a real makeshift operation, with him leaning back as far as he could in the metal-framed hospital chair while I tried, with no success at all, not to spill water down his back as I scooped it up from the brown plastic basin with a white plastic cup to wet and rinse his hair. I gently massaged lotion into his hands and feet several times a day. It was almost as if a gravely injured wild animal was, out of abject need and surrendered trust, allowing me to caress it. I studied his hands as I stroked them. He had such beautiful hands, such long, slender fingers—not unlike my own, I realized. The lotion disappeared almost instantaneously into his skin. He was parched throughout, body and soul. When I finished massaging one hand, he'd lift the other toward me. My touch relaxed him; it brought him a small pleasure and brief respite from his pain. It brought me profound solace.

***

I accepted a teaching assistantship at Penn State's College of Arts and Architecture and made plans to move to State College to begin my doctoral work. I made my decision in favor of Penn State several weeks before Daddy died, so he had known of my plans and, although he did not say it straight out, I knew he was proud of me. That July I loaded my possessions and my two cats into a U-Haul truck and drove to Happy Valley. A faculty member's wife helped me find the sweetest place to live—the carriage house of the Boal Estate. Boalsburg, the self-proclaimed birthplace of Memorial Day, is right next to State College on its eastern side, and is picture-perfect charming. I don't believe I ever drove down the gravel driveway of the estate, past the historic mansion on the left and the little stream-fed pond on the right, without thinking how lucky I was to live there. I immediately purchased a road bike and a mountain bike, and set about exploring the spectacularly verdant two-lane-blacktop loops and off-road trails in every direction.

My time at Penn State was a satisfying fusion of curricular and extracurricular activities. Penn State and Ohio State have held fast to the top two positions in graduate art education studies for well over four decades. My faculty adviser and dissertation committee chair was Brent Wilson, a highly respected, innovative thinker in the field. My fellow doctoral students were smart, accomplished, and—I soon discovered—gung-ho for potluck dinners. State College was a northern version of Chapel Hill—a quaint, cozy college town, but more geographically isolated and outdoorsy. When the academic grind got to be too much, my colleague Anne and I struck out on a long hike through the state forests that surround Happy Valley. We'd wander the mountain trails for hours, pondering the possibility of changing our major to parks and recreation.

I was able to get to know many more people outside the university than most of my peers by residing in the close-knit community of Boalsburg (rather than in a neighborhood close to campus) and by teaching step aerobics at a local fitness club. Bonnie, an able seamstress and every Boalsburg Elementary School student's favorite teacher, helped me make lace curtains for the carriage house. I met Faye, a truly gifted healer, herbalist, and massage therapist, at the fitness club. Faye lived in an old farmhouse fifteen miles south of State College, in the middle of Amish country. When the weekend weather was pleasant, she and I would set out from her house on a forty-mile bike loop alongside rushing mountain streams and over hill and dale. On our return we'd shower, stretch, make a huge vegetarian feast, and lie out on her front porch and stargaze while drinking a two-thirds/one-third mix of semidecent white and strawberry wine from a vineyard down the road. Faye's circle of friends included a lot of hippies and New Agers in and around Happy Valley (an area chock-a-block with both). She brought me along to several thoroughly pagan affairs replete with all the cosmic essentials—bonfires, sweat lodges, chanting, drumming, dancing, and full moons. I imagine most PhD candidates don't have nearly as much consciousness-raising fun.

I was the only doctoral student in Penn State's art education department who had not taught art at the K–12 level. Most of my peers planned to move into university teaching, where they would educate the next generation of K–12 visual arts teachers. I had no intention of teaching, but envisioned myself as the director of a state or municipal arts council, or at a private foundation that awarded grants to artists and arts organizations. I was interested in arts and arts education program administration and policy making related to the focus and funding of such programs. My work at Pratt and my close association with Jerry and Charles inspired me to pursue what was, at the time, a markedly unconventional course of study within the realm of art education. Congressional attacks in 1989 on the National Endowment for the Arts over "obscene" art further spurred my fascination with the role of government in the arts. I took courses in policy research and evaluation offered by the departments of economics and psychology, since none were available within the College of Arts and Architecture. The grim reality of having flunked my one and only undergraduate economics

45

course was ever present in my mind as I toiled day and night for a mercy B in my graduate-level econ class.

In 1991, I along with four other doctoral students in art education received $12,000 grants from the J. Paul Getty Foundation to finish writing our dissertations. It was the first year the Getty Foundation made such grants. Throughout the 1980s and well into the 1990s, the foundation sponsored groundbreaking research in K–12 curriculum development in the visual arts. Its patronage was an enormous boon to a small academic field that had never before (and has not since) received much attention from any entity with such money and power. Being named a Getty doctoral fellow was a huge honor, one that carried significant prestige in our little corner of the world. My dissertation was titled "Artists in the Classroom: An Analysis of the Arts in Education Program of the National Endowment for the Arts." As I rummaged through library stacks hunting down old legislative documents, I would sometimes say to the ghost of my father, "Daddy, you more than anyone would have loved this! What conversations we might have had." It made me sad that he hadn't lived to see me become a scholar. At the same time, however, I felt less encumbered than ever before—which is a blessing when you're in the midst of getting a PhD.

To make the Getty grant money last longer, I decided to move back to my mother's house in Burlington. My mother had also found a new life: she'd recently remarried. Olin was a local radio personality with a delightfully genteel South Carolina accent. He was kind, sociable, and jovial. He was the anti-Clifton. He and Mother were both in the choir at Front Street Christian Church, the small church where Mother had taken me almost all my life. (Daddy never went to church.) Olin's first wife had died a year before my father. I was pleased for my mother because, as much as she had always wanted to be away from my father, she was lonely once he died. She moved into Olin's home, so her house was available. I didn't want to leave Happy Valley, and it felt a little creepy to return to the unhappy house in which I grew up, but I was grateful to have a rent-free place to live, few distractions, and the precious time to write. I waved a sage smudge stick through it a few times to get rid of the bad vibes and set up shop.

I began looking for a job several months before my scheduled graduation, interviewing at three arts agencies and an art museum.

All rejected me. My dissertation research had led me to conclude that many of the National Endowment for the Arts' educational policies and programs were largely self-serving, doing more to undermine support for rigorous K–12 arts instruction than to advance it. I suspect this point of view did not endear me to those with hiring power at institutions receiving NEA funding.

I was in a screw-it state of mind when I skipped out of a mind-numbing lecture at the 1993 National Art Education Convention to exorcise my funk in the exercise room of the conference hotel. Fortunately, I was not in such a mean mood as to dismiss a request from a nearby gentleman for assistance in figuring out how to program a newfangled elliptical trainer. This person turned out to be Michael Parsons, the chairman of the Department of Art Education at Ohio State University, who was also playing conference hooky.

"Aren't you Brent's student?" he asked. "And a Getty fellow?" Double affirmative. "You did a policy-oriented dissertation on the NEA?" That's me. "We're starting a new graduate program in arts policy," he said, "and we're looking for someone to help us with it." A month later—the day after I received my diploma at Penn State—I drove west six hours to Columbus to interview for the Ohio State job.

4

The Yellow Dress

I FIRST MET PRESIDENT E. GORDON GEE at *The* Ohio State University. (Yes, "The" is part of the university's given title and on its state seal. Same thing for *The* Pennsylvania State University, by the way. I suppose that leaves no room for confusion with imposter Ohio or Penn state universities.) It was September 1993 and I walked into Gordon's trademark "new faculty reception," which was held at the university president's residence at the start of each new school year. I was wearing a short, swingy silk cocktail dress in unabashed cadmium yellow. Being a fashion plate in academia is like shooting fish in a barrel—cruelly easy and more than a little demented. The room was a sea of neutrals. In my black sling-back heels and attention-grabbing dress, I stood out like a sunflower in a vat of oatmeal. My relative glamour dazzled the president, although I wouldn't know it until months later.

Gordon likes to compare his looks to those of Orville Redenbacher or the former college football coach Lou Holtz, depending on his audience. I saw a fellow blue-eyed redhead with a wide, toothy smile, who was readily approachable and nice looking in a geeky, professorial way. He wore a dark gray suit, a bowtie of scarlet and gray stripes, and horn-rimmed glasses. A jaunty set of red braces (I would have called them "suspenders" at the time but quickly learned better) peeked out from under his unbuttoned jacket.

I had landed the job that I first heard about beside the elliptical machine. My mission was to create a new graduate program at a time when the Ohio Board of Regents was cutting graduate programs statewide so legislators could redirect more of the budget toward prisons. I was an unintended beneficiary of a circuitous hookup between a donor's interest and a dean who knew an opportunity when he saw it.

The donor, Larry Barnett, was an alumnus of the business school and a former president of the Music Corporation of America's (MCA) talent division during the 1940s and 1950s. His wife, Isabel Bigley Barnett, won a Tony Award for the lead role of Sarah Brown in the original Broadway production of *Guys and Dolls*. Larry believed that artists needed to know more about the "bidness" side of art. The process by which this concept would become a master's program in arts policy and administration under the auspices of an art education department constitutes a helpful case study in Creative Turf Expansion 101. Suffice it to say that a solicitous art college dean and alert department chair were involved, and that Ohio State's business school wasn't all that interested because the initial donation was significantly less than seven digits. Larry's dream of teaching aspiring artists entrepreneurial skills and how to negotiate contracts was about to morph into the nation's first degree-granting program in nonprofit arts management and public sector arts and arts education policy analysis.

As fortune would have it, there were only two newly minted PhDs in the country who had coupled the study of policy analysis with arts education and who could be brought in at the quasi-faculty level of "lecturer" (translation: will work for peanuts with no health benefits) to develop the proposed graduate program. My sole competitor had just graduated from Ohio State and might well have beaten me out for these particular peanuts had he not managed to piss off his doctoral thesis adviser. The last I heard, he was teaching part time at Tierra del Fuego Community College. Feeling flush with victory as the newest winner of the graduate job lottery, I was hired with a one-year contract.

While creating the new graduate program, I would be teaching a full load of courses, all of which I would make up along the way. The trick would be to try and stay a chapter or two ahead of my students. I was already feverishly condensing my doctoral dissertation into a publishable format, knowing it would have to appear in print my first year or there would be no second year. Of course, there also wouldn't be a second year if I didn't fully execute an Ohio Board of Regents–approved graduate program. There were times that year when I daydreamed about less stressful employment opportunities in Tierra del Fuego.

***

So there I was, hell-bent for glory in a short yellow dress in the university president's kitchen, face to face with the president himself. I was determined to talk up the exciting and newly proposed arts policy program, knowing from experience that such moments should not be squandered. Also, thanks to my friendship with Jerry Pratt, I knew that university presidents were people, too (although I've heard there are exceptions), so I was not intimidated to approach the head honcho. I learned then that it was Gordon Gee who had closed the deal to secure the funds that brought me to Ohio State. "I have a special interest in that program," he said.

A few weeks later, I ran into Gordon Gee on campus at an exhibition opening at the Wexner Center for the Arts. Art openings are good sport if you like sipping white wine while gazing at unusual-looking people. I enjoy both of these activities. The art at Wexner openings was usually good, as well, which was an unexpected bonus—not that anyone paid much attention.

I was not on the guest list for the Wexner's private openings but attended with my faculty cohort and comrade Carol Gigliotti. Carol had an appointment in the Wexner's education department, which meant that, happily, she got invited to these fashion-forward affairs that were entirely devoid of drably attired math and history professors. Wexner openings are as close to New York art experiences as one gets in Columbus, Ohio. I never missed one.

Neither did Gordon. He also never missed me. He would always find his way through the adoring throng to ask how I was doing and inquire about the progress of the arts policy program. Witnessing this process at the third Wexner opening that school year, Carol cocked one dark eyebrow, smiled conspiratorially, and whispered, "He likes you."

I looked at her in surprise. "What do you mean?"

"I mean he *really* likes you," she clarified. "His eyes twinkle when he looks at you."

"Isn't he married?" I asked.

I had no reason to think previously about his marital status, and had just assumed that university presidents usually had spouses. Besides, I'd long ago learned that just because a man is attentive doesn't mean he has ulterior motives. Sometimes it's plain old-fashioned manners. Carol informed me that Gordon's wife had died two years earlier.

"Let's just stand here and see if he comes back around," she smirked.

She positioned herself so that she was facing the crowd into which Gordon had disappeared. We resumed our chitchat, trying to act nonchalant, as she kept tabs on the president's progression around the room. Not more than ten minutes had passed when she gestured with her eyes over my left shoulder. "Here he comes."

"So how do you like the show?" he asked, looking at me.

"It's very good," I said, choking back a nervous titter and managing to add, "I especially like that piece." I nodded almost randomly at a large painting not far away, attempting to redirect his attention away from my stupid grin and rising color. I glanced at Carol, who was struggling to maintain a relaxed, grownup expression but not doing very well.

Gordon agreed the painting was also one of his favorites. We talked for a few more seconds until someone tapped him from behind and he turned away to greet the person. Carol and I couldn't get out of the building fast enough. Grabbing our coats and fleeing into the frosty January night, we burst into girlish giggles.

On the way home, Carol jerked the car to the side of the road, stopping it violently to turn to me and pronounce, "You're going to marry Gordon Gee!"

"Oh! That's ridiculous," I laughed.

"No," she said. "This is an epiphany. I have them. I know it."

***

A week later I reached into my mailbox to discover an envelope with an "Office of the President" return address. I opened it and read, "I would like to invite you to join me and a small number of your faculty colleagues for dinner at my home on Tuesday, February 1, at 7:00

p.m." As much as I had been trying not to think about Carol's words or replay Gordon's and my conversation at the Wexner, my heart leapt: *Wow! Maybe he really* does *like me!*

I sat down to collect myself. Nervously, I dialed the RSVP number to say I would attend. A woman answered, made note of my response, and was about to hang up when I simply had to ask why I, a first-year faculty member, was invited. I felt a lot less special when she told me that invitations to these dinners were "done randomly," their purpose being to bring together faculty from across disciplines who might not otherwise meet one another. I chided myself for my thoughts of presidential romance, but I just couldn't leave it alone.

The next day I meandered into the office of one of my favorite senior department colleagues. We chatted for a few minutes, and then I edged into the topic of the dinner.

"I received an invitation to a faculty dinner at the president's residence."

It was as if I had said, "NASA just telephoned to see if I want to take a ride on the space shuttle."

His eyebrows shot up, but no words escaped his half-open mouth.

"When I called to accept, the secretary told me the guest list was put together 'randomly'—that the dinners were held to bring together faculty from different academic areas," I added half apologetically, still waiting for him to respond.

"Have you ever been invited to one of these dinners?" I tried again.

"No," he finally managed, eyeing me suspiciously.

***

The burning question over the next few days was, What shall I wear? For me, clothes are costume. I've never been dedicated to one particular fashion look or signature perfume. I like to mix it up according to mood and occasion. My closet harbors an assortment of styles and attitudes: '20s Hollywood, '40s man-tailored, '60s mod, '70s glitter disco, urban minimalist. (I used a three-inch-long, black-enameled and silver-inlaid cigarette holder during my sophomore and junior years of college, and I've always had a tender affection for cloche hats. It is very possible that I was a flapper in a former life.) I decided on "1920s demure sophisticate" for the president's dinner, donning a deep blue-violet drop-waist dress, an opera-length strand of not obviously faux pearls, and low black suede heels. My chin-length, pageboy haircut nicely completed the effect.

Armed with a spiral-bound copy of the recently completed Ohio Board of Regents proposal, which I intended to present to Gordon Gee upon either my arrival or my departure, I told my concerned-looking English setter to "be a good boy," returned my little brown-and-white dwarf rabbit to his cage, and climbed into my pale-yellow Toyota Tercel. It was already five minutes till seven; I was going to be late to dinner at the president's house. I tried my best to breathe slowly and deeply during the twenty-minute drive across town to Bexley, an affluent township east of downtown Columbus.

I had read that morning in the campus newspaper that President Gee would celebrate his fiftieth birthday the next day, 2 February 1994. It was the first time I thought about our age difference. We were a decade apart.

The residence was a lovely gray two-story, cedar-shingled house. It had a Cape Cod, cottagelike quality that welcomed rather than imposed. The golden glow of the lights through its windows contrasted deliciously with the sharp nip in the night air and the blanket of snow on the lawn and shrubbery. The door opened instantly as I stepped up to ring the bell. The greeter—a young, nice-looking fellow dressed in a business suit—gave me a warm smile, pried the proposal from my grasp, whisked away my coat, and delivered me into the drawing room.

Gordon was standing among a cluster of guests but facing the entrance. He immediately walked over to welcome me. I realized with embarrassment that he had been awaiting my arrival. He quickly introduced me to his ten other guests, all super-senior faculty, most from the medical school or other areas of science.

I had taken one sip from the promptly delivered glass of wine when Gordon abruptly took me by the arm, steered me toward the kitchen, through the buffet, and into the raspberry-colored formal dining room. In a single motion, he seated me to his immediate right at the long mahogany table, plucked his chair from the head of the table, and propped it against the wall in the hallway. Clearly, no one else was going to sit in that spot. As I was still recovering from the buffet march, the deliberateness of this action further flustered me.

The young man who had greeted me at the door surveyed the scene with a bemused smile. I hoped that by the time Gordon returned with his plate and chair, the flush would leave my face.

After some brief pleasantries, our host requested that we introduce ourselves to one another by describing our research interests. "Tom, why don't you begin?" he nodded to the bearded fellow at his left. Each guest dutifully complied: astrophysics, econometrics, infectious disease, finding the cure for cancer . . . With each daunting pronouncement, my heart pounded harder in agonizing anticipation of my rapidly approaching reciprocation. *Oh God*, I thought, *how do I make what I am doing sound important?!*

Two recitations away from my intellectual Waterloo, I was saved. One of the guests introduced herself as Moon Womyn. She proceeded to inform us of her research in feminist theory and sexual oppression. There's a saying in Alabama that goes, "Thank God for Mississippi." "Thank God for Moon Womyn," I murmured into my barely forked food. In the middle of a game of macho-science one-upmanship, a feminist-speak discourse delivered by a mascara-less women's study dweller with a pretentious, self-inflicted name is a true godsend. *Thank you, Jee-sus.*

My turn came. I smiled demurely, gazed admiringly at my colleagues, and expressed my awe over the wonderful work they were doing and how honored I was to be in their venerated presence. Stressing the impressive word "policy" over the suspect word "art" (and the decidedly unimposing word "education"), I gave a three-sentence explanation of my five months of scholarly labor at Ohio State. I was the last in line to speak. Gordon smiled in benediction, a signal that we could now chat among ourselves.

Gordon turned toward the man seated on his left, so I began a conversation with the fellow on my right. Within three or four minutes, however, Gordon gently tapped the table and interjected a comment into the conversation unfolding on his right. Apparently, he had performed his duty toward his other dinner companion and was now free to turn his attention to me. In short order, it was only the president and I, as all other conversations seemed to fade away.

We quickly got around to the topic of New York. Gordon and his late wife, Elizabeth, had spent a few years living on the Columbia University campus while he worked on his law degree. Their daughter, Rebekah, was a freshman at Columbia, he proudly told me. He visited her often, and had great fun taking her shopping and out to eat. We began swapping stories about favorite New York restaurants, favorite things to do, and favorite areas of the city. It could have been like one of those speed-dating experiences where you get five minutes to impress someone or it's over, but this was different. We really wanted to know about each other.

One of the things I loved to do most in New York was go dancing, I said, especially at the Rainbow Room. Gordon, too, loved dancing at the Rainbow Room! He had taken Rebekah there for her eighteenth birthday last December.

I'd lived for many years on Sullivan Street in SoHo and enjoyed exploring Lower Manhattan. So did he!

Had he ever taken the train to Brooklyn Heights, strolled the Promenade, and walked back to Manhattan over the Brooklyn Bridge? He hadn't but would love to do so.

Here I was, flirting openly with the president of the university where I'd just been given my first postdoctoral career opportunity. This was where a more cautious woman would have stepped back and thought a moment about the wisdom of such an unrestrained tête-à-tête with the big boss—but not me. I'd always led with my heart and I wasn't about to change.

"I read in today's *Lantern* that your fiftieth birthday is tomorrow; I had my fortieth in December," I said.

"You're forty!" he exclaimed so loudly that for a moment everyone stopped talking and turned to look at us. "I thought you were much younger," he added more softly.

***

I proudly presented my proposal to him after he helped me into my coat. I had lingered for a few minutes so I wouldn't have to give it to him in front of the other guests. "I look forward to reading it," he said, as we walked toward the door. I floated out into the crisp winter air.

Gordon later told me he had thought I was in my early thirties, as are most new PhDs. He was relieved and encouraged when he discovered I was forty. An age difference of ten years seemed more personally and professionally acceptable than one of fifteen or more. He also told me later that he immediately arranged a meeting with the OSU board chairman and provost just to make certain there wouldn't be a problem with his dating a faculty member.

As for me, I tended to find older men more alluring than men my own age. Not men old enough to be my *father*, mind you—my daddy complex wasn't that severe—but a decade or so older seemed to work out nicely. Older men did more interesting things, or so it seemed to me at the time. (Most men ten years older than I am now are retired and playing golf in Florida, which doesn't exactly blow my skirt up.) Intellect and dedication to a creative endeavor or societal cause have always been the things that most attract me to a man. When a women is in her twenties and thirties, smart men in their forties and fifties often have a lengthy leg up on their juniors. I had found that to be the case early on, first with my undergraduate painting professor, and later with a lanky, athletic former Penn State psychology professor turned workplace communication skills counselor who broke my heart when he telephoned ten minutes before he was suppose to arrive for dinner to say he wasn't coming.

"Are you not feeling well?" I asked.

"No, I feel fine," he said. "I've decided I don't want to continue this relationship."

"Could we talk about this . . . face-to-face?" I gulped.

"No, nothing to talk about," replied the communication skills expert.

But back to the budding romance at hand.

After Gordon met with the chairman and provost, he dropped in to see Donald Harris, dean of the College of the Arts, and while "casually" inquiring about the progress of the arts policy program, wondered aloud if Harris thought I was a lesbian. A lesbian? Gordon reasoned that an attractive, never-married forty-year-old could very likely be a lesbian. (Hmmm . . . Well, I know that my own gaydar goes up around attractive, never-married forty-year-old men—especially those who like to go dancing at the Rainbow Room. But I'm certain I hadn't mentioned my bartending stint at the lesbian club during any of our previous conversations, and it wasn't on my résumé.)

Gordon telephoned two nights after the faculty dinner on the pretext of discussing my proposal. I was at my computer, concentrating on my final revisions to a journal article based on my dissertation.

"Hello?" I answered absently, glancing at my watch, and realizing with a flash of annoyance that it was well after ten o'clock.

"Hi, Constance. It's Gordon Gee. Sorry to be calling so late."

"Oh, that's all right," I said, taken completely by surprise but trying to steady my voice. "I'm at my computer writing," I added like a good student.

"It's good to know the faculty is working so hard," he joked with a nervous chuckle. "I finished reading your proposal," he continued, "It's excellent. You deserve an A-plus."

"Well, thank you," I murmured, grateful beyond measure he could not see my cheeks, suddenly hot to the touch. I had very much wanted his approval. Why was I now so shy about getting it?

An awkward silence followed.

"Do you think it would be too forward of me to ask you to dinner?" he stumbled.

"I'd love to have dinner with you," I said, recovering myself.

"I'm traveling a lot this week and next. I've got a lot going on, so not sure when," he said.

What's this about? He calls to ask me out and then says he doesn't know when?

"What about Sunday night?" he added after a brief pause. As in three days from now.

"This Sunday?" I asked in amusement, now with my antennae up. *Maybe I shouldn't make this so easy. Oh, what the heck.* "Okay."

"Could I ask a favor?" he rushed on. "I've got an event at the house earlier that evening. Would you mind driving over to the residence?"

He's not going to pick me up? That's not very gentlemanly. "Okay," I said again, slightly miffed.

"Around eight?"

Late for a school night, I thought. "All right," I said. "See you then."

After hanging up, I pondered the conversation I'd just had with the Ohio State president and my acquiescence to each and every one of his eyebrow-raising maneuvers. *Well, he's not a southerner, and he is the president; he is very busy and probably doesn't think about such things*, I reasoned.

***

On Sunday, I drove into his driveway a few minutes after eight. He had been on watch from the kitchen window and quickly came out to my car. "We've got reservations at the Bexley Monk. It's just up the street. I'll drive."

The maître d' came over to greet us as we entered the restaurant, obviously pleased to see Gordon. He ushered us into the dining room and toward a cozy booth. The restaurant was only about half full. Almost everyone looked up and smiled at the president and his dinner companion. Several people called, "Hello, Gordon!" He waved back and we stopped to speak with two of his neighbors, a handsome couple who lived across the park from the residence. I felt a few eyes lingering on me as I slipped self-consciously into the booth across from Gordon.

I quickly learned he was Mormon. He joked that this meant he "didn't drink or smoke, but watch your women." I told him that the chair of my thesis committee at Penn State, Brent Wilson, was Mormon (or "LDS" [as in the Church of Jesus Christ of Latter-Day Saints], as Brent preferred). I informed Gordon that I had worked closely with Brent and with his decidedly non-Mormon wife, Marj, who was also on the art education faculty and my thesis committee. "I adored them both," I said.

What I didn't tell Gordon that evening was that I knew what Mormon underwear looked like. Marj had provided this useful tidbit. I had dropped by their home one afternoon so she could show me how to format a graph on the computer. Marj was a whiz at all things technological. In the midst of my tutorial, the dryer buzzed. I followed her downstairs as we continued our conversation. Pulling the warm clothes out of the dryer, she suddenly brandished a pair of strange white-cotton-knit long-john shorts three feet in front of my face. She smiled evilly. "Want to see Brent's underwear?"

"Nooooooo!" I yowled. It was too late. I could now imagine what my revered professor looked like in his magic skivvies.

(While disconcerting at the time, this image actually came in handy during my dissertation defense.)

Like many Mormons, Brent wore the undergarment as a daily religious observance. As I would come to know, Gordon preferred boxer shorts of Brooks Brothers plaid and snappy Vineyard Vine beach motifs. He wore his "garmies" more as a talisman against plane crashes and football game losses.

***

Gordon seemed to appreciate my casual reception of his announcement that he was Mormon. He had no idea that I was using the "imagine the audience in their underwear" approach to calm my fluttering stomach. The fact was and remains that I don't much care about a person's religion, as long as there's not an oversupply of it.

Our conversation progressed easily, and by the end of dinner had become soft and intimate. Gordon told me about Elizabeth's death after her long struggle with cancer. It was terribly difficult on him and their daughter. Rebekah was sixteen when her mother had died. Like most teenage girls, she had an emotional push-pull with her mother, made all the more intense by Elizabeth's protracted illness. He and Elizabeth had adopted Rebekah when she was four days old. Elizabeth had wanted a large family, but she learned in her midtwenties that she could not have children. After a few years, they decided to adopt. Gordon told me that Mormons often adopt children, even when they have their own.

My heart went out to him and Rebekah. My heart ached for Elizabeth, who was only six years older than I when she passed away. I smiled through the tears that blurred the flickering candle between us, revisiting his earlier remark about "watching your women." This bespectacled, bow-tied guy was clearly women-*un*worldly. It was more than that, though. He was earnest, sweet, and self-effacingly funny—a refreshing combination for a woman who had long majored in darkly handsome and too cool.

We were the last patrons to leave the restaurant, and it was quite late as we pulled into the residence driveway. He came around to open my door. I got out and stepped over to my car.

"Thank you, Gordon. I had a wonderful time."

"Me, too," he said, standing close but not moving forward to embrace me.

I turned to open my car door and then, without thinking, whirled around and quickly kissed him goodnight squarely on the lips. I surprised both of us. I scrambled into my car and pulled out of the drive, heart pounding. A few blocks up the street, I pulled over and thought: *I cannot believe you just did that!*

***

Elizabeth, true to LDS tradition, always kept a journal. A selection of her journal entries was published posthumously as a book, *The Light around the Dark*. It chronicles the years of her fierce battle with breast cancer and her thoughts about life as she moved ever closer to death. It's a bittersweet, stoic story and offers her own poignant observations about the challenges of being both a university president's wife and Gordon's wife, in particular.

Gordon mailed me a copy of her book the day after our dinner at the Bexley Monk. I looked at the inscription: "To Constance Bumgarner—with best wishes and the hope that you, too, will always find the light around your own life."

I was taken aback. It seemed like such an intimate thing to share after a single date, but then our conversation the previous evening had been remarkably intimate. *He wants me to know him*, I thought with a stab of deep affection. I began leafing through the book, reading passages at random.

It was all so sad. Elizabeth seemed disturbingly isolated in her marriage and in her illness; that much I garnered quickly. I sat down on the sofa and read it through from the beginning. Her portrayal of Gordon was complex—of a man attentive and focused when a crisis arose, but largely absent, physically and emotionally, in the day-to-day. He was there to help her procure an experimental medical procedure, but would withdraw within himself afterward, when she really needed the intimacy of his company.

I closed the book and wondered why he wanted me to know these things about him. Did he not see the disquieting picture Elizabeth had painted of him? Had he read it so long ago that he had forgotten, only remembering the tender parts about their life together? Or was this a confession of sorts? A tacit acknowledgment that he had done the best he could in a terrible circumstance? An admission by an imperfect human who craved understanding from a younger woman who wanted to give it?

***

That was the beginning of a romantic courtship made all the sweeter because we kept it secret. We took long, exploratory drives in the rolling countryside outside Columbus, first in one direction, then another. Gordon knew the state well. He traveled it constantly to meet with alumni, parents, high-school students and teachers, farmers, physicians, veterinarians, and business people—basically anybody and everybody with a possible connection to Ohio State. He had been identified as a close second, right behind the governor, in a statewide name-recognition poll and had been approached by both political parties as a possible gubernatorial candidate. He had declined.

Gordon took pride in his knowledge of the small townships. He enjoyed regaling me with humorous and touching stories about the people he had met when speaking at a Rotary or Lion's Club. I pointed out the natural beauty of the landscape: the woods and fields greening into spring after a long, cold winter; the slant and hue of the sunlight and shadows; an enormous flock of black birds peppering a sea of cornstalks.

One day a brand-new crescent moon hung in a deep blue, late-afternoon sky like the bright-white grin of the Cheshire Cat. "The perfect swing," I said.

He delighted in my whimsy. "I can see you up there," he chuckled.

Gordon often told me he loved my visual descriptions of nature and my excitement over the birds and animals I pointed out from the car. He didn't usually notice such things, he admitted.

We talked about all sorts of subjects, personal, political, and university related, as we meandered over the back roads. Our conversations were broad and deep, relaxed, and always interesting. He took great pleasure in my comically irreverent observations on human behavior and academic rules and regulations. My junior faculty perspective of the university, and my unabashed willingness to share it with him, intrigued him. We expanded each other's thinking, and laughed a lot along the way. He steered with one hand, holding mine with the other.

***

In mid-March, Gordon asked me to spend a weekend with him in New York. This would be the first time we'd spend the night together. We arrived at the hotel in the late afternoon. We unpacked, dressed, and headed to the Rainbow Room.

I still have the menu and a photograph from that evening. In the image we hold each other on the rotating dance floor, paused in midstep, smiling brightly at the photographer. A black headband sweeps my hair away from my face, revealing the drop faux-pearl earrings I had bought especially for the occasion. I wear a simple black knit dress and sensibly low-heeled black pumps, perfect for dancing. Gordon looks handsome and proud. His hand is spread wide across my lower back. "When the world was ours," reads the Rainbow Room inscription on the green-and-blue cardboard photo jacket.

On the back of the menu Gordon wrote:

Gordon and Constance's Big Adventure:

1. Danced at the Rainbow Room and into my heart!
2. Won the "Most Beautiful Woman in N.Y." Prize.
3. At the same time—won the "Best Dancer in N.Y." Prize.

Our dancing was as enjoyable and inventive as our conversations. We moved smartly across the floor, impressing ourselves with our well-matched steps and agility. Other couples smiled and nodded at us. We glowed in return like starry-eyed young lovers in a 1950s movie. We fell in love that night at the Rainbow Room.

We made love for the first time when we returned to the hotel. We were good together. Afterward, we ordered up a banana split and two spoons.

Although Gordon had booked a separate room for me at my request, its bathroom and closets were the only areas that would be put to use that weekend. I had no interest in leaving his side, and he did not want to leave mine. In Columbus, there were scores of distractions—hands reaching out for him to shake, his name yelled out as he crossed the street, throngs of people jostling to speak with him, his car phone ringing incessantly. For these stolen forty-eight hours in New York, his focus was on me.

This concentrated attention was as seductive to me as our original organic connection. Aside from knowledge and talent, the kind of charisma that it takes to rise to the top in any field is what makes a great leader. People often talk about Bill Clinton, Bill Gates, and Oprah having that kind of personal magnetism. In the world of academia, Gordon was that person. He had dedicated his life to making a difference in education, and I could sense that he was now committing himself to me. At least that's how it felt when the world was ours.

5

Prenuptial Requisites

GORDON AND I KEPT OUR romance confidential at first because we wanted to get to know each other in some degree of privacy. We continued our secrecy into late spring, at my insistence. Larry Barnett had donated additional funding, so a tenure-track faculty member could be hired to direct the newly approved Arts Policy and Administration Program. I had recently been chosen as one of four candidates in a national search to fill the position. I didn't want my relationship with Gordon to positively or negatively influence my chances of winning the appointment. One never knows how one's colleagues might respond to such news.

Everything was hunky-dory for me at Ohio State, with one significant exception: *teaching*. I had completed and submitted a solid proposal to the Board of Regents for the establishment of a Master of Arts in Arts Policy and Administration. I had gained Larry's confidence, which had helped secure the additional program funds. My dissertation research, analyzing the intent, structure, and effects of federal arts education policy and programming, had been published in a respected scholarly journal and had attracted serious attention. My love life was better than a Hollywood romance. I was even teaching a step-aerobics class twice a week at the nicest exercise facility in town. University teaching, however, was whuppin' my behind.

I was having a tough time, in terms of both course content and methodology—*what* I was teaching and *how* I was teaching it. My only previous teaching experience had been as a TA at Penn State. Any college undergrad can testify that just because someone has spent three years as a teaching assistant (and another two or three or seven writing a dissertation) does not mean that person knows much about teaching. The operative word in the phrase "teaching assistant" is *assistant*. To make matters more desperate, at Ohio State I wasn't teaching undergraduates. I was teaching graduate students, a few close to my age, with more experience than I had in day-to-day nonprofit arts management. I feared that the rubber-meets-the-road realities of teaching were careening me over a steep embankment. I was scrambling to commit to memory today what I would be teaching tomorrow. I had no inkling of "classroom management strategies" or of how to jump-start a class discussion. I was excruciatingly aware of my knowledge and experience deficits and terrified of my students standing up en masse and calling "Bullshit!"

A Gary Larson cartoon came out around that time, picturing an oafish student, with his hand raised, asking: "My brain is full, may I go home now?" With the slight variation of substituting the word "fried" for "full," that was precisely the way I felt after cramming for each and every class, and crawling toward the finish line of its conclusion.

***

The unpublished rules of the game for fledgling faculty at most research universities go something like this:

> OK, you're hired. You can teach one course related to your dissertation research. The other three or four will be on something about which you know very little, if anything. We have no idea, and don't much care, about your teaching abilities. We'll find that out along the way when the students submit their anonymous evaluations of your teaching, facial expressions, and fashion sensibilities. This will occur at the end of the semester—after they know what grade they've received in your course. (By the way, be certain to keep up our rigorous grading standards!) If, for one reason or another, they don't like you, they'll

rip you to shreds. This information will go in your permanent file and will be considered if and when you make it to your fourth-year review. At that point, we will decide whether you may or may not proceed toward the ultimate goal of tenure. If not, you will need to clean out your teensy office forthwith so we can replace you with another pitifully eager, college loan–burdened desperado. Of course, if you publish a lot of articles in academic journals (*peer reviewed, please!*) or, Lord Almighty, a BOOK, then we won't pay much attention to what those little dweebs have to say. And if you bring a big fat grant into the department coffers, then you're golden. Anyway, in the meantime, here are your assigned courses. Oh, and there's the community service component (*snicker*). Break a leg.

Two months into my first semester at Ohio State, a gangster band of three students had decided I should be deep-sixed. They'd become used to having direct and frequent access to Dean Harris, as there had been an eight-month lag between the departure of their former faculty adviser and my arrival. They saw themselves as student pioneers in arts policy and administration. They liked things better before I came along and got between them and the dean in the academic flowchart. I did things differently than my faculty predecessor did; they didn't like that, either. Being much too accustomed to the ideological sparring that spiced my own recent grad school experience, I offhandedly described the Republican grandstanding against the National Endowment for the Arts as "self-righteously really fucked up." (Oops!) I then frolicked on to compare the difficulty of describing an "aesthetic experience" to that of describing an orgasm. (I still think this is a fitting analogy, however shocking it was to those chaste twenty-something graduate students.) The band of three scurried off to the dean to inform him of my pedagogical transgressions.

I was swiftly made to understand that these students were out for blood, which they just might get if I didn't immediately cease my use of profanity and "sexual innuendo." Sucking up to them was also advisable. My department chair (who was truly sympathetic about the entire mess) broke this news to me moments before my first class of the day on the morning of my fortieth birthday, 1 December 1993. It was touch and go for about a month. I thought I was going to lose my job.

I honestly think my memories of that incident undermined my confidence in the classroom for my entire teaching career. I will always be grateful to my faculty colleagues and students who stood beside me during that rough patch.

***

The Ohio Board of Regents approved the proposed master's program in mid-April 1994. A few days later I learned that I was to be its director and the new tenure-track professor.

The following weekend, on a Saturday night, Gordon and I attended our first public gathering together. It was a black-tie dinner for the Ohio State University President's Club. I was so nervous that I have no memory of what I wore—only that it was floor length and uncontroversial. Five hundred heads swiveled when Gordon and I entered the ballroom. We stood motionless for a brief moment as though pressed in amber by the viscosity of their gaze and their collective will to hold me immobile for a probing once-over. If Dean Harris had detected some interest on Gordon's part with the lesbian inquiry three months earlier, his expression did not indicate it. He and his wife, Marilyn, were seated directly in our path, and I witnessed the dangerous lurch of his chair as he whipped around to see what had caught the attention of his tablemates.

Other than our grand entrance, my only clear memories of that evening were Gordon's empty seat beside me, and the distinct feeling of being peeped at from every direction. Gordon, you see, rarely remains seated for more than a few minutes at large dinner parties where there is schmoozing to do. It is apparently part of his job to bestow on each table three or four minutes of his attention, whether or not he is the event host. (All political spouses will know exactly what I am talking about.) He'd be able to do more room-working prior to being seated for dinner but for his habit of arriving toward the end of the cocktail hour. He always has his busy schedule to use as cover for his late arrival, but the truth is that it's not much fun for someone who doesn't drink to watch others do so for an hour or more *before* he has to sit down with those same people for another two hours and three or four courses. I can't blame him—I feel the same, and I drink. Anyway, Gordon is frequently AWOL during multiple-tabled dinner parties, and it falls to his escort to hold down the fort and divert attention away from his absence with lively conversation. I would soon become accustomed to his dinner-table disappearance act, but that first evening I felt a bit like Little Orphan Annie after Daddy Warbucks departs on one of his business trips.

Sunday afternoon was rainy and cold, so Gordon and I decided to do some shopping at the downtown mall. Gordon enjoys shopping more than any man I've ever known; he particularly likes strolling around a mall. If I need an item, I go directly to the store I think might have it—a small boutique, if possible—and buy it. I've always disliked the hermetically sealed aspect of indoor malls, along with their chain-store sameness. I love the zombie movie *Dawn of the Dead*, in which the decaying denizens lurch by JC Penney and concrete fountains as mall music plays.

"What are they doing? Why do they come here?" asks the female protagonist.

"Some kind of instinct, a memory of what they used to do. This was an important place in their lives," explains her male counterpart.

But going to the mall that Sunday with Gordon was an entirely different experience. It was the academic equivalent of going out with Bruce Springsteen. People smiled, heads turned.

"Hello, Gordon!"

"Hi, President Gee!"

"Go Bucks!"

Gordon was enjoying the excitement elicited by his mall stroll and, I suspect, relished showing off his popularity to me. It was clear, however, that my presence on this stage set was less than incidental. If we'd been in a movie, I'd have been a ten-dollar extra—not that I was expecting anything more. It was fun in a disconnected sort of way to observe his interaction with his fans. He was Mr. Ohio State and he was taking pleasure in his job. I didn't fault him for that, but if I'd been a more reflective person I might have caught the flicker of a foreshadowing that I was to become an extra in my own life.

***

It seemed everyone was lying in wait on the third floor of Hopkins Hall when I walked toward my office on Monday morning.

"So what's all this about?" queried my department head, waving me into his office with a fatherly smile.

"You're dating Gordon Gee?! How long have you been going out?" asked faculty and secretarial staff.

"Not long. We're just getting to know each other," I assured them with as much composure as I could muster, even as I was about to burst with excitement.

My students (with the sheepish exception of the mutineers who had tried to get me fired) were thrilled. I was close with many of them. They crowded into my office to get the scoop.

I was now an authentic tenure-track faculty member, the director of the new arts policy program, *and* the president's girlfriend. I noted that what I had to say at faculty meetings was suddenly given more weight. This realization brought me more discomfort than satisfaction, in that I was still as much of a smart-mouth as I'd always been. Jests that my colleagues previously would have laughed at, or simply ignored, were now parsed more closely. Fortunately only a month remained until the end of the school year. Maybe I could take an intensive summer course in gravitas and tongue curbing.

***

It was right about then that Gordon announced he had gotten a vasectomy. We had talked about that possibility once or twice, but only in the most preliminary manner. I'd never had a burning desire to have children, except for a brief spell in my early thirties. I was dating a lunatic at the time, a very sexy lunatic to be certain, but neither husband nor daddy material when I really thought about it. Somehow, by the time we broke up, the urge to be a mother had passed. I decided to pursue my doctorate and just never got back around to a mating-and-procreating state of mind.

Two popular T-shirts at the time pretty much summed it up for me and for a surprising number of my girlfriends: "Oops, I forgot to have children!" and "Nuclear war? What about my career?" My parents had never encouraged me toward matrimony, much less raising a family. If not downright opposed to the idea, my mother was definitely on the negative side of ambivalent. "I don't care if you ever have children," she'd opine breezily. Although she'd usually follow up with "Don't misunderstand, I'm glad I have you," motherhood never seemed like something to aspire to. And what daughter in her right mind would want to risk being trapped in wedlock by a baby, as her own mother had been? Besides, the world was an overpopulated, violent mess; why bring more people into it?

To my way of thinking, there are at least as many reasons for women *not* to have children as there are to have them. But then reasoning doesn't play much of a role in procreation. For the human species, contemplation of the creational consequence of copulation seems to exist in inverse proportion to the situational logic of multiplying. In Margaret Atwood's futuristic novel *Oryx and Crake*, Crake comments on the inevitability of human overpopulation and its disastrous end: "You can't couple a minimum access to food with an expanding population indefinitely. *Homo sapiens* doesn't seem able to cut himself off at the supply end. He's one of the few species that doesn't limit reproduction in the face of dwindling resources. In other words—and up to a point, of course—the less we eat, the more we fuck."[1]

It wasn't that I was against having children (although I do think there ought to be a nontransferable, worldwide limit of one per person for the next hundred years). It was more a case of not having found any compelling reason to do so—the first and foremost consideration being that I didn't have a husband and was not especially eager to acquire one. I know husbands are not required for childbearing, but I always thought it was a sound idea.

For the first time in my life, I had fallen very much in love with a man with whom I could envision spending the rest of my years—not that we had yet spoken of that possibility. Nevertheless, Gordon was a person I wanted to have a long future with. I was also forty and moving into the now-or-never female life phase of yea or nay to motherhood. As most women in my circumstance might imagine, I was not altogether pleased by Gordon's vasectomy revelation, and I was more than a little hurt and insulted by the implications of his apparent rush to have one. But I could not rationally argue that at this point in our relationship the decision wasn't his to make. As it turned out, this would be only the first of many major decisions affecting the two of us that were his to make and mine to react to.

***

In June, Gordon asked me to marry him. He had just arrived back in town from traveling on university business. He telephoned to say he was heading back out the next morning, so we wouldn't have time to get together.

"Darn," I sighed, "I miss you."

"I miss you, too," he said. "I wish you were here right now."

"Me too. When do you get back?"

"Day after tomorrow, but I have a board dinner that evening."

"Oh," I sighed again.

A few beats passed. "Let's get married," he said.

I gulped, totally surprised. A *whoosh* of emotion flooded me; I felt the blood surge to my head. *He's asking you to marry him*, my brain shouted. *Respond!*

"I'd like that very much," I managed.

Gordon immediately began tossing out possible dates, in his characteristic plan-ahead, get-it-on-the-calendar, decisive manner. I was still trying to process the fact that he had just asked me to marry him, and that I had just said yes.

We're getting married! I wanted to reach through the phone and squeeze him tight. I wanted him to reach through the phone and squeeze me back.

I regretted accepting his proposal the moment we hung up. I didn't regret that we were to be married. I loved him! I loved his wit, his energy. I especially loved talking with him about, well, *everything*. I knew he loved me, too. He always seemed to take such delight and pride in my presence. We had many common interests. We were intellectually compatible and terrific dance partners. The contrast between our religious and regional backgrounds was almost comical—a Mormon from Utah and a Disciple of Christ turned Druid-Buddhist from North Carolina. "*You're* dating a *Mormon*?!" my friends would chortle.

At the time, we saw our differences as complementary, as broadening for both of us. We were a good pair. We made a good *team*.

My regret was that this personally historic moment had occurred *over the phone*. This wasn't the way it was supposed to happen. It was supposed to happen during a candlelight supper at a corner table in some cozy, rosy-hued restaurant. It was supposed to happen at a picnic lunch, as we sat eating juicy peaches in a beautiful garden. It was supposed to happen in a parked car along-side a field of wildflowers during a drive through the countryside. It was supposed to happen when we were *together*. He would take my hand, look into my eyes, and say: *I love you. I want to be with you forever. Please be my wife.* And I would say, *I love you, too. I would be honored to be your wife. Please be my husband.* Then we would embrace and kiss. That's the way it was supposed to happen.

Why hadn't I had the presence of mind to say: "Gordon, I want to marry you, too! But please, ask me again when we are together, side by side in the same room." Maybe part of me was a little afraid that, if I didn't say *yes* right then and there, he might change his mind.

All I knew for certain was that—for the first time in my life—I'd just told a man I would marry him and, a few minutes later, I was staring at the phone. *Alone.*

***

I quickly learned that all things revolved around the university and its calendar. Our wedding would take place over Thanksgiving break, with the honeymoon scheduled for the following June, after graduation ceremonies.

We decided to have the nuptials in Salt Lake City rather than North Carolina or Columbus, for two reasons. First, Gordon's mother, Vera, was too frail to travel comfortably. And second, I wanted to avoid what in Columbus would have been a huge, public affair. While it was great fun accompanying Gordon to university events and other festivities, I did not seek a spotlight on our private affairs.

I understood nothing of how swiftly and radically my life was to change. Gordon was so used to living such an intensely public life that he did not think to prepare me for those changes.

***

We kept our engagement confidential until after Labor Day, announcing it as the new school year began. I was completely unprepared for the media frenzy. Gordon's top two public relations men immediately summoned me to the president's office for a coaching session on how to deal with the reporters who were calling his office and my home. I had no idea what to expect. Were they serious about this? Would I have to go into some kind of training?

Gordon was immensely popular. He was Ohio State personified—the No. 1 bow-tied Buckeye. There was considerable public interest in his private life, what little he had of it. Elizabeth had died a year and a half after their arrival in Columbus. The good folk of Ohio had been very sympathetic to the family's struggles, and genuinely wanted to see their university president both happy and happily matched. His engagement to a new assistant professor was like the prince marrying Cinderella. So romantic! It was a real-life, happily-ever-after story.

The two-man PR team conducted a mock interview with me so I could practice answering likely questions:

"How did you meet?"

"At a bar—just kidding."

"Amusing, but don't be flippant. How did you meet?"

"At a new faculty reception Gordon held at the residence a year ago last September. I don't think I'm going to let him have any more of those; all those young professors, you know."

"Where do you plan to go on your honeymoon?"

"We're going to fly from Salt Lake to New York so we can go dancing at the Rainbow Room. We're only staying two nights. Gotta get back for winter quarter. We've talked about driving through England's Lake District and up into Scotland for a couple of weeks in June. Afterward, we might take the Chunnel from London to Paris!"

"Where is your home?"

"North Carolina. Tar Heel born, Tar Heel bred."

"How do you like Ohio State?"

"What's not to like? The president is awfully cute!"

And so on.

This isn't so difficult, I thought. Besides, the media in and around Columbus were very supportive of Gordon. From what I'd read, the *Columbus Dispatch* seemed to love him. There had been some initial problems with the *Cleveland Plain Dealer*, Gordon had told me, but he'd worked them out. I had no idea what a media master he was, nor any conception of what that entailed or how truly important it was. This interview business seemed relatively straightforward to me: just answer the questions. That one-hour session was to be my only media tutorial as a university first lady, until twelve years later when Vanderbilt's lawyers would tell me precisely what to say: "I have no comment."

**

My public life officially began on 7 September 1994, on the front page of the *Columbus Dispatch*, with an ego-deflating reality check: "Gordon Gee to Wed Assistant Professor." What was I expecting? "Gordon Gee to Wed Constance Bumgarner"? Still, it seemed a tad dismissive to a forty-year-old woman with her own academic career who thought of herself as an actual person.

In sisterly solidarity, to her dying day, Mrs. Gigliotti (mother of my soothsayer friend Carol) referred to Gordon as "the man who married Constance." Flowers for you, Mrs. Gigliotti.

**

As September flew toward October, I forced myself to turn to a sad task. Gordon had made it clear in the early days of our engagement that my beloved English setter and dwarf rabbit were not welcome at the residence. Mr. Beauregard Jones, a.k.a. "Beaujo," was a wild, beautiful dog—bred for birding, hardwired to run, and impossible to keep fenced in a suburban backyard. I had no choice but to tether him to a tie-out stake with a fifteen-foot cable when I wanted to let him lounge in the backyard on nice days. If I didn't tie him, he would climb the fence like a five-year-old boy on a set of monkey bars and be off in a flash cavorting through the streets.

There had always been a dog in the Bumgarner household— along with a couple of cats and, at other points in my childhood, two hamsters (Sam and Herman), two chicks (one yellow, the other black), and of course the baby squirrel Rutherford Lucius. The cats were always strays that "followed" me home with the encourage- ment of some cheese slices or baloney. Mother and Daddy were indulgent in this regard, loving animals as much as I did.

I continued to rescue stray dogs and cats into my adulthood. I had never considered parting with any of them, with the exception of my last two cats, Chopin and GG Marie, whom I left with my mother when I moved to Columbus. They had been shuttled from

New York to State College to her house in Burlington. They were getting older and enjoyed lolling around on her deck and roaming a more ample backyard than I would have in Columbus, and she'd grown fond of them. I had taken young Beaujo and BW, the dwarf rabbit, along with me to Ohio State.

BW stood for "Bunny Wabbit." It was my former professor Brent Wilson—known to all his graduate students as "BW"—who suggested the name. I had been smitten by a litter of baby bunnies curled up in a bedding of hay in a State College pet store window. I don't usually patronize pet stores because there are already so many homeless animals that need adopting, and I don't want to support the breeding of more. That day, however, my friend Anne and I happened to walk by the shop, spotted the bunnies, and were overcome by their cuteness. It was lagomorph love at first sight. (I understand that's the way a bundled-up infant in a pram affects some women, which accounts for a lot of irrational behavior.) The following day I was walking across campus with BW, pondering the name of my bunny, when he said, "What about BW?" When I shot him an amused glance, he followed up, "for Bunny Wabbit."

Chopin and GG Marie (named for the GG subway line, where I rescued her from inside the tunnel at the Hoyt-Schermerhorn station in Brooklyn while on my way to Pratt one morning) taught BW to use the litter box, and he did, mostly. I would let him out of his cage for a few hours each day to play with GG while Chopin looked on in disgust. As I worked at my computer, GG and BW would take turns chasing each other up and down the hallway. The first time I saw GG tear down the hall after BW, I was up on my feet hollering, "Noooo!" In an instant, BW was chasing GG back the other way. And so it went until they retired to their respective napping spots. GG would stretch out atop the sofa while BW rested securely underneath it.

BW allowed me to place him on his back on my lap, which is the ultimate in bunny trust. He was crazy for chocolate and could hear the crinkle of an M&M's packet being stealthily opened two rooms away. He would bound across the room, leap into my lap, place his front paws on my chest, and gently pluck the M&M that I held for him between my teeth. I knew I shouldn't give him chocolate but figured one morsel once in a while wouldn't hurt him. Being a chocolate lover myself, I knew his joy.

BW was a mighty sweet wabbit, except that wabbits do what they must do: they *chew*. I would place him on a towel on my lap (to catch the wood shavings) and hold an untreated, foot-long two-by-four for him to munch on each evening while I watched TV. This generally kept the monkey off his back, but occasionally a chair leg, the edge of a bookcase, or the spine of a book would prove too tempting. Thus, much of my furniture and just about any book I left in his reach fell victim to a gnawing. My mother will never forgive him for his repeated assaults on her walnut china cabinet. Hopefully, she will never realize the full extent of the molestation, as I always kept wood putty and a medium brown marker close at hand. Gordon made it clear the residence furniture was not going to suffer the same fate. BW would be relegated to his cage, which would be kept in the basement. The thought of this made me very sad, for that was no life for a free-range bunny.

Remarkably, the special assistant to the president stepped forward to say how delighted his family would be to adopt BW. His children, a boy and girl of around seven and five, respectively, were positively delirious with the notion, so I took BW over for a trial introduction. The kids couldn't have been sweeter, gentler, or more excited to meet him. Their father had already built an enclosed pen under the shade of a tree for BW's pleasure on warm days. BW did so enjoy a good supervised hop around the backyard now and then. With tears and lengthy instructions on how to care for and handle a rabbit, and on BW's own special preferences (minus the chocolate), I left him with the children.

***

In early October during a dinner party at the residence, I fell into conversation with Dr. Charles and Barbara Sinsabaugh, a kindly older couple. They lived in Newark, Ohio, an hour's drive east of Columbus. I confided in them that, although I was looking forward to my nuptials, I was terribly troubled about what I should do with my two-year-old English setter.

"An English setter? We'd love to have him!" they both agreed right then and there. They owned a cabin on a pond surrounded by two hundred acres of woods and quail. Beaujo would be very happy there, they assured me.

The next weekend, Gordon, Beaujo, and I drove out to see them. We met them at their home in town, where Beaujo went sniffing all around and Barbara and Charles were just fine with it. We then followed them out to "the farm." Beaujo launched himself out of the car, made a beeline for the pond, and jumped in with a big doggy grin on his face. He liked it there. That was for certain. I agreed they could adopt him, but I would keep him until just before we were to leave for Salt Lake.

While I hated giving up Beaujo, I had to acknowledge that he was much better off with our new friends in Huntin' Dawg Heaven. Not only that, but Gordon was not going to change his mind, no matter how much I pestered him. I don't think he cottoned to Beaujo's protective male energy toward his betrothed; plus Rebekah was allergic to animals, at least all shedding animals.

Gordon and Elizabeth had bought two shih tzus for Rebekah when she was in her early teens. There names were Bad Boy Birk and Mitz America, better known as Birky and Mitzy. "Dumbest dogs in the continental United States," Gordon would say in semifond remembrance. He promptly gave them to Yvonne, the residence housekeeper (and the only person who really loved them), the moment Rebekah departed for college.

He enjoyed describing the time Mitzy slipped out the front door one snowy winter morning and ran across the street into the park. Still in his pajamas and bathrobe, Gordon jammed his feet into a pair of galoshes and took off after her.

"Mitzy! Mitzy! Come here right now!" he bellowed as she scampered around him always just out of reach.

Cars slowed to watch the irate Ohio State president chasing the little white fluffy menace around the park, his bathrobe flapping open in the wind.

***

Beaujo thrived. His chest grew broad from running and swimming. After a few months, I ceased my regular visits to see him. He would greet me with a nuzzle and tail wag but return immediately to Charles's side. He was their dog now.

BW died. His adoptive family went out of town for several days, leaving him in the care of a neighborhood girl. She inadvertently poisoned him by giving him some toxic plant matter she thought he would find tasty—which he did.

The family called to tell me he'd died. I telephoned my friend Anne.

"BW died," I sobbed.

"BW died?!" she shrieked.

"BW, my bunny," I corrected, realizing what she was thinking.

I couldn't stand the thought of BW dying alone in his cage, and cried over him for days. Gordon couldn't understand why I was so upset over a rabbit. "I'm sorry, I know you feel bad," he attempted by way of comfort. I didn't feel bad; I felt *awful*. I had betrayed that trusting little creature, something no animal had ever done to me. I will never get over it.

6

First Time First Lady

WE WERE MARRIED ON THE morning of 26 November 1994 at the White Community Memorial Chapel, a little jewel of a church perched on Capitol Hill and overlooking Salt Lake City. The chapel was decorated very simply, but Mother Nature had gone all out. There had been a plump snowfall the night before of dry, perfectly formed demitasse-saucer-size flakes, the likes of which one seldom sees in the East and I'd never seen growing up in the South. Hardly anyone was about as our little procession drove through town and up toward the chapel. Every tree branch and conifer needle glistened like the lovely diamond on my finger. The sky was Carolina blue.

Gordon and I, along with my small party of out-of-town guests, were staying at a downtown hotel. Rebekah had opted to stay with her aunt Cherie and uncle Malcolm. Cherie, Gordon's older sister and only sibling, had kindly served as my wedding planner because we were having the ceremony on her turf. Gordon and I drove together with my best friend, Cat, who was my matron of honor and only attendant. Rebekah rode with Cherie and Malcolm. Cat's husband, Jerry, drove my mother, stepfather, and friend Betsy, who had been my comrade-in-mischief since our raucous days together in the church nursery. The remainder of my entourage piled into the car with my cousin and surrogate older brother, Carl, at the wheel. Gordon was already dressed in his morning suit, looking fresh and handsome. I would dress at the chapel.

My cream-colored gown was simple and elegant, with a tailored bodice, square neckline, and Eisenhower jacket. I had bought it with the thousand dollars I got for my Toyota, "ol' Yeller," as Gordon called it. I splurged on an exquisite Tuscan wedding cap, which the New York milliner Suzanne fashioned for me. It was a neat little rounded pillbox number with a delicate cluster of peach silk roses fastened at the back. I carried a bouquet of long-stemmed white calla lilies.

Gordon appeared completely relaxed, but I was edgy. He joked that I was going to bolt and leave him at the altar. There is a photo of me in our wedding album pretending to flee the church—gown hiked up with one hand, hairbrush in the other.

I was out of my element and already immersed in his. Most of our seventy guests were Gordon's extended family, including his late wife Elizabeth's mother, stepfather, brother, and stepsister, and all their children and grandchildren. My entourage was much smaller; only six of my closest friends, along with my mother, stepfather, and cousin, had made the trek from eastern to mountain time. I was grateful for their reassuring presence.

I needed reassurance. Rebekah, then a week short of nineteen, was extremely upset that her father was remarrying and missed no opportunity to express her displeasure. The night before the wedding, at the rehearsal dinner, she spent most of her time boohooing in the hallway outside the restaurant bathroom, as various guests attempted to console her. Her morose mood was probably not improved by her uncle Malcolm's slipping her rum-and-Cokes. (Rebekah always had to drink on the sly when her devoutly Mormon grandparents were on hand.) The restaurant had set up a single long table for our party of twenty in a private dining space in the wine cellar. The composition of our rehearsal dinner guests was almost evenly split down the middle—teetotalers, responsible adults (including the groom), and Rebekah (when she wasn't weeping in the hallway) to the bride's left, rowdy friends of the bride to the right. Stranded in the middle with a bright smile plastered on her face, the bride nursed a glass of white wine, occasionally stealing a longing glance at the children's end of the table, where laughter reverberated and no one was nursing anything. The scene would have made for a perfect *Seinfeld* episode, although I failed to grasp the hilarity of it at the time.

Thinking back on it, I should have asked Rebekah to be my maid of honor, but the little time that I had spent with her during her father's and my engagement had not been loads of fun. There was that time when she purposely let Beaujo dash out my front door. He went tearing across a busy street, getting clipped by a car, with me screaming my head off in hot pursuit. (Mercifully, he only suffered a bruised flank.) There was that time when Gordon and Rebekah drove over to pick me up. She was in the front seat, so I climbed into the back. After a block or so, she rolled down the car window (I was being blown to bits) and produced a series of catlike sneezes. "Your perfume!" she gasped, as if I'd taken a bath in Eau de Cheap. There was that time . . . well, you get the picture.

"Why does she dislike me so much?" I naively asked her doting daddy. "I have no children. There is no threat to her on that account." (I was still nettled by Gordon's emergency vasectomy and wondered if Rebekah might have had something to do with instigating it.)

"She'll come around," Gordon assured me.

***

The wedding ceremony was about as simple as they get, which was exactly what we wanted. A trio of musicians from the Salt Lake Symphony played a few classical arrangements. Cousin Carl escorted me down the aisle and handed me off to Gordon, who, as I already noted, looked spiffy in his morning suit. The only hitch came when my stepfather, Olin, read a passage from the Bible that was given to me by my uncle Gene and aunt J. Dean upon my "accepting Christ as my personal savior" at age eight or thereabouts.

It was a white Bible, King James Version most likely, which I'd kept in the drawer of my bedside table when I was growing up. I hadn't seen that thing in years, and for some reason, when Olin held it up and announced that he was going to read from it, I almost burst into tears. As Olin's richly sonorous voice resonated throughout the small church, I stared down at my bouquet trying to get a grip. *Oh! My nose is running!* I thought in panic. "Kleenex?" I whispered desperately to Cat, who was standing next to me. "No!" she whispered back, eyeing the space between my nose and upper lip in alarm as she fought hard to keep from laughing. I wanted to

81

kill her. She swung around and mouthed "Kleenex" to my mother, seated in the front row, who, God bless her, having already divined the crisis, thrust a tissue at Cat, who delivered it to me a split second too late to catch the *blop* into my pretty bouquet. I didn't hear a word Olin read, and I don't remember anything else about the ceremony other than exchanging *I do*s, and being deliriously relieved to exit the sanctuary on Gordon's arm.

The reception luncheon was held at the Town Club, a small private ladies' club to which Cherie belonged. It was all very nice. Gordon and I welcomed our guests, and two or three of them rose to propose a fruit-punch toast to the happy couple. There were no spirits being served, out of deference to our large Mormon contingent. Just below the sober pleasantness meandered an undercurrent of melancholy. Elizabeth's many family members were doing their collective best to be cheerful, but it was all too easy to read the sadness in their eyes. My marriage to their former son-in-law was a stark reminder that Elizabeth was dead and life goes on. It all finally bubbled up and over me when Elizabeth's sweet but emotional younger brother attempted to simultaneously convey his best wishes to me and his sorrow over his sister's death. "I miss her so much!" he gave way, draping his heavy arm over my shoulders to support his six-foot-four, sobbing personage. I could have used a double scotch about then.

It was a relief to conclude the nuptial celebrations and board the plane to New York for the two days that remained of Thanksgiving break. Our Rainbow Room photographs this time framed two beaming newlyweds—one in a tuxedo, the other in a beaded, bronze, backless gown. My hair is longer and wavy. In my favorite of the two images, my head is thrown back, my mouth open in an elated smile. Gordon's face is buried in my neck. The following afternoon we saw the Broadway play *Sunset Boulevard* and had supper at a wonderful Italian restaurant on the Upper East Side. The next morning we were on the plane heading back to Columbus.

I finished moving into the university president's residence over the Christmas holiday, a small feat as everything but my clothing, computer, and research papers went directly into storage. Gordon, Rebekah, and I hung a lifetime of Gee family ornaments on the tree, along with two of my childhood treasures (a Styrofoam bird spray-painted gold, with a few remaining patches of glitter, and a small, framed black-and-white photo of my mother holding me as a newborn), and several new "first Christmas" ornaments that Gordon and I received from friends. Although Gordon did his best to make me feel welcome, I was, in truth, a stranger in a strange land of Gee family holiday ritual. There were father, daughter, and the ghosts of Christmases past—and then there was me, lurking around, trying to sustain delight over this or that family tradition or artifact. (How I missed my dog and rabbit!)

It was the first time Rebekah had been home since I'd moved into the residence. I remember feeling half embarrassed when we'd meet in the hallway in our pajamas and very embarrassed when, with only a brief knock and not waiting for a "Come in," she'd stick her head into my bathroom. She also seemed to enjoy popping into my walk-in closet and leafing through my clothes in a sorority-sister manner, while I attempted a nonchalant conversation in my underwear or less. I didn't want to discourage her impromptu drop-ins, but I was genuinely discomforted by my own naked vulnerability. It took me several days to get up the nerve to ask her to wait until she heard me answer before she entered. The truth was that Rebekah intimidated me, especially on her home turf, and most especially during the granddaddy of family holidays—that most won-der-ful time of the year.

I think we were all thankful to leave the confines of the house and head down to Orlando for the Florida Citrus Bowl. The New Year's bowl celebration is a time-honored Ohio State tradition. Great season or middling, Ohio State will play a bowl game (with the ouchy exception of 2012), because major college bowls are *big business* for the university, the athletic conference, the corporate sponsors, and network television and because Ohio State football has a huge draw. This was my first bowl game and, although we lost to Alabama, 24–17, it was a wild ride. We attended scarlet-and-gray events morning, noon, and night for four straight days. A thousand Buckeyes celebrated New Year's Eve at Liberty Square in the Magic Kingdom. On New Year's Day, Mickey, Minnie, Donald, and Goofy led a buoyant Buckeye parade down Main Street, USA. The only thing I remember about the game was that a large yellow dog ran out onto the field. The poor animal must have been frightened out of his wits, but not so badly that he didn't manage to deftly evade all manner of capture, delaying the game for seven or eight minutes. Instead of getting perturbed, Coach Stallings should have recruited Rover as quarterback, strapped the football on his back, and put a big slab of roast beef in the Ohio State end zone. We might have won that game.

***

Being Gordon's consort and the first lady of Ohio State was a full-time, 24/7, very public affair. We entertained relentlessly. By most human standards I would be considered a sociable person. I have many friends. I enjoy entertaining and being entertained. I have been known on occasion to be the veritable life of the party. Yet I need chunks of quiet, private time to rebalance and recharge in equal or greater measure. I have found this to be especially true when the social events I am attending aren't small gatherings of good friends, but huge affairs where one does not so much partici-pate as *reign*. Unlike Gordon, who actually derives energy from adoring throngs, the task of being "on," fabulously on—shaking hands, nodding convivially, smiling, smiling, *smiling*—drains me. I am happy to have my dog by my side at all times. I do not feel that way about members of my own species.

University presidents are politicians, and politicians must be skilled at the art of working a crowd. Gordon is so good at it that the US Congress should hire him to offer a seminar on the subject. The object of the game is to move through a sea of people, alight-ing briefly with small clusters or an occasional individual, without getting "captured." Each guest is either a current or possible donor, and each has to feel that he or she has made a personal connection with you, even if the actual contact time is less than a minute. (You lose points with each additional ten-second segment after the one-minute chat-up.) Remembering names is a key skill that master movers take very seriously. The gravest faux pas is to not remem-ber that you have previously met the person standing expectantly before you. (We *Homo sapiens* have a deep-seated need to be remembered.) The less industrious attempt to remedy this situation with the noncommittal "Good to *see* you," rather than the far too committal "Good to meet you."

Gordon had assumed his first presidency at West Virginia University in 1981 at the record-breaking age of thirty-seven. By his second college presidency five years later, at the University of Colorado, he had adopted the Lapel Pin Strategy. He would always carry a pocketful of specially made lapel pins sporting the logo of the particular university he was at—Colorado's buffalo, Ohio State's red block "O," Brown University's coat of arms, and the Vanderbilt "V"—that he, and only he, could bestow. When meeting someone for the first time he would "pin" the person, informing the recipient that this was the president's own special pin. Alumni and devoted fans of the university football team ate it up. Forever after, they would proudly wear "the pin" to university functions. Little did they realize they were now marked.

Spotting a lapel with a president's pin, Gordon could say with great confidence to its owner, "Good to see you *again!*" Knowing he had previously met the person would often jog his prodigious memory enough to remember *where* he had met the person. From there, he might even conjure up a first name or some other detail, such as, "How's your grandson liking Ohio State?" Forgetting about the visual clue emblazoned on his jacket, the person would be tickled pink to be remembered by the university president after that one thirty-second encounter, three years earlier at the Wapakoneta Rotary. Lapel Pin Strategy aside, Gordon moving through a crowd was a wonder to behold.

The initial thrill soon wore off for me, however, after a few months of scurrying along at his elbow repeating, "Nice to meet you, too! Oh, yes, I just *love* Ohio State. What about those Buckeyes?! Yes, [sigh], he is amazing." Although I did mean it—it was nice to meet good-hearted Ohio Staters; I did love Ohio State, and still do; Buckeye football truly is the best there is; and Gordon was amazing—there are not many people in this world who can recite that shtick 180 times over the course of a 120-minute reception and come across as being genuine.

Success as a crowd-whisperer appears to depend more on a person's ability to stifle completely any creeping cognizance of absurdity than on whether or not the person at the other end of the exchange believes you are authentically, fully present. After about twenty minutes of meet-and-greet, I have an involuntary out-of-body experience. I find myself floating above the parade like a Bullwinkle balloon, cringing at my own superficiality and that of the entire human race. Then, like a driver snapping out of a deep reverie the moment the car begins to veer off the road, I overcorrect and attempt to make a "real connection." This invariably gums up the works.

Gordon would grouse about my impeding the flow: "You allow yourself to get captured!" The truth was that I initiated the capture to save my own soul and alleviate the hot ache of a jaw muscle locked in The Everlasting Smile. I soon learned that it was best if I peeled away from Gordon after a few minutes of shake-and-smile and found someone I could have a five- or ten-minute all-out conversation with. It was a relief.

***

Elizabeth had been fond of jesting that Gordon enjoyed nothing more than a nice dinner at home with five hundred of his closest friends. I was quickly learning that it was no joke. Together we would host or attend events five or six nights a week, sometimes two or three in a single night. Home football games, parents' weekends, commencements, and other university-wide celebrations would constitute all-day, all-weekend event marathons. It was wildly exhilarating and utterly exhausting.

I would labor all day, every day, in my various roles of professor, hostess, and social escort. On my one or two nights off each week from entertaining, I tried as best I could to keep up with my faculty duties and to get some writing done on the perpetually overdue journal article. I struggled to keep myself together emotionally and physically, but the hectic juggling wore me down. I always felt I was not doing something as well as I should or could.

I could see that my emotional swings were hard on Gordon, too. This further distressed me. *Maybe I need to talk with someone*, I thought. Maybe it would be even better if we could *both* talk with someone. Such thoughts were not easy for me. No one in my immediate family had ever seen a psychiatrist. God forbid! That sort of thing was only for navel-gazing whiners or the truly insane. "Y'all are gonna drive me to Dix Hill," was the only psychoanalysis I heard growing up. (Dix Hill was the "lunatic asylum" near Raleigh that was established by the mental health activist Dorothea Dix in the mid-1800s.)

Although Gordon had joined Rebekah for several counseling sessions after Elizabeth's death, he seemed to view my adjustment

86

difficulties in a different, more problematic light. He refused vehemently when I asked if we could get some couples therapy. I think he feared that someone would find out everything wasn't perfect. Maybe he didn't think it was necessary, or he simply didn't want to put the time into it. I don't really know. I do know that he wanted no part of it.

Gordon made an appointment for me to talk with a senior member of the psychiatry department of Ohio State's medical center. The doctor came to the residence so that I would not be seen going to his office. I was grateful for this privacy measure, although it further reinforced my feeling of shame about needing mental health support.

At the end of our first session, the doctor informed me that he was going to report all that I had said to Gordon. "Why would you do that? What about doctor-patient confidentiality?" I asked. The doctor explained that since Gordon was the one who had requested the meeting, and since he was, after all, the president of the university, he felt he had a duty to tell Gordon what I had said—especially with regard to what I had said about *him*.

It was not as if I had said anything awful about my husband to this man. The worst of what I had to say was that I felt terribly alone in my struggles to adapt to my new life and its demands. I told him that I didn't know how to talk to Gordon about my anxieties without sounding like a crybaby. I also felt he didn't want to hear it, that he *couldn't* hear it without feeling personally reproached. I didn't know how to approach him so he *could* hear it, I admitted. These were not deep, dark confessions that I didn't want Gordon to know, but I certainly didn't want my supposed confidant to report to my husband after our sessions. It reeked of chauvinistic paternalism to me, so my first meeting with the good doctor was also my last.

I elected another type of therapy. Every few days, I would retreat into the sanctuary of my walk-in clothes closet (my only private space in the house), shut the door, and cry. Then I would wash my face, take a short nap, and prepare for class or yet another event. Looking back, I'm surprised I didn't wind up in a rubber room.

***

One morning, after having hosted a large event the prior evening, I tottered into the kitchen in my pajamas to make some coffee. I looked a mess, was slightly hung over, and was grumpy because I had overslept and now needed to rush to get to class on time. There *they* were—the head of special events, a chef from university catering, and two waiters. For an instant, I thought they were still there from the night before but realized, as my precaffeinated brain came into semifocus, that they were laying out a breakfast buffet. I felt my face flush from a surprised blanch to hot pink to purple.

"Good morning!" they chimed.

"What are you *doing* here?" I growled.

"Preparing for the breakfast meeting. Coffee's made, want some?" someone chirped.

I had forgotten that Gordon had scheduled an eight o'clock meeting with a group of black ministers.

"No, I want you out of here! I just want to have a cup of coffee *by myself* in *my* kitchen!"

They scattered like bowling pins out of the kitchen, into the hallway, and out of sight. I made my own coffee and stomped upstairs. After I showered, dressed, and thought about what an ass I had been, I skulked shamefaced back into the kitchen to beg their forgiveness. "Just call me the Dragon of Drexel," I joked apologetically. (The residence was on the corner of Commonwealth Park North and Drexel Avenue.) To my chagrin, the nickname stuck.

***

Clearly, I required some self-imposed partying parameters. Gordon was either in full motion (eighteen hours a day) or asleep (five hours in the bed, the other hour wherever he could: at a performing arts event, in the dental chair while having his teeth drilled, or on occasion in staff meetings). If he sat still and was not talking, he fell asleep. When nudged after drifting off during a staff meeting, or hearing "Gordon, wake up!" during a rare, just-the-two-of-us supper at home, he had the uncanny ability to repeat verbatim the last five seconds of conversation—proving that his subconscious remained in attendance even though his eyes had been closed, his breathing slow and deep, and his chin on his chest. I, on the other hand, required eight hours of sleep and at least a little time to rock in the porch swing and watch the squirrels dig up the tulip bulbs.

I would not entertain or be entertained four nights in a row, I announced. Three consecutive nights was my new limit. I also lobbied to reinstitute private-time Sunday, something to which Gordon and Elizabeth had adhered, but which had lapsed with her death and Rebekah's going off to college. Gordon suggested that he and his office staff mark events on my calendar as A (must do), B (would be good to do, but not mandatory), or C (only if you want to go, but otherwise don't bother).

We tried to carve out a weekly date night, where we would enjoy supper at home and a video, or occasionally go out to a restaurant. Our date nights out were often spent talking with affable Buckeyes who would stop by the table to say hello and comment on the eternally upcoming football, basketball, or bowl game. Buckeyes love their university, and they loved this guy who loved their university. Gordon reveled in the adulation, absorbing it through every pore. It was fun and flattering, and I genuinely enjoyed seeing him in his element, but I, too, wanted his attention.

This was the beginning of the weekly calendar scuffles, which were generally held on Sundays around 5:00 p.m. at the kitchen table or, weather permitting, on the screened porch. After reviewing the upcoming week's event schedule, we would sort through the requests from various arms of the university's development office for us to host cocktail receptions, and small and large dinners at the residence or elsewhere on campus. Invitations to charitable fundraisers, bar and bat mitzvahs, and birthday, holiday, and graduation parties would be considered and negotiated as either events we would go to together or events he would attend on his own. A, B, and C status would be discussed and duly noted, with me holding as firmly as possible to the no-more-than-three-nights-in-a-row rule.

We planned our schedule of major development events and related travel one to two years into the future. There were many such events with much travel nationally and internationally. I was game for most of it, especially as we considered the extraordinary opportunities months and years out while sitting at the kitchen table. But when that weekly review rolled around with more—always more—to squeeze in, I would invariably feel that I had been gobbled up by the university. I learned the more you give, the more it wants. "The university is a jealous mistress," Gordon told me. From my perspective, she wasn't just jealous—she was insatiable. And she clearly came first.

7

Wicked Stepmother

A JEALOUS MISTRESS IS ONE force of nature. A jealous stepdaughter is quite another. I continued to hope that Rebekah would gradually "come around," as Gordon had assured me she would. We would be friends—*girlfriends*, I thought naively. I wouldn't try to mother her. She already had a mother, who by then seemed to have been canonized in Rebekah's remembrances. Besides, having no children of my own, I didn't know how to be a mother. But I did know how to be a friend. The problem was that I had never tried to be friends with someone who didn't want to be friends with me. If a person didn't like me, then so be it. But this wasn't just someone. This was my husband's daughter and only child, whom he loved immensely. I needed and wanted her acceptance.

I began to comprehend that I was in for a tougher time than I had anticipated when, during a weekend home from college, Rebekah proclaimed, "Homosexuals *deserve* to die of AIDS!" It was midmorning, and she and I had faced off across the large kitchen island. Her father was standing on the sidelines at a safe distance, fidgeting with the newspaper. We were all still in our pajamas and bathrobes. There had been an article in the paper about the AIDS epidemic and her commentary on the subject was reaching its dramatic crescendo. Gordon had not uttered a word. Spurring her forward was my obvious agitation and a growling reminder that I had many gay friends, several of whom had died of AIDS-related infections.

The Pratt student Jerold McCain had been my first friend to die of AIDS. Shortly after Jerold's death, my dear friend Stuart Blake told me he had been diagnosed as HIV positive. Stuart and I had been kindred spirits since ninth grade. We had both studied art at East Carolina; he had majored in graphic design. We had held our senior art exhibition together. Stuart moved to New York after I graduated from Pratt and camped out in my apartment for a month until he found his own place. Stuart had a quintessentially whole-some, all-American look—wavy brown hair, green eyes—and spent a couple of years modeling in Japan before returning to New York and landing an art director job at Condé Nast. We had briefly attempted a boyfriend-girlfriend relationship in the tenth grade, accompanying his older brother, Walter, on a double date. After the requisite movie at the Paramount and burger at Skid's Drive-in, Walter had found an out-of-the-way spot to park and proceeded to get hot and heavy in the front seat with his girlfriend. Stuart and I tittered and whispered self-consciously in the back seat, our braced-teeth glinting in the moonlight. "Be quiet!" Walter com-manded. It was time to get down to business, so we gave it a go for about two minutes until, coming up for air, we began giggling uncontrollably at the absurdity of it all—ruining any chances of further romance that night for Walter, who drove me home pronto. *The absurdity of it all*—Stuart and I saw that in ourselves and in the world around us. We prided ourselves on the adolescent perversity of our humor and pretend wickedness. We always knew exactly what the other was thinking or could communicate it in a glance. We were the male/female flip side of each other. "My Narcissus," he called me. Stuart died on 17 January 1990 from cryptococcal meningitis, a truly horrific, opportunistic AIDS-related disease.

Rebekah delivered her judgmental declaration with full knowl-edge of Stuart's terrible death, a personal sorrow I had confided to her during an earlier, more civil conversation we'd had about AIDS. Fortunately, I was on the side of the kitchen island closest to the din-ing room, so I could turn and stomp out of the room without having to pass within strangling distance of her. Though she surely would have demolished me in hand-to-hand combat. At a statuesque five feet, eleven inches, Rebekah was the tallest and, no doubt, strongest among us.

A half hour later she knocked on the door of my bathroom, where I had taken refuge. She tearfully apologized, saying that she "didn't really feel that way about gays." She explained that she had said those things just to make me mad. She knew how strongly I felt about the issue and wanted to see how far she could push me. I was genuinely surprised at her admission and grudgingly impressed by her personal insight and apparent honesty. I also couldn't stay in the bathroom the rest of the weekend. I told her how much I appreciated her apology and that I admired her for being able to own up to having deliberately provoked me. I said that I wasn't always so good at admitting my mistakes. I reached out and embraced her, and felt the tears spill down my cheeks when she returned the embrace. For that moment, there was no impediment between us. Maybe we were *all* coming around, I thought. I hoped so, because this moment felt a thousand times better than any other she and I had shared up to then.

To my chagrin, a familial behavioral pattern was established or, perhaps more accurately, reestablished. The three of us would be in the midst of a conversation when Rebekah would latch onto and begin scraping at a belief or opinion that I had expressed or she knew I shared. I would counter, trying to reason with her, as I would with any of my very bright college students. She would then begin making increasingly outlandish statements, at which point Gordon would offer up a "Now, Rebekah." I would fall silent for a bit, trying my best to project some semblance of control and dignity when all I really wanted to do was smack her. Four or five minutes would pass as I seethed and she sulked. Then she would start up again, picking, poking, and finally puncturing through to my molten anger until I would either blurt out something I quickly regretted, flee the room, or both. Soon afterward, we'd have the tearful reunion. She'd apologize for picking the fight; I'd apologize for losing my temper. Her father would stand by looking relieved. For a day or so we'd all be on our most cheerful best behavior, pretending nothing had happened.

***

Gordon told me I shouldn't take Rebekah's attacks personally because she had goaded her mother in much the same manner. I didn't know about that, but it was true it wasn't just me she attacked. I watched her behave similarly toward him, although she seldom went at her father as cattily as she came after me. After a few patient repetitions of "Now, Rebekah," he would finally snap, "That's enough!" Just as she would do with me (and, I suppose, as she had done with Elizabeth), she would later go to him and apologize. Rebekah's apologies always seemed so sincere, and they were always accompanied by tears and hugs.

Nothing good ever came from our altercations. The tearful reunions became less heartwarming as time went on, and my impulse to embrace and forgive began to harden into wary cynicism—even as I kept taking the bait. It seemed to me that Gordon rarely stepped in with a "That's enough!" when Rebekah was going after *me*. My temper, so reminiscent of my father's, shamed me. I would berate myself for days; after all, as Gordon pointed out, I was "the adult" and should have had more self-control.

Gordon's tantrum tolerance was undoubtedly higher than mine, but then he'd been dealing with it since his daughter was old enough to jump up and down while screaming her lungs out. He told me he and Elizabeth were so undone by Rebekah's childhood fits that they would just sit and watch her until she'd finally collapse exhausted on the floor. Rebekah was diagnosed as being hyperactive early on, and later as having attention deficit disorder. Her parents had worked patiently with her, centering their domestic lives around her, as would any couple who had long wanted a child and finally got their hearts' desire in the form of a beautiful blond-haired, blue-eyed, kewpie-doll-lipped baby girl.

I did not feel the same sense of unconditional love toward Rebekah. Not even close. Gordon was right—I should have been more measured and intelligent in my response—but he was not as right about "the adult" thing. I had my own anger and abandonment issues. I'd stuff them down, but they'd claw their way back up, and I'd rise to the bait like a stupid wide-mouth bass—knowing that was her intention and hating myself for playing the losing game. Not having had children or younger siblings was a serious handicap in my dealing with Rebekah, although I doubt if Gordon would have married me if I'd had any children in tow. I'd never developed the tools to calm an angry child or been forced to sit through a two-year-old's tantrums. Yet it was my own temper, not hers, that was my most debilitating handicap and worst enemy. Rebekah and I had that in common.

The truth of it was that we had a lot in common—strengths, weaknesses, and happenstance. We were both only children. Our birthdays were within three days of each other's, albeit twenty-two years apart. We were high-spirited, adventurous, impetuous, determined, and opinionated. We both had difficulty dealing with life's transitions. We could be charming and funny, or impatient and sharp-tongued. Her father, however, was what we had most in common. It seemed that was one thing too many.

***

I don't pretend to understand the psychological ramifications of being abandoned by your birth mother, but it must be deeply traumatic. Even if the stars align perfectly and you are adopted at four days old by the most loving couple imaginable, as Rebekah was, a black hole of need and insecurity must remain. Imagine, then, at sixteen, what it must be like to have your adoptive mother die!

If one didn't know about Rebekah's early losses, it would be difficult to empathize with her constant need for reassurance. She seemed to have it all—looks, intelligence, and a loving and enormously privileged upbringing. Over the years, I would repeatedly tell her how much her father loved her, how proud he was of her, how proud *I* was of her, and how she had nothing to fear. No one would ever take her place in her father's heart or threaten her material security—a seemingly constant source of worry to her. I had no children; she remained "the only one." Everything her father and I had would go to her.

In spite of this, her ferocious rivalry with me continued, much as it had, Gordon explained, with Elizabeth. She had always been her father's daughter. "Da-da," she affectionately called him in mock baby talk. Following Elizabeth's death, Rebekah took to wearing her mother's Escada suits and other dress-up attire. She became her father's consort, attending university functions on his arm and welcoming guests to gatherings at the president's residence. My presence had dethroned her. She had been demoted from mistress of the manor back to daughter.

The destructive dynamic of abandonment drove the worst of our family interaction—but I hadn't begun to grasp the extent of it at the time. Years later, after I'd been deposed and Rebekah was back on her father's arm, I ruminated about how hard it is to give up the glittering spoils and attention that come with Vanity Fair. Although Rebekah would always be the princess daughter (never the exile), it is better to be queen. Having claimed that position at sixteen, how it must have galled her to surrender it before she turned nineteen. And though I felt sincere sympathy for Rebekah over her maternal losses, I neither understood nor appreciated her desperate attachment to her father. It seemed to me that she received substantially more paternal love and attention than most children. She certainly got more than I ever did. Gordon took the morning shift when she was growing up. He'd awaken her and, when she was very young, get her dressed. They'd have breakfast together and he'd drive her to school. He went to her sporting events whenever he could. He was sober and conversational at the dinners they shared. So what if he was frequently unavailable in the evenings, either because he was away on university business or simply too drained to do anything more than watch television? I'd never known a father who wasn't remote. The largess of fatherly attention that was Rebekah's was unimaginable to me. Even so, I now recognize the double-edged truth of the statement "You can never love your children enough."

***

Over the years Rebekah and I managed to build a friendship, although our closeness ebbed and flowed. When it was just the two of us—neither one competing for Gordon's attention—she and I had great fun together. We shared many unforgettable experiences. We climbed the 272 steps to the entrance of the Batu Caves north of Kuala Lumpur, Malaysia, stepping in bat guano and shrieking with laughter and a little alarm as the macaque monkeys grabbed at our sleeves and the fruit treats we'd bought for them. We stood together in amazement inside that Hindu shrine, gazing up a hundred meters at the dripping stalactite ceiling of Cathedral Cave. We downed a bottle of Champagne and danced and whooped in the pouring rain one dreary New Year's Eve on a deserted stretch of Bahamian beach, where we'd been stuck for an entire chilly, wet week with only her dad (who had disappeared into a six-hundred-page Civil War history), a golf cart, and one bad restaurant/tacky souvenir shop for amusement. We climbed the steep, narrow steps of the Buddhist temple Wat Arun in Bangkok, where, as we stood on the balcony of the central tower, our guide said he could feel the heavy tension between us. "It's like you're both carrying around a brick. Throw it away," he urged. With tears streaming down our faces, we pulled the bricks from our hearts and heaved them into the air. We picked up new bricks after a while, but the lightness was lovely while it lasted. We scuba dived through underwater stalactites in the Great Blue Hole of Belize at 120 feet below sea level, where the dense water was alight with minuscule fluorescent sea beings like a universe of stars. In the throes of nitrogen narcosis—similar in effect to a liberal dose of nitrous oxide (laughing gas), and which Jacques Cousteau called "rapture of the deep"—I began swimming farther down and out toward the center of the 400-foot-deep hole. Rebekah seized my foot, reached for my hand, and led me back toward our dive group, which had already begun the measured ascent to the surface. I suppose that made up for the time she tried to kill me on a black diamond ski slope in Park City, Utah.

Rebekah's energy, imagination, and willingness to take a risk could make an adventure out of the mundane. In good times, we would jokingly acknowledge our stepmother-stepdaughter détentes. I would sign my letters to her "Your wicked stepmother." That is, until I began to understand she truly perceived me that way. In 1995, however, we were just embarking on the age-old, infamously perilous journey of stepmother and stepdaughter. I know it was as hard on her as it was on me.

8

Executive Search Stealth

PRESIDENTS OF TOP UNIVERSITIES are most often stolen property. The objectives of the presidential search game are to (1) locate and preapprove the desired nominee; (2) arrange a clandestine meeting with the nominee to secure a commitment to accept the job when formally offered; (3) round up the board for a quick vote; and (4) release the triumphant news to the press—all before the university that is about to lose its president has time to react.

As it turned out, the University of California botched the game in 1995 when it tried to recruit Gordon. Ohio State won it with an end run around the University of Colorado in 1990 and around Vanderbilt in 2007. The 2007 Ohio State victory, it bears noting, was more a result of Vanderbilt fumbles, unsportsmanlike conduct, and roughing penalties than any stellar offensive strategies by the Buckeyes. The Buckeyes simply picked up the battered ball and sauntered across the goal line.

***

Gordon began entertaining the notion of leaving Ohio State four years into his presidency, his head turned by the series of offers from the State University of New York, Johns Hopkins University, the Kellogg Foundation, and the Museum of Modern Art. His presidency at West Virginia University and the University of Colorado had each lasted five years. Five years seemed to be his expiration date, after which he began to feel as if he were "running a marathon around the block," a demanding but rather monotonous activity.

The Museum of Modern Art had attempted to recruit Gordon as its president a couple of months before our wedding. MoMA had decided to expand its facilities, and it needed a proven fundraiser to make that happen. The traditional role of museum director was to be divided into two positions—a president, who would serve as CEO/fundraiser in chief, and an artistic director. Although the vision of living amid Klees and Pollocks was alluring, I wondered aloud how Gordon would fare in the New York art world. Running the largest university in the country is one thing. Surviving art-world politics is another.

The thought of the MoMA board looking for a friendly, populist, hands-on kind of guy to head up the church of modernism amused me. I could just see Gordon walking around the museum lobby or intercepting visitors as they prepared to exit and asking them where they were from and what they liked most about the museum. That was probably precisely what MoMA needed—what most art museums need—but was that what Gordon needed?

"Before you proceed with this," I cautioned, "why don't you meet with the senior department heads, just to get a feel for the environment—to see if you're simpatico?" I knew he'd be hightailing it back to Columbus.

"I barely escaped alive," he reported after he returned. "They thought I was some hayseed from Ohio."

MoMA ultimately decided not to change its directorship structure.

***

Roy Brophy, a University of California Regent and the chairman of the presidential search committee, knocked on the door of the Columbus residence the morning of the June 1995 Ohio State commencement and flat-out offered Gordon the job. Brophy wanted an answer right then and there. It appeared he could not imagine anyone turning down the opportunity to run UC's nine-campus system, the largest and most academically acclaimed in the nation. It remains the pinnacle of power for a public university presidency. Gordon told his suitor that he wanted to meet with the entire search committee before making a decision.

Gordon, Rebekah, and I were scheduled to leave the next day for a two-week university development trip to Asia. Our first stop was to be Seoul, then Kuala Lumpur, Manila, and Hong Kong. We agreed to a brief layover in San Francisco so Gordon could meet with the search committee and we could all see the UC president's residence. While Gordon met with the committee, Rebekah and I were given a tour of the Berkeley campus. Then the three of us were escorted to the residence and driven past the UC corporate office complex in Oakland that housed the president's offices.

The residence was spectacularly located in Berkeley Hills on a sizable piece of property designated as part of the university arboretum. It had a breathtaking view of San Francisco Bay. Like so many university residences, it had been poorly maintained, but it was not difficult to envision the restored elegance of its modernist lines and Asian antique furnishings. Although I was resistant to the idea of leaving Ohio State less than two years after I had arrived, and at a time when the arts policy program was beginning to gain real traction, it was impossible not to be impressed.

Gordon was favorably inclined, but he told Brophy he needed a few days to mull over the offer. The search committee grudgingly agreed to his request.

Over the next week Gordon, Rebekah, and I discussed the offer from every angle. Two aspects of the job concerned him—the location of the system president's offices, and the controversy in California over Governor Pete Wilson's attack on affirmative action.

Gordon's office had always been in the thick of campus life. He was well known for walking the Morgantown, Boulder, and Columbus campuses, chatting with students, faculty, staff, and anyone else wandering by. A corporate complex in Oakland was not his style. How would Berkeley's chancellor deal with the system president showing up regularly on his turf to get his student hug fix?

Of greater concern, however, was the vociferous debate over affirmative action in California. Governor Wilson had entered his second term in office the preceding January with an eye on capturing the 1996 Republican presidential nomination. Affirmative action was a key hot-button issue both nationally and in California. Although Wilson had supported affirmative action policies as mayor of San Diego in the 1970s, he now stepped forward to say those policies were misdirected and should be rescinded. Angling to position himself as the political leader of the anti–affirmative action movement, Wilson announced his intention to eliminate, by executive decree, all California affirmative action programs not mandated by federal and state law. The headline of a 4 June 1995 press release from his office summed it up: "Wilson Becomes Nation's First Governor to Issue Executive Order Rolling Back Affirmative Action." Less than a week later, as Regent Brophy made his pitch to Gordon on our screened porch, the governor was in the process of dismantling affirmative action policies throughout all state operations, including the University of California system. Any preference given to minorities or women in university admissions, hiring, and contracting would be discontinued.

Gordon had his own reservations about affirmative action, but being a smarter politician than the governor, he kept them to himself. This was not the most desirable of circumstances in which to begin a new university presidency—caught between a hard-charging governor with "Hail to the Chief" ambitions and angrily protesting university faculty and students, with the state legislature divided as well. But then, it was not uncommon for some political or fiscal trauma-drama to accompany the changing of the guard at a major university. Gordon had handled some political hot potatoes before, and although this one had already reached combustible temperature (Jesse Jackson had called Wilson "a glorified George Wallace"), he felt he could avoid any blistering. Besides, he doubted the governor's ability to nix affirmative action policy entirely.

Also of concern was the threat by a Republican-controlled US Congress to drastically cut federal research grants and student financial aid, the impact of which would hit UC especially hard. The UC system received $4.6 of its $9.3 billion budget from federal sources, with state funding coming in a distant second at $1.9 billion. The university had already suffered serious cuts in state funding: $340 million had been stripped away over the previous five years.

Gordon had already confronted the matter of pending fiscal difficulties, as well. In fact, steering large universities away from financial doom through political maneuvering, massive restructuring, and mega-fundraising campaigns was his forte. The Ohio legislature had sliced $80 million from Ohio State's budget just six months after Gordon's arrival. So he had gone on a restructuring and fundraising rampage that ultimately boosted the university's bottom line and improved its academic standing. The UC system posed some major challenges, but it also offered many seductive opportunities, one being that it provided the most visible bully pulpit in the country for a public university president.

On the other hand, Gordon's administrative and programmatic restructuring at Ohio State was far from complete; he was smack in the middle of several important development initiatives. The vibe in Columbus was good—very good. He would be leaving behind some important unfinished business and an enormously supportive environment.

***

I weighed in on the side of remaining at Ohio State. We'd been married for less than seven months. I was just beginning to remember the names of some of the hundreds of faces we encountered weekly. I was building a terrific graduate program and had just recruited my second round of students. I needed to catch my breath, and I wanted to continue the development of the arts policy program. Couldn't we stay at Ohio State for a few more years?

The California job wouldn't wait, Gordon countered, and there would never again be such an offer. Heading up the University of California was the most prestigious position in public education in the country. And, San Francisco! What a great place to live! Around and around Gordon and I went—with Rebekah touting California's undeniable coolness, and predictably taking her father's position against any reservations I expressed. This was our conversation on the flight to Seoul, during our stay in Seoul, and throughout Kuala Lumpur.

***

By the time we arrived in Manila, Gordon was leaning heavily toward accepting the job. My resistance had worn down, and I was trying to focus on the possibilities of a new adventure on the West Coast. When we checked into the Hotel Manila, the clerk handed

Gordon a batch of telephone messages. He scanned them with increasing agitation. "They're from the press—the *New York Times*, *Los Angeles Times*, *San Francisco Chronicle*, and the [Columbus] *Dispatch*," he ended, wincing. The chairman of the Ohio State board of trustees had left several urgent messages, as had numerous television and radio reporters. There had been a leak at UC.

Gordon telephoned Roy Brophy, who apologetically assured him the leak had been unintentional. Gordon wasn't so certain; it appeared to us both that this was an attempt to force his hand. He was highly irritated at this breach of confidence. He immediately phoned the Ohio State board chairman to assure him that he had not yet accepted the job, and that he would be sure to let him know when or, at this point, *if* he decided to.

The *Los Angeles Times* called our room the following morning. There is a sixteen-hour time difference between California and the Philippines, so it would have been around four o'clock the previous afternoon in Los Angeles—Sunday, June 18. "I have not yet accepted the position," Gordon informed the reporter. A few minutes later a second reporter called. At that point, Gordon got the hotel manager on the phone and told him to make certain that no other calls reached the room. For the next four days, he refused all contact with the media.

***

In the meantime, the press was having a field day. On the 16th, Brophy had announced to his entire Board of Regents that the presidential search committee had unanimously chosen a nominee, but he had refused to indentify the nominee. It took less than twenty-four hours for Gordon's name to surface throughout the larger board—and to be released to the media. The front page of the Sunday *Los Angeles Times* proclaimed: "A University of California Board of Regents committee has decided to recommend the president of Ohio State University to be the next UC president, reaching outside the nine-campus system for the position for the first time in at least three decades, sources said Saturday."[1]

The rumblings began immediately. Regents who were not on the search committee, and who were miffed at being offered only a single candidate, grumbled publicly about the exclusionary selection process and about the nominee. An especially telling commentary was offered by the UC Regent Glenn Campbell and reported by the *Los Angeles Times*:

> "I've never heard of him before until I heard about him on the car radio," said Campbell, a fellow at the Hoover Institution, a conservative think tank at Stanford University. Were it up to him, Campbell said, he would have "stolen a distinguished person" from a university better known for its academics.
>
> "I would've preferred someone that would be accepted to Harvard or Stanford. . . . I understand [Gee] is big on affirmative action, and he's a big supporter of gays. . . . I'm sure the governor will love that."[2]

Campbell, who simply could not contain himself over the horrific thought of the bespectacled, bow-tie-wearing barbarian at UC's golden gates, plunged forward: "I don't know Gee except that he's president of a Big Ten university and us Harvard types consider them second-rate at best."[3] The *San Francisco Chronicle* humor columnist Herb Caen observed: "Well, you can always tell an Ivy Leaguer but you can't tell him much about grammar. It's 'we Harvard types,' Glenn. 'WE.' Go to your room in the ivory tower."[4]

The three-ring media circus was now at full tilt. Not being able to dig up any delectably nasty stuff in Columbus, the media shoved its trowel into Boulder and scooped up some smelly undercover bonus deals. "UC Nominee Gave Secret Bonuses; Controversial Deals While in Colorado," announced the *San Francisco Chronicle*. The front-page article went on to report that a year after Gordon had left for Ohio State, the University of Colorado regents "were angered to learn that he had bypassed the board to grant hefty bonuses of $10,000 to $13,000 to his four top lieutenants."[5] He was also criticized, the article continued, for giving a $232,400 golden parachute to a Colorado chancellor he had fired and a $75,000 bonus to the football coach for winning the Orange Bowl—both deals that the board had approved, although it later claimed it had not known the full amount of the packages. The *Chronicle* attributed the delayed kvetching to sour grapes over

Gordon's leaving for Ohio State: "Gee was extremely popular during his tenure in Colorado, but when news of the secret deals broke, editorials accused him of 'doing his very best imitation of Machiavelli' and 'see[ing] himself as bigger than the regents who appointed him or the citizens who paid his salary.'"[6]

When asked by the press if the UC presidential search committee had been aware of the controversy, Regent Brophy replied, "I don't know a thing about it, and I don't care a thing about it. It's nothing we're aware of."[7]

A follow-up headline read: "Lawmakers Troubled by UC Choice; They Want Probe of Deals by Presidential Candidate." Marguerite Archie-Hudson, a state senator from Los Angeles and chair of the Assembly Committee on Higher Education, weighed in: "If the allegations have some foundation, we would like to know from the university how they could come to the place of appointing the new leader of our flagship institution without having settled what to me is a rather serious allegation. We want an explanation."[8]

Brophy and other regents from the search committee frantically called Gordon, applying the full-court press for him to accept the job. Ohio State trustees and friends begged him not to. We were at the Regency Hotel in Hong Kong by then, ragged with exhaustion and drained by the emotion of it all.

Thursday evening over dinner we discussed it one final time. I pointed out how shabbily Gordon was *already* being treated in the press and by grandstanding state legislators and disgruntled UC regents. Gordon acknowledged that the UC presidency could be a rough gig, but he maintained that he was ready for the challenge. It was the leadership opportunity of a lifetime in higher education. He determined that we should accept the offer. I acquiesced; it was time for me to set aside my reservations. Gordon telephoned Brophy that night. He would fly to San Francisco the next day to meet with the full board and to hold a press conference announcing his acceptance of the presidency of the University of California.

I fell into bed relieved that a decision had been made, but I was awoken throughout the night by my husband's tossing and turning. Before dawn, the hotel manager knocked on the door of our room. He had brought up two large boxes overflowing with paper. "Sorry to wake you, but I thought this must be important," he apologized, nodding at the boxes. "We've received so many faxes that it burnt out the machine."

Gordon hauled the laden boxes into the bathroom so I could get a little more sleep. I stood watching as he sat down on the toilet and read the first few. They were from Ohio State alumni and supporters all over the world. Tears welled up in our eyes. I hugged him, closed the bathroom door, and returned to bed. A couple of hours later, he woke me. "We're not going," he said, tears streaming down his face. I started to cry too. "All right," I said, "that's good." We sat in bed and read the faxes from Buckeyes everywhere, with the same message: *Please don't go!*

The fallout in California was swift and furious. "Top Choice to Lead UC System Declines Post: 11th-Hour Decision by Ohio State Head Stuns Regents and Sparks Criticism That Process Was Botched," declared the *Los Angeles Times*.[9] Suddenly, the news about the "secret bonuses" was characterized as having been "taken out of context" and "not that big of a deal."

Much finger pointing ensued. The Board of Regents pointed at the media and legislators. Legislators, faculty, and several regents pointed at the search committee, and at Brophy in particular: the process was too secretive; it was not kept confidential enough; the search committee had not anticipated predictable publicity and had failed miserably at damage control; the board had not stood together; legislators and media had once again stampeded into the china shop, ruining everything. "When the most prestigious public university system in the world doesn't get its first choice, that's— how shall I say it?—embarrassing," observed Robert H. Atwell, chairman of the American Council on Education in Washington. "This is very unfortunate for the University of California."[10]

Over the years, whenever the topic of that harrowing week in June came up, Gordon would say, "If not for that leak, I would have been president of the University of California."

***

California's shame was Ohio's triumph. Upon his return Gordon received a hero's welcome. The entire Ohio State marching band struck up "Carmen Ohio" as he stepped into the airport terminal. The Ohio State trustees raised Gordon's salary from $168,500 to $220,000. The biggest honor was the marching band's invitation for

Gordon and me to "dot the i" at the first football game of the season. Anyone familiar with college football knows about TBDBITL and the dotting of the "i" in "Script Ohio."

TBDBITL—pronounced "tibidle," accent on the middle syllable—stands for The Best Damn Band in the Land. And in my unbiased opinion, it is. Fans cheer wildly when, at the beginning of each home game, the Voice of the Buckeyes cries out, "The Ohio State Marching Band!," and the scarlet-and-white-uniformed drum major struts out onto the field to the heart-swelling strains of "The Buckeye Battle Cry." The band marches in place behind him (or her) as he tosses his baton high into the sky, catching it with showmanly grace. Then he executes a backbend, touching the ground with the scarlet plume atop his mountainously tall white hat—at which point the crowd screams even louder. He then takes off in a flying high strut, leading the largest all-brass-and-percussion military-style band in the world onto the field. My God! We *will* win this game, every beating Buckeye heart cries in unison.

The game highlight (for those of us more in love with the band than with football) is during halftime, when TBDBITL forms the word "Ohio" in perfectly rounded script across the length of the field, while playing "Le Régiment de Sambre et Meuse." The drum major jauntily high struts to the top of the "i" and, with a tap of his baton to the ground, indicates for the chosen sousaphone player— the luckiest sousaphone player in the universe at that moment—to dot the "i." The sousaphone player marches into position, bows low to both sides of the riotous stadium, and stands straight and tall, the bell of the sousaphone providing the perfect dot. It gives me chills just describing it.

The band's formation of "Script Ohio" at halftime is one of the greatest traditions in college sports, and to be asked to dot the "i" is the highest honor. Having someone other than a senior sousaphonist dot, or "tittle," the "i" is a most rare occurrence—a privilege that cannot be bought, although more than a few wealthy donors have tried.

Gordon and I were only the sixth non-sousaphonist tittlers since the tradition began in 1936, joining the esteemed company of the legendary Buckeyes coach Woody Hayes, the comedian Bob Hope, and the golfer Jack Nicklaus, all famous Ohioans. We stood side by side at the fifty-yard line watching the band move into formation. The drum major marched over and with a nod indicated we were to follow him. He led us onto the field and motioned with his baton that we were to pause a few yards away from the dotless "i." Turning crisply, he began the spirited high strut to the "i" and, with a flourish, tapped the ground above it. Completely caught up in the moment, I broke into a high strut right behind him with Gordon walking beside me, grinning broadly. We were the first to umlaut the "i" in "Script Ohïo."

***

Less than two months after the University of California drama, the chairman of the University of Utah presidential search committee came to the residence to offer Gordon the job. Gordon was gracious, telling the man he would think about it. The University of Utah, or the "U" as they refer to it in Salt Lake, was Gordon's undergraduate alma mater. We discussed it only briefly. He had no desire to return to Utah, having escaped its religious and familial confines three decades earlier. Besides, he had just turned down California to stay at Ohio State. Why go to Utah?

9

Residence Renovation
and Spousal Packaging 101

IT WOULD BE TWO YEARS before the next presidential search surge, two very busy years during which I took my first course in how to renovate a president's residence. Renovating, or worse, building a university president's residence is a politically hazardous undertaking, one that Gordon had already lived through and learned from. The University of Colorado had built an eight-thousand-square-foot residence on ten acres for its new presidential family soon after the Gees' arrival in Boulder. Gordon and the university trustees received a lot of criticism for building the mansion. It had been an unpleasant experience for both him and Elizabeth, which taught them a painful lesson about the political perils of university residence construction: *Always use private money.* Even so, Gordon always made certain to live in the official university residence. Living in one's own home can be filled with fiscal landmines. It is not uncommon for a university president to be fired over disagreements about expenditures on a private home, even when the home is used frequently for university-related entertainment.

Ohio State University had purchased the house on Commonwealth Park to serve as a temporary residence for the Gees while a larger home, more suited to oversized entertaining, was being renovated (with private donations) several streets away. The house was given a minimal, but nice, touch-up in anticipation of the

Gees' relocation in the near future. Then Elizabeth passed away, Rebekah left for college, and Gordon decided just to stay put.

***

I loved the house, but I had no place of my own within it. There was only one guest suite, a cramped set of rooms above the garage and accessible by a back stairway off the kitchen. I had been using the tiny guest sitting room as a makeshift office. My computer took up most of the small writing desk, so I had fashioned a short L-extension using a board atop a filing cabinet. The guest bedroom and sitting area were separated by a set of French doors that I always left open so as not to feel closed in. When we had guests, I was unable to use my "office."

One morning I walked into the guest sitting room and, out of the corner of my left eye, caught a movement. I swung around just as a startled, bare-chested man lurched up in bed. I screamed like a soon-to-be-totally-dead teenage girl in a slice-'n'-dice horror movie—and yes, I was in my nightgown. The perpetrator was Jim Delany, athletic commissioner of the Big Ten (and former Tar Heel basketball player). He had arrived late the prior evening, after I had gone to bed. Gordon had forgotten to tell me that Jim was spending the night. The rattled commissioner departed hastily that morning.

***

The university's board of trustees had agreed to a partial renovation of the president's residence after Gordon's decision to remain at Ohio State. A catering kitchen would be constructed in the basement, an office for me would be built off the master bedroom, and the screened porch would be enlarged so a couple dozen people could be seated there for dinner. A few other "freshening-up" changes would also be made. The board wanted the renovations to be as inexpensive as possible, which was understandable, because this was the second time the house was to be worked on in the space of five years. The trustees themselves stepped forward, making and soliciting the personal donations for the planned renovation.

I was eager for the work to begin, overjoyed that I was to finally have my own office and domain. It would be so nice to put my stamp on a house where I had lived for almost two years as a virtual visitor. I came to understand swiftly, however, that a renovation of a state university president's residence is a public enterprise, even when paid for with private money. Several layers of people felt the need to weigh in at every turn. One university financial officer, in particular, seemed to think her design expertise was required on a frequent basis. Early one morning, she telephoned to inform me that she liked the window curtains above the kitchen breakfast table just as they were. She saw no reason at all to change them; in fact, she liked them much better than the proposed ones. I thanked her for her concern, certain that she'd been up all night thinking about it.

Architectural plans were drawn up during autumn; construction began after the holidays. We remained in the house the first month of the renovation, naively believing we were going to continue to live there for the duration. After all, it was a relatively small project that would be completed in a couple of months.

The catering kitchen turned out to be more of an ordeal than we thought. The problem was that the basement ceiling was only six feet high; additional headspace was needed. Down was the only direction to go. That meant the original concrete floor in that portion of the basement had to be excavated and a new, lower foundation had to be poured. Gordon was generally out of the house before the jackhammering began in the morning and did not return until well after the workers had left for the evening. Unfortunately I was often in my sitting-room office, preparing for class or trying to get a research paper ready for publication—ten feet up and over from the excavation site.

I had discovered foam earplugs several months after we married as a defense measure against Gordon's snoring. This marriage-saving device had kept me from suffocating him with my pillow. The earplugs did not completely block out the heart-jarring pound of the jackhammers, or Gordon's snoring for that matter, but they made it bearable. It was the dust that almost did me in, as I contracted a mean lung infection. Gordon and I, along with our new puppy, Lucy, decamped to a large two-room suite at the Crowne Plaza Hotel in downtown Columbus.

Lucy B. Gee, a.k.a. "Lucy Belle," or "Lucyfer" when she was naughty, was a beautiful black standard poodle. Lucy was my forty-third-birthday present, undoubtedly the best present I have ever received. I had been pining for a dog since giving up Beaujo two years earlier. I wanted a large, smart, obedient dog—a dog that might actually come when I called, unlike her sweet but hard-headed predecessor. Equally important, I had to find a breed that didn't shed so that the dog could coexist with Rebekah. I had the excellent fortune of making the acquaintance of Max, a handsome black standard poodle who was occasionally allowed to come into the bar area of one of my favorite Columbus restaurants. What a terrific dog he was—calm, affectionate, college smart, and no shedding. Bingo! Gordon finally succumbed to my pleading and doggy research data, buying Lucy from the same breeder who'd bred Max.

Lucy was three months old when she joined our family just before Christmas in 1996. She was housetrained within a week and ready for the high-rise life when Gordon and I set up our temporary quarters at the Crowne Plaza in mid-February. We joked about Lucy being Eloise at the Plaza. I could take her almost everywhere except into the restaurant. Whenever she made her daily rounds, everyone seemed tickled to see her. She was treat rich.

Gordon and I did surprisingly well in our close quarters throughout that cold, blustery Columbus winter. I think we both enjoyed the relative simplicity of it all, and it *was* temporary. Our entertaining schedule slowed considerably, and what entertaining we did took place at one of several campus facilities. Our closet space was limited, so we'd only brought along the basics for dressing. It was sort of like camping out, or about as close to that abstract reality as Gordon was likely to submit willingly. (Gordon once told me that when he was a Boy Scout, his father would have his equipment delivered to the designated campsite. If his tent weren't already set up when he arrived, Gordon would direct other boys to do it. I believe Gordon achieved Eagle Scout by amassing a record number of badges for skills such as supervision and administration, logistics outsourcing, and motivational induce-ments.) Rebekah stayed in an adjoining room when she came to visit. With perpetual maid service, who cared if she left dirty dishes all over the place? Even so, it was mighty sweet to return that spring to the newly renovated residence.

I was thrilled to finally have a room of my own, a generously proportioned office-studio overlooking the back garden. The basement catering kitchen was a bit tight for the tall, but a very welcome addition; and the new kitchen curtains looked much better than the old ones. I set about putting the house back together, proud of how it had turned out—beautiful, yet cozy and a little whimsical.

The event schedule slammed back into fifth gear before we had unpacked the boxes from our two months at the hotel. Now that we had a larger entertainment space and a catering kitchen, it was time to use them. The money that had been spent on the renovation had to be justified by bringing in a lot more of it.

***

It would be inaccurate to imply that I was practicing Zenlike juggling of life's demands during our move back into the residence and the rapid reacceleration of our entertaining schedule. We were smack in the middle of spring quarter, careening toward the end of the school year—an intensely busy time for educators, whether one teaches first graders or grad students. It was also the time of year when student applications must be reviewed, admission decisions made, and acceptance or rejection letters mailed. My assistant and I were drowning in paperwork.

Flying into a tirade one morning after sloshing coffee down the front of my blouse, it came to me that I was an irritable mess. I'm not known for being the world's most patient person, even when I'm not stressed out. Let's just say that, depending on the situation, I'm about a three on the Lizzie Borden–Mahatma Gandhi Patience Continuum, Lizzie being a one and Mahatma being a ten. My favorite lapel button in my small but well-curated collection reads: "Gandhi would have smacked you in the head."

I realized I could not endure the pressure of two demanding, full-time jobs. I also realized that those closest to me could not endure the radioactive fallout from my having two full-time jobs. I proposed cutting back to a fifty-percent faculty appointment beginning the spring quarter of 1997, a year hence. I would remain director of the arts policy and administration program throughout the 1996–97 academic year, when a national search could be conducted to find a new director.

I was extremely torn about stepping down as program director. I had put tremendous effort into creating and developing the program; it was building great momentum and gaining national recognition. I knew, though, that I had to let something go. I had to acknowledge that being married to Gordon was being married to the university. I made the decision to do what many professional women have done when facing the choice between career and family: I prepared to take my foot off the accelerator and steer out of the left lane, into the right.

***

That May, Gordon sent a memorandum to the Ohio State board of trustees informing them of my intention to decrease my faculty responsibilities over the upcoming two years and to "assume more university obligations in [my] spousal role." He wrote:

> I am grateful for her willingness to do so, although this does represent an awkward professional move for her. I am therefore requesting that we implement the rest of her spousal privilege over the next several years, as necessary. When Constance and I were married, I talked with Chairman Kessler and the Board regarding the need to reinstate spousal support at the same level agreed upon for Elizabeth Gee when we joined Ohio State in 1990. . . . Let me reiterate the spousal package provided for Elizabeth Gee:
>
> one administrative assistant
> one research associate/writer
> one secretary
> one Foundation officer assigned to Critical
>   Difference for Women
> two student workers
> $25,000 in salary support for a part-time academic
>   appointment

Oh my! Although I had been vaguely aware that Elizabeth and Gordon had negotiated an extensive contract on her behalf, I had no idea of its parameters. Elizabeth had earned an EdD in higher education from West Virginia University and had helped to establish the Center for Human Caring at the University of Colorado College of Nursing. She served as the center's interim director during the time of its founding, from 1985 until 1987, when she was first diagnosed with breast cancer. She held an adjunct appointment in the nursing school until she and Gordon left for Ohio State in 1990. Critical Difference for Women, an Ohio State program that provides scholarships and professional development grants to female students, faculty, and staff, was of special interest to Elizabeth up until her death in December 1991.

Seeing in writing the comprehensive support Elizabeth had been provided brought my own situation into stark focus. I'd been directing a graduate program, teaching a full load of courses, writing research papers, and performing night and day at university functions as first lady—all with the help of a single assistant. My assistant and I had spent innumerable hours the previous year on organizing and promoting the second Barnett Symposium on the Arts and Public Policy. Two months into its planning we realized we needed *HELP* and had petitioned for and received it in the form of one part-time, highly competent grad student. At some point during the two-and-a-half-day symposium, we each took our turn having a tearful meltdown. Our grad student lost it the first day. I lost it the second afternoon, when the audio-visual equipment in the law school auditorium had its own personal trauma. My assistant burst into tears the final morning, when the caterers arrived half an hour late to set up the continental breakfast. Our staggered meltdown schedule worked out nicely, allowing us to crawl victoriously over the finish line toward a chilled bottle of Moët & Chandon.

No wonder I was driving in the "nervous breakdown" lane. And what of my assistant, who was putting in over fifty hours a week without paid overtime, serving as both the program secretary and my liaison with the Office of the President's secretarial staff? That I'd had to ask for everything I had managed to get thus far— my assistant and an office large enough to house the two of us along with all the program materials and student files—stung further. Nothing had been offered up; no one had informed me of any hefty spousal-package keg sitting in the president's office, just waiting to be tapped. As far as I knew, Gordon had not negotiated anything on my behalf when we were married. My only "contract" was the one that all untenured faculty have: You can work here until we decide otherwise.

I guess I had thought I should have been able to do it all. Perhaps, on a subconscious level, I didn't think I was worthy. I felt I had to prove that I was not getting off easy because I was married to the president.

***

University employment and support packages for presidential spouses assume many shapes and sizes, depending on several factors, including the size and prominence of the university, whether it is public or private, what the spouse asks for, and how well her husband negotiates on her behalf. I describe this process in terms of president and first lady, rather than "first gentleman," because that was and remains overwhelmingly the case at major research universities.

As I write this, there are fourteen male spouses of university presidents with membership in the Association of American Universities (AAU), the organization that represents the interests of the sixty-one major research universities in the United States and Canada. In 1996 there were only two male spouses, or "partners," as we were called. Several surveys were conducted among the AAU partners between 1995 and 2000 to ascertain the amount of time they spent on university business related to their role as presidential spouse, the specific nature of the work, and whether they received compensation. Questions were also posed regarding whether and to what extent partners were professionally employed in any other capacity.

Compensation was an ongoing topic at AAU partner meetings, where a few partners reported refusing compensation not only because they felt it was their duty to support their husbands professionally, but also because they were wary of the demands and expectations that would come with payment in any form. Many did receive compensation by way of the use of a car, secretarial assistance, or a modest stipend that almost always came attached to an official title such as "university associate."

Survey conclusions and, ultimately, spousal-package policy recommendations were difficult to make because of the broad range of spouse-university compensation arrangements; the individual ways that each first couple approached their tenure within the unique cultures of the various universities; and the increasing lack of partner response to the surveys over the years. However, a longtime AAU staff member recently noted two constants across the survey years and into the present: private universities generally offer more generous spousal compensation than public universities, and significantly more university involvement is expected of female spouses than male spouses, regardless of the spouse's own employment status.

***

Elizabeth's hefty spousal package was an anomaly, truly exceptional at a public university and rare even for a private one. Yet there it stood, head up, chest out, black on white. I felt very stupid. Gordon's letter to the board continued, "She would like to add more support over the next eighteen to twenty-four months as she moves from her academic to university role."

I'm really not so certain about all this, I thought. I was in so far over my head that I couldn't imagine how I would coordinate the efforts of up to six assistants, a shortcoming that seemed sort of lame for someone directing an arts policy and *administration* program. At this juncture, I reasoned, I just needed to focus on stepping back from my faculty workload. I could figure out later what to do with an extra assistant or two. Let's not pile on more when trying to arrive at less.

Cutting back to a half-time faculty appointment in the spring of 1997 didn't mean I would be scarfing bonbons on the sofa while blissfully watching *Mary Tyler Moore Show* reruns. Although I would be teaching only one course, I would still be advising twenty-five students, recruiting new ones, overseeing student internships at local arts organizations, chairing thesis committees, and serving on departmental committees and on the boards of two of the major arts organizations in town. My academic research and publishing would continue steadily.

***

At that very moment, I was neck deep in a wildly ungainly and time-consuming research project. Carol (the epiphanic soothsayer of matrimony) and I were codirecting a "partnership" among six Columbus public schools, three arts organizations, and OSU's College of the Arts. I place the word partnership in quotations to signify the effort's essential unpartnership-ness.

Ménages à trois between schools, cultural organizations, and businesses are still loudly touted as the solution to the failures of public education. In my limited (thank God!) experience, however, I have come to believe that for such fundamentally incongruent co-conspirators to have so much as a slim chance of bedfellow bliss, a 9.5 on the Lizzie Borden–Mahatma Gandhi Patience Continuum must be required of all participants.

I couldn't blame anyone other than myself (and Carol) for getting enmeshed in that labyrinthine muddle. In a fit of unbridled, we-can-save-the-world enthusiasm, Carol and I had written a grant proposal to the Ameritech Corporation, and had been awarded $76,000 for the consortium's establishment and first year of work. Our mission was to engage middle school and high school students in exploring and documenting historically important public spaces in and around downtown Columbus, thereby igniting the students' civic passions; their embrace of history, design, and architecture; and their love of hands-on, kinetic, arts-infused learning . . . or something like that. Frankly, I can't remember precisely, as I happily threw out my bulging files on the project years ago.

With the help of two other dedicated but misguided souls and another grant from Ameritech, we managed to hold the project together through a second year, wrongly thinking it would eventually work if we just kept at it. This is referred to down South as "polishing a turd." I remember the giddy relief the four of us felt, huddled together at poodle Max's bar, after voting unanimously *not* to apply for a third grant. Drinks all around! "If you're such a crackerjack fortuneteller," I asked Carol, "why didn't you foresee this fiasco?"

***

Two concerns about cutting back to a part-time faculty appointment kept circling around in my academic hamster brain. Would I be allowed to remain on the tenure track and undergo my fourth-year review as scheduled during the 1997 fall quarter? If the review went well, might I then "slow the tenure clock" so I could go up for tenure in 2003 rather than 2000?

"Tenure" is defined as the holding or possessing of anything, or the status granted an employee, usually after a probationary period, indicating that the position is permanent. Many newly tenured associate professors might define it as the dazed, haggard state of being that follows seven years of hazing, after which one feels like not doing a damn thing for the next seven years—out of both exhaustion and revenge. Yet there really is no other option if you aspire to be a *real* professor rather than a (ahem) forever untenured, "clinical" one, relegated for time eternal to the academic no-man's-land of practical skills training. You make the run for tenure *and get it*, or you're out on your PhD behind.

I realize that academics suffering the hardships of the tenure process elicit little sympathy from . . . well, come to think of it, no one else except other academics suffering the hardships of the tenure process. You might think that those who have tenure would exhibit a smidgen of empathy for their bedraggled underlings. You would be wrong. Once you get tenure, you suddenly and fervently believe that everyone should have to jump through those same damn hoops, by God.

Academics are conditioned to this way of thinking by the dissertation writing and defense process. After you have spent way too many years researching and writing a five-hundred-page tome on something only a handful of people find marginally interesting, and that will most likely never, ever be read in full by another soul in the universe (including members of your own thesis committee), you are pretty much certain that any other person who wants to put a PhD after her name should be required to write a five-hundred-page tome that no one else will ever read.

One of my favorite cartoons shows a woman socking a guy in the jaw, with an impressive uppercut. The woman is a doctoral candidate; the man, one of three tweedy professors facing her at la table de l'Inquisition. One of the other professors exclaims: "Great defense! Let's give her the doctorate."

All in all, however, it is reassuring to know that once tenured—unless you are convicted of a federal crime—you can hunker down in that cramped office amid your research data and student exams for the next four decades. If you relish thinking obsessively about one slice of a subject area, enjoy lugging satchels of books and papers through green spaces littered with sunbathing undergrads, and don't mind having homework every day for the rest of your life, it's a dream job.

***

My faculty colleagues voted to allow me to remain on the tenure track, undergo fourth-year review as scheduled, and slow the tenure clock. I received a letter from the board of trustees stating:

> In recognition of the numerous and important duties you perform as spouse of the university president, the Board wishes to provide you with an additional 50% appointment with the title Associate of the University. The annual compensation for this appointment will be equal to the salary and benefits of your 50% faculty appointment. . . . The effort, energy, and skill you bring to generating goodwill, private support, and increased appreciation of the university among its various constituencies are invaluable assets to Ohio State. We hope that you will view this as a sign of our appreciation for the many things you do to benefit The Ohio State University.

This was welcome news, as I had assumed that my $35,000 salary would be cut to $17,500. I was still paying off college loans.

***

Spring of 1997 arrived and my half-time faculty appointment officially began. A new arts policy program director had been hired but would not begin until the following fall, so I continued to serve in that capacity. It was a huge relief not to be teaching that quarter. I felt as if I were getting into a groove; it wasn't the first time around for everything and everyone. I could walk into a crowded reception and greet scores of people by name.

A semblance of balance was obviously too much for the Fates.

10

Executive Search Redux

THE UNIVERSITY OF NORTH CAROLINA Board of Governors sent a search firm emissary to gauge Gordon's interest in the system presidency that spring. This was not going to end, I understood. Forget about the plans we'd made for another couple of years at Ohio State. Forget about the fact that we had just settled into a newly renovated house, and that I had finally unpacked my paints and brushes for the first time in years. Gordon was completing his seventh year in Columbus, and he had a big itch. He was restless for new challenges and tired of forever fending off state legislators from Ohio State's piece of the budget pie. "This is not a state university. It's a *state-located* university," he would grouse, referring to the shrinking percentage of the university's budget that the state provided.

If we must leave Ohio State, I thought, *let it be for UNC.* Most of what little family I have on my paternal side graduated from UNC Chapel Hill. My father received his law degree there in 1952. My cousin Carl, his wife, and their three sons all wore Carolina blue graduation robes. (If God is not a Tar Heel, then why is the sky Carolina blue?) My grandmother, Margaret Greene Bumgarner, graduated from Appalachian State (a member of the UNC system) on her fiftieth birthday, after teaching for three decades in a one-room schoolhouse in Crossnore. The president of Appalachian had graciously scheduled commencement to be held on her birthday to celebrate her achievement. My alma mater, East Carolina University, was also part of the UNC system. This seemed to me like an advantageous trans-state spread for the UNC system job.

When I was growing up, both "UNC" and "Carolina" meant *the* University of North Carolina—the one in Chapel Hill. UNC was the first public university in the nation; most native North Carolinians are mighty proud of that. UNC Chapel Hill has always been the premier public university in the state. There are a good many of us who would say it is the best university in the state, period. Oh, we are aware of Duke, contemptuously known as "Dook," a southern extension of the "University of New Jersey." Duke is to UNC on the basketball court what Michigan is to OSU on the football field—a perennial thorn in our side and no one sweeter to beat. Although the UNC system had, since 1931, included North Carolina State University and UNC Greensboro (originally Women's College), everybody knew that "UNC" was that great university in Chapel Hill—that is, until 1969, when legislators voted to absorb three small state colleges into the system. They would be renamed UNC Charlotte, UNC Asheville, and UNC Wilmington. In 1971, the state's remaining ten public universities and colleges would be brought into the system. Now, in large part because of serious sibling rivalry and the little guys' need to put the "big man on campus" in his place, the original UNC had to be called UNC Chapel Hill. People have adjusted, but at the time, the political correctness of it all rankled hardcore Tar Heels, a demography that included my entire family.

Infighting among smaller and larger institutions within state university systems is more common than not, and a primary reason Gordon was no fan of system presidencies. The UNC system was particularly rife with such squabbling, a circumstance that concerned Gordon but did not deter his earnest consideration of the job. Having acquired by marriage a family whose college degrees and birthplaces stretched the length of the state was not politically inconsequential. Gordon harbored romantic notions about the South and had long admired UNC Chapel Hill for its academic quality and the gentlemanliness of its sports programs, as personified by basketball coach Dean Smith. We were both enamored with the lovely town of Chapel Hill, where the president's office and residence were located. To my mind, Chapel Hill offered the best of both worlds, with its southern easygoing grace and not so southern political liberalism.

We met the UNC Board of Governors search committee in a Charlotte bank office complex. There were about a dozen of us in the room. I wore a Carolina blue skirt and jacket. The softball interview was very convivial. I chatted about my love of and family ties to the North Carolina mountains, growing up in the Piedmont, and family vacations at the shore. I was thoroughly at home among the various Carolina drawls.

It looked like a clear win until an African American board member said, "I understand you're a Mormon."

"Yes?" Gordon replied with eyebrows raised at the conversational detour.

"Well, Mormons used to not allow African Americans into the church . . . ," the man continued as everyone else at the table held their breath, including me.

I could see Gordon tense up momentarily, but to everyone's visible relief, he nipped the inappropriate and illegal line of inquiry about religion in the bud with a lighthearted comment about how things had long since changed, and that polygamy might be of greater concern to the board. We all laughed gratefully and the interview was concluded.

The board chairman expressed his embarrassment at the final interview topic as we walked to the limousine that would return us to the airport. He was a gracious host who wanted very much to lasso Gordon for the system presidency. He well understood what a coup for UNC it would be should Gordon accept.

Once we were alone, Gordon vented about the implications of the board member's comment, though I was more irritated than he was. I knew that although he was interested in the job, it wouldn't take much for him to become uninterested. Gordon always wanted his suitors unanimous in their adoration. He was willing to set the incident aside, however, since everything else had gone so well.

***

Various board members made it clear that they wanted him to commit as they telephoned in quick succession over the next two days. A day of silence followed, after which the board chairman telephoned and asked apologetically if Gordon would be available for a conference call the following day to speak with several board members who had not attended the Charlotte meeting. This did not bode well, as it signaled disagreement among the board. Gordon agreed to the second interview, but he was not pleased. I knew at this point it wouldn't take much for him to bail.

He took the call at home and I stood by listening to his responses. It seemed to begin well enough, but then, after a few minutes, he said crisply, "My record is clear; I have long been a supporter of affirmative action." With his jaw set, he terminated the conversation then and there. A second board member had noted Gordon's Mormonism while pressing him about his commitment to affirmative action—and that was that for UNC.

***

I believe at this point the Ohio State board of trustees was about as worn out as I was by the courtship dance marathon. It was no longer a matter of whether Gordon would leave; it was just a matter of when he would leave and what school he would leave for. We all hoped the next university in line would be a worthy successor to Ohio State, but what state universities or university systems were left? The University of Michigan was clearly out. The University of Texas wasn't looking, and besides, Gordon is not a Texas kind of guy.

About that time, my friend Morgan sent Gordon a clipping from the *St. Croix Avis* announcing a presidential search for the University of the Virgin Islands. "University residences on St. Thomas and St. Croix," she had underlined in red. She also sent him a UVI sweatshirt and bumper sticker. I began wearing the sweatshirt around the residence and saying "Hey, mon" a lot.

"Land Grant Gordon," as he was known among some of his wittier colleagues, had no place to go except . . . somewhere that was *not* a state university. Suitors from the J. Paul Getty Museum and Brown University arrived on cue and in tandem a month after UNC had been crossed off the dance card. Gordon flew out to Los Angeles to visit with the Getty search committee, but quickly reconfirmed that the art museum business was not for him. He might not have so readily dismissed the Getty but for the Ivy League attentions of Brown.

***

Brown was a questionable match for Gordon. It is thought of as the most liberal of the Ivies, which in some people's estimation is a little like saying this woman is more pregnant than that one. Five years earlier, he had steered Rebekah away from Brown, characterizing it as "Granola U"—gooey with political correctness. Although Gordon is fairly liberal in terms of many social issues (he is pro-choice and has some gay friends who keep a low profile with regard to their sexuality), he is conservative with regard to economic policy and the funding of social welfare programs. He often joked that he had never seen a non-Mormon or a Democrat before he left Utah in his early twenties.

Gordon's status as a registered independent allows for chameleonic colorations from bright red to blue violet, as necessitated by his environmental surroundings. This is an important survival mechanism for university presidents, especially public university presidents, who spend a lot of time walking the halls of state legislative buildings with their hands out. This capacity would enable him to adapt to Brown's social liberal leanings. He would just have to keep his politically incorrect gag reflex in check. His fiscal conservatism was a nonissue; anyone in power wants to be thought of as a good steward of the commonwealth. No one wants a profligate at the helm.

Size was another imperfect fit factor with Brown. Gordon was used to running massive university complexes. Ohio State was a $2.5 billion operation with 60,000 students and 30,000 faculty and staff. It owned hospitals, huge sports arenas, and athletic training facilities and offered advanced degrees across the professional spectrum. Brown's annual budget was $600 million; it had 7,200 students, employed 8,000 faculty and staff, and was primarily an undergraduate institution. "What will I do after 11:00 a.m.?" Gordon asked only half in jest. In a small business, everyone is looking over your shoulder. A large enterprise provides its CEO many more layers of hierarchical cover—a structural buffer zone that affords substantial policy-making freedom, as long as you have the backing of your board. The same is true of universities. However, Gordon mused, "You can shift the direction of a speedboat much more readily than that of an aircraft carrier."

***

Once again we found ourselves in "should we or shouldn't we" purgatory. Gordon was impressed by Brown's Ivy League status. I was apprehensive. I'd experienced a few doses of Ivy League snobbery. Who among those working in academia hasn't? I'd also experienced it at home. Rebekah had just received her bachelor's degree from Columbia and would be starting medical school at Cornell in the fall. As she was growing up, the only universities that had been deemed worthy of serious consideration for her education were the more prominent Ivies. The daughter of a public university president, she declared vehemently one night over dinner that her (as yet unborn) children would *not* be going to Iowa State! No indeed; they would go to Harvard or Princeton or Columbia, which meant that her father should establish a trust fund to enable them to do so.

Discussing the pros and cons of Brown with Gordon, I wondered aloud how I would fare personally as first lady of an Ivy League school. I hadn't even gone to a top-tier public university for my undergraduate education. East Carolina was probably easier to get into than Iowa State! Sure, I had a PhD, but from Penn State, not the University of Pennsylvania. Also, what about my professional interests? Brown had no art education or arts policy program of any kind.

Gordon brushed aside my concerns, assuring me that I would do "just fine" both personally and professionally. (My academic appointment would be to Brown's Department of Education, although I would teach within the Taubman Center for Public Policy and American Institutions.) He also reminded me that his own educational pedigree was not solidly Ivy League. His undergraduate degree was from a public university, way out in Utah, no less, though he did have two graduate degrees from Columbia.

I threw in the towel early on in the discussion. "I'm OK with whatever you decide," I told him. I knew he was ready to leave Ohio State. Others tried to dissuade him, but they knew it too. Nevertheless, our lives were absorbed by the decision as he continued to wrestle with it and needed a sounding board. After three weeks of back-and-forth, he accepted the position. The next day we boarded a plane to Providence for a press conference.

11

Welcome to the Ivy League

I KEPT MY HEAD DOWN throughout most of the press conference as tears threatened to spill down my face. "Smile!" hissed Brown's public relations director, who was seated in the front row. It wasn't that I was terribly unhappy to be coming to Brown, but the finality of our Ohio State days moved me deeply. I tear up easily. I weep at weddings (including my own). I wept singing "America the Beautiful" while standing next to John Glenn at the opening of an Ohio State football game. At such moments the poignancy of our collective humanness overwhelms me.

Here we were, in a hot, oxygen-deficient room stuffed with people and cameras, standing together beside the podium as Gordon was being introduced as the seventeenth president of Brown University. The speaker turned and handed us baseball caps with "Brown" stitched on the front. Gordon put his on for a brief moment, removing it as he stepped up to the microphone. I kept mine on, its brim providing some cover from the glare of the lights in my watering eyes.

The photograph on the front page of the following day's *New York Times* showed Gordon at the podium and me standing next to him, wearing the baseball cap. Ohio State fans criticized me for keeping the hat on my head; they thought that I should have taken mine off, just as Gordon had. I understood that they felt betrayed and needed someone to blame. First ladies are good for that when you can't bring yourself to lay your anger and grief at the feet of the beloved leader who has failed you.

***

It was late June 1997, two months before the beginning of the next school year. We should have immediately begun preparations for our move to Providence. Instead we decided to stay in Columbus through the fall term. Gordon maintained that he did not want to leave Ohio State in the lurch, so he offered to remain and assist with the transition. The board readily accepted. They were proud their president was going to an Ivy League school, but no one really wanted to let go. Meanwhile I was focused on the transition of the arts policy program. The new director was scheduled to begin in the fall, and I'd been looking forward to working with her as planned. Also, how does anyone leave Ohio State just as a new football season is approaching? In hindsight, it is easy to see that our reluctance to leave clouded our judgment. Once you make the decision to go, you should go.

As would become increasingly apparent, we weren't the only reluctant ones in this presidential changing of the guard. Brown's outgoing presidential couple, Vartan and Clare Gregorian, also seemed disinclined to make an abrupt exit. Dislodging them from the president's residence was a tricky task, and a harbinger of times to come. Vartan, who had served as Brown's president since 1989, would now be heading up the Carnegie Corporation of New York. By most accounts he was much loved—a "teddy bear" of a fellow known for his jolly greetings and engulfing hugs. Thus, both emeritus presidents led their former schools into the new academic year.

Welcoming the freshman class to Ohio State consists of a few informal events and a cheery, motivational, "glad you're here, study hard, don't drink too much" speech by the president to eight thousand bright-eyed eighteen-year-olds. Welcoming the freshman class to Brown, called "convocation," is a different kind of affair, second in pomp only to the university's three-day commencement celebration. Both these treasured Brown traditions involve grand processionals through the ornate wrought-iron Van Wickle gates, which stand proudly on Prospect Street at the main entrance of campus. The gates swing inward to welcome new students during

convocation ceremonies, then open outward for the commencement processional. At all other times of the year they are closed.

This would be the last year Vartan Gregorian led a freshman
class through the Van Wickle gates as university president, but, as
it turned out, would not be the last time he was front and center at
graduation ceremonies. Standing onstage in full academic regalia
before the class of 2001, Vartan proclaimed that he would return
for every commencement until they graduated. Several freshmen
later told us they were a little confused by this grandstanding.
Wasn't the guy seated behind Gregorian their president? Their
president was experiencing "absolute heartburn" over the supposedly outgoing president's promise to hang around for years to
come.

Gordon was beginning to feel a tinge of buyer's remorse.

***

Only moments after I first set foot on College Hill in Providence,
a man asked me, "Where did you go to school?" I was so surprised
that for a second I thought he was inquiring as to where I went to
high school. I half expected him to follow up with, "What does
your daddy do?" In my experience, that was just not a question that
a middle-age person asks another middle-age person. I quickly
came to understand that, at least among the older Ivy Leaguers I
was meeting, the pressing question of where one went to college is
the Ivy League version of the southern query "Where do you go to
church?"

Finding out where a new acquaintance went to college or goes
to church is a useful social indicator and sorting tool. I have never
scored high on either question, being a mostly public school graduate and a "none of the above" on organized religion. Apparently,
just as Presbyterians differ from Episcopalians, so the various Ivy
League tribes differ. I got the distinct impression that Yale alumni
are imbued with certain characteristics, Princeton alumni with others, and those with a Harvard sheepskin . . . well, what more is
there in this world?

The all-important question of where one went to school is
focused almost exclusively on one's *undergraduate* alma mater.
After all, the minute possibility exists that someone from Iowa
State just might make it into grad school at Yale. Although that per-

son would have technically graduated from Yale, he didn't *really* graduate from Yale. As best I could surmise, the pecking order on the impresso-meter at cocktail parties across the Northeast is: (1) Harvard, (2) Princeton and Yale, (3) Columbia, (4) Brown and Penn, and (5) Cornell and Dartmouth.

I realize fully that, with the exception of Harvard graduates, I have just insulted every other Ivy League alum on the planet. I also understand this is a witless thing to do, seeing as they pretty much run the universe. Please take note, however, that this is not a *U.S. News and World Report* ranking, but merely the impression one outsider garnered from the physical posturing, facial expressions, and vocal tones of Ivy Leaguers and those fortunate enough to be in their presence while sipping a highball and munching a skewered shrimp.

I went through four distinct phases in answering The Question, once I ascertained that Walter Williams High School was not the information being sought. Phase one was honest and friendly, lasting about a month: "East Carolina." Seeing the puzzled look on my interrogator's face, I would add, "in Greenville, North Carolina . . . They have a good studio art program; that's what I studied."

Phase two was evasive and a little apologetic. "In North Carolina," I'd reply, glancing over the person's shoulder in search of diversion.

"The University of North Carolina? Chapel Hill?" the inquisitor would inevitably pursue hopefully, over her glass of white wine.

"Er, no, East Carolina."

"Where?"

Phase three was more proactive. Heck, I had three degrees; most of my tormentors only had one.

"Oh, undergraduate at East Carolina University, master's at Pratt Institute, PhD at Penn State," I would recite nonchalantly.

I well understood that having *three* degrees from non–Ivy League schools did not come close to having a single degree from one of the Ivies (even Dartmouth) in the mind of the Ivy Leaguer. At the very least, however, my mention of the other institutions provided the expectant face before me with more ample opportunity for a follow-up remark. For example:

"I had a distant cousin who was friends with someone who went to Pratt." Or, "Now, *where* is Penn State?"

Phase four?

"Harvard '76."

"Aaah."

"Just kidding. Iowa State."

***

We moved to Providence the first week of January 1998. The Brown president's residence, at 55 Power Street, was undergoing a major renovation at the suggestion of Brown's board of trustees, otherwise known by the scary name "the Corporation."

The twelve-thousand-square-foot, Georgian-revival mansion needed work. Gordon and I requested that the renovations include the addition of a large space for seated dinners, as well as a catering kitchen. The Corporation readily agreed; its members liked the idea that its new president and first lady would be entertaining frequently at the residence. We unpacked as little as possible, settling temporarily into a smaller, university-owned house just down the street. This was the third time in three years I had packed and unpacked. I would be doing so again in a few months when the residence was ready. I grumbled about feeling like a Bedouin; moving vans were our camels.

I was not scheduled to begin teaching until the fall semester, so I was able to spend much of my time that spring semester working with the renovation design team. The residence is located at the south edge of campus, providing a leisurely ten-minute walk up Brown Street and across the green to the president's offices in University Hall. Fifty-five Power Street is a stern structure—a three-story, red-brick fortress of a house surrounded by high stone walls, with a front entrance guarded by imposing wrought-iron gates. It looms close to the sidewalk, as do so many houses in older northeastern urban neighborhoods.

Its interior architectural detailing is impressive. An ornate white-marble fireplace stands directly opposite the front door in the foyer, with its handsome black-and-white-checkered marble floor. Two pillared archways bracket the foyer, offering a stately first impression. Despite its good bones, the house had a cold sterility when Gordon and I first saw it. Its walls were painted white, making its large, high-ceilinged rooms seem cavernous. A few thin area rugs were scattered about, but there was little other fabric to absorb sound or provide warmth. The drawing room opened onto a brick patio that was tented to accommodate large dinner parties—a pleasant enough arrangement in nice weather, but uncomfortably chilly or damp much of the time. There were no porches or covered outside areas.

The architect engaged by the Corporation suggested constructing a conservatory off the drawing room that would open into the garden. It would be a light-filled, airy space that could be used throughout the year, whether the gardens were covered in blossoms or snow. Interior walls were repainted in rich, warm tones of Tuscan yellow and browns; the drawing room was painted a fresh spring green. A William Morris pomegranate-and-lemon wallpaper replaced the worn, dull-green grass cloth on the dining room walls. Huge trellises for climbing roses were installed in the side garden. The smartly designed and perfectly proportioned conservatory was a delight, accommodating up to seventy people for a seated dinner.

The interior designer and I combed through the university's storage areas for historically important pieces showcasing Brown's heritage. I worked hard to make the residence warm and inviting—hanging art, taking and framing photos of new Brown and Providence friends, and meticulously arranging bookshelves. The finished house was grand, sparkling, and elegant.

We moved into the residence in April, just in time to prepare for its commencement debut over the Memorial Day weekend. The house would be open to faculty, alumni, and students and their parents for a series of receptions throughout graduation. People loved to come to the residence, and we entertained frequently. I loved that house; it was my architectural favorite of the three university residences that Gordon and I shared.

***

I was completely unprepared for the intricacies and longevity of the Brown commencement celebration. Graduations at most universities are several hours long. Students and faculty march in the morning; the commencement address is given; degrees and honors are conferred. Usually, it is a morning of "Congratulations, go forth, be strong, and don't forget to pay your alumni dues." By early afternoon, graduates are eating and drinking with family and friends. This is not how it is done at Brown.

Commencement events at Brown include a pops concert, a campus-wide dance, ongoing faculty lectures, five-year class alumni celebrations, academic departmental gatherings, processionals up and down College Hill, and many speech and cocktail opportunities. The trees on the campus green are strung with thousands of twinkling Japanese lanterns before the pops concert on Saturday evening, staying up throughout Sunday night's campus dance. The baccalaureate procession is held on Sunday morning. Donned in caps and gowns, graduating seniors follow the president and his entourage through the Van Wickle gates; through a human corridor of proud parents, friends, and alumni; and down the steep decline of College Street to First Baptist Church (literally, the nation's first Baptist church) for the baccalaureate service. The church is filled to the rafters with soon-to-be graduates; parents and guests are seated on the green, viewing the service on large-screen monitors. After the baccalaureate, the entire procession marches back up the hill to rejoin family and friends.

The following morning, Memorial Day, students gather once again, along with faculty, trustees, and alumni, for a second march down and back up College Hill through a larger, more boisterous crowd of well-wishers. Finally, it is commencement; everyone is giddy with the excitement of spectacle and lack of sleep. By late afternoon, several thousand revelers and one university president and his partner are laid out on sofas, staring into space.

Our first commencement was also to be Gordon's presidential inauguration, or "the coronation," as we jokingly called it. He had declined a formal inaugural ceremony when we first arrived in Providence. Presidential inaugurations at Brown are grand affairs, costing the university $150,000 or more. Gordon allocated the money set aside for the inauguration to financial aid and library support, which was a very savvy political move on his part.

I was swallowed up in the preparation of the residence for its public debut during the weeks before commencement, and I had not been well briefed on the intricate choreography of the three-day fete. Gordon, of course, had worked intimately with the commencement planners. He was instructed precisely on where he had to be and at what time. His handlers made certain he moved seamlessly through his back-to-back appearances. I, on the other hand, was handed an events schedule and mostly left to figure it out for myself. I was still unfamiliar with many of the buildings and gathering points on campus, a deficiency his staff didn't fully comprehend. They largely assumed I would be where I was supposed to be, when I was supposed to be there.

I remember frantically chasing down my academic robe just minutes before the baccalaureate procession was scheduled to roll. I had been told to robe in Manning Hall with the rest of the faculty, only to discover that my robe had been brought to Gordon's office, which by then was locked since everyone had left to watch the procession. I finally located a guard to unlock the office, grabbed my robe, and ran to join the procession. Catching sight of Gordon just as the march began, I sprinted up to join him. "There you are," he smiled, oblivious to my discombobulation. He hooked his arm through mine and we walked side by side through the Van Wickle gates, with Vartan on our heels.

***

Gordon Gee and Vartan Gregorian had vastly different personal and managerial styles. Both men had come to personify the spirit and values of their former universities, which made Vartan as difficult to follow at Brown as Gordon was at Ohio State. It was no secret that Gordon was selected as Brown's seventeenth president largely in reaction to the sixteenth president's lack of ability or interest in structural and strategic management. Gordon was well known as a CEO-type university president, a strong manager who would shake things up administratively and programmatically. Apparently, those responsible for bringing him to Brown had thought that was what they wanted, what the university needed. It turns out that intellectualizing the need for change is one thing; suffering its application is quite another.

It was also no secret that the Brown faculty viewed Gordon with a jaundiced eye from day one. As at every other university, most members of the professoriate couldn't give a hoot about the administrative and management side of things. Professors tend to say "the administration" in the same contemptuous tone that most people say "the guv'ment." Vartan, however, had been provost of the University of Pennsylvania prior to serving as Brown's president and also CEO of the New York Public Library. He had a bachelor's and doctorate in history from Stanford, had taught at the university level for many years, had raved about his absolute *love of teaching*, and had waxed philosophically with the best of the faculty. In short, the Brown faculty considered Vartan a fellow scholar, one of them. From their perspective, Gordon's academic credentials just didn't measure up.

Vartan relished the roles of magnanimous philosopher-king on campus and close friend of Brooke Astor in New York society. He would stride through campus dispensing insight and bear hugs with bravado. He and his wife, Clare, maintained a pied-à-terre in New York and were there as much as they were in Providence. *Charismatic* and *enigmatic* were words associated with Vartan. He was cosmopolitan European in style, speaking seven languages.

Energetic and *affable* were words used to describe Gordon. He was midwestern in style, if not origin. He spoke a smattering of German, left over from his Mormon missionary days in his early twenties. Gordon walked around campus wearing a Brown baseball cap. He was an unapologetic, rah-rah college sports booster—a rather uncool thing to be in his new environment. Although he joked about coming to Brown "to get as far away from college football as possible," he immediately set about nursing Brown's football program and trying to get students to show up for games.

He'd appear at the Brown bookstore and bag purchases at the checkout line. He'd go to fraternity and sorority parties so frequently that they learned to keep a six-pack of his signature drink, Diet Dr. Pepper, on hand for the bow-tied guy. He'd spend two or three nights each semester at a residence hall and order in pizza for everyone. He'd join the students for lunch in the campus dining hall and in the evening at one of the popular bars on Thayer Street.

At first, the Brown students didn't know how to react to the new president's chummy ways. The *Brown Daily Herald* published a cartoon of Gordon running after a group of horrified students, calling out:

"I want to sleep in your dorms and eat in your dining hall!"

"Who *is* this guy?!" cried the harassed, fleeing students. "Leave us *alone!*"

The students came around much faster than the faculty.

***

A lot of eyes rolled when, upon first arriving, Gordon announced his new mantra for Brown: "A private university with a public purpose." Brown's attitude toward Providence was manifest geographically in its physical position atop wealthy College Hill, overlooking a struggling downtown. From the perspective of someone who had been a public university president for seventeen years, the town-and-gown disconnect was immediately apparent. Not only did Brown need to connect locally, as Gordon saw it, but it needed to build relationships statewide and regionally as well. Faculty who considered themselves scholars in the purest sense sniffed disdainfully at this pedestrian interpretation of their academic mission.

The humanities faculty at Brown wields significant power, which is no small feat considering the money-first, corporate environment of higher education in the United States. Brown's forty-year-old humanities curriculum, still called the "New Curriculum," had long been its pride and joy, and is considered to this day to be a defining characteristic of the Brown experience. Mr. Shake Things Up promptly endeared himself to the humanities protectionists by suggesting it was high time the old New Curriculum be rethought and updated. "Any four-decade-old program referred to as 'new' begs reappraisal. Brown thinks of itself as progressive; it's time we examined the output of this course of study," Gordon brashly pointed out to faculty and board members early on in his tenure.

"It was as if I had attacked the pope," Gordon griped when recounting faculty reaction to his executive decree. Apparently, any fool could see that the "output" of the perfectly formed humanities curriculum was four decades of perfectly formed Brunonians. According to Gordon, the New Curriculum—along with a few other things at Brown—was "embedded in academic concrete."

Swiftly adding insult to injury, Gordon announced his intent to upgrade the biological sciences at Brown and construct an $80 million life sciences building. Most university department heads and their faculty view budget apportionment as a zero-sum game— what one academic area gains, another loses. With fundraising efforts now focused on a new life sciences building, to be designed by a signature architect, no less, the general feeling among the Brown humanities faculty was that they were losing ground.

Gordon believed that the university had serious core problems both structurally and strategically. There was no clarity in terms of what it was trying to accomplish, no strategy in terms of fundraising and community relations. Although Brown was considered a "hot" school with a steadily rising pool of applicants, Gordon thought that by the time Vartan left office, it was "running on fumes." Brown had a jazzy reputation, but, in Gordon's estimation, it "needed a lot of restructuring work across the board." He also announced plans to begin examining Brown's graduate programs, with the goal of enhancing the strong ones and consolidating or eliminating the weak.

Overall, members of the Corporation were more responsive to proposed curricular and structural changes than were members of the faculty. The "arrogance of 'we've always done it this way'" piqued their new president, who believed that the "heavy hand of tradition" had stuck this speedboat in the muck. Much of the faculty, along with a few members of the Corporation, saw this new president as the arrogant one, striding into their tranquil domain and punching too fast and hard. I'm sure they thought, *Who does this guy think he is?*

Less than a year into his tenure at Brown, Gordon summed up the difference between Ohio State and Brown by how he was treated day in and day out. The Ohio State faculty and administration had immediately made him feel welcome and valued. In word and ambiance, it was, "We're so happy and fortunate to have you!" At Brown, it was, "What have you done for us today? Prove you deserve to be here."

***

The success of a university president is predicated on his or her ability to work closely with the board of trustees. Ohio State had a board of nine trustees, appointed by the Ohio governor, that met up to ten times a year. The downside of political appointees is *politics*—which is not the best ingredient to mix with education. But then, who am I kidding? Politics is as much a part of education as it is a part of religion, which means it is heavily under the influence of money, money, money. Of course, *academic* politics may be more about credit, prestige, and hanging on to your small slice of the ideological pie than it is about actual money, but all in all, it is still a pernicious influence on education.

With a governor-appointed board of nine, there may be one or even two clunkers, but if the president is tight with the other seven, he can hold the reins. Seven semi-likeminded trustees and one determined president at a public university can make things happen, especially if state legislators see fit to fund the university (a bigger and bigger if these days, as more states teeter on the brink of financial disaster).

Whereas Ohio State's governance structure was streamlined, Brown's was awkward, unwieldy, and divisive. Gordon quickly discovered that the speedboat had more admirals than the aircraft carrier. The Brown Corporation had sixty-one members, both active and not so active, plus numerous honorary senior fellows who enjoyed offering advice and had considerable sway, although no voting power. The Brown faculty was also intimately involved in university governance, often more so than many members of the Corporation. The Corporation met only twice a year, making it difficult to maintain momentum from meeting to meeting. Its real power rested in a more frequently convened executive committee, which had about a dozen members. A large board provides ample opportunity for schisms, factions, and sidelining; the Corporation had its share of each.

The New York City membership of the Corporation and its alumni supporters were an especially strong contingent of Brown's governance. It was as if Brown had two seats of power, one in Providence and the other in New York, with two distinctly different orientations.

The head of the Brown Corporation is its chancellor. Artemis "Arty" Joukowsky was the acting chancellor when Gordon and I came to Brown. Arty's father had started the financial corporation American International Group (AIG), and Arty was a wealthy man. He was also soft-spoken, kind, and generous. He and his wife, Martha—a highly respected Brown professor and the mistress of Brown's archeological dig site at the Great Temple of Petra, Jordan—loved Brown beyond measure. The Joukowsky family was Brown's undisputed biggest donor, but they were low-key and unassuming about it.

Soon after our arrival, Stephen Robert became Corporation chancellor. Steve's personal style differed greatly from Arty's. Steve gave little money to the university until, at the height of the hullabaloo following our announced departure from Brown two years later, he strutted forward with a $5 million peacock contribution—a gesture for which he expected, and received, mounds of publicity. Steve lived in New York, and now, as president of the Carnegie Corporation of New York, so did Vartan Gregorian.

Vartan seemed to pride himself on his fundraising abilities. It must have galled him when Gordon raised more than $109 million his first year at Brown—more money than Vartan had raised during his last two years. One way Gordon set about adding to the Brown endowment was to insist that Corporation members "give, get, or get off" the board. With a few exceptions, Arty being far and away the biggest exception, the Corporation was a miserly group. Gordon was aggressive in his stance, explaining that he couldn't ask others for money if his board was not giving. When Gordon's year-one fundraising numbers were first reported, we began to hear that Vartan was whispering that his successor was cooking the books.

It was clear that Vartan was not going away. Not only did he remain within the NYC-Brown trustee circle, but he would frequently come into town, where he would stay at the home of the publisher of the *Providence Journal*. The publisher lived *right next door* to 55 Power Street, overlooking the residence's back garden and our bedroom windows. I began referring to Vartan Gregorian as "Vartan Gargoylian."

***

I have my own special memory of Vartan. Well into our time at Brown, Gordon and I attended a large, black-tie Brown alumni dinner at the Waldorf in New York. The pioneering investor and philanthropist Sir John Templeton, then in his nineties, was the speaker. Gordon was being recognized for his fundraising and restructuring contributions. I was feeling less insecure about my un–Ivy Leagueness, by then knowing a lot of people by name and enjoying the cocktail chitchat. Adjustments were finally beginning to be made all round. In short, we were settling into Brown, and Brown was relaxing with the two of us.

The dinner bell had rung when, as guests filed slowly into the ballroom where the tables were set, I made a quick detour into the ladies' room. A few people were still conversing on the dance floor when I entered the ballroom, although most had taken their seats, including Gordon. Vartan came toward me smiling as I walked across the softly lit dance floor.

"Ah, Constanz!" he exclaimed in his courtly manner. I reached out my hand to his, but instead he pulled me to him for the trademark bear hug. He then gave me a kiss on the lips, which was no huge surprise, but just as the quick kiss should have ended, he jammed his tongue into my mouth. I was stunned. I pushed him away and literally staggered backward toward the table. I plunked down in my chair and sat in silence, trying to absorb what had just happened.

When Gordon turned to me after a few minutes of conversing with a dinner companion, I said to him, "Vartan just stuck his tongue in my mouth."

Gordon looked at me quizzically.

"I'm serious, Gordon, he just accosted me on the dance floor. I ought to go throw this glass of wine in his face."

"Don't make a scene," he warned.

"Aren't you going to do something—*say* something?!" I sputtered.

"Just calm down," he replied. With that, he turned back to resume his conversation. I sat there, my cheeks stinging with anger and humiliation.

Most women experience an unwanted and inappropriate advance from a man at some point in their lives. That is simply the way it is. It is something so common as to not merit mentioning, normally. Vartan's, however, was a more invidious transgression. This was a dog raising his leg on another dog's territory. It hurt me to learn that my dog didn't much care.

12

From Brown to Gold

THE ASSOCIATION OF AMERICAN UNIVERSITIES (AAU) meets twice a year. Its spring conference is always in Washington, D.C., with its fall conference at one of its member institutions. The 1999 fall conference would be held in October at Ohio State. We were looking forward to returning to Columbus to see old friends, and we had planned to stay an extra day for the unveiling of Gordon's presidential portrait.

Vanderbilt University trustee John Hall telephoned Gordon a couple of weeks before the conference to see if he would advise the board's search committee on possible candidates for the soon-to-be-available position of Vanderbilt chancellor. (Vanderbilt calls its president "chancellor.") John and Gordon had known each other since Gordon's West Virginia University days, and they had later served together on the Banc One board, which was then head-quartered in Columbus.

John, along with Vanderbilt Board of Trust chairman Martha Ingram and vice chairman Denny Bottorff, arrived at our hotel suite the first morning of the conference. I was invited to sit in on the meeting. They explained that it had been eighteen years since Vanderbilt had been in the market for a new chancellor. They needed some updates on the kinds of packages university presidents were receiving these days, what would make Vanderbilt appealing to a candidate, and who Gordon would recommend be included in their candidate pool. They also expressed interest in my perspective, as they acknowledged that they would likely be recruiting a spouse along with their next chancellor. What was it like being both first lady and faculty? What types of arrangements had Ohio State and Brown made to accommodate me? It was a very friendly meeting; Gordon and I were relaxed and spoke openly.

As they prepared to leave, Mrs. Ingram smiled and said, "We wish you could be a candidate, but I know you haven't been at Brown very long."

Gordon and I both laughed, and he said, "Well, I'm not a candidate."

They would still like to stay in touch, they said.

After they left, we stood there looking at each other with surprised expressions.

"Don't even *think* about it," I said.

"Don't worry," he replied.

***

I was then into my second year of teaching at Brown and felt on firmer footing than I had since leaving Ohio State. I no longer seemed to be as much of a student curiosity as I had been the previous year, when close to a hundred students showed up the first day of class for a seminar with a capacity of fifteen. Most of them weren't interested in the class; they just wanted to get a look at the new president's wife and hear how she pitched her course. Apparently, I either did very poorly or very well, depending on how you look at it, as only fourteen returned for the second class.

I've had many different types of jobs in my life, requiring a variety of knowledge and skills, but in my experience teaching was undoubtedly the most challenging. Teaching shone a klieg light on my number-one insecurity: the terribly undermining fear of not being smart enough.

As each new semester began, I suffered anxiety dreams about arriving the first day of class and not having prepared a syllabus, having forgotten to order the required reading materials, or running late and not being able to find the classroom—basically, the exact same nightmares most third graders have about school. I prepared hours on end for each class session, thinking I should know the answer to every conceivable question that might be asked of me.

It took me years to accept that it was OK to not know the answer *and to admit it*. I finally learned to say: "That's a good question, Megan, but I don't know. Could you please do a little research on that and get back with us next class?" In the meantime, I would conduct a little research of my own so I could validate and augment whatever information Megan might bring back to class. And then I made certain to ask Megan to share the fruits of her inquiry at the beginning of the following class. Megan either enthusiastically related her findings or henceforth asked fewer difficult questions. Although the first outcome was much more preferable, I have to admit that sometimes the second proved to be a relief.

My fate in regard to teaching offers convincing evidence of the existence of karma, because I had been such an impertinent thorn in the side of more than a few of my own teachers. Mrs. Alspaugh and Mrs. Mosley—God rest their souls—might gain a measure of satisfaction knowing that all the pain I inflicted on them came back to me tenfold. Brown students relished playing "gotcha" with flappable professors like me. In turn, I spoke often of the joys of teaching, and of how rich their lives would be should any of them decide to become educators. It is my sincere and sinister hope that many of them did.

***

All in all, my teaching slowly improved as I became more relaxed with (and appreciative of) the jousting character of student-teacher relationships at Brown. I had been made to feel welcome by my faculty colleagues at the Taubman Center, where I was provided an office. Tom Antoine, director of the center, had generously expressed interest in my academic area when I had first arrived, encouraging me to begin a program at Brown similar to the one I had developed at Ohio State. I declined his offer for the short term, needing some recuperation time from the demanding move from one university to another. Also, I wasn't so keen on providing immediate competition to the four-year-old Ohio State program. How many degree-granting arts policy programs did the world need?

For the time being, I would teach an undergraduate arts policy course and focus on my research and writing. I had been serving since the fall of 1997 as an executive editor of the scholarly journal *Arts*

Education Policy Review and would continue proudly to do so. My salary at Brown was $37,000. Half was paid out of the university administration budget, the other half through my academic department, just as it had been at Ohio State.

The tiny portion of a life I had outside university parameters was also gaining momentum. I'd made a good number of friends, most of whom were associated with Providence's richly talented arts community. Providence is home to the Rhode Island School of Design (RISD) and the Trinity Repertory Company. RISD is one of the top art schools in the United States, just as Trinity Rep is one of the country's best regional theaters. I had been appointed to the Rhode Island Council on the Arts and was on the board of Trinity Rep. I was also a member of the Providence Art Club. In short, I was finding my own place in Providence.

It is true that my appointments to the boards of the arts council and Trinity Rep came about by virtue of my being married to the president of Brown. Spouses of university presidents (and, of course, the presidents themselves) receive numerous invitations to serve on cultural and educational nonprofit boards. I had served on the ballet and symphony boards in Columbus, but there was something especially satisfying about my warm welcome into the Providence arts community. Perhaps it was because I was beginning to feel more confident professionally and I felt I had something to contribute. I knew a fair amount about the visual arts, as opposed to symphonic music or ballet, and I adored theater. In my twenties, I devoured plays like most of my friends ate up novels. It was delicious to listen to the Trinity Rep director Oskar Eustis offer nuanced interpretations of various dramatic roles and discuss the merits of staging one play over another.

I also had an inner circle of girlfriends, none of whom taught or worked at Brown. Unfortunately, it seems almost impossible to have close friends within the university if you are married to its president. I think this must also be true of women who are married to corporate CEOs and top-dog politicians. Anything you say or do will be scrutinized and passed along, seldom with kindness. I was grateful for the protected space this circle of new friends afforded. Good girlfriends are life support both when the going is good and when it's not.

Over the Thanksgiving break following the AAU conference in Columbus, I finished unpacking my studio art materials and set up a painting workspace. Before beginning that pleasantly anticipated task, I had asked Gordon if this was safe to do. We *will* be staying here at Brown, right? This is not going to be like Columbus, where I finally got settled into my new workspace and we moved two months later?

I was mostly joking with him, but I also felt an ominous vibe in the air. I wanted to hear Gordon say that everything was all right, that I could relax and settle in. Although he reassured me that we would remain at Brown for many years, I was unable to set aside my apprehension. For all his recent restructuring and fundraising successes at Brown, he would sometimes say that he felt "like an antelope in a telephone booth."

Two weeks later Gordon remarked off-handedly: "The darnedest thing just happened. Denny Bottorff called and offered me the chancellorship of Vanderbilt."

Seeing the color drain from my face, he added, "I told him I wasn't interested . . . but he asked me to think about it."

"No, Gordon, no thinking about it," I demanded. "And please stop talking with them!"

***

Denny telephoned a few days before Christmas to ask whether Gordon had thought further about the offer. Had he changed his mind? This time, Gordon told Denny that he couldn't leave Brown because he had a "moral obligation" to stay. It wasn't because he didn't *want* to leave, but because he felt he *couldn't* leave, he explained.

That reasoning constituted a whole different fishing strategy. Denny knew the bass was eyeing the bait and quickly offered up the name of an ethicist whom he encouraged Gordon to contact. An ethicist! Gordon frequently joked about getting "special dispensation" for this or that from the LDS Church. I sarcastically asked him if this ethicist friend of the Vanderbilt Board of Trust vice chairman might find it in his heart to bestow a special dispensation of moral obligation in this case.

I was adamantly against leaving Brown and Providence. We had just gotten there. We had just settled into the residence, for goodness' sake. It was absurd and exhausting to even think about it. I was beginning to feel part of the community, especially the arts community. Besides, it would be *scandalous* if we were to leave.

Gordon once more declined the offer, but I could see Vanderbilt's persistent attentions had turned his head. He was *not* not thinking about it.

I knew that Gordon liked being pursued. It's only human nature to want to be wanted; it's an addictive ego trip for anyone. Some people—certainly a lot of entertainers and politicians among them—crave attention. Gordon was voted "Best Actor" his senior year in high school. He was class president his sophomore and junior years, and (of course!) student body president. I won't venture any further down Psychoanalysis Lane, but I think most people might see a tendency there. Granted, it was a small high school; maybe he was the only one who auditioned for the lead role in every school play. (I was named "Wittiest" my senior year. The prescience of high school superlatives is truly amazing.)

***

Gordon was scheduled to fly to Naples, Florida, for a fundraising event the first week of January. John Hall called to persuade him to stop over in Nashville. He would send his private jet to Providence for Gordon. Gordon would meet with Mrs. Ingram and Denny and be given a brief tour of Nashville and the Vanderbilt campus. He would then be delivered to Naples in time for the scheduled reception. It would be quick and easy; no one would be the wiser.

"You're kidding," I said, astounded by their audacity. "Isn't that rather unseemly, kind of like, well, cheating?"

Two days later Gordon boarded John's plane for Nashville.

"It was all very impressive," he reported. "The campus is beautiful. It's a very complex university for its size—sort of a perfect mix of Ohio State's intricacy and Brown's intimacy—and Nashville's much nicer than I expected."

He was so buoyed up by the attention and sparkle-eyed at this greener grass that I couldn't help but be a teensy bit happy for him. On the other hand (my much more dominant right hand), I wanted to shout: What about the life we've built *here* and all the work *I've* put into it? *You're* the one who couldn't wait to leave Ohio State and now, *less than two years later*, you want to go to Vanderbilt

145

because those sneaks are whispering sweet nothings in your ear? What about what *I* want?"

I knew that he and, by extension, *we* were now walking the edge. "So?" I asked impatiently.

"I told them no."

"Good," I exhaled.

After a beat, he continued: "I'm going to tell Steve that I went. I think he should know."

"*No!* Do *not* do that!" I shrieked. "Why do you want to do that?"

"He'll find out at some point anyway. Better for me to tell him now."

"So *now* you're having twinge of conscience? *Now* you have an overwhelming need to be forthcoming? *Really*, Gordon, how do you expect him to respond?!"

Gordon, with me strapped to his back, was hell-bent on stepping over the edge. I prayed for a huge circus net or large trampoline to stop our freefall. I tried to envision a white light surrounding us as the recently hired president informed his corporate executive board chairman that, en route to a major fundraising event, he had taken a detour to check out a job offer at another university.

"Thank you for telling me, Gordon. I appreciate your honesty. Let's just move on from here," Steve would respond with a beatific smile.

***

The next day Gordon told Steve about the Nashville detour, adding that Vanderbilt had offered him "a very nice compensation package." Gordon had told me the previous evening of Vanderbilt's salary offer of $1 million. We had discussed and, I thought, dismissed it, even though it would have meant a 333 percent pay increase. We already lived royally. Most of our living expenses were paid for by the university: housing, travel, two cars, and house staff, including a chef. Gordon sat on several corporate boards, bringing in another sizable chunk of cash. What else did we need?

As reported by Gordon, the conversation went smoothly. "We agreed I should say no to Vanderbilt, and that we'll discuss my salary when we get back from Asia."

From Steve's perspective, the conversation went a tad less agreeably. As later reported in the *Brown Alumni Magazine*, he told Gordon that his continued communication with Vanderbilt was "entirely inappropriate" and "a violation of his commitment to Brown."[1] Gordon was to give Vanderbilt his final, *final* no and, while we traveled on a two-week development trip through Seoul, Hong Kong, and Japan, the Brown Corporation would review his compensation package and see what they could do.

At this point, the "just say no" reprise was getting to be like the joke about the protesting girlfriend: Don't! Stop! Don't! Stop . . . Don't stop. Gordon had told me that he had declined the offer at the end of the Nashville visit. So now he would tell them no again? Hmmm . . .

He phoned Denny on our way to the airport. This time Denny responded to no by telling Gordon that the job would be his until they hired another person. Denny must have scored a lot in high school.

***

We had just arrived in Seoul when Gordon's sister, Cherie, telephoned to say that their mother was critically ill and had been admitted into the hospital. Vera was ninety-one, and Cherie called with reports on her condition throughout the trip. One day, her death was imminent and we should come home; the next, she seemed to rally and we should complete our trip.

I thought we should cancel the remainder of our trip and fly directly to Utah to be with his mother. Gordon was clearly worried, but he maintained that since the Asian trip had been planned so intricately and almost a year in advance, we needed to keep to our itinerary. We would fly directly to Salt Lake from Asia, he decided. Gordon's choice in this matter didn't altogether surprise me, but it did sadden me. "Gordie" was everything to his mother. Her dining room table, completely covered with large silver-framed photos of him, was a shrine to her youngest child and only son. It was a bit of a family joke. Cherie, the daughter who tended daily to her mother, merited a couple of smaller photos on a coffee table. It seemed that, for Gordon, work took precedence over everything. Or maybe it was that he couldn't deal with the vulnerability he felt over his mother dying, and his work gave him the illusion of being in control.

John and Denny immediately telephoned Gordon from Nashville to express their concern about Vera. Gordon continued to speak with them throughout our travels, from Seoul to Hong Kong to Japan. We never heard a word from Steve or any of the Brown trustees. This bothered me. My husband was dealing with the death of his mother, and they were in a snit over his flirtation with Vanderbilt? Gordon was in daily contact with his office, so it was highly improbable that the entire Corporation was unaware of the situation. It was true that Steve was traveling in Cambodia, but, even so, it was odd not to hear from him. Phnom Penh was only two hours' time difference from Seoul, an hour from Hong Kong. Gordon was feeling decidedly unloved, and by the time we got to Hong Kong, he began to reconsider Vanderbilt's offer.

***

This time I entered into the should-we-or-shouldn't-we speculation, as I was becoming increasingly piqued over the Brown communiqué blackout. Besides, the possibility of moving to Nashville (code name Dogpatch) still seemed remote. It was a travel game of sorts, something to take our minds off worrying about Vera and airport weariness. Sitting on our futons in a Kyoto hotel one night, we made a "leave Brown for Vanderbilt" pros-and-cons list. "Big Scandal!" was the first item on the con list.

Also on the con list was: "not good for CBG professionally." A move to Vanderbilt would be devastating for me as an untenured professor. Each time we moved, the possibility of tenure receded further into the future. Brown's Faculty Executive Committee had extended my tenure review for *twelve years*, until 2010—in other words, to a galaxy far, far away. It was clear that little of what I'd accomplished at Ohio State would be acknowledged during the Brown tenure process. I had been hired at Ohio State on my own merits and had been considered a productive, bona fide member of the art education faculty. At Brown I was the trailing spouse and would be so again at Vanderbilt, where I would have to start over once again. Although neither Brown nor Vanderbilt offered any coursework in art education or exhibited much interest in it, at least Brown had a solidly functioning policy center, which Vanderbilt did not. Things looked rather bleak for me at Vanderbilt, with the university's lack of interest in both art education and arts policy.

If Vanderbilt wants you as much as they seem to, I told Gordon, then this is the time to negotiate tenure for me. He agreed and assured me that he did not foresee the request as posing much of a problem. I did not relish the prospect of obtaining tenure in such a manner. I had always stood firmly on the ethic of making my own way through hard work, a rudimentary value that had been ingrained in me at an early age. I was learning quickly that is not the way of the rough-and-tumble, grab-the-ring worlds of big business and American higher education, which are essentially one and the same.

***

Vera passed away two days before we were to leave Asia. We completed our scheduled business and flew to Salt Lake City for her funeral. Although he did not say it, I know Gordon must have felt awful about not having seen his mother before she died. I certainly did. She had always been kind to me, and happy to see someone else love her "Gordie," too.

We arrived back in Providence somber and weary. Steve never bothered to contact Gordon either to offer his condolences or to inquire about our long trip on behalf of the university. It was an ominous silence.

***

The day after we returned from Utah, my beloved dog, Lucy, and I met up with Sammy and Sheila Blumstein for a play date on the campus green. Sammy was a brown Labrador retriever and Lucy's best friend. Sheila had served as interim provost during our first year at Brown after Gordon had sacked the former provost, which was the common fate of provost leftovers when he assumed office. Gordon always insisted on bringing in as much of his own executive team as possible.

I told Sheila of Steve's rude inattentiveness, of Vanderbilt's continued aggressiveness, and of Gordon's growing ambivalence. I asked if she could pass the word along to the powers that be that they need to do something *tout de suite* to reassure Gordon of their affection.

A meeting between Gordon, Arty, and Brown Corporation vice chairman Marie Langlois was arranged for that evening, with Steve calling in from Cambodia. They all assured Gordon that they did not want him to leave. Steve told Gordon to meet the next morning with the university's chief financial officer, Donald Reeves, to reexamine his compensation package.

It was during his meeting with Donald that Gordon realized he had been lowballed when hired by Brown. He maintains that he was led to believe that his salary was in the midrange of Ivy League presidential compensation, but instead he discovered that it was at the bottom rung. A pay hike of $50,000 would be required to move him into midrange level.

Several hours later, Arty and Marie arrived at Gordon's office to affirm that the Corporation would approve the salary increase. He now needed to cut off communications with Vanderbilt once and for all, they informed him. Gordon accepted the arrangement and, with Arty and Marie present, telephoned Denny to inform him of his recommitment to Brown.

It was over! I was jubilant when I heard the news. The next afternoon—a cold but crystal-clear New England Sunday—Gordon and I stopped by Arty and Martha's home while out on a walk with Lucy. Standing in their kitchen, we hugged and raised a toast to our future together at Brown. Even Gordon took a sip of Champagne.

***

Gordon was scheduled to make a business trip to New York the third of February, the day after his fifty-sixth birthday. Although Steve had been back in New York for well over a week, he had not contacted Gordon. "Isn't that a little strange?" I asked Gordon. "Why don't you stop in, see what's up, and make sure everything's OK."

Gordon telephoned me late that afternoon, as he was standing outside Rockefeller Center, where Steve had his offices. "We're going to Vanderbilt," he said.

"What?" I managed to squeak, utterly stunned, as my heart thudded *No, no, no!* I was alone at a house we'd bought a year earlier in Westport, Massachusetts, on the Westport River, a thirty-five-minute drive southeast of Providence. The sun was setting, and I stared in a daze at the bleeding water as Gordon related what had happened over the past half hour.

Steve appeared to be angry when Gordon entered the office.

"How are you doing?" Gordon asked.

"Not very well," Steve answered.

"Why is that?"

"The fact that you held us up for that $50,000. The Corporation needs to think about this."

"We both need to think about it," Gordon replied as he turned and left the office.

The moment he stepped outside the building, Gordon called Denny. "Is that job still available?" Denny said the Vanderbilt board of trust would call an emergency meeting the next day to make the appointment, and a press conference would be scheduled for Monday.

Gordon waited until Sunday to inform Steve that he was leaving Brown for Vanderbilt, and to expect a press conference to be held in Nashville the next afternoon announcing the appointment. Steve was caught completely off guard.

"You can't do that!" he said.

"I just did," Gordon replied.

Steve had to pull it together, and fast. He called for an emergency meeting the next day, where he related a very different version of the president's defection to Brown's shocked faculty. Steve said that Gordon had walked into his office the previous Thursday soliciting a counteroffer from the Brown Corporation, citing "an actual figure that would have elevated [his salary] to the top of college presidents in the country."[2] He told the faculty he had turned down Gordon's request, and that the meeting ended with the mutual agreement that Gordon should accept Vanderbilt's offer.

***

We boarded John Hall's plane for Nashville early Monday morning. I had barely slept since hearing the news. My face was puffy from crying. I was exhausted.

We met first with the Vanderbilt board. I told them that, as a southerner and native North Carolinian, I felt I was "coming home." Of course, I didn't tell them that I did not *want* to come home, that I liked it fine up north, thankyouverymuch. Nope, my new home was now Nashville, Tennessee, the "Buckle of the Bible Belt," where men are men and women are expected to stand by them no matter what scoundrels they are.

Doing my duty to God and country, I marched alongside my man to Kirkland Hall with a big smile on my pale face. There I stood, gazing adoringly, as Gordon accepted the seventh chancellorship of Vanderbilt University—a university purchased 127 years earlier by Cornelius Vanderbilt to "heal the wounds between the North and the South," or so the story goes.

I continued smiling even as I heard my husband tell the world—his speech was being broadcast live on television, radio, and the Internet—that it was "our" decision to come to Vanderbilt, that he and I had discussed it and come to the joint conclusion that it was the right move, the right "fit." *What a crock*, I thought, nodding demurely. *If I could edge a little closer, I could pinch him really hard and no one would see.* Coming to Vanderbilt, he continued, was "a rendezvous with responsibility." Keeping a straight face at this point was almost more than I could manage.

I glanced up at Vanderbilt's founder and mascot as he cynically surveyed the scene from his full-length portrait behind the podium. Crude, virtually illiterate, and "actively hostile to formal education," Cornelius (a.k.a. "the Commodore") Vanderbilt had been persuaded by a Methodist minister relative of his devout new second wife, Frank (yes, Frank!), a native Alabamian forty years his junior, to donate $1 million to jump-start a small Methodist school in Nashville then called Central University.[3] In 1873, Central was a "school" on paper only. It was immediately renamed Vanderbilt University, its first classes being held in the fall of 1874.

Hail, Frank! There should be a statue of Frank instead of Cornelius at the main entrance of Vanderbilt. Personally, I would have felt better about things if literate, lovely Frank had been witnessing the seventh chancellor's press conference in place of her dour old husband. As it was, the frugal Dutchman looked positively disgusted that the fast-talking fellow gesticulating beneath him would be putting more in his pockets each year than the entire amount on which the university was founded. Maybe the Commodore's expression was more of grudging admiration—it was hard to tell with those squinty eyes and muttonchops. I think I was hallucinating by then.

"Is there any wine on this plane?" I asked as we climbed aboard for the flight back to Providence. I knew that the return trip would force us to face music less agreeable to me than country. Not since my father's alcoholic rages and mistreatment of my mother and me had I felt so powerless and *lonely*.

***

Brown University went a little insane. Students burned Gordon in effigy on the campus green. An especially motivated if uncreative gang egged the university residence. Gordon was not allowed to return to his office. I slunk into mine over the weekend to gather some needed books and papers.

Brown faculty and alumni wrote scathing diatribes about Gordon's avarice and abject failure as a moral leader. Even ol' Cornelius was getting the what-for. "It should be noted that Cornelius Vanderbilt, after whom Vanderbilt is named, was an unscrupulous railroad magnate, known along with many of his peers of that era as robber barons," an irate citizen pointed out in a letter to the editor of the *Providence Journal*. "His namesake university has continued to follow in his footsteps."[4] Never mind that the original Brown family wealth was derived in large part from slave trafficking. Righteous anger rarely faces a mirror.

Vartan Gregorian cannonballed into the fetid Brown pool of indignation. "There is an etiquette among educational institutions, that you do not go after a person who has been in an institution for two years only," he lectured. "And if you're the president of an institution for two years, you do not leave, either. I am stunned, utterly disappointed and dismayed."[5] He may have been stunned, but he was not so immobilized that he couldn't hold himself up as a model of integrity: "When I was offered the presidency at Columbia [in 1996], I turned it down. . . . You don't use offers to hike salaries. I didn't go to Brown and say, 'Match Columbia's offer.' . . . There's a convention you respect. It's not like the corporate world, raiding each other."[6]

Martha Ingram, the chairman of Vanderbilt's board and chairman and CEO of the mega-conglomerate Ingram Industries Inc., begged to disagree with Vartan's idealistic portrayal of the American university system. "I don't see the difference between the corporate world and the academic world," she stated. "A university is a really big business, and the chancellor is the CEO."[7]

A morally affronted Steve Robert, the former chairman and CEO of Oppenheimer & Company, beseeched the heavens above: "God, I hope she's wrong. I pray that she's wrong. If principle is not paramount at a university, where in our society is it going to be?"[8]

I had been grimly following this who's-who volley between Brown and Vanderbilt. Until I read Steve's supplication to the Almighty, I was having a lot of trouble finding any humor at all in the fine mess my husband had gotten us into. I was in a deep funk—so much so that even Vartan's antics failed to amuse me, and I usually got a big kick out of such obvious self-aggrandizement. Martha's corporate-macho response certainly didn't make me feel better about going to Vanderbilt. When I read Steve's rejoinder, however, I choked with laughter on my morning coffee.

***

A little comic relief was exceedingly welcome in what had turned out to be a really bad week. It was being speculated widely that someone else was behind Gordon's decision to leave Brown: the first lady. "Was it simply the money?" asked the astute editors of the *Brown Alumni Monthly*, or "was it that Vanderbilt had offered his wife tenure, something Brown had refused to do?"[9]

An Ivy League president jumps ship for a less prestigious university, creating a scandal in the process, because his wife is offered tenure . . . Makes sense to me, fellows.

It was said that I had never liked Brown and, as a native North Carolinian, had persuaded my husband to move south. Gordon fed this truly idiotic conjecture when, grasping for justification for jilting Brown, he told a reporter: "My wife is from the South. There is really quite a high comfort level in moving to the South again. And professionally, there was a clear match given her interest in arts policy. We're a partnership, and I want her to feel as professionally fulfilled as I do. At Brown, that would have taken much longer."[10]

What recourse is available to the trailing spouse in such a situation? I so much wanted to set the record straight, but to do so would be matrimonial murder and social suicide. Oh, how I wanted to dial the news hotline and say something like this:

Hello, news hotline? This is Constance Gee. I'd like to report some real bullshit perpetrated by my dear husband, whom I've just punched in the nose:

1. Any "comfort" I derive south of the Mason-Dixon line comes from personal friendships. I am, in fact, very discomforted by the South's overtly sexist attitudes and conservative political values.

2. Vanderbilt offers nothing, zip, nada by way of arts policy; thus, any "clear match" for me professionally is total baloney.

3. The decision to leave Brown for Vanderbilt was not a mutual one—so spare me the politically correct talk of "partnerships."

4. My professional "fulfillment" has nothing to do with this defection. If that had any bearing at all, we'd have stayed at Ohio State.

5. I have no friggin' idea what my husband's remark about my professional fulfillment taking longer to achieve at Brown than at Vanderbilt is supposed to mean, although it sure *sounds* like a direct reference to my short-circuiting the tenure process. Please know that was an act of professional survival, not fulfillment.

Of course, I could not make that phone call. Publicly refuting Gordon's characterization of my involvement in the defection would be a lose-lose-lose proposition whereby I would have undermined my husband and myself, possibly even destroying our marriage. I would have lost, he would have lost, and Vanderbilt—home of the Corporate Commodores—would have lost. The only winners would have been our attackers. I wasn't about to let that happen, because I was even more incensed at the hysterical moralizing of the Brown community than at Gordon. I limited my public response (my private response was another matter) to an email to the *Brown Alumni Monthly* I pounded out on my computer:

> For Brown to have "refused" to offer me tenure would mean that someone had made that request. I can assure you that is not the case—neither Gordon nor I have ever considered making such a request. I had served four years as an Ohio State faculty member when we came to Brown. To have asked for tenure at that point in my career would have been as presumptuous and poorly reasoned as has been much of the reporting about our decision to move to Vanderbilt.
>
> I am not the scapegoat that some members of the Brown community appear to require. I suggest that those who love Brown and care about its dignity accept my husband's graceful explanation of his resignation.[11]

"My husband's graceful explanation of his resignation." *I deserve some sort of matrimonial loyalty award*, I huffed, as I reread my supportive close to the electronic missive. It was worth at least a substantial pair of diamond stud earrings.

Gordon told reporters that he had listened to his "inner soul," which had told him that staying at Brown would be "the easy way out." He was being "courageous" in going to Vanderbilt. My inner soul was really irked with his inner soul.

In spite of myself, the more Brown howled and threw sticks, stones, and eggs, the stronger my allegiance grew to my husband and to Vanderbilt. The final straw for me was when the *Providence Journal* published a letter to the editor calling Gordon "a mercenary bastard."[12] I telephoned the *Journal* that very morning, proudly identified myself, and canceled our subscription. Maybe he is a mercenary bastard, but he's *my* mercenary bastard.

Vanderbilt was reveling in Brown's impotent temper tantrum. Its slick thievery of an Ivy League president and ability to plunk down such a huge wad of cash were a point of pride. Vanderbilt had just scored a victory for Dixie that, from the southern perspective, actually did help heal the lingering wound of inferiority left over from the War of Northern Aggression—or, as a friend's very proper North Carolina Tidewater grandmother called it, "The Late Unpleasantness."

In a voice dripping with incredulity and disdain, a *New York Times* reporter had asked Gordon, "*Why* would you leave Brown for *Vanderbilt?*" I could not deny my southern pride when he replied, "I'm not naïve enough to think the world begins and ends with the Ivy League." Damn, I loved that. Of course, that little exchange never made the paper.

So why did Gordon Gee leave Brown University? Certainly the huge salary increase was a factor, but it was not the money per se. It was what the money represented in tandem with Vanderbilt's relentless pursuit: They *wanted* him. Gordon's long-time assistant Kate Wolford summed it up most perceptively: "He can't keep his knickers up." Steve's duplicity over the promised salary increase relieved Gordon of any and all compunctions he had about leaving Brown for Vanderbilt.

***

We lived as exiles in the Brown president's residence until mid-March, when we were able to finish our packing and put our belongings in storage. Once again, I had to dismantle what we—what *I*—had carefully and lovingly constructed. The ill will and media attacks were hard on both of us, but Gordon had weathered negative press coverage before. He had a "thick skin," he maintained. I had no experience with public flogging. Each blow brutalized me.

Gordon was the rock star, already focused on the next sold-out performance. To hell with the unappreciative, angry audience he'd left midperformance in Providence. Feeling more and more like a mere roadie on this tour, I envied his ability to flip 'em the bird and move on. That ability can come from being solidly self-determined and in control, or can be arrived at (so I have read) by accepting that one has no real control of anything. Being neither that powerful terrestrially or that evolved spiritually, I was mired in a Prussian-blue mood. I couldn't escape the demeaning realization that I had become increasingly dependent on my husband's career and life choices and less self-directed than I'd ever imagined I would be.

I was unable to visualize my future in Nashville. Even though I had been granted tenure, I knew the move to Vanderbilt was not professionally advantageous for me. I had played my tenure ace, but I still had no academic home. Art education courses there were nonexistent, and the Art and Art History Department's faculty exhibited no interest in my arts policy work. In fact, they flat-out denied my request for appointment to their department.

The Vanderbilt board leaned on the Department of Leadership, Policy, and Organizations in the Peabody College of Education and Human Development. I was appointed associate professor of public policy and education. I would teach a class on arts and arts education policy each year in the spring semester and continue my research and writing and my editorial work with *Arts Education Policy Review*.

***

We retreated to our home in Westport, which Kate Wolford had dubbed "Chez Consuela" in my honor. Gordon had bought the house for me, he said, because he wanted to make certain I had a home if something should happen to him. (At that point, I believe the "something" he envisioned happening was more along the lines of meeting his maker rather than "See you later, alligator.") He had done very well on the sale of some Banc One options, and his lawyer advised him that, for tax and investment purposes, we should purchase some real estate. The moment I walked into the house, I fell dead in love with it—or, more precisely, with the view.

Chez Consuela is not large—only two bedrooms, on a postage-stamp-size parcel of land—but it is about as close to the water's edge as a house can be without being a houseboat. It looks across a grassy flat, where scores of delicate snow-white egrets gather at low tide for a seafood buffet. They step prissily, pulling up one slender black leg and surveying the spread with a critical eye, like your aunt Matilda at a church dinner when not just any piece of fried chicken will do. When an egret makes her unhurried decision on which dish looks the most worthy, she plucks it from the buffet lightning fast but so very gracefully. Ospreys patrol overhead for fish to serve up to their ever-hungry young. A blue heron stands sentinel while seagulls drop surprised clams on the dock with a *thwack*.

I once witnessed—up close and personal, thanks to an excellent pair of image-stabilizing binoculars—a kingfisher capture, stun, and swallow a silverside. It's interesting that kingfishers are so named, because they often miss their prey. I had kept my spyglasses trained on the bird as he dived back and forth between our neighbor's dock and ours, intent on supper. Then, *bingo*, he swooped up with the silverside flipping in his beak and perched atop a piling on our dock about twenty feet away from where I was stationed. In a fluid set of motions lasting only about three seconds, he grasped the little fish by its tail, whacked its head against the piling, and tossed it up in the air so that it did a half somersault, landing head first in his open mouth. The silverside slid neatly down his throat, emitting a little spurt of blood and entrails out its rear as the kingfisher closed down on it. I would later clearly remember that image from the perspective of the silverside.

***

Chez Consuela had become my spirit's refuge. It was my place to disconnect from the constant demands and confinements of public life and plug into the rhythms of the natural world. Gordon proposed selling it and purchasing another retreat home near Nashville. At that point, he didn't care if he ever set foot in that part of New England again. Besides, Gordon doesn't like water. He doesn't mind *looking* at it for a few minutes, but he hates being *in* it and doesn't particularly like to be *on* it. His favorite moment on a watergoing vessel of any type is disembarkation, that instant when his socked and tightly sneakered foot makes contact with dry land, preferably the concrete of a large city. With the exception of salmon and tuna (both well done), he does not eat fish.

Actually, Gordon doesn't eat much of anything except pasta pomadora, grilled chicken breasts, taco chips and salsa, ice cream (always straight from the container), and an occasional cheeseburger or cheese enchilada. Rebekah observed that her father's palate seems limited to the food he grew up eating in Vernal, Utah—a clear case of arrested taste bud development.

All things considered, it was big of him to agree to the counterproposal I made halfway through that cold, rainy spring in exile. I said that I would cease bemoaning our move to Nashville and get with the program if, in return, we could keep the Westport property and I could spend July and August there each year. He consented, saying that he'd visit for several long weekends and come up for an *entire week* each August. (With the exception of our honeymoon to England and Scotland, we'd never taken an entire week of vacation together.) The extraction of these prizes from my husband—the grand prize of Chez Consuela and summers in Westport, and the pleasant surprise of his committing to a weeklong vacation—made me feel somewhat better about the move and us.

During the spring and early summer, Gordon flew frequently from Providence to Nashville to prepare for his 31 July assumption of the Vanderbilt chancellorship. I joined him every few weeks, first to help select and then to meet with the design and construction team that would execute the vast restoration of Braeburn, the twenty-thousand-square-foot Vanderbilt chancellor's residence.

Gordon left for Nashville in mid-July. I wanted to linger in Westport since summer had finally arrived. After Labor Day, Lucy and I began the drive south.

13

Down in Dixie, Again

SO THERE I WAS, RELUCTANT, rebellious daughter of the South, driving down to Dogpatch, trying hard to muster up my dormant southern pride. It had helped considerably that Yankee newspapers had belittled Vanderbilt and, by association, the South. I don't think too many southerners would mind if a *New York Times* reporter snidely intoned the name "Duke," but Vanderbilt, for all its "Harvard of the South" pretensions, is a quintessential southern university. Not as southern as Washington and Lee, where the doors to the stable are left open so the spirit of General Robert E. Lee's beloved steed, Traveller, can freely come and go, but still very southern nonetheless. Say something mean about Vanderbilt and you've said something mean about the South. That's just the way it is. Truly, there is no better fatwood than Yankee disdain to fire up southern pride. As I crossed the Mason-Dixon Line, I conjured up all the Ivy League snottiness I had endured over the past two years, opened the car window, and gave a rebel yell: *As God is ma witniss, the South will riiiise agin!*

I was proud of my southern/northern bilingualism. After twenty-four years up north, I could understand, if not fluently converse in, various Yankee dialects—Rhode Island's being the most challenging. It had taken me a full two weeks to be able to follow a conversation between native Rhode Islanders. For a few days I didn't think they had any "art," until I realized it was "ott." But it took only one experience of ordering a chocolate milkshake, and being handed a glass of milk with chocolate syrup that had been shaken up, to grasp that the Rhode Island word for milkshake is "cabinet." I later learned that just over the Massachusetts border, it's a "frappe" (pronounced "frap"). Some words are important to know in any language.

For all my manufactured bravado as I crossed the fortieth parallel from Pennsylvania into Maryland, I was worried. Vanderbilt seemed awfully conservative, and from what I'd seen so far, so did Nashville. After all, it was the South, wasn't it? But maybe the South had become significantly less socially and politically conservative over the past two decades, and maybe Middle Tennessee was a smoldering hotbed of liberalism. Somehow I doubted it. Whatever the case, I'd best put on my steel-magnolia game face and, as I'd promised Gordon, get with the program.

***

During our first trip to Nashville as the newly appointed chancellor- and chancellorette-elect, I had noticed two pervasive phenomena that told me I was not in New England anymore, as well as distinctions between middle-class South and society South. They were (1) black waiters in white jackets serving an all-white crowd and (2) facelifts.

I promptly "ingratiated" myself with the hostess, Martha Ingram, about half an hour into an elegant reception she was holding at her home in our honor. Around a hundred people were in attendance, including Vanderbilt trustees, senior administrators, and other well-heeled denizens of tony Belle Meade (the old-moneyed township in west Nashville). Gordon and I were stationed in the entry hall so Martha could introduce us to arriving guests. After we shook the last hand, a white-jacketed black waiter whisked up with a glass of white wine and a Diet Dr. Pepper on a silver serving tray.

Surveying the scene as we stepped into the drawing room, I whispered to my hostess that it felt very strange to me to be in the midst of an all-white crowd being served by an all-black staff.

"I can see where Northerners might . . ." I burbled forth stupidly, cut short by the astonished look on her face that clearly indicated she could not believe my crassitude.

"You don't understand," she said curtly. "They control this business and take pride in their high standards of service."

I was left to mull over my obvious breach of etiquette in this brave new world. I felt as if I'd stumbled onto an antebellum movie set—but was it an idealized movie about the past or a sardonic one about the future? It certainly wasn't *my* past, or was it? With my middle-class North Carolina upbringing, I'd never before experienced such a genteel panorama of race-based demarcation between those being served and those doing the serving. This early impression of my new habitat, and my elevated-by-marriage place within it, made me flush with embarrassment. It also added more weight to the already burgeoning knapsack of cynicism that I'd been hauling around since third grade. There was a flash of self-recognition in my intense reaction, a reaction born out of my own racist guilt. It was similar to the indignity one feels when a blood relation does or says something unsavory in front of a new acquaintance—a gaffe to which the nonrelation might react with a shrug of her shoulders and let it go at that.

When I got up my nerve again a few months later, I pursued the topic more delicately with a Belle Meade grand dame who had befriended me. She explained that yes, indeed, a couple of black-owned waitstaff organizations had kept a virtual lock on the high-end service business, passing control down from father to son for generations. The godfather of one of these businesses also runs a private detective firm, she added. She did not use the nomenclature "godfather," but that was how her description of high-society Nashville waitstaffing came across. Nobody was sleeping with the fishes after trying to horn in on the family business, but she couldn't imagine a white person making such an attempt. It just wouldn't look right. If a white man in a white jacket were to meet you at the door, you might mistake him for a fellow guest. It would all be too confusing.

***

Another striking difference between the middle-class South of my youth and the upper-crust version I now inhabited was the ubiquity and extremity of facelifts. It wasn't as if I hadn't seen hundreds of facelifts at cocktail parties and fundraising galas all over the country, but the Nashville facelift aesthetic mesmerized me. It is likely that my reaction may have been exacerbated by having just moved from old-moneyed New England, a place where some women rarely bother with makeup and sport the exact same flipped-up hairdo they wore forty years earlier at Wellesley.

At my first few Old South cocktail parties in Nashville, I could not hear a word that was being drawled by some of my new acquaintances. Their mouths were opening (although not so widely as their eyes) and words were coming out, but all I could focus on were their achingly taut faces—bless their hearts.

I realize this is a dangerously delicate topic, so allow me to say that I myself have always thought I'd get a facelift at some point, but I still haven't worked up the nerve or cash reserve. The scary thing is that people don't always look better after one, and wouldn't that just be *awful*?! There are the fortunate "rested" recipients of a good facelift and the "should be arrested" perpetrators of bad ones. I believe we need intervention in the form of public pillories for plastic surgeons who do this to people. Right outside the Belle Meade Kroger would be a satisfying location. A genteel Nashvillian friend of mine never says that someone "had too much to drink." No, the person was "overserved." Since no person of good breeding would knowingly overindulge, his or her inebriation would indubitably be the result of a bartender with a too liberal pouring hand. Clearly, the extremely-surprised-to-be-trapped-in-a-wind-tunnel look is the fault not of the overlifted but of the overlifter.

Remarkably, it only took a year or so on the Nashville social circuit before most of the nips and tucks began to appear perfectly normal to me. In fact, I'm a wee bit embarrassed to admit that they started looking enviably good. Perhaps everyone had rushed out and gotten their facelifts two weeks before we arrived in town and, over the course of the year, scores of hiked-up malar fat pads and nasolabial folds had "settled." Or maybe, as my own jaw line crept toward a jowl, I was undergoing an aesthetic paradigm shift of my own.

***

There are few things more important to a southern woman than being "attractive," hence facelifts, wearing flattering colors, and jewelry—serious jewelry, if at all possible. Every southern female over the age of four with anything on the ball knows what "season" she is and, therefore, which color palette looks best on her.

My blue-eyed, strawberry-blond mother is a spring. I'm an autumn. I'd bet ten to one that Reese Witherspoon, who was raised in Nashville, is a summer. As good as Oprah, who spent her teens in Nashville, looks in white, she's got to be a winter. There is no doubt in this world that Scarlett O'Hara, with her "magnolia-white skin," pale green eyes "without a hint of hazel," and black hair, was also a winter—a fact that her love of apple and emerald green dresses confirms she was fully cognizant of.

Here is seventeen-year-old Scarlett critically surveying the flirting belles in their gorgeous frocks while she herself is dressed wrist to chin in hot black taffeta, most unhappily relegated to the sidelines of the ball "all because" her young husband, Charles Hamilton, had died ingloriously of the measles: "'How sweet I'd look in that dress,' thought Scarlett, a savage envy in her heart. '. . . That green is just my color and it would make my eyes look— Why will blondes try to wear that color? Her skin looks as green as an old cheese.'"[1]

Your season is not zodiac related; it is based on your skin tone. Is your skin tone warm or cool? If it's warm, yellow-based colors are more flattering; if it's cool, blue-based colors look best on you. There are warm reds and cool reds, warm greens and cool greens. Springs and autumns are warm; summers and winters are cool. Spring and summer colors are lighter versions of a given hue; autumn and winter colors are deeper shades of the hue. A southern woman not only dresses in her seasonal palette, she also decorates the entire house in them, especially her boudoir, where flattering skin tones are most essential.

***

Nashville has two white-tie affairs every year—the Swan Ball in June and the Symphony Ball in December—and a black-tie event just about every week, sometimes twice a week, depending on the season. These are "pay parties," held in support of arts, cultural, or health service organizations. To name but a few black-tie events, there's the Ballet Ball, Opera Ball, Hunt Ball, Library Ball, Heart Ball, and (I swear I am not making this up) Eye Ball. (Frist Center for the Visual Arts supporters will feel slighted at having been omitted, but theirs is a *gala*, not a ball, and being so named does not contribute to the literary cadence I am working hard to achieve.)

The party to be seen at is not the actual ball itself but its requisite patrons' party. The patrons' party is generally held two or three days before the ball at one of the many grandiose private homes in Nashville. The per-couple price of admission to most balls is around $1,500. Patrons' parties cost almost twice that, making them more select and thus more desirable.

If one attends the patrons' party, one really *should* go to the ball, but, with the exception of the Swan Ball (deemed one of the top five benefit balls in America by *Town and Country* magazine, no less), more than a few patrons' partiers eschew the "main event." During our first year on the Nashville white- and black-tie circuit, I asked a friend if she and her husband were going to the Heart Ball. She rolled her eyes and said, "No, we just had to draw the line. We don't go to parties for individual organs."

The Swan Ball, a benefit for the Cheekwood Botanical Garden and Museum of Art, is hands down the center jewel in the tiara of Nashville balls. Being anointed co-chair for the Swan Ball is on par with being voted homecoming queen. You and your sister co-chair (it is a shared title because of the workload and the danger of giving a single female that much queenly power) spend an entire year organizing the ball and the numerous events leading up to it. You must decide on its theme and colors (it helps if the co-chairs are of the same color palette); secure underwriters and superstar entertainment (Diana Ross, Donna Summer, Tony Bennett, and Johnny Cash have all played at the SB); select the orchestra; and entice reluctant friends and acquaintances to serve as chairs for the fifty or so committees (including a cleanup, or "swansong," committee). A jeweler must be selected to set up shop at the patrons' party, the ball, and several of the more prestigious committee parties. (Having a jeweler exhibit his or her wares has become *de rigueur* at all Nashville balls and patrons' parties. Wives and girlfriends are bound by local custom to drag their hopefully-by-that-point-in-the-evening well-lubricated men by the wallet through rows of display cases. Pausing now and then to try on a glittering bauble, the hopeful one smiles wistfully while whispering a promise of a special carnal post-ball favor, should desired bauble be purchased. If the lady scores, the jeweler hands over ten percent of the take to the house.) These and thousands of other tasks are accomplished with the assistance of a full-time Cheekwood staff member and more than five hundred individual volunteers, most of whom have never been, and never will be, invited to the ball itself. It is important to note that getting on the Swan Ball invitation list is in and of itself a significant social achievement. Few dare dream of the honor of handing over $2,500 to attend the patrons' party. A decade or so ago a man promised to give $100,000 to Cheekwood if he and his wife could attend the ball: not the patrons' party, mind you, but the ball. One can only imagine the pitiful whimperings of the Cheekwood administrative staff when the SB senior sisterhood nixed the man's request. To quote a friend in the know, "Invitations to the ball are highly sought after and stingily given."

***

But I regress—or, pardon me, digress—as is easy to do when broaching the tangential topic of fancy dress parties in Nashville within the protuberant parameters of a tale about love, power, money, betrayal, illegal substances, and D-I-V-O-R-C-E, as Tammy Wynette famously referred to it in the presence of little J-O-E. The issues at hand are *glamour*, *sparkle*, and the critical feminine function of this version of attractiveness in Nashvegas.

It took me about ten minutes into my first Symphony Ball to realize just how *dowdy* I'd become residing among academics and hobnobbing with New England blue bloods. It was a shock to my feminine southern soul. I wore a long black skirt and a cream blouse. *A long black skirt and a cream blouse*, I repeat. *Good God, what has become of me?* I thought dejectedly as kaleidoscopic satins and iridescent silks and taffetas sashayed around us.

My husband had contributed significantly to my fashion demise. Sure, he loved my apparel pizzazz when we were courting, but soon after we were betrothed, a critical eyebrow would be raised at a dress deemed too short or revealing. He once gave Rebekah and me identical floor-length, powder-blue pinafore dresses—sort of a Laura Ashley–polygamous prairie dress hybrid. Like a good sister wife, I actually wore mine a couple of times.

Rebekah, to her credit, immediately returned hers for something skintight and low cut.

My friend Laura, who was raised in Cincinnati but has spent the past forty years in Providence, delights in contrasting upper-crust southern and northern signifiers of affluence. Although Laura insists that Cincinnati qualifies as a southern city since it is just over the river from Kentucky—an assertion I gave up arguing about long ago—she does have legitimate southern heritage in her Georgian grandparents and is very close to her cousin and his wife, who are socially prominent Atlantans.

Laura believes it was her ties to the South in her formative years that infused her with a passion for sparkly things—a yearning that precludes her from ever passing as a New Englander, not that she would want to when it comes to personal adornment. She has an impressive collection of rhinestone-encrusted dress shoes. She opened a high-end jewelry store and habitually wears much of its inventory. After spending two-thirds of her life in the North and truly preferring it to the South, most decidedly in the realm of politics, she still laments over "everybody smashing around in L. L. Bean and ancient ball gowns." But then, practicality, understatement, and frugality are defining measures of sound Yankee character, she observes, and "virtues" that are so *not* southern. A few years back, I received a postcard from a girlfriend (southern, of course) picturing a well-coiffed, bejeweled woman wearing an expression of pained disdain. "Frugal is such an *ugly* word," read the caption.

According to Laura, moneyed New Englanders would rather show up at a party DOA than overdressed. For a party in Belle Meade, "casual dress" verges on what "cocktail attire" means to the rest of the industrialized world. Although difficult, it is *possible* to be overdressed for a soirée in zip code 37205; but then, one can always say she's on her way to a cozy, black-tie supper at the club. "You have no idea what you're in for," warned Laura as I had prepared to depart Providence for the Old South.

She was right. Nashville is the buckle on the Bible Belt and the brooch on the ball gown.

through the third floor to a skylight in the roof. The house was completed in 1914, and the ladies, both of Scottish descent, christened it "Braeburn," a combination of the Scottish words *brae*, meaning "sloping bank," and *burn*, meaning "brook." Aptly named, the house sits atop a slight hill that gently slopes down toward Richland Creek on the northwest side of the property.

Vanderbilt University purchased the property in 1964 from the Caleb T. Haun family, Braeburn's third owners, as a residence for its new chancellor, Alexander Heard. Chancellor and Mrs. Heard had four children and petitioned the Board of Trust to construct a large swimming pool on the southwest side of the house. It was a lively and well-used house for the Heards' eighteen years of residence. No doubt it required some work by the time Joe B. Wyatt became chancellor in 1982.

***

As I mentioned, I wanted to turn and run when I first saw Braeburn in February 2000, because it was all too evident the massive amount of work it would require. The problem was that I would not, nor could not, *not* be involved in it up to my elbows. Just as I had worked on every detail of renovating the Ohio State and Brown presidential residences, I would work on Braeburn. Making a home was my gift to Gordon, to the university, and to myself. It was something I could contribute to both our marriage and our partnering as university president and first lady. It was also something I knew I was good at and for which I received praise, most meaningfully from Gordon.

Frankly, I just couldn't help myself. I had always felt compelled to *arrange* things in my personal space. I suppose that was a means of asserting some control, of creating a small sanctuary within a house where the volatility of an alcoholic father threatened an emotional hurricane every night. I suppose it has also been a way to satisfy my aesthetic sensibilities, to make my environment pleasing for me to look at and live in.

But it felt as if I'd barely completed the Brown residence—as if, only a moment ago, I had made that offering to Gordon's and my life together. I had finally refocused on my academic research; I was trying hard to meet my duties as journal editor amid the emotional and physical upheaval of leaving Brown. Now Denny was asking: "Would y'all like to live here? *Would* you live here?"

171

We were standing on the expansive front porch, looking across the front lawn at the ravaged remains of several trees a tornado had assaulted the previous spring. "The board has thought about selling the property, but they'd be pleased if you'd agree to live here. Of course, it's going to take a lot of work. We understand that," he said.

Gordon and I looked at each other and then back at him. "All right," Gordon said, "but we'd like to add two main areas for the purposes of entertaining: a conservatory and a catering kitchen."

"I don't think that will be a problem," Denny replied.

The renovation process began almost immediately. The Board of Trust's renovation oversight committee mailed me packets of information on three architectural firms and three interior designers. In early March, I had been flown from Westport to Nashville to interview and select an architect and an interior designer from the candidates the committee had preselected.

Detailed renovation and interior design plans had been drawn up; cost estimates were made. Everything had been submitted to the renovation oversight committee, sent out for a construction bid, and approved. Gordon had insisted on not being involved in the renovation budget approval process, saying firmly, "Boards should renovate presidents' houses; presidents shouldn't." So it had been at West Virginia, Colorado, Ohio State, and Brown, and so it would be at Vanderbilt.

***

We moved into a nicely furnished townhouse that had been leased by the university. It was clear that the board was trying to accommodate us as graciously as possible. I knew that and appreciated it, but the fact remained that I was having a hard time coping with this move.

Once again I was unpacking boxes and placing photographs here and there, trying to make a temporary living space feel a little like home. I accompanied Gordon to university events, struggling to remember the hundreds of names and blur of faces.

I was seriously depressed—shell-shocked, actually. I was a genuine posttraumatic-stress-disorder basket case. I had also begun having hot flashes. I tried to take pleasure in what I was accomplishing, but I didn't, *couldn't* feel much of anything except my own waxing and waning incandescence throughout the night and day. I was losing my mind and my youth. And, there was just no denying it, I was still very angry with Gordon.

I felt I did everything I could to create a home, only to have him decide he'd rather be someplace else. I built it and he tore it apart, or so it seemed to me at the time. Now I was supposed to put on a smiley face and act as if everything was hunky-dory? Of course I knew the answer to that question was *yes*—that is precisely what a good wife is supposed to do, especially one whose husband holds a prominent leadership position and needs her support both publicly and privately.

I had begun seeing a psychiatrist soon after we'd fled to Westport after the Brown blowup. By that point, I'd decided I really needed to talk with somebody, regardless of the "shame." Besides, the psychiatrist's office was on a secluded property several miles away from the Brown campus. (I'd asked Gordon to join me for one of the sessions, but he refused, so I didn't ask again.) The doctor had prescribed an antidepressant, which I was still taking. The medication alone, however, did not seem to be as helpful as it had been when coupled with our counseling sessions.

Once again, I felt that I had no place to turn. Gordon was caught up in the excitement of his new job and didn't want to hear my complaints, and he wasn't about to ask around for a psychiatrist. I understood his reticence. I also didn't want to begin my relationship with Vanderbilt by asking strangers where I might get some psychiatric counseling: "Yes, so thrilled to be here! By the way, can you recommend a good shrink?" So I just kept slogging through the thick gray muck, hoping to get to the other side.

***

Lucy and the 2,700 acres of wooded hills and streams of Nashville's Warner Parks were my saving grace during that difficult time. I took solace in Lucy's sweet, steadfast company, as well as in the peace and beauty of the parks. She and I soon learned every possible hiking trail and horse-path loop combination. I truly do not know what I would have done without my dog, those woods, and bio-identical hormones.

Thank God for girlfriends and the secrets they pass along. The go-to guy for menopause was Dr. Joel Hargrove, a kindly, older gynecologist who years earlier had retired from Vanderbilt to open

173

up his own menopause clinic in the little town of Columbia, an hour's drive south of Nashville. We love you, Dr. Hargrove.

Meanwhile, Gordon was doing the thing he seemed to like best in the world: meeting everybody for the first time. He was a walking, bow-tied smiley face, chanting, "Better fit, better fit." Clearly Vanderbilt was a much better fit for him than Brown. I hoped it was a damn good fit, an Yves-Saint-Laurent haute-couture fit, a better fit than his birthday suit, because I never again wanted to rev up for another university debut. He swore that Vanderbilt would be his last university presidency—but then, he'd said that about Brown. We would remain at Vanderbilt until he retired into a nice nonprofit or corporate foundation presidency, preferably in or near New York or Washington, he promised. That was the plan.

***

The renovation of the chancellor's residence was moving along at a remarkable pace, considering the top-to-bottom, inside-and-out scope of the project. The third floor (which Ida Hood and Susan Heron had left unfinished, thinking they would later make it into a ballroom) had been transformed into a combination office–art studio and exercise room. The second floor was being reconfigured, as the original bedrooms had been apportioned not as suites but rather as single rooms with baths off the hallways. The residence would often be filled with university guests over graduation and football weekends. Visiting scholars and speakers would stay overnight throughout the year. It would not do to point guests to a shared bath down the hall. The new floor plan would allow for an ample master suite and three beautifully appointed guest suites: the Commodore Suite, the Iris Suite, and the Acorn Suite. The Acorn Suite would serve as Rebekah's bedroom when she came home for visits.

I was into themes by that point in my university residency interior-decorating career. Braeburn's theme was All Things Vanderbilt, including a few humorous nods to the nautical origins of the family fortune. A fanciful clipper ship–shaped crystal chandelier would hang at the center of the drawing room. Historical _cy would have dictated a steamship-shaped chandelier, _ornelius built his fortune in the steamship business ferry- _ight and passengers first between Manhattan and Staten

Island, then between New York and New Jersey, and later across the Long Island Sound. But who cared about historical accuracy when presented with the opportunity to hang a glittering, three-masted sailing ship from the ceiling? The ship chandelier became a favorite of Braeburn guests.

Paintings of ships from the university's art collection were hung in the Commodore Suite, which was decorated handsomely in the school colors of black and muted gold. An oak leaf and acorn are featured on the university's crest; hence the Acorn Suite with its subtle acorn-motif bedspread and rich autumnal color scheme.

The iris is the Tennessee state flower and adopted symbol of the Peabody College of Education and Human Development, formerly the George Peabody College for Teachers, which Vanderbilt took over in 1979. It was a perceived act of aggression that still rankles crotchety Peabody old-timers. I'd been scouring the university, doing my best to charm deans and department heads out of antiques and artwork. It takes a lot of stuff to furnish and decorate a twenty-thousand-square-foot house, and we were beginning with virtually nothing.

I had my eye on a massively magnificent nineteenth-century mahogany armoire that the Peabody dean kept imprisoned all by itself in a teensy room near her office. Originally given to Peabody College in 1937 by Mrs. Henry W. Peabody, the piece sat in its little enclosure day in and day out, looking lonesome and unloved. When I first saw the armoire, I dropped a subtle hint that I would like to have it for the residence. The comment went something along the lines of: "Wow! What an amazing armoire! It sure would look good in the entry hall of the residence." The dean laughed uncomfortably and changed the subject.

I tried a different tack several weeks later, inviting her over for a private tour of the residence during the latter stage of its renovation. I walked her through the entire house, saving the front guest suite, the Iris Suite, until last. Its walls had been painted a spectacular shade of leafy, spring green. Flowing, floor-length draperies with a finely wrought iris flower pattern adorned the two large windows overlooking Braeburn's broad front lawn.

"This is the Iris Suite—in honor of Peabody," I told the dean, who smiled approvingly.

"It's absolutely beautiful," she said.

The liberated Peabody armoire lives in Braeburn's grand twelve-foot-wide by fifty-four-foot-long entry hall, in happy proportion to its surroundings. At least the Peabody armoire will always remember me kindly.

***

My favorite room in the house was a cozy little reading room on the second floor. It opens onto an ornate balcony that extends about five feet over the front door of the house, protected from the elements by the fly-speck blue ceiling of the columned portico. It was the perfect spot from which to survey the front and side lawns, and to watch the lone blue heron that resided on Braeburn's picturesque section of Richland Creek for as long as we resided at Braeburn. The reading room once served as Connie Heard's dressing room. When coming home past curfew, she and her older brother Stephen would scale the limestone face of the house and climb up and over the balcony, slipping quietly into their respective bedrooms as their parents slept unaware.

The Hauns had built a family-size sunroom off the front end of the drawing room in the 1950s. A thirty-by-forty-foot conservatory was being constructed in its place. The drawing room and rear gallery would open into the conservatory, which would open onto a newly designed garden that would displace the now badly cracked and leaky Heard Memorial Pool. The pool, I understood, would not be missed. Guests had long grumbled about having to circumnavigate it, cocktail in hand, hoping to maintain dryness and dignity. While the ceiling height of most of the conservatory was fifteen feet, its lantern would rise to twenty-three feet, providing the perfect spot to place a towering Fraser fur that would glitter with multicolored lights and ornaments each December.

***

Braeburn's eight acres pleaded for attention. "Help me! *Help* me!" beseeched the ragged trees and bushes and parched, patchy grass, sounding to me (I swear) just like the tiny half-insect, half-man creature in the excellent 1958 horror flick *The Fly*. I don't think a r seedling of any sort had been planted on the grounds for a of decades.

The Board of Trust hired a landscaper, who drew up plans for the transformation of the property. A horseshoe-shaped driveway would provide a stately solution to the party-clogging problem of moving hundreds of guests to and from the residence in an evening. Valets would deliver the cars to the ample parking lot of the Temple Congregation Ohabai Sholom, our Reform Jewish neighbor, with whom Braeburn shared a property line. Flower beds were dug, trees and bushes planted, irrigation and lighting installed.

Braeburn's grounds were my special love. Lucy and I would walk them daily throughout the year, lingering over every detail. When the landscaping budget had dwindled, I would appeal to Gordon every planting season to contribute funds for more trees, shrubs, and flowers, which he would do. We donated well over a hundred trees and bushes to Braeburn's eight acres. We received the city's permission to plant a dozen good-sized magnolias on the other side of Richland Creek, property not owned by the university. I was obsessed. I may have lost control over most all other aspects of my life, but the grounds were mine—mine, the squirrels', the blue heron's, and Lucy's.

The spring after we planted the magnolias, it rained and rained; Richland Creek rose fifteen feet, becoming Richland River. I watched as the swollen stream flattened all the trees we had planted on both sides of the creek. I plunged out into the torrential rain, trying to get close enough to pull trees upright while the grounds crew, which I had summoned to "get here as fast as you can and bring sandbags," yelled at me to get away from the rushing water.

The next day, after the rain finally stopped, I ventured back outside to survey the damage. Two sentences came to my mind as if I were reading them in a novel: *The day smelled like a wet dog. Richland Creek had overflowed its banks, knocking flat all the trees she had planted the previous fall.* I still think that would make a good, foreboding opening for a novel. I'm just not sure what happens next. *She stood in the mud and cursed?*

***

The residence required new mechanical systems, including heating and air conditioning, electrical, and plumbing. Tons of debris were hauled out of the basement to prepare for the construction of a restaurant-grade catering kitchen, an updated laundry room, two large storage areas, and a walk-in security vault. An elevator was installed in order to meet Americans with Disabilities Act standards and to enable large warming bins of plated food to be ferried from the catering kitchen to the main floor. A house manager's office was constructed off the family kitchen. The house had to serve dual roles, private and institutional—although, for a house of that size and a renovation that extensive, the institutional function was paramount.

Beyond the big brushstrokes, there was also much fine detailing to do. Braeburn needed some artwork and heirlooms—items that would weave an impressive narrative about the university, intrigue the thousands of people who would gather there each year, and inspire them to write big, fat checks to carry on Vanderbilt's proud heritage. My study of art, my tours (almost to the point of numbness) through European palaces during my sophomore year abroad, and my more recent exposure to the lovely homes of wealthy university donors enabled my quick study of symbols of wealth and their use to beget more wealth. I'd also had an excellent tutor in the creation of an interior "story," as she termed it, in the interior designer of the Brown president's residence, Nancy Taylor. It was she who had first suggested ransacking the university's archives and attics to apprehend historical objects to enhance the legend of Brunonia. I was intent on crafting a similarly splendid saga for Vanderbilt at Braeburn.

The associate vice chancellor for planning and construction, with whom I got along well both personally and aesthetically, helped ferret out treasures stashed willy-nilly in basements, attics, and offices across campus. He contacted the curator of the Vanderbilt Fine Arts Collection and explained that we were looking for some artwork for the residence. Apparently word had already gotten around that I was pillaging the campus, snatching precious treasures from the death grasp of deans, department heads, and small children. The curator agreed to let us *look* at the collection, but he made certain we understood that it was under the vigilant protection of the Fine Arts Department. I assured him I had no intention of spiriting off a single item that he and the fine arts faculty wanted to keep for exhibition or teaching purposes. Gordon and I would be hanging every piece of available art we owned; even so, I explained, a vast amount of wall space would remain forlornly empty.

The curator led us down into the dark, dank basement of the then-crumbling Cohen Building, where *la collection* (really more *la mishmash*) sat moldering. Prior to our visit the curator had met with the fine arts faculty to determine what works they might consider lending us, so he had his list on hand as we picked our way through the catacombs. I selected a number of paintings, most of which were torn, scuffed, or water damaged, and asked if there might not be a few more available pieces. Anything we borrowed, I reiterated, with the associate vice chancellor nodding beside me, would be restored and reframed. It would be well cared for and hung in a nice, dry place where people would actually see it. I added that we would be *forever grateful* to the Fine Arts Department.

He guided us into a small room containing several flat-file cabinets and began pulling out prints and vintage travel posters, all in fairly good condition. He would see if we might be able to use a few of them.

A reporter from the student newspaper, the *Vanderbilt Hustler*, contacted us the next day. (The paper was named after old Cornelius, whose other nickname was "the Hustler.") My plan to exhibit some of the university's art collection had generated student interest. A *Hustler* editorial stated:

> The Gees are going to rescue part of a collection that hasn't seen the light of day in years. With all the talk of the Gees, their personal charisma, interest in students and dedication to learning the inner workings of the University, this is yet another example of the attention that Vanderbilt needs from a chancellor.
> . . . For the Gees to take this extra step in favor of representing Vanderbilt in their home is hopefully a harbinger of the commitment we hope they will give during this era of new leadership.[1]

The *Hustler*'s editorial applause aside, it is easy to read my and the associate vice chancellor's defensiveness in the accompanying interviews. "If there's any reservation whatsoever about us using the pieces, we won't use them. The last thing we would want to do is take pieces the faculty doesn't feel good about us taking," I told a student reporter. The associate vice chancellor added: "We're trying to work with things that literally have tears and rips in them and have never been deemed worth restoring from an art standpoint, but they could be nice to look at. The work we're talking about has not seen the light of day. It's sitting in a molding basement in Cohen."[2]

I emphasized that the main purpose of the residence was to raise money for the university. The associate vice chancellor pointed out that productive fundraising could ensure the construction of a new fine arts studio building, a project which was then in the preliminary planning stage.

Hello? Earth to fine arts faculty?

In the end, numerous paintings were restored and prints nicely framed (all out of the residence renovation budget). They continue to reside high and dry at Braeburn. A new studio arts building was completed in August 2005. Restoration of the Cohen Building began in 2007; it now houses the state-of-the-art Vanderbilt Fine Arts Gallery and storage facilities, the Department of History of Art, and the Department of Classical Studies. The studio and art history faculty had to be divided into two separate departments because they couldn't play nice together.

***

The procurement of historically important tableware for display and, on very special occasions, use at the residence was a vastly simpler and more enjoyable experience. In fact, it was a big thrill—rather like stumbling into Aladdin's cave. I will never forget it.

Several tense staff members stood at attention beside a large conference table that had been moved to one side of a meeting room in one of the administrative buildings. Two eight-foot tables were placed perpendicularly at both ends of the table. Three hundred square feet of gleaming treasure covered the tables. Thankfully, I had requested that someone knowledgeable about antique silver and china be present to help. The Vanderbilt senior historian and a gentleman from Nashville's best giftware shop stepped forward to greet me. Mouth agape, I looked at the largess and squealed, "*I get to choose?!*"

There was the Bishop McTyeire tea set, given to the bishop's wife, Amelia, by the Methodists of New Orleans in 1858. Amelia was Frank Vanderbilt's first cousin. It was Bishop McTyeire who had convinced Cornelius to fund this new college in the South. The bishop would serve as the first chairman of Vanderbilt's Board of Trust.

There were silver candelabra and candlesticks ranging from simple to highly ornate. My favorites were four English silver-plated candlesticks, circa 1800, made for the Scottish Order of the Thistle. A small dagger and broken sword were engraved at their bases, along with the Latin inscription *Nemo Me Impune La Cessit* ("No one provokes me with impunity").

There was an exquisite circa-1800 Old Sheffield Plate soup tureen and numerous finely made sterling bowls and serving pieces. It was love at first sight for a set of Elizabeth-Tudor hammered flatware and Harold Stirling Vanderbilt's porcelain dinner plates, which were decorated with the boar's-head emblem of the Harvard Porcellian Club (and its motto, *Dum vivimus vivamus*—"While we live, let's live").

An elegant single place setting of gold-rimmed china, monogrammed "WVK," caught my eye.

"What's this?"

"A set of tableware from Marblehead, William Kissam Vanderbilt's home in Newport, Rhode Island. Harold Stirling was his son. There are sixty place settings available for your use at the residence." Sixty place settings! Now *that* was a fun afternoon—a wild shopping spree and history lesson rolled into one.

***

Braeburn, the given name of the residence, had not been used since the university purchased it from the Haun family in the 1960s. After learning of the two ladies who had lovingly built the house, I decided it should once again be called Braeburn in their honor. It is such a lovely and appropriate name. We had a rectangular piece of limestone engraved with the name and set into the new stone wall at the entrance of the driveway. An ink drawing was made of newly renovated Braeburn and printed on the front of folding note cards that Gordon and I used. These cards also were left in all the guest suites for the use of visitors. In a fine typeface on the back of the cards, its story was told:

Braeburn, the Vanderbilt University Chancellor's Residence, was built in 1914 and acquired by the University in 1964. The name "Braeburn" is of Scottish origin, composed of two words: "brae," meaning hillside, slope, or bank of a river, and "burn," a brook or rivulet. The original owners, Miss Ida Hood and Miss Susan Heron, both being of Scottish descent, named their home appropriately, because of its situation on a sloping hill leading to Richland Creek.

We began our move into Braeburn in early May 2001, immediately following commencement. Gordon arranged his clothes in his dressing room and returned to work. I worked all day, every day for two months on unboxing and placing things around the house with the help of Nancy, our good-natured and hardworking housekeeper. Chef Bunny (who had been our chef at the Brown president's residence and whom we had happily persuaded to join us in Nashville) set up the family and catering kitchens.

I was determined to get everything as shipshape as possible by the end of June, as I was hell-bent on returning to Westport in early July. I desperately needed some time to myself. Although I was immensely proud of Braeburn's beautiful renovation, the process had been grueling. It is hard to imagine the pressure on a first lady who chooses to be involved intimately with the renovation of a university residence. Hundreds of eyes watch and judge every step along the way.

***

A forty-foot, lime-green-and-turquoise iguana resided on the roof of the Lone Star Cafe at the corner of Fifth Avenue and Thirteenth Street in New York from 1976 to 1989. "Iggy," for that was its name, predated me there by a year and lingered until a year after my departure. Iggy cracked me up, as did the large banner that hung just under him, declaring, "Too Much Ain't Enough."

"Too much ain't enough" (a line in the Billy Joe Shaver song "Old Five and Dimers Like Me") seemed to have become Gordon's and my motto. At the exact same time we were moving into Braeburn, we bought a house in Monteagle, Tennessee.

A lot of Nashvillians had told us about Monteagle, which was right down the road from the University of the South. The University of the South owns thirteen thousand acres of indescribably beautiful forestland, referred to as the Domain. There are more than fifty miles of hiking trails within the Domain, including the spectacular Parameter Trail. Thousands of square miles of state parks can be accessed from every direction within fifteen minutes of Monteagle. It's a hiker's paradise.

Gordon was keen on buying some property in Tennessee, as much to prove his long-term commitment to Vanderbilt as anything else. We had rented a house in Monteagle from January through March 2001 in order to check out the area and find a little weekend peace from time to time. I promptly fell in love with the forests, bluff views, waterfalls, and hiking trails. Gordon wasn't much of a hiker, but he accompanied Lucy and me on occasion with the stipulations that the hike would not exceed two hours and that I knew where we were *at all times.* You see, I enjoy exploring new paths, getting "lost," and finding my way back out again just before dusk. This was not Gordon's idea of a good time. Anyway, we ended up buying a "cabin" (actually a good-size house, but constructed from logs) on five wooded acres that were perched at the edge of a bluff overlooking forty miles of ridge after ridge of undisturbed forest. Its given name was "The Cabin Door." We changed it to "Cabindore," in honor of the Vanderbilt Commodores.

Cabindore was to be our stress-reducing retreat. Of course, it would be a huge stress inducer, both financially and timewise, until we had it fixed up to our liking. As with any house, there would always be scores of things to maintain, repair, and trim back. That was true times two with the Westport house, with its being right on the water. I left behind Braeburn and Cabindore to attend to Chez Consuela in July. Too much was par for our course.

***

What is it about being on the water that is so healing? Tranquillity, renewal, and release are what my little spot on the river brings me. It is blissful to lay down the burden of attainment and have the luxury of time and clarity of mind to write, garden, and think, or not.

Gordon joined me toward the end of July for a long weekend and, as promised, for a week in mid-August. I always looked forward to his visits, although it would take me a day or two to adjust to his presence and energy in my serene abode. It's not easy getting married for the first time at forty after having lived by oneself for so long. One likes having things one's own way—at least I did (and still do). Although always a challenge, sharing space was less difficult within a university residence. After all, they were large houses, but perhaps more essentially, the residences were never ours per se, and certainly not *mine*. They were primarily public spaces, even though I fought to find and keep a small private place within each one. Once I had escaped to Chez Consuela and had a few weeks to myself, however, I got sort of territorial. So it was good when Gordon was there for a week rather than a long weekend, as we both were able to settle back into each other.

The previous school year had been tense not only between Gordon and me but for Rebekah and me as well. She knew that I had been furious with her father over the Brown fiasco, and that I continued to harbor resentment throughout much of our first year at Vanderbilt. She had understandably allied herself with Gordon, expressing annoyance with my lingering bad humor. We'd all had an uneasy Christmas trying to fabricate the holiday spirit in our temporary quarters in an unfamiliar city, and had then flown off to that thoroughly sopping week on Abaco Island in the Caribbean. Happily, the strain between Rebekah and me was eased with our pagan, Champagne-infused beach boogie in the pouring rain. (There's nothing like a wild romp 'n' howl in a downpour to build camaraderie.) She had returned to complete her third year at Cornell University Medical College, while I threw myself into the Braeburn renovation. She and I were getting along much better by the summer, so I was pleased when she decided to take the train up from New York to visit me in Westport—just the two of us. She also came up for part of her dad's August vacation.

Heart and arms opened wide to the river, with Lucy standing next to me at the end of the dock, I said my Labor Day farewell-to-the-river prayer for the second time: *Please protect this house and let Lucy and me come back safely next summer.* Lucy and I climbed into my overpacked car, beeped goodbye to the neighbors, and drove southwest. This time around I was ready, even eager, to rejoin Gordon in Nashville.

***

I'd left one task incomplete when I'd departed the residence for Westport: I'd hung only a small portion of the artwork. Hanging artwork is, for me, like frosting the cake—the fun, finishing touch. Selecting what piece to place where is a personally expressive act, something I give great consideration to and take much pleasure and satisfaction from. We were still awaiting the restoration of several pieces that I'd finagled out of the fine arts collection. I wanted to wait until everything was on hand before beginning this final phase of Braeburn's adornment. Also, I had simply run out of steam and wanted to be fresh for this special undertaking. Before leaving for Westport, I told Gordon and the residence staff that I would hang the remaining artwork when I returned in September, and explained my reasons for wanting to wait.

Imagine my delight when, after three days on the road, I walked into Braeburn to find that two members of the design team had taken it upon themselves to finish hanging the artwork on the main floor. Not only had they placed pieces at odd juxtaposition and in a rather willy-nilly manner, they'd hung artwork I'd never approved. In fact, several oil paintings were hung that I had rejected out of hand as being *bad art*. (A large, screaming-orange-and-baby-poop-yellow painting of globular, abstract shapes pops into mind as I write this.) Yet there they were like smirking hooligans on the once pristine, hand-scumbled walls—the repair of which would entail substantially more than simply spackling the nail holes and repainting a solid color on top.

I had a jumping-up-and-down fit right then and there, probably reminiscent of the tantrums Rebekah had when she was four, except I was a perimenopausal forty-seven. How *dare* they! I telephoned the culprits and ordered them to take the paintings down and repair the walls, *now!* They told me they'd thought the house would look better if all the artwork was up; they thought I'd be *pleased*. It was supposed to be a nice surprise. Gordon said he hadn't known they were going to hang the artwork; he'd arrived home one evening, and it was done. No one, including Gordon, could understand what I was so upset about. They seemed unable to comprehend what an astounding invasion of privacy I considered their little "surprise" to be. Their offense was doubly compounded for me in that the medium of their blundering intrusion had been the very artwork that I'd taken such pains to attain and refurbish. That they had chosen to impose themselves through *art*—the area of human endeavor that meant the most to me personally and professionally—was especially insulting. Yet how were they to have understood the depth and complexity of my feelings of having so little control over my life? How were they to understand my treasured privacy in Westport and how jolting it was to be reminded within five minutes of arriving back "home" that there was no such thing in Nashville? I didn't understand it myself—I just knew how it *felt*.

I overreacted terribly. I knew it even then. Still, I think it requires an inordinate amount of audacity to take it upon oneself to nail stuff to another person's walls. Of course, that's the hitch: they weren't *my* walls.

***

Gordon had held four or five luncheons or small dinner parties a week at Braeburn throughout the summer. That pace picked up considerably with the beginning of the academic year. The entire Board of Trust and their spouses got their first tour of newly renovated Braeburn at the board's November meeting. The residence's grand public unveiling was the Symphony Ball patrons' party that December.

The Nashville Symphony is largely the creation of one person, Martha Rivers Ingram. Martha served as chairman of the Vanderbilt Board of Trust for sixteen years, from 1995 to 2011. She followed her late husband, Bronson Ingram, as board chair. Bronson served on the board for eighteen years; his father, Orrin Henry, had joined the board in 1952. Two of her four children are members of the Vanderbilt board. The Vanderbilt campus abounds with buildings, programs, endowed chairs, and students on scholarship linked to the surname Ingram. Mrs. Ingram was then involved romantically with the debonair conductor of the Nashville Symphony, Kenneth Schermerhorn. When she requested that the Symphony Ball patrons' party be held at Braeburn, everyone agreed it was a very good idea.

Hundreds of strands of blue and white lights were wound sculpturally up the trees. It was the holiday season, and I had chosen blue as a nod to our ever-gracious temple neighbors. That and because I just really like blue lights. The grounds looked as if Moss

Hart had risen from the grave to remake Braeburn into Camelot. The Knights of the Round Table and their ladies had never seen so much tented acreage. A tented walkway ushered two hundred guests from their auto-steeds to Braeburn's stately front entrance. A large, clear tent extended off the conservatory and into the garden, encircling a colorful mosaic fountain, which an artist friend of mine had inlaid. The magic fountain was Gordon's and my personal gift and tribute to the garden. A second tented walkway stretched seventy yards through the garden, across the back drive, and onto the south lawn—delivering post-cocktailed patrons to the huge, high-topped dinner tent glowing inside and out with candlelight. A catering services tent was attached to the dinner tent. Even the Porta-Potties were nestled under candlelit his-and-hers tents.

After dinner, Delicious, a fantastic local disco band ("fantastic" and "band" being synonymous in Music City, no matter what the genre), struck up KC and the Sunshine Band's "Get Down Tonight." At one point, Maestro Schermerhorn, a dozen other people, and I were dancing onstage to "Shake Your Booty." The maestro wore the lead singer's blue feather boa around his neck. There was widespread booty shaking and boa waving that evening, testimony that even classical-music aficionados like to shake, shake, shake it from time to time.

***

Braeburn averaged three thousand guests a year for the six years we lived there. We hosted intimate suppers for six, receptions for three hundred, and everything in between; and we did so five and occasionally six days out of the week. Sunday was the only day decreed off limits; even then, exceptions were made. We made a special point of inviting people to the residence who had never before been invited to a chancellor-hosted function, which meant just about everyone connected with Vanderbilt, given the introverted character of the previous administration.

Every year we hosted employee celebrations, new and emeritus faculty luncheons and dinners, twenty-five-year alumni reunions, pregame and other sports-related events, faculty and alumni book signings, various university club luncheons and teas, and intimate student gatherings. We hosted patrons parties and other large fundraising events for Nashville's nonprofit organizations, such as

187

Second Harvest Food Bank, Artrageous (benefiting Nashville Cares), Nashville Humane Society, Garden Club of Nashville, Nashville Film Festival, Actor's Bridge Ensemble, Friends of the Ballet, and Cheekwood Botanical Garden and Museum of Art, to name only a few. We held a Ugandan AIDS Activist luncheon and a party in honor of civil rights leader and Vanderbilt alumnus Reverend James Lawson. We held receptions welcoming the new presidents of Belmont University, Fisk University, Meharry Medical College, and Tennessee State University; the new executive director of the Frist Center for the Visual Arts; and the new Metropolitan Nashville chief of police. Gordon and I stood at the front door at every event, personally welcoming each guest into the Vanderbilt chancellor's residence.

Our first Christmas at Braeburn, we held a holiday party on three consecutive nights so we could keep all the serving tables and party decorations set up and reuse the flower arrangements and center pieces. Close to a thousand people—a festive carousel of town and gown—swirled through the house, danced around the Christmas tree, and expressed delight to be there. By the third night, the entire staff was slaphappy with exhaustion. Interestingly, that night turned out to be the best of the series. By then no one was fretting about details; we were on the home stretch. Thereafter, we limited our holiday parties to two consecutive nights.

***

Vanderbilt's isolation from Nashville had been readily apparent to Gordon and me almost from day one. Nashville mayor Phil Bredesen had famously called the university "the eight-hundred-pound gorilla up the street." Vanderbilt was known as being bossy, territorial, and insular—shrouded "behind the magnolia curtain" from a city at which it sniffed with its big, upturned gorilla nose.

Vanderbilt was old Belle Meade. Downtown Nashville was the Grand Ole Opry. Elite Nashvillians cringed at the city's honky-tonk hillbilly image. "Nice shoes. I didn't think people from Nashville wore them," was the clever comment heard all too frequently by Nashvillians visiting New York, Vail, and Palm Beach. Never mind that more than a few Belle Meade fortunes came from the production and performance of country music; by and large, the two worlds did not mix.

Gordon and I made a pact to try to change that, not only because it would be good for Vanderbilt and Nashville, but also because it would be *fun*. Although we ourselves had playfully derided "Dogpatch" prior to moving there, it took me a nanosecond, once there, to realize that being "the home of country music" is the coolest thing about the city.

Nashville is awash in music-making talent. Nashville's heart and soul are its songwriters. These poets laureate of Americana reside all around Music City, even in Belle Meade. It is virtually impossible to not hear great music in just about any honky-tonk one might stagger into, any time of the day or night, within a half-hour's drive of the city. Karaoke in a Nashville bar is blood sport. You'd best be good—real good—or you'll creep, humiliated, off that small corner stage. I know this.

Gordon and I instituted our Vanderbilt–music industry dinners to help bring the two communities together. We scheduled the gatherings every couple of months throughout our time at the university, and always held them in Braeburn's impressive formal dining room, which seated twelve people. At first it was not easy persuading celebrated singer-songwriters, musicians, and producers to join us. These were busy people. Dining with the Vanderbilt chancellor and his wife was not exactly at the top of their thousand-things-to-do-before-I-die lists. Besides, most of them had few dealings with Vanderbilt, with the exception of the well-respected Vanderbilt Medical Center. Undoubtedly, many of them thought, *That sounds about as exciting as watching paint dry. What do they want from me anyhow?*

Key to our initial forays into Music Row were Marshall Chapman, a singer-songwriter, author, and Vanderbilt alumna, and Elaine Wood, our newly hired director of chancellor events. Elaine had been the public relations manager of Nashville's Hard Rock Café, so she knew just about every musician in town. Cowboy Jack Clement—singer-songwriter, producer, filmmaker, and all-around legend—attended our first music industry dinner. After dinner he sang a couple tunes, then passed his guitar to Marshall. She played a song, and then another guest took a turn. This is called a "guitar pull." A few musicians are sitting around shooting the bull, a guitar materializes, and someone plays a tune. The person next to him pulls it away, eager to play, and the instrument makes its way around the circle. There is hardly anything better that can happen after supper than for a guitar pull to spontaneously combust.

It was a fascinating evening, with all the guests telling stories, laughing, and strumming a song or two. Cowboy began telling his friends that the Vanderbilt chancellor and his wife were a lot livelier than might be imagined, and that they should come to one of our soirées. Those evenings will always be some of my fondest memories of Nashville.

Braeburn embraced a wide swath of local musicians and musical genres, from bluegrass and R&B to jazz and classical. The conservatory turned out to be the perfect concert and dance hall. Beautifully renovated Braeburn was filled with music, laughter, and warmth, just as Ida Hood and Susan Heron had wanted it to be.

***

Gordon and I were drawn together as we partnered in these efforts. My anger receded, replaced by the satisfaction of our work, our evolving affection for Nashville, and the pleasure of new friends. Our next three years at Vanderbilt were our best as a married couple and as a presidential spousal team. I did all I could to be the wife and partner I wanted to be and I thought he wanted and needed. He was a bold leader in those years. Although I did not agree with everything he did, I understood why he believed he needed to do it. I fell in love with my husband all over again.

15

Perks and Privilege

THE LIFE OF A PRESIDENT of a major university is remarkably privileged. A significant income is only part of the package, as are the many domestic services provided to presidential families who live in university residences. But the single most important hallmark of the privileged life is *access*—that is, *whom* one gets to meet and *what* one gets to experience. Major American universities are renowned internationally, prodigiously expanding one's prospects for meeting the highly accomplished and the powerful and for partaking of adventures worthy of the Discovery channel.

Gordon and I usually took two extended overseas trips each year. One would be a multicountry business tour, the other, an alumni tour—still business, of course, but conducted in a more relaxed atmosphere and in resort wear. We made three business tours to Asia (Seoul, Tokyo, Beijing, Hong Kong), one for each university. We traveled to Europe at least once a year. We represented Ohio State in South Africa and Uganda; Brown in Jordan, Turkey, and Greece; and Vanderbilt in Brazil and Guatemala. We flew business class if available, but were often upgraded to first. We stayed at five-star hotels and entertained at fine restaurants with spectacular views of the surrounding city.

The ambassadorial feel of our international business trips cannot be overstated. We were representing not only the university but the United States as well. There are many high-level government officials and powerful business leaders on every continent who are proud of their Ohio State, Brown, or Vanderbilt diplomas. They actively seek to maintain professional and personal connections with their alma maters, as do their alma maters with them. Major universities cultivate impressive political, commercial, and social networks across the globe.

A visiting university president and his entourage are treated as foreign dignitaries. There are state dinners; motorcades to attend national memorial services and celebrations; audiences with heads of state; meetings with secretaries of education, agriculture, and commerce; and receptions at the homes of ambassadors and corporate leaders. There are tours of scientific and medical research facilities. Every trip includes visits to other major universities to initiate, shore up, or expand joint programming and faculty exchanges. All along the way, people with great knowledge of the host country's political climate, economic policies, and social and cultural issues share their insights and tell their stories. It is a heady and profoundly intellectual experience to travel the world in this manner.

It is a wonderful thing to have to get an additional insert for your passport because you've run out of room for stamps. All our travels were fascinating. The people who hosted us were gracious beyond words. To provide a sense of the privilege and thrill of access, I'd like to recount three of my favorite adventures: traveling in South Africa and Uganda on behalf of Ohio State; visiting Brown's archaeological dig site in Petra, Jordan; and trekking to Vanderbilt's archaeological dig in the middle of the Guatemalan jungle.

***

Ohio State was the first university invited by the South African government under the new Nelson Mandela administration to send a collegiate delegation to tour the country. The OSU delegation would include the president and his family, several top-level administrators and professors with ties to and research interests in South Africa, and a dozen members of our men's basketball team. Our accompanying fresh-faced student athletes, most of whom were African American, would provide basketball clinics and, presumably, serve as positive role models for young boys in impoverished townships along the way. We would begin our ten-day journey in Cape Town, then fly up to Durban and over to Johannesburg. A brief respite in Sun City was planned as a special treat before the students and most of our entourage headed home. We, along with the dean of the Ohio State College of Agriculture, would then travel on to Uganda.

Brenda Gourley, vice chancellor of the University of Natal, had played an important role in arranging our South African portion of the trip. She would be our host in Durban, which is in the South African province of KwaZulu-Natal, the homeland of the Zulu nation. The title "vice chancellor" in the British university system is equal to that of "president" at American universities. Gourley was South Africa's first female vice chancellor.

Nelson Mandela was scheduled to deliver a speech at the University of Natal, so Gourley arranged for Gordon, Rebekah, and me to attend. The cavernous auditorium was packed with people; it was standing room only. We were seated toward the front and center, within a few yards of Mandela. After his speech, an aide escorted us down several hallways and into a large room to meet him. We each shook his hand and were invited by him to sit down. He exuded calm kindness while inquiring about our visit to South Africa. Gordon told him about the unique composition of our delegation and related a little of what we'd experienced thus far. We were all a little overwhelmed to be in his presence. Even the unflappable Gordon was so overwhelmed that he left his prescription sunglasses on the end table beside his chair. They were returned to him at the hotel the next morning.

The mood on the bus was somber as we drove past miles of wretched lean-tos and shanties on our way from the Johannesburg airport into the city. Gordon, Rebekah, and I had seen equally gut-wrenching poverty during our trip to Manila the previous summer, but this was the first time our student charges had witnessed horizon-to-horizon filth and misery. Our arrival at a fine hotel in the wealthiest part of Johannesburg—where every house is surrounded by an eight-foot-high wall, crowned with another two feet of razor wire—did not make us feel a whole lot better.

Our group would often split up during the day throughout the trip, attending to different matters and meetings. As a result, we had not seen many of the basketball clinics. Our first morning in Johannesburg, we all climbed aboard our bus and headed out to

Soweto (*South Western Townships*) at the southwestern edge of the city. We watched as our Ohio State basketball team worked with thirty or forty adolescent boys, explaining teamwork strategies and showing them ball-handling techniques. It was hot and dusty on the hard-packed red dirt "court," but no one minded. The children were enamored with the players, trying their best to mimic their moves. Our students were having a wonderful time, laughing and kidding with the boys. Elementary-school-age boys and girls cavorted around the sidelines, sometimes dashing in to grab a ball, heaving it with all their might toward the rusty hoop, and cheering loudly for any shot that miraculously made its mark. It was a wonderful sight to behold. Maybe there is reason for hope in this world.

While in Soweto we stopped to see the Hector Pieterson Memorial. Hector Pieterson, age twelve, was one of the first people to be killed on 16 June 1976 during the Soweto riots. That day thousands of black schoolchildren marched in protest against a decree by the apartheid Afrikaner government forcing black schools to use a fifty-fifty instructional language mix of Afrikaans and English. Afrikaans was seen as the language of the oppressor, a stinging reminder of the Dutch colonists; students wanted to study in English only. The march had been carefully organized and was intended to be peaceful, but a few students began throwing rocks at a police patrol that had barricaded their way. A police officer fired into the crowd, panic ensued, and more gunshots followed.

Twenty-three protesters died that day. Fifteen hundred heavily armed police officers were deployed to Soweto the next morning; before the end of the day over five hundred men, women, and children were dead and over a thousand more were wounded. The Soweto massacre was the beginning of the end of the Afrikaner government and apartheid. Parents and grandparents of the boys and girls who had followed our bus down the road that very day, waving and calling out "goodbye, goodbye," had undoubtedly been witness to the killings and violence.

I remember my acute embarrassment as we piled out of our big, gleaming, air-conditioned Elwierda bus to view the memorial. Pedestrians paused to study us as we walked conspicuously around the site. The basketball team wore their scarlet-and-gray Ohio State warmup suits. They looked so young, so vigorous—and so privileged. No one said much on the ride back to Johannesburg.

The following evening we were strolling the expansive gardens of a government official's residence located a few miles north of Johannesburg. The residence was magnificently situated atop a high hill overlooking miles of verdant, rolling land. A cocktail party for forty or so guests was being held in our honor. Our hostess walked us toward a nice-looking, compact gentleman wearing a white, knee-length achkan jacket over white pants. Slipping her arm around his waist she said, "President and Dr. Gee, I want to introduce you to Joseph Shabalala of Ladysmith Black Mambazo."

I had been a fan of Ladysmith Black Mambazo, an isicathamiya singing group, since first hearing them in concert during their 1975 college campus tour in the United States. Isicathamiya originated in Zulu South Africa and is a style of a cappella, incorporating all the idiosyncratic click consonants of the Zulu language. The singers execute tightly choreographed dance movements while performing. Mr. Shabalala founded Ladysmith Black Mambazo in 1960.

I knew Mr. Shabalala had been born in Ladysmith, a town about 140 miles northwest of Durban, and had named the group after his hometown. "But who or what is a 'Black Mambazo'?" I asked. His eyes twinkled with good humor as he explained that "black" signified the black ox, a symbol of strength, and "mambazo" meant "ax" in Zulu. The young a cappella group had been determined to "chop down" its competitors at choir competitions. "That's a very warlike sentiment for a bunch of guys who sing so sweetly," I observed.

I later learned on our visit to South Africa that Ladysmith—a word as gentle as Mr. Shabalala and his isicathamiya harmonies—was the site of an important battle of the Anglo-Boer War in the early 1900s. Mahatma Gandhi had led a stretcher corps to assist the British wounded. Young Winston Churchill was there as a war correspondent. Mandela later employed Gandhi's strategy of nonviolent resistance to destroy the apartheid state that Churchill helped to create in his support of South African self-rule by the Afrikaner government. Churchill well knew the intent of the Afrikaners to strip all nonwhite South Africans of their rights. The seven-year mass protest movement launched by Gandhi against the South African government ensured that Indians who resided in South Africa retained some of their rights, unlike blacks, who lost all means of redress. Gandhi fought for the rights of Indians, not "Kaffirs," a disparaging epithet for blacks, whom he then believed to be vastly inferior to Indians. When Mandela came to power in 1994, after spending twenty-seven years in prison, he publicly honored Churchill with his declarative intent to follow the elder statesman's motto: "In Victory, Magnanimity." I marveled then, as I do now, over the infinite web of connections to be found in a single place and time. And I continue to think about how hard is it to move beyond self-interest and prejudice, whether one is white, black, or Gandhi.

After all we had seen and experienced, traveling on to the Sun City luxury casino and resort was surreal. Sun City is located two hours north of Johannesburg toward the border with Botswana. It was carved out of the "bantustan" of Bophuthatswana. Bantustans were territories or "homelands" established under apartheid for the purpose of concentrating black Africans into designated ethnic groups—similar in concept to the US government's establishment of American Indian reservations.

Opulent, all-white Sun City became an international symbol of the injustices of apartheid when, in 1985, Artists United Against Apartheid pledged to boycott performing there. Forty-nine top recording artists collaborated in the production of the protest music video "Sun City," in which they declared, "I ain't gonna play Sun City."

Eleven years later, Gordon, Rebekah, and I were spending the night in the King Suite of the Palace of the Lost City, the most resplendent accommodations one can imagine. From our balcony we could see our basketball players bodysurfing on hydraulically manufactured six-foot waves in the Roaring Lagoon of the Valley of the Waves. The next day we would once again drive past the seemingly infinite shanty landscape en route to the Johannesburg airport. The disparities between South Africa's wealth and poverty were mind-boggling.

As we flew into the Entebbe-Kampala International Airport, Gordon (my resident history buff and frequent tutor) reminded me of "Operation Entebbe," the ingenious hostage-rescue mission carried out by Israeli defense forces in 1976. Palestinian and German terrorists had hijacked an Air France jet en route to Paris from Tel Aviv and, after refueling in Libya, forced the plane to land at the old Entebbe airport on 27 June. The terrorists vowed to begin killing the Israeli and Jewish hostages if Palestinian prisoners held in Israel and several other countries were not released by 1 July. The Israeli government negotiated with the hijackers and Ugandan president Idi Amin, who supported the terrorist action, to extend the deadline to 4 July. The Israeli forces landed at 11:00 p.m. on 3 July, killing all seven hijackers and about forty Ugandan soldiers. The entire rescue operation took less than an hour. After landing at the Entebbe airport, Gordon and I were escorted to see the old terminal building where the hostages were held for that horrific week—almost exactly twenty years before the date of our visit.

Churchill had called Uganda "the Pearl of Africa," so taken was he with its beauty. Of course, he was in Uganda when it was part of the British Empire, had a functioning government, and had one of the top education systems in Africa. Entebbe, located on the northern shores of Lake Victoria, was the first seat of British colonial administration in Uganda. By the time we drove through its broken streets, its once lovely colonial-era architecture was falling into ruins. I could not help thinking that, at least in the case of Uganda, the British left too soon and too abruptly. Twenty years of murderous coups and countercoups would ravage Uganda after Great Britain granted it independence in 1962.

The three things I remember most clearly about Kampala were our visit to Makerere University to lunch with its gracious president; the chaos of the Taxi Park, where four thousand beat-up, dusty, sardine-packed commuter vans come and go from the crack of dawn until two in the morning; and the biggest, ugliest birds I have ever seen, standing atop mountains of garbage piled in the streets. Kampala was a squalid mess, with the exception of the Makerere University campus, which was also in dire need of maintenance. The campus, however, was a veritable oasis compared to the surrounding city. Fortunately, we spent most of our time on day trips outside the city visiting the sites of Ohio State's agricultural and fish-farming projects.

Working in close alliance with Makerere faculty, the Ohio State College of Agriculture basically ran the Ugandan government's agricultural programs. It was fascinating to view the various projects that were located one or two hours by car outside

Kampala. We traveled with the dean of our College of Agriculture, meeting up along the way with the head of Makerere's Department of Agriculture and other faculty specializing in food science, agronomy, plant pathologies, and animal husbandry. We drove down two-lane blacktops to large single-crop fields and modern plant breeding facilities. We spent hours bouncing over narrow dirt roads through lush rain forest to see family farm experiments in crop rotation and organic vegetable gardening. Most memorably, there was a fish-farming project operated by one determined woman in a pond the size of a small-town municipal swimming pool.

A village feast was held in our honor by two of our Makerere faculty hosts, during which Gordon was inducted into the Hippopotamus Clan. He was given a Swahili name meaning "Big Wave." Rebekah and I amused ourselves—more than him, I think—coming up with other names prefaced by "big," our favorite being "Big Wind."

There was food of all kinds—none of which passed Gordon's lips. He had his stash of granola bars back at the hotel. It was up to Rebekah and me to make a show of tasting every dish with appreciation and delight.

Eating the food at state dinners, rather than pushing it around on our plate (as Gordon did), was one of Rebekah's and my most important diplomatic duties. Gordon would later hit on the idea of having his travel planners tell foreign hosts that he was a vegetarian, so as to avoid being subjected to mystery meat. (He would claim his religious beliefs disallowed meat. There must be scores of foreign dignitaries who think Mormons are vegetarian.) I was grateful for that ruse, as it had been fifteen years since I had eaten meat other than fish—with the uncomfortable exceptions of when well-meaning hosts would serve chicken, lamb, cow, or pig. At those times, I would take a few bites and then employ my husband's food rearranging strategy.

Somewhere in the jungle outskirts of Kampala, percussionists played, a singer warbled, and everyone—except Gordon and the most high-ranking Hippos—joined in a line dance snaking around and under a tent that was lit from outside by torches and from within by strands of generator-fed, multicolored Christmas lights.

Toward the end of our time in Uganda, we stood overlooking the forceful waters of the Kagera River. Originating in Burundi, the Kagera forms the border between Uganda and its neighbors Tanzania and Rwanda, as it flows north and east into Lake Victoria. Our guide told us that only two years before, the water was teeming with bodies. Thousands of politically moderate Tutsis and Hutus had been murdered on its banks upstream in Rwanda and dumped into the river.

Ida Amin murdered more than three hundred thousand of his countrymen during his eight-year reign of terror from 1971 to 1979. The flagrantly corrupt president Milton Obote had terrorized and tortured his opponents from 1966 to 1971, before Amin seized power, and then again from 1980 to 1985, when he took it back. Those two despots and a cast of other vile characters drove Uganda into the deepest poverty and despair.

Yet the Ugandan people remain incredibly resilient and generous of spirit. The question we kept asking ourselves during our time in Uganda was, *How can the Ugandans be so happy?* How can a people who have withstood so much, and who still struggle so hard, smile so readily and genuinely? Maybe it is simply because they have withstood, and in having done so, know what life is worth. Maybe it is their nature. We didn't know, and out of respect we didn't ask, but we admired and were humbled by them.

I returned from Uganda all fired up to collaborate on a research project with an art education professor I'd met at Makerere University. She and I had really hit it off and had decided we'd conduct a comparative study of elementary-school arts instruction across Uganda. What was being taught? What teaching materials were commonly available? In what manner were the programs funded and to what extent? What were the educational and experiential backgrounds of the art teachers? The Makerere professor had a general idea about what we might find in terms of curricula content and materials, but not much beyond that. There had never been resources available for such a study. I wrote a grant proposal to the Kellogg Foundation, hoping to secure some support for such a project, but was turned down. She and I continued to correspond and plot for the next year and a half; we would make it happen somehow. But then Gordon and I moved to Brown, and our project plans and budding friendship got lost in the shuffle.

Traveling throughout South Africa and Uganda on behalf of Ohio State was a pivotal life experience for every person on the trip, I believe. It shook me to the core spiritually and intellectually. Its emotional impact brought Gordon, Rebekah, and me closer together. I would bet that every one of the Ohio State basketball players remembers his trip to South Africa, sixteen years ago, with awe.

***

Gordon and I traveled to Jordan in June 1998, at the end of our first semester at Brown. The school has strong ties to Jordan, primarily because of three intertwining factors: Brown's two-decade sponsorship of the American Center of Oriental Research (ACOR), the capital city Amman's largest archaeological, social, and scientific research institute; nineteen years of excavations at the site of Petra's Great Temple; and the university's education of many members of elite Jordanian families, including Prince Faisal bin Al Hussein, the younger brother of King Abdullah II. The archaeology professor Martha Sharp Joukowsky and her husband, Arty, initiated, funded, and continue to direct the Petra excavation. Arty served for many years as the chairman of ACOR's board of trustees. The Joukowsky Family Foundation is perhaps ACOR's top private benefactor. It would not be a stretch to say that the Joukowskys are the mortar in the foundation of the Brown-Jordanian partnership.

We were in Amman only two days, during which time we accompanied Arty to ACOR and were invited to the Basman Palace within the Royal Court. Our primary destination was Petra, the circa-sixth-century BC capital city of the Nabataeans, where we spent an entire week. We stayed in a small hotel a ten-minute stroll from al-Siq (the shaft), which is the main entrance into Petra. Every morning as we walked the mile through the cool, narrow gorge (the walls of which stand as close as ten feet apart and three hundred to six hundred feet tall), we stared up in amazement at the cobalt blue slit of sky above. Every time we walked around the final turn of the passage, we gasped as the Treasury loomed into view.

Like most of the structures hewn into Petra's rose-red sandstone cliffs, the Treasury is more an architectural relief than a three-dimensional building. With its shallow, largely unadorned interior, it looks like a fantastic towering Greco-Roman-Hollywood movie set. Its tall, two-story façade, however, is finely detailed, with twelve Corinthian-capped columns (six on the face of each story) in graceful balance. It was the perfect Spielbergian sacred temple for the Holy Grail in *Indiana Jones and the Last Crusade.*

Martha, Arty, and the Brown students and research staff stayed in a rough, one-story dormitory at the Great Temple excavation site. With the exception of the day he arrived with camels, Arty met Gordon and me each morning at the Treasury in his jeep and drove us to the Brown dig about a mile or so northwest. Feeling a little too perky on the second day of our visit, we insisted, against Arty's advice, on walking from our hotel to the dig site. Drenched in sweat, with sand in our mouths, noses, ears, and eyes and sunburn on every patch of uncovered skin, we limped into camp late morning, sheepishly acknowledging that we weren't as macho as we thought. Every evening we'd totter back dirty and exhausted to our air-conditioned hotel room, having not done much of anything except enjoy a perpetual walking tour of the surrounding dig sites with Arty, eaten lunch, and talked with students and staff. This was in stark contrast to the Brown students, who worked like immigrant day laborers—and were paying the university for the privilege.

Later that week, His Royal Highness Prince Faisal arrived in his helicopter and took Gordon and me on an aerial tour of the beautifully rugged mountains that flank the western edge of Petra. We landed atop a high plateau to see a temple ruin that I have no idea how anyone would get to without a helicopter. Amazingly, a small dwelling stood about a hundred feet from the temple entrance, where an enterprising, leathery-faced man and a magnificent peregrine falcon entreated us to buy a coffee and pastry. I can't imagine that he and his bird get much business. I recovered my machismo on our return flight, leaning Indiana Jones–style as far out of His Royal Highness's helicopter as the harness would allow, snapping photos of Petra, the glowing-rose Wonder of the World.

Her Majesty Queen Noor was our guest at the Brown president's residence the following spring during graduation exercises. She was to be awarded an Honorary Doctorate of Humane Letters and to accept the same award on behalf of her late husband, King Hussein. (Interestingly, given the Indiana Jones–Petra connection,

Steven Spielberg was also present at that commencement to receive an honorary doctorate.)
I was standing on the outside patio atop the stairs leading down into the garden, where a large postcommencement lawn party was in progress. Lucy was lying in front of me, front paws crossed and head held high, surveying the scene below. Queen Noor, a truly elegant woman, stepped out of the conservatory onto the patio. She silently appraised Lucy and, with a wry, self-deprecating smile, remarked, "It's terrible to be outclassed by a dog."

I later explained to Lucy that this was pretty much the highest compliment she could receive, but, of course, she already knew that.

***

I'd been in Nashville for only a few days when I unfolded the 8 September 2000 issue of the *New York Times* and read, "Splendid Maya Palace Is Found Hidden in Jungle." Salivating over every word in the front-page headline, I charged forward:

> In a remote jungle of Guatemala, among the remains of a little-known ancient city with a name meaning Place of Serpents, archaeologists have uncovered one of the largest and most splendid palaces of Maya kings ever discovered. Its 170 high-ceiling rooms were built around 11 courtyards and spread over an area greater than two football fields.
>
> "No one has found anything like this since the turn of the last century," Dr. Arthur A. Demarest, an archaeologist at Vanderbilt University in Nashville and leader of the discovery team, said yesterday in describing the palace, which dates from the eighth century A.D.[1]

"Gordon!" I hollered, scrambling out of bed and into his bathroom, where he was shaving. "Look at this! It's Vanderbilt! Let's go see it!"

"Place of Serpents?" he read in his *fat-chance* tone of voice.

The following April, thirteen intrepid souls (plus Gordon) departed Nashville for Guatemala City. Arthur (or "Tennessee

Demarest," as he had been nicknamed for his Indiana Jones–like bravado and crazy jungle-man persona), his stoic wife, and two jungle-boy teenaged sons were at the airport to meet us, cheering and holding aloft a huge banner that read, "Welcome Vanderbilt!"

Early the next morning we were off to Tikal, a Maya ruins site, flying north toward the Belize border in a small chartered plane. Conversation ceased abruptly as we all stared down at tens of thousands of charred, barren acres of former rain forest. We had arrived amid "the burning season," when farmers burn the jungle to plant corn in what will remain fertile soil for two or three years at best. After the corn crop fails, the land is used to graze cattle. The cattle ranches fail when the cattle can no longer subsist on the sunscorched, brick-hard land—a process that takes a couple more years. The sky was hazy with smoke as the fires burned in every direction.

We spent our first night in the jungle at a small eco-lodge at the edge of the Tikal ruins. Sitting on the top steps of an ancient palace watching the sun set over the rain forest, we listened to Arthur describe the Mayas at their pinnacle and in decline. It was early lights-out that evening, as we were all exhausted from little sleep and lots of adrenaline.

Around midnight, the howler monkey family that had so amused us in the daylight hours swooping from tree to tree among our huts began to *howl* and *screech*. It sounded somewhat like a stadium full of University of Tennessee football fans at a conference championship. Gordon flung himself out of bed, dazed and confused, thinking we were under attack. The cacophony lasted *all night long.* Even with my anti-snorer plugs jammed into my ears and the pillow pulled tightly over my head, it sounded as if the critters were hanging from the (nonworking) ceiling fan directly over our beds.

When I finally gave up all hope of sleep about six in the morning and took out my earplugs, I truly could not believe the decibel level. I lay in my bed and chortled wickedly at the harrowing night my fellow travelers must have spent. Had I known what the night would bring, I could have sold my extra set of plugs for an easy C-note.

The following afternoon we landed on a clandestine, druglord-owned-and-operated runway on the edge of the Guatemalan highlands, where the entire village turned out to see who or what was being unloaded from such a relatively large plane in the light of day. Since there was no car rental agency for hundreds of miles in any direction, the drug lord was nice enough to provide us with three vans (two for us and one for our luggage and provisions) and drivers to take us on the two-hour, hot-and-humid, bum-bruising, bumpy-dirt-road drive to the Pasión River. Tennessee Demarest had reached a live-and-let-live (literally) agreement with the head jungle drug thug so he could get to and from the dig site.

Once at the Pasión, we climbed aboard two thatch-covered, motorized longboats and shoved off for the hour's journey upriver to Cancuén. The sun was already low in the sky, the water reflecting tangerine and scarlet as it set.

Arriving at dusk meant we had ten minutes to find our tents, stash our gear, and get a quick visual memory of the camp's lay-out before dark descended—pitch-black jungle dark. A two-foot-wide path led up from the water's edge to every small building and tent in the camp. The path was covered with lime, glowing bright white against the inky terrain. We were told to stay on the path to and from our tents, especially at night. Snakes and scorpions do not like to slither and crawl across lime. Lime was our friend.

No one had to be told twice. Arthur had scared the heck out of us—something he would relish doing for the duration of our trip—with tales of snakes and scorpions eager to bite and sting any human body part that came within lunging distance.

We grabbed the plastic bath totes that had been thoughtfully prepared and placed on each of our sleeping bags and dashed en masse for the camp's two showers, taking great care not to step off the lime. Covered in a thick inch of grime and perspiration and peering around anxiously for snakes and scorpions, we demonstrated remarkable orderliness as we each waited our turn at a cold shower. One slithering black shadow, however, and all pretense of civilized behavior would have vanished in an every-man-for-himself stampede in the opposite direction.

Arthur expounded cheerfully on the rich variety of venomous Guatemalan vipers as we strapped on our snake guards the next morning before heading off to the dig site. The rigid plastic guards wrapped completely around the leg from ankle to just above the knee, causing us to lurch through the jungle like a lost corps of Tin Man extras in a tropical *Wizard of Oz* sequel. The Guatemalan rain forest boasts snakes that leap at you from ground level and snakes that fling themselves onto your head from above. The jumping viper strikes with such force that it catapults itself through the air. "But don't worry," Arthur reassured us. "They're really rather slow; sometimes you can dodge them."

The eyelash pit viper prefers to hang out in low-hanging trees and drop down on its victims. The lovely fer-de-lance can eject its venom at a victim more than six feet away, causing mortal hemorrhaging and tissue necrosis. It also doesn't mind swimming or climbing trees to reach its prey, and enjoys nothing more than curling up inside a sleeping bag (along with a buddy scorpion) and springing out like a jack-in-the-box. "Make certain to zip up your tents after you enter and the moment you leave," warned Arthur.

The eyelash viper and fer-de-lance are both described as having "irritable dispositions," striking often and with little provocation. The jumping viper is a laid-back fellow compared to his Cancuén colleagues.

We had arrived early in the excavation process, so the splendid Maya palace looked to our untrained eyes like a big, jungle-covered hill. Fortunately, we had Arthur there to describe each room, courtyard, and unearthed stone in minute detail as we maneuvered stiff-legged around the site, glancing nervously for signs of slithering at every tree root. He had "discovered" the palace by falling through some dense vegetation into one of its courtyards—which, of course, in his spinning of the yarn, was filled with snakes.

The discovery of Cancuén was causing scholars to revise their views of Maya civilization as being preoccupied almost exclusively with war and with religious rituals aimed at ensuring success at war. No traces of a pyramid had been found at Cancuén, nor would there be. A stepped pyramid was the religious heart of a Maya metropolis and was usually located near the king's palace. Cancuén's power and wealth came from commerce rather than military conquest and were strengthened through royal intermarriages with neighboring kingdoms.

Cancuén was built at the beginning of the navigable part of the Pasión River as it flows north, down from the Guatemalan Highlands into the jungle lowlands. Cancuén's rulers controlled trade between the two regions, dealing in precious commodities such as salt, jade, pyrite for making mirrors, and obsidian (black volcanic rock) for razors and knife blades. The people of Cancuén had formed a very advanced society, with superior skills in architecture and building construction. Homes and workshops of highly skilled artisans surrounded the palace.[2]

Guatemala's Institute of Anthropology and History, the National Geographic Society, and Vanderbilt were sponsoring the expedition. Arthur and Tomás Barrientos from Guatemala's Universidad del Valle were the expedition's codirectors. Their intention was to unearth only as much of the palace and its surroundings as was necessary for future ecotourists to envision its structure and understand its significance. Protection and preservation of an excavated ancient metropolis in the middle of a rain forest are extremely challenging and expensive. The plan was to have the local descendants of the ancient Mayas become invested in the expedition project.

Arthur and Tomás were already training some men from the closest village—El Zapoté, a half-hour's trek from Cancuén through the jungle—to help with the excavation. Some of the village women had been hired to prepare meals and do laundry. Arthur and Tomás were on good terms with the village elders and its inhabitants, who eked out a living with subsistence farming. The villagers understood that they would ultimately inherit the Cancuén site, having already assumed responsibility for guarding it when excavation work ceased during the rainy season. Vanderbilt's Institute of Mesoamerican Archaeology would assist them in building a small ecotourist center. It would also establish an educational program to train them in the skills they would need to operate the center and to preserve and protect the site. It was hoped that continued archaeological study, rainforest conservation, and indigenous community development would be interwoven to create a better, more sustainable model for future archaeological research in developing countries.[3]

Late that night, we boarded our longboats and proceeded an hour upriver to El Zapoté. The village had begun a three-day festival. We were present to witness a special religious service to dedicate and "make Mayan" a small, generator-operated electric gristmill that Arthur had given the village on behalf of Vanderbilt. The women of the village had beseeched Arthur for the mill to assist them in grinding their corn, an arduous daily task that consumed much of their time.

We had been told that only the men of our group would be allowed to participate in the ceremony, but, at the last minute, the elders relented and we were all ushered inside the small hut that had been built to house the mill. The hut was lit dimly with tallow candles; the air was heavy with smoke and the musky smell of perspiring bodies. Eight or ten elders awaited us, dressed in their Sunday best of short-sleeve white shirts and dark cotton trousers. The ceremony was very somber—a Maya-Catholic mixture of ritual blessings to the north, south, east, and west, incorporating animal blood, cocoa, and rum.

After the gristmill ceremony, we followed the elders up through their fields toward the village. They lit the way with hand-held torches. Our processional entered the small, brightly painted church that stood in the center plaza. The women and children, like the elders, were dressed in their best clothes. Thirty or forty small children were sleeping under wooden benches and in the aisles. Their parents' singing and worship had already been going on for hours. We followed the elders toward the front of the church and took the seats that had been reserved in our honor.

The elders spoke, presumably praising the dedication of the electric mill and introducing us, since everyone turned our way and smiled, nodding their heads. The singing resumed. People wandered in and out. We watched and listened for well over an hour. The crowded church was uncomfortably hot and humid.

I finally walked outside for some fresh air, watching from the doorway. Several other members of our group meandered outside, including the eldest and tallest man in our group, the Vanderbilt trustee Rodes Hart. After about fifteen minutes, most of us returned to our seats. We were all exhausted, as it was well past midnight and we'd had a hard day in the jungle, but the ceremony was just beginning. A fermented chocolate concoction was served to us in small earthen cups. Gordon (who should probably receive treatment for his paranoia over food sanitation) looked as if he'd just been handed a cup of phlegm. His stricken expression struck me as so hysterical that I almost induced an aneurism trying not to laugh. He lamely feigned a sip, holding the cup a full inch away from his lips and giving it a slight tilt.

All of a sudden the village elders stopped the ceremony, noticing Rodes was not present. They demanded he rejoin us, for they perceived him to be our "founder," or our preeminent elder. Poor Rodes was hauled back inside and made to toss back the fermented cocoa right then and there. We all grimaced in sympathy; the stuff was not exactly a Godiva cordial. After the sacrifice of Rodes (an act we were more than happy to go along with, if it meant we had fulfilled our ceremonial obligations) and Arthur's receipt of a major Maya award of some sort that none of us comprehended (he and the villagers appeared pleased), we were allowed to retreat to our boats.

It was about two o'clock in the morning when we began our return trip. The rapids were treacherous in places and the swift current more difficult to navigate downriver than up. Arthur had terrified us during our first boat ride with horror-flick descriptions of the thousands of hungry crocodiles that lived in the river. Gordon, the Eagle Scout who had never learned to swim because of his fear of water, and who still refuses to put his toe in the most enticing of swimming pools, was hyperventilating in anticipation of capsizing into the pitch-black, reptile-infested waters. I turned to him and said in a low voice, "Gordon, if we capsize I will save you. Do *not* freak out and start thrashing about. You'll be OK, if you remain calm. Whatever happens—*don't panic*. Do you understand?"

"OK," he squeaked, peering off into the rushing water and gnawing on his cuticles.

Having imbibed liberally of the cocoa beer, Arthur snoozed peacefully in the back of the boat throughout our two-hour ordeal, blissfully unaware of the glares directed his way by senior university administration.

I suspect I overstepped the limits of Gordon's adventure tolerance with the Cancuén trip. Our future university excursions were a bit more sedate.

***

University alumni tours are usually uniquely interesting, civilized affairs. A group of alumni from one or more universities fly to and then bus or boat around some desirable faraway land. A couple of professors are generally in tow to augment tour-guide commentary with scholarly asides and after-dinner lectures on history, politics,

flora, and fauna. At Ohio State, Gordon instituted an annual President's Alumni Tour, advertised as such and always to some wonderful part of the world we wanted to see. These were high-end,
smaller group tours offering wealthy alumni, otherwise known as
present and potential donors, the opportunity to get to know their
president and his wife up close and personally.

We sailed the Greek Islands on a spectacular three-masted clipper ship with a convivial mix of Buckeyes and Tulane Green
Waves. We navigated the Danube from Regensburg to Budapest
with Brunonians. We bused around New Zealand and the Amalfi
Coast of Italy with Commodores.

Group transportation by bus and boat require a lot of sitting;
eating goes far too well with sitting. Biking and hiking tours were
my preference, which we finally got to take during our time at Vanderbilt. We went on a bike trip through France's Loire Valley and a
hiking trip in northern Italy near Lake Como.

Here's a valuable tip: If you are a Type A(+) personality on a
biking or hiking trip in high temperatures, a bandanna soaked in
cold water tied loosely around your neck will allow you to push
yourself to even greater extremes. Soon everyone in the group
will be following your lead so as not to be outdone, because they
are most assuredly Type A as well—otherwise, they'd be on a bus
or boat.

***

Whether one is embarking on a two-week, multicountry business trip or giving a supper for six at the university residence, every
detail must be carefully conceived, organized, and executed. The
more a president and first lady travel and entertain, the greater their
needs and expectations. Herein lies the source of two unattractive
features of the privileged, *managed* life: dependence and confine-
ment. I want to make it clear that I am not speaking of the merely
wealthy, but of those who have large hunks of their lives scheduled
far in advance and who must rely on others to help them juggle it
all.

Representing the university day in and day out, despite all the
perks, is extraordinarily demanding. When a lot is expected of you,
you expect a lot from those whose jobs it is to assist you in doing
yours. It is easy, almost to the point of inevitability, for someone in

such a lofty yet responsibility-laden position to begin to feel entitled. Things are done for you. They *have* to be done for you in order
for you to do your job. But it gets confusing.

At first the special treatment and kowtowing are embarrassing,
but soon it all can become the norm. You begin to expect it, and
then you can begin to think you *deserve* it—after all, you're working so hard and trying to move so fast. What was once an embarrassment can become a necessity. Service and deference can be
both enabling and enjoyable, and both disabling and corrosive.

I believe it is almost impossible to live such a life without
becoming dependent and, worse, arrogant—a somewhat counterintuitive combo when you think about it, unless you're currently
living with a fourteen-year-old. Perhaps those effects are more pronounced when one enters suddenly into such a life, as opposed to
gradually working her way into it or having been born with "Her
Highness" in front of her name. But then, maybe, it's the relative
newcomer who can see more clearly how privilege changes people—herself, first and foremost—because she has a more recent,
keener memory of what life was like before being handed a VIP
badge. I do believe that no matter how you get there, it requires
ongoing vigilance not to succumb to the pernicious influences of
the VIP life. Those who were born into it are probably no less
affected, but they may simply lack the perspective to recognize the
extent of it.

I was born determined and impatient. Being an only child
probably did not help temper those traits. Moreover, I was raised to
be *independent*. My mother especially liked using that word. "Your
father and I have raised you to be independent," she'd say. It was a
characteristic that my parents admired greatly in a person, and a
reality that I worked hard to achieve.

I'm uncertain as to the origins of my arrogance. Maybe it
comes from the fragile artistic ego, the self-justification an artist
must manufacture just to keep doing what it is she wants and needs
to do. (The same might be said of academicians toiling in less
respected and monetized fields, such as almost all subjects identified as part of the liberal arts.) I'd never thought of myself as arrogant, until several people had taken the trouble to point it out to me.
Even so, I never really acknowledged it. But then, isn't it the very
nature of arrogance not to notice itself? When everything was

twisting and turning in on us at the end of our marriage, Gordon flung the word *imperious* at me. Ouch. I do so dislike imperiousness in a person.

The almost complete reliance on a seemingly unending number of people that came along with my marriage to Gordon was a continual irritant to independent me. I strained against it like an unbroken horse does against a bridle. (Bride, bridegroom, bridal, bridle—the etymology is the same. It pretty much boils down to a woman/horse being restrained/trained/broken by a man.) I remembered rearing up in anger when Gordon insisted on holding on to my passport the first time we traveled abroad together. Eventually, I relented and handed it over. He kept it for twelve years.

I had to accept the fact that the complexity of our lives required 24/7 reliance and dependence on many people, but while I happily enjoyed the spoils, I never fully surrendered to them. It didn't take me long to give in to the deliciousness of not having to deal with large chunks of the mundane, such as grocery shopping and keeping my car gassed and serviced. It was great not having to spend time on stuff I didn't want to do, but I did resent it when the responsibilities and restrictions of my position stood in the way of what I wanted to do and, perhaps more to the point, how I wanted to *be*.

I tried containing my anger. I tried being (or at least *acting*) nice and appreciative. Sometimes, though, the dam would rupture and I would lash out at the people closest to me, the ones trying their best to help, the ones dependent on the paycheck the job provided them.

A friend familiar with my struggles sent me a card that summed up my frustrations a little too revealingly for comfort. Pictured on the front was a Persian cat wearing a pink sweatband and a peevish expression and sitting haughtily on a yoga mat. The caption read, "I meditate, I do yoga, I chant . . . and I still want to smack someone!"

Enrollment in a graduate-level seminar called something like "How Not to Be Viewed by Others as an Imperious Pain in the Ass" should be required of those who arrive abruptly into societal positions where they must rely on other people to manage their lives. (I daresay there are many members of the lucky sperm club who also might benefit.) The seminar would be three-pronged: (1) grace under pressure, (2) public and media relations, and (3) maintaining strict boundaries between oneself and those employed in one's service. At the very least, there should be a contraindication warning label on the back of all VIP badges: *Can cause severe bouts of ill temper in those persons with tendencies toward willful independence, impatience, and arrogance.*

16

Faux Pas and Politics: His

"FRIENDS MAY COME AND GO, but enemies accumulate."[1] The veracity of this statement is proven time and again, Gordon maintained. It is rarely a single mistake or affront that takes down someone in power, but an accumulation of missteps, resulting in an ever-expanding constituency of the offended.

Gordon made several major decisions during his first two years in Nashville that would come back to bite him, and swallow me, as he set forth like a Maya warrior to, in his exact words, "change the culture of Vanderbilt." In a region of the country where "he needed killin'" is a justifiable legal defense, going up against the sentinels of the Old South may have been more perilous than telling an Ivy League faculty that it needed to rethink its precious forty-year-old humanities curriculum.

***

Vanderbilt's student population was predominantly white, Protestant, and affluent when we came to town in 2000. It still is, but a little less so thanks (or not, depending on how you look at it) to Gordon's determination to expand minority enrollment. "Minority" doesn't always mean black or Hispanic and poor. It can also mean white, affluent, and Jewish, especially if the institution has a well-deserved politically conservative reputation and happens to be the shiny gold star on the rhinestone buckle of the Bible Belt.

Less than four percent of Vanderbilt's students were Jewish. Vanderbilt had the lowest percentage of Jewish students of the country's top twenty-five universities with the exception of Notre Dame. ("Too many crucifixes," surmised a Jewish friend regarding Notre Dame's skimpy Jewish student population.) About a quarter of the students at most Ivy League institutions were Jewish—the same percentage of Vanderbilt students who identified themselves as born-again Christians.

Washington University (in St. Louis) and Emory (in Atlanta), two of Vanderbilt's major regional competitors, had Jewish student populations of thirty-five and thirty percent, respectively. *U.S. News and World Report*'s 2002 Best Colleges ranking had Washington at fourteen, Emory at eighteen, and Vanderbilt at twenty-one.

The College Board's 2001 statistics showed that Jews had the highest SAT scores of any religious group other than Unitarians. Only 2,354 students who took the SAT that year identified themselves as Unitarian, but 27,120 said they were Jewish. Clearly, if an elite, conservative, predominantly Protestant university wanted to further elevate its academic profile *and* expand its cultural diversity, Jews were the ticket. (Unitarians are still Protestants, albeit *liberal* ones.)

Gordon set out immediately to recruit more Jewish students, hiring Rabbi David Davis (the former head of the Swig Judaic Studies Program at the University of San Francisco) in July 2001 to head up the intensive effort. This was part of what Gordon termed his "elite strategy," the purpose of which was to raise Vanderbilt's ranking into the realm of the Ivy League. Surpassing Brown, in particular, was his heart's desire and plan for revenge.

Rabbi Davis immediately began an aggressive marketing campaign to spread the word among top Jewish students and their teachers about why they should consider Vanderbilt University. He himself visited (and dispatched Vanderbilt admissions officers to) private Jewish high schools and academically rigorous public schools with large Jewish student populations. Jewish students were told straight out that Vanderbilt was looking for more Jewish students. Rabbi Davis set up an exhibition booth at the annual convention of the Union of American Hebrew Congregations—an appearance that surprised attendees, not only because Vanderbilt and Judaism were not exactly closely associated, but also because it was the only university represented at the convention.

The focused recruitment of Jewish students was not a new strategy for Gordon or for scores of other university presidents around the country. Judaic studies programs and Hillel centers had become the norm, rather than the exception, at the nation's better universities and those aspiring to be better. Gordon had overseen the construction of a new Hillel center while at Ohio State and the renovation of the Hillel facility at Brown. At Vanderbilt, both a brand-new Hillel center and a new program in Jewish studies would be open for business by the fall of 2002.

It was not the general idea of recruiting more Jewish students to Vanderbilt that attracted media attention and ruffled feathers on and off campus and within and outside the Jewish community. It was the unabashedly blatant way the high-profile chancellor went about it, all under a bright-white media spotlight. He was a national leader in higher education and the second-highest-paid university president in the country. He was also the cad who had recently ditched Brown for Vanderbilt, but who now seemed to be trying to turn Vanderbilt into Brown. Media attention was a certainty. There was just nothing subtle about his motives and methods beyond a slight nod toward "cultural diversity" to divert the gaze of the squeamish away from his pursuit of higher rankings.

"Yes, we're targeting Jewish students," the *Wall Street Journal* quoted him as saying at a Vanderbilt Hillel board meeting. "There's nothing wrong with that. That's not affirmative action. That's smart thinking."[2]

The dean of undergraduate admissions disagreed. He was concerned that the administration's heavy-handed approach would backfire and incite guidance counselors at predominately Jewish high schools to dissuade students from applying to Vanderbilt. He reported that several guidance counselors had already expressed their disgust over the "self-serving and repre-hensible" character of the recruitment strategy. They saw the tar-geting of Jews for any reason as having anti-Semitic overtones. "A positive stereotype is just as pernicious as a negative one," stated a spokesperson for the academically renowned Roslyn High School on Long Island, New York.[3]

Vanderbilt's Baptist chaplain was also irked, but on behalf of the southern white Christians who dominated the student body. He didn't believe that Jews were better students than Christians and demanded "to see factual information" to support such a claim.[4] Someone must have forwarded him the College Board statistics, because the next semester the reverend appeared to be doing penance by accompanying a group of Vanderbilt students to the Holocaust Museum in Washington, D.C.

***

At the same time that Gordon was whipping up media attention with his elite recruitment strategy, he and two of his vice chancellors decided to take a stand against the Confederates. Gordon, David Williams (vice chancellor for university affairs, general counsel and secretary of the university), and Mike Schoenfeld (vice chancellor for public affairs) decreed that the offensive word "Confederate" would be eradicated from the front of Confederate Memorial Hall.

Confederate Memorial Hall had been built in 1933, with a sizable donation from the United Daughters of the Confederacy, to house young women studying at the George Peabody College for Teachers. The name of the dormitory had caused bouts of heartburn in pockets of the Vanderbilt community since the 1960s. For the past several years, black students had simply refused to live there. Henceforth, proclaimed the new chancellor, the name of the dormitory would be Memorial Hall—never mind to whom it was built in memoriam.

Gordon knew he could never get the Vanderbilt Board of Trust to approve the name change, so he announced it without informing them.

"A president gets two or three passes to do something without board approval and ask later for forgiveness," he explained.

"You're in big trouble," I observed.

A few days later, Gordon came home crowing about a meeting he and his two vice chancellors had that day with a band of blue-haired Daughters of the Confederacy. The ladies had visited him in his office to discuss the matter at hand. He and his comrades were feeling rather smug about the multicultural character of their little trio—a Mormon from Utah, an African American from inner-city

216

Detroit, and a Jew from New York. They had shown those old ladies a thing or two!

"You're in *really* big trouble," I observed.

As a native of the South, I had mixed feelings about the name change. On the one hand, there was no getting around the fact that the word "Confederate" had some mighty ugly connotations that were inextricably bound up with the enslavement of Africans and the denigration of generations of African Americans. If I were a black student, I would not reside in a dorm named Confederate Memorial Hall. On the other hand, most of the men who fought and died under the Confederate flag did not own slaves. They were fighting to protect their families and homes from an invading and brutally destructive enemy.

Regardless of how one views the immensely complex and still hurtful subject of the Civil War, one thing is certain: *it happened*. It is a part of our American history and heritage. I did not think trying to erase that history by sandblasting the word "Confederate" from the façade of a building would serve anyone well, but it seemed especially antithetical to the educative and reflective mission of a university. I told Gordon my thoughts on his decision, but he dismissed me.

"Even if you're right ethically," I pressed, "you're going about it wrong." Three non-southern men—white, black, or purple—should not try to intimidate a group of super-southern elderly ladies over the Lost Cause.

The student publication *The Slant* offered the only humorous perspective on the otherwise humorless Confederate Memorial Hall debate:

> The University administration today announced a new series of sweeping name changes and regulations. "We need to purge this campus of anything that could possibly be construed as politically incorrect," said Vice-Chancellor David Williams. Williams unfortunately shares a name with a former Confederate soldier and will be forced to change his name under the new regulations.
>
> . . . Administration officials agonized over the new name Furman Hall would be receiving. It was

first suggested that the name be changed to
Furperson Hall to remove the gender bias. However,
officials decided that this name had a species bias
that needed to be removed, so the name became simply Fur Hall. The administration decided to scrap this
idea as well because of possible complaints from
People for the Ethical Treatment of Animals (PETA).
Thus, Furman Hall will now be known as Synthetic
Faux Fur Hall. Cotton growers were offended by the
new name, but because of cotton's connection to
slavery, they were ignored.

The University itself will be forced to undergo a
name change as well, owing to the fact that Vanderbilt is named after a robber baron. "We suggested
changing the name to Ralph Nader University, which
would be the opposite of the cutthroat businessman,
but we thought that would offend libertarians. We
thought of God University but that offends atheists.
Mother Teresa University? Offends feminists who
don't think women should be forced to be mothers,"
said Williams. Finally, the administration decided
that the University's official name shall be That Place
With Students.

. . . Suffering the most from the name-change
policy, however, will be the history department,
which will be completely cut at the beginning of next
semester. "We tried to keep history, but it just got too
hard," said Williams. "We started with just telling
American history teachers to leave out the Articles of
Confederation in the hopes that people offended by
the use of that word would feel comfortable. But then
we discovered that American history was filled with
topics like slavery and racism that might cause some
people to feel uncomfortable, so we decided to scrap
American history altogether. But then someone
pointed out that things like slavery and racism are
fairly global phenomena throughout history, so we
decided to eliminate the department rather than force

people to confront the former existence of these disquieting topics."[5]

Finding no humor at all in the onslaught, the Daughters of the Confederacy took Vanderbilt to court. The lower court sided with Vanderbilt, allowing the name change.

Soon after that, a pint jar of one-inch tacks was tossed on the gravel drive at our home in Monteagle. A tinny recording of "Dixie" was left repeatedly on our Monteagle voicemail service. For the next two years, perhaps after downing a flask of Southern Comfort, Johnny Rebel Jr. would telephone during our visits to the cabin and repeat the Dixie performance whenever we answered. Occasionally I'd join in on "Look away, look away, look away, Dixie Land" before hanging up. I had to wonder if Junior knew all the verses to Dixie and realized it was as much about an ungentlemanly "gay deceiver" named Will who broke the heart of "Old Missus" as it was about wanting to live and die in the South. Somehow I don't think Junior was much of a gentleman, either.

The Daughters appealed and, in May 2005, the court ruled unanimously in their favor. The appellate court opinion read:

> Allowing Vanderbilt and other academic institutions to jettison their contractual and other legal obligations so casually would seriously impair their ability to raise money in the future . . .
>
> It is not within the purview of this court to resolve the larger social and cultural conflicts regarding whether and how those who fought for the Confederacy should be honored or remembered.[6]

At first Gordon declared that he would fight the ruling, but he later decided to back off. "We won anyway," he said. Although Vanderbilt could not remove "Confederate" from the building itself, the word had already been eliminated from all references to Memorial Hall in campus publications, maps, and websites.

I didn't think he had won. It all seemed like a poor expenditure of political capital to me. It certainly didn't seem like a smart choice to use for one of the two or three get-out-of-jail-free cards that Gordon believed a university president got from his board.

***

The next bastions of the Old South to feel threatened were the Greeks—as in Betas, Deltas, and Kappas. In 2002, Gordon announced that the university would restructure its student housing into a residential hall system similar to those of Harvard and Yale, which were themselves modeled on Oxford and Cambridge (the English "Oxbridge" system). The first phase of the projected quarter-century-long restructuring would be the construction of the Commons, a freshman residential hall composed of a central building and ten "houses" (one of which would be Memorial Hall) on the Peabody campus. The Commons Center would have a large dining hall, a well-equipped exercise facility, a living room with a concert-grade grand piano, meeting/study rooms, academic support services, and administrative offices. Each house would have seminar rooms and a cozy lounge and refreshment area, offering a familial atmosphere for its residents. The Commons, as Gordon would say in speeches to board and faculty members, was to provide first-year students with a "unified and unifying living and learning experience."

Unlike the passé dormitory model that most of my friends and I somehow managed to endure until we could finagle off-campus living quarters as upperclassmen, the residential hall system sought to provide undergraduates with such a wholesomely holistic living/social/educational environment that they would happily elect to reside on campus all four years. Consequently, they would graduate into the world having had a vastly more satisfying college experience than could ever have been imagined by those of us who had to live in a twelve-by-fifteen-foot dorm room with a sink, a hot plate atop a small refrigerator, and a perky cheerleader from Fayetteville as a roommate.

Faculty members and their families would live on site in special quarters as "heads" or "deans" of the various houses and, as the Yale residential college site once advertised, "hold study breaks with tasty snacks in their homes during reading weeks and exam periods."[7] Whereas many of us who attended college circa 1970 would not have considered a chummy on-site adult and his or her family a real boon to our college experience (tasty snacks notwithstanding), it seems the much-better-adjusted (or perhaps simply more docile) undergrads of today do.

"Just like Hogwarts!" I enthused on hearing of Gordon's plans for a Vanderbilt residential hall system. "Will there be a 'sorting hat' to determine each student's housing assignment?"

We were both great fans of *Harry Potter*. Gordon believed himself to be a Gryffindor, while I felt more of a kinship to Slytherin. For readers sadly unfamiliar with *Harry Potter*, the difference between the house of Gryffindor and house of Slytherin is roughly the equivalent of "works and plays well with others" and "runs with scissors."

The Alphas, Omegas, and all letters in between were concerned that the Commons was to be built far, far away (a fifteen-minute hike) from Greek Row. Although conspiracy theories abounded, the physical separation of first-year students from the fraternity and sorority houses was not some diabolical plan. It just so happened that Peabody had the best space configuration for the proposed complex. The Peabody administration and faculty very much wanted to see it built there as well.

While the prospect of being physically isolated from the freshman class worried Greek upperclassmen, it was the possible *unification* of the freshmen that was seen as the biggest threat to Greek life and recruitment. What if first-year students really got to *like* each other, had a good time in a Kumbayah/everybody's-beautiful-in-their-own-way fashion, and decided they didn't need to join a fraternity or sorority to have a great college experience? Disaster!

Greeks young and old rose up in opposition. The word went out that the new administration was bent on destroying Greek life at Vanderbilt. All hands on deck! Vanderbilt's Greek alumni, including several major university donors and a few good-ol'-boy board members, led the charge, with their little brothers and sisters in tow.

A card-carrying member of Pi Kappa Alpha (inspirational motto: Once a Pike, Always a Pike), Gordon had no intention of waging Panhellenic and panfrat warfare. Frankly, he liked dropping by parties at the fraternity and sorority houses too much to contribute to their demise. (It has always been my theory that Gordon's own stultifyingly respectable undergraduate experience, during which he spent two years as a Mormon missionary, infused him with a latent desire to hang out with inebriated nineteen- and twenty-year-olds.) Nevertheless, a lot of Greeks on and off campus got their togas in a collective wad over Chancellor Gee's Culture-Changing Overture No. 3.

I found the Commons versus the Greeks to be highly amusing Théâtre de l'Absurde, an entertaining counterweight to his War on the Confederacy. The cliquishness of many of the more popular fraternities and sororities had always seemed silly and mean-spirited to me, an unfortunate extension of the worst part of high school. Several college friends of mine had formed two "frarorities": I Eta Pi and I Phelta Thi. Anyone could be a member of one or both, depending on your mood or appetite.

***

Gordon used his second free pass to dismantle Vanderbilt's Athletic Department. He did not inform the Board of Trust before he made public his plan to fire the athletic director and place varsity programs within the domain of the Office of Student Life—all under the ever-expanding auspices of General Counsel David Williams, the Confederate-fighting vice chancellor for university affairs.

The summer of 2003 had brought a string of collegiate sports scandals to the attention of both the general public and the National Collegiate Athletic Association. (As of late, what summer, autumn, winter, or spring hasn't?) Although Vanderbilt was not associated with any of the misdeeds, the bad-boy behavior of Division I-A athletic directors, coaches, and athletes was the catalyst Gordon needed to take a stand against a culture that enabled athletic departments to act "as islands, answerable to no one, spending ridiculous amounts of money." He told the press he was "declaring war" on a "culture of separation" that coddled student-athletes while isolating them from their peers and "protect[ing] them from the university in general."[8]

This was a brave move, but not one he would have dared to make at a university that had a nationally competitive football program. "If I tried this at Ohio State or Colorado, I'd probably be pumping gas in Vernal, Utah," he admitted.[9] Gordon was not interested in working for an oil company—at least, not in his hometown for minimum wage. He was taking his stand on this important moral issue at a place where he thought he might be able to get away with it.

Vanderbilt had long been at the bottom of the Southeastern Conference in its ability to compete in the two most important sports at American universities: football and men's basketball. This was and continues to be primarily because Vanderbilt requires a tad more academically of its student-athletes than other SEC schools. Vanderbilt requires its incoming top-ranked athletes to be able to read and cipher at an above-average high school level and, furthermore, heartily encourages them to *graduate from college*. One can scarcely imagine the severe recruiting handicap such academic expectations place on the Harvard of the Southeastern Conference.

What did a southern university whose certifiable football heyday was in the early 1900s (kudos to Coach McGugin!) and whose last winning football season was in 1983 stand to lose? Apparently quite a bit, if the howling of sports fans—and more important, major-donor sports fans—was any indication.

"Of all the things I did at Vanderbilt, that received the most negative publicity," Gordon reminisced after his departure for Ohio State. I heard later that the Ohio State trustees made it clear to their returning president that no such shenanigans would be going on anywhere near the Horseshoe—a stance I doubt will be changed by their football-memorabilia-for-tattoos turmoil that ultimately ended the tenure of Buckeyes coach Jim Tressel.

* * *

Targeting Jewish students for recruitment, dropping "Confederate" from university references to Memorial Hall, moving toward a residential hall system with the construction of a freshman commons, and dismantling the athletic department—these were all early policy decisions initiated by Chancellor Gordon Gee himself to improve the university's ability to compete nationally and internationally. Although many important Vanderbilt supporters disagreed with one or more of his initiatives (not to mention his frenetic, chain-saw, un-southern approach), just as many applauded his efforts—especially years afterward, when the Commons proved to be a resounding success, fraternity and sorority membership remained steady, and the football team won a few more of its games.

While the chancellor may have underestimated the intensity of the resistance, the discontent fomented by those changes in the university's culture was more political than personal in nature. It was the personal that was ultimately to do us both in.

An enemy made through a personal affront—that is, someone who feels in some way personally slighted or disrespected—can be much more vicious than a political adversary, whose focus is on a public point of disagreement. A university board can become a Guatemalan snake pit if two or three key trustees believe they have been unjustly treated. A person might never know precisely which snake bit him, only that he has been bitten. That is the viperous nature of palace intrigue: it coils and strikes in the shadows.

17

Dangerous Frenemies

THE US SECURITIES AND EXCHANGE Commission sued
Dollar General Corporation in 2002 for accounting fraud. Fraudu-
lent or improper accounting practices were alleged during the fiscal years 1998–2001 and included (1) intentionally underreporting
at least $10 million in import freight expenses; (2) engaging in an
$11 million sham sale of outdated, essentially worthless cash reg-
isters; (3) overstating cash accounts; (4) manipulating the company's reported earnings; and (5) failing to maintain accurate
books and records, and filing inaccurate financial reports with the
SEC. Dollar General's CEO, Cal Turner Jr., was personally
indicted, as were Dollar General's president, its chief financial officer, and its controller. According to the SEC, the officers "were
motivated in part by a desire to report earnings that met or
exceeded analysts' expectations and to maintain employee
bonuses."[1]

Cal Turner Jr. had taken over as CEO of Dollar General in
1977, following his father, Cal Turner Sr., who had founded the
enterprise in 1939. Cal Turner Jr. was on the Vanderbilt Board of
Trust. The Vanderbilt board's vice chairman, Denny Bottorff, was
on the Dollar General board of directors. Gordon joined the Dollar
General board immediately after arriving at Vanderbilt.

Sitting on corporate boards can be very lucrative. Gordon was
then on the board of five Fortune 500 companies, easily bringing
in $400,000 or more annually in retainer and per–board meeting

payments and stock shares. Gordon considered his board director-ships as a way to sharpen his business acumen and open doors for himself and the university, as well as a sort of "therapy." "The uni-versity can be very isolating," he told a reporter from the *Nashville Scene*. "I get to see how other people do their work, how they attack problems. It's very empowering."[2]

Most universities encourage their presidents to sit on boards, and presidential recruitment packages are often sweetened with the offer of one or more corporate board memberships. Gordon was a director of ASARCO (copper mining) during his University of Colorado tenure. He joined Banc One and The Limited while at Ohio State, Hasbro at Brown, and Dollar General, Gaylord Entertainment, and Massey Energy at Vanderbilt. The *Scene* reported: "The trend toward university presidents sitting on for-profit corporate boards seems to have originated about 25 years ago as presidents became more involved in fundraising. In those two decades a kind of hierarchy had been established. Presidents of Division One research institutions are often invited to join corporate boards of Fortune 500 companies."[3]

Not only do universities actively connect their presidents with corporate boards, but corporations often solicit university presi-dents. "It's easy to see what corporations receive from university presidents: credibility and integrity," the *Scene* article continued. Gordon acknowledged that, as the president of a major university, "he's viewed as independent of the conflicts perhaps tarnishing the reputations of other corporate directors." A university president's role is to serve as a sort of moral compass, "to dress up all the fancy terms like company values and morality and education," in the words of the Vanderbilt philosophy professor John Lachs. "He's an educator and as such he has a special responsibility to teach the fundamental rules of morality."[4]

In April 2001, Dollar General disclosed that its financial state-ments had been wrong for the preceding few years and, as a conse-quence, it had fired its auditor. An SEC investigation was already under way. Dollar General's officers and board knew the commis-sion was preparing to file suit.

The company's market capitalization fell from more than $7.5 billion to roughly $5.2 billion after the announcement of its accounting problems. During the same period, Dollar General shares declined by 13.6 percent, at a time when a stock index composed of retail peers increased by 4.7 percent.[5] Over twenty class-action law suits were swiftly filed against the company. The lawsuits were consolidated into a single action, with the Florida State Board of Administration and the Teachers' Retirement System of Louisiana as lead plaintiffs. The primary allegation was that Cal Turner Jr. and other Dollar General officers and directors had intentionally misrepresented the company's financial results.[6]

Turner received an $800,000 bonus for FY2001—the maximum amount allowed by the company's bylaws. About the same time Cal received his bonus, Dollar General agreed to pay $162 million in damages to the plaintiffs of the class-action suit. That "scandal-plagued year," as Nashville Post.com described it, was the year "in which his company disclosed possibly the most damaging accounting scandal the city has ever seen."[7]

Gordon, Denny Bottorff, David Wilds, and one other man constituted the executive compensation committee that awarded Turner the bonus. Denny and Cal were close pals. David Wilds and Cal had been fraternity brothers at Vanderbilt. Wilds was Cal's trusted adviser and the CEO of the Family Office, an investment firm owned by the Turner family, which managed a sizable portion of the family's wealth. While such intertwinement might seem ethically problematic to the naïve outsider, it doesn't seem to raise an eyebrow in the corporate world.

As a board newcomer, Gordon was asked to chair an ad hoc shareholders committee. Gordon explained to me that the board formed the shareholders committee to review the company officers' actions relative to the SEC investigation. The committee was charged with determining what had happened and who had known and approved of the alleged financial improprieties.

SEC investigations take a long time, and so it was with the Dollar General case. Gordon told me that over the next four years, he and Dollar General's lawyers did everything they could to protect their CEO. However, the shareholders committee's primary responsibility was to the shareholders, just as the responsibility of Dollar General's lawyers was to the company. Gordon said that the more he and the committee learned, the clearer the merits of the SEC's allegations became. There was no getting around it. The best way to save Cal from the distinct possibility of felonious prosecution and to shore up the integrity and worth of the company was to order him to step down as CEO and force him off the Dollar General board. It fell to Gordon, as the shareholders committee chairman, to deliver that message to Cal. Turner resigned as CEO in November 2002 and left the board chairmanship in June 2003.

The suit was settled by an SEC enforcement action on 7 April 2005. Dollar General and all four indicted officers pleaded *nolo contendere* (no contest)—that is, without their admitting or denying the SEC's findings, fines would be paid and stipulations against any future service as corporation officers or corporate board members would be accepted. (Good luck, naïve outsider, on understanding the ethical justifications for the "neither admit nor deny" legal fiction used so frequently by the SEC and other government agencies.) Under the agreement, Turner, who had remained connected to the board in an advisory capacity, now had to sever all ties with the company his father had founded. Dollar General and Turner paid civil penalties of $10 million and $1 million, respectively.

Both at the time of the SEC–Dollar General settlement and again years later, Gordon told me that he had been "enormously relieved" at the conditions of the settlement and relatively lenient penalties. He felt that, as chairman of the shareholders committee, he had done a good job for the company and for all concerned. Cal Turner Jr. could well have ended up "in the hoosegow."

Turner, however, did not appear to view his forced retirement from the family business in such a positive light. Although Turner did not directly confront him, Gordon would hear "from a lot of people, including John Hall, that Cal was enormously angry over the way things were handled"—more specifically with the way *Gordon* had handled things. "My position as chancellor of Vanderbilt made me a target," he surmised, when I asked why Cal would blame him above other shareholders committee members. It seemed that Turner, a fundamentalist Christian, did not embrace the university chancellor's interpretation of "the fundamental rules of morality" as they applied to corporate governance. Years later, Gordon observed, "It was a classic case of shooting the messenger."[8]

If there were any other way around this part of the story, I would gladly take it. I believe that indiscretions of the heart (and loins) between two consenting adults should remain private affairs. (The exception to my thinking on this is loin-based indiscretions perpetrated by preachers and politicians who proselytize about family values.) Unfortunately, the rumor of this particular alleged indiscretion is germane to later events.

In 2004, Martha Ingram announced that she was ready to step down as the chairman of Vanderbilt's Board of Trust. Gordon said that he, along with most of the board, assumed Vice Chairman Denny Bottorff would succeed her. Gordon told me that the Vanderbilt trustee Monroe Carell came to his office the day after Martha's announcement to deliver a message on behalf of a determined segment of the board. Monroe told Gordon that *Denny must not be allowed to succeed Martha as board chairman.*

According to Gordon, Monroe related the rumor that Denny had been having an affair with the much younger wife of a federal judge who resided in Nashville. This was not the first time Gordon had heard the rumor. I had told him about it several weeks earlier, after hearing a lengthy recitation of the alleged affair by a gaggle of shoppers and sales clerks at a local clothing boutique.

Monroe warned Gordon that there would be a bitterly divisive board battle if the possibility of Denny's assuming the chairmanship proceeded further. Gordon asked Martha if she would continue as chairman, thereby avoiding the question of who would be named as her successor. She agreed, and the rest of the board concurred.

Gordon said he believed that Denny long held a grudge against him for his support of Monroe's position and his subsequent role in Denny's not being allowed to assume the Vanderbilt chairmanship. Gordon's constituency of seriously offended trustees, or "restive trustees," as the *Wall Street Journal* would later characterize them, was growing. And two of them were tight as ticks.

18

Faux Pas and Politics: Hers

GORDON WAS NOT THE ONLY ONE accumulating enemies along the way. I dug a hole for myself our first year at Vanderbilt that I was never able to climb out of. My resentment at our Providence exodus and my depression about having to start all over again at another university slopped over onto my personal assistant, who worked directly under Gordon's chief of staff, two or three other staff members with whom we worked closely, and, Lord knows, more than a few other innocents I happened to bump up against. I felt beleaguered with demands and expectations, although I have come to understand that I, not others, am the most demanding critic of Constance Gee.

Gordon's extended office was like a harem. A dozen or so females did whatever he needed doing. The only male in the chancellor's office other than The Bow-Tied One himself was the tech support guy.

"You can't deny your polygamous persuasions," I would joke. "You have Office Manager Wife, Assistant Office Manager Wife, Appointment and Travel Scheduling Wife, Board Liaison Wife, Events Planning Wife, Filing Wife, Phone Answering Wife, and Miscellaneous Wife at your office alone. At Braeburn there's House Manager Wife, Chef Wife, and the Keep Everything Spotless Wives. I suppose I can live with it, as long as I get to be Credit Card Wife."

Don't get me wrong: I like other humans of my gender. In fact, in most well-lighted circumstances, I prefer the company of women (and gay men) to that of the straight, sports-obsessed male. I have extremely limited tolerance (0.5 on the Lizzie Borden–Mahatma Gandhi Patience Continuum) for the macho man. Let's face it: a landslide majority of one gender of humanoids, female or male, makes for an icky environment. Too many females, and things get petty and bitchy. (There's even the small fact that when women spend a great deal of time together their monthly cycles merge.) Too many males, and it's a world of odoriferous one-upmanship. I am not making this point as an excuse for my bad behavior (there were instances when Gandhi *should* have smacked me), but in a harem, when Wife #1 has a meltdown, or even a little frisson, it's everybody's business.

Perhaps it would have been a better strategy to have taken my sister wives to a two-martini lunch once a month, but I did my best to stay physically out of Gordon's office. The place I couldn't avoid was Braeburn. And the person I most clashed with, but could never get rid of, was House Manager Wife.

***

We hired House Manager Wife upon moving into Braeburn. She seemed nice enough at first, but it soon became apparent that she was massively passive-aggressive. She would sit for hours in her office off the family kitchen typing detailed memoranda into her computer. She was extremely sensitive to any brusque word or perceived personal slight from Chef Bunny or me. The housekeepers dared not cross her. Everyone, myself included, tried to steer clear of her, yet she always seemed to be lurking within earshot. There was the ever-present, burdensome feeling that she was watching, judging, and keeping score. "She's always trying to find something to make me look bad," Bunny complained. I knew exactly how she felt.

House Manager Wife habitually showed up for work one or two hours late and went AWOL in the afternoon, expecting Bunny or one of the housekeepers to meet with repairmen or accept deliveries. She was lenient with herself but strict with those who reported to her. She fawned over people she deemed important but was rudely dismissive of those she considered inferior. "You two.

Wait outside!" she once ordered two Vanderbilt employees who had accompanied their department director on an errand to Braeburn. Descriptions of such incidents would regularly trickle back to me through residence and catering staff.

I was told by one of the housekeepers that House Manager Wife bought a set of lower-thread-count bed linens for guests she did not consider worthy of the good sheets. I was not surprised to learn that many of my personal guests slept on the cheap sheets.

House Manager Wife actually presented my friend Diane with a detailed memo scolding her for having put her "bloody underwear" in a plastic bin under the Acorn Suite bathroom sink. Diane was the artist who inlaid the garden fountain with colorful mosaic tiles and blown-glass rosettes at my and Gordon's personal request and commission. It was a bear of a job, as the fountain was ten feet in diameter and she didn't get started on the project until early June. We had only just moved into Braeburn.

Diane would work in the morning, take a break during the heat of the day, and put in two or three more hours in the early evening. It took her over two months to complete the project, during which she stayed at the residence. Things were going fairly well until I left for Westport in July, leaving Diane to fend for herself with House Manager Wife. "When you left," Diane said, "my status dropped from artist and friend to manual laborer."

Diane had tried her best to hand scrub a pair of panties that had suffered an unexpected and forceful "visit" from the monthly curse. She hung them to dry in the bathtub and went back to work. A housekeeper came out to the fountain to inform her that a plumber was being sent up to the Acorn Suite to fix a leak in the tub shower, so Diane rushed upstairs, tossed her underwear in a plastic container, and stashed it under the sink. Later that day, another housekeeper discovered the underwear and apparently reported it to the house manager. The house manager promptly sat down and wrote Diane a page-long memo on how she should not expect the housekeepers to deal with her bloody underwear, including instructions on how she should handle future laundry emergencies. Diane completed the fountain, departed Braeburn, and never again came to visit me there.

My dear friend Morgan was diagnosed with lung cancer in the fall of 2001. Morgan lived alone in St. Croix and was terribly worried about the quality of the medical care available to her on the island. Gordon kindly arranged for her to have her surgery at the Vanderbilt Medical Center, after which she stayed with us during her monthlong convalescence. Morgan is a stubbornly independent soul, so she was up and about the moment she was able, insisting on doing her own laundry and tidying her room. One afternoon, Morgan was struggling to put on a pair of tights, lost her balance, and put her foot through the top of a rather fragile red leather trunk that served as a sofa table in the Acorn Suite. Horrified, she immediately went to the house manager to report the accident and offer to pay for its repair. The house manager proceeded to tell my friend what a valuable piece of furniture she had destroyed. When I arrived home from work that evening, Morgan showed me the trunk, apologized profusely, and reiterated her offer to pay for it.

"[The house manager] said it was an antique," she ended glumly.

"Oh, please," I said. "It came from Pier 1. Don't worry about it!"

It didn't actually come from Pier 1. It was an antique of sorts, although I don't know how terribly valuable it was. But really—to take someone to task who is recovering from cancer surgery?

When Morgan returned for her six-month checkup at the medical center, she refused to stay at Braeburn. My dear friend of twenty-five years insisted that she would rather stay at a motel than subject herself to the one who considered herself "Queen of the House."

"She was so unpleasant to be around," Morgan said years later. "I don't know how you stood it for so long."

House Manager Wife and I did not get along. I wanted her transferred to another universe, or at least a different part of the university, and I pleaded with Gordon to make that happen. He replied that he couldn't just let someone go for no good reason, that a substantial file would need to be built against her.

Who had the time to meticulously build a file documenting her habitual morning tardiness, afternoon hiatuses, and bullying nature? No one who witnessed or bore the brunt of it, I argued.

He questioned the need for her dismissal, discounting my criticisms. The subject annoyed him. He was tired of hearing about it, since he heard it from a few other women on his staff besides me. "Can't you all just get along?" he'd groan. She was, of course, sweet as Karo syrup to him and ingratiated herself with Rebekah, his sister and brother-in-law, and key university people.

House Manager Wife knew how I felt about her. This was a humongous tactical error on my part. I am bored by, and therefore lousy at, the maneuvering and manipulation required to play, much less win, the passive-aggressive game. I like to know when someone is irked with me right then and there. Certainly, I bestow that favor on others. My philosophy is, Let's have it out and move on. But in a harem, I learned too late, to be passive-aggressive is a much wiser and more effective strategy.

***

One of my father's favorite jokes pretty much summed up the different worldviews and gender expectations between the North and South, as he saw it several decades ago. Yes, I know attitudes have changed in Dixie, but there's still a mighty sizable kernel of truth here:

The northern girl says, "Men are all alike."

The southern girl says, "Men are all *ah* like, too!"

Southern men continue to take comfort in that story line, and smart southern women are not about to dissuade them from believing in its absolute veracity. While women's subversive manipulation of men (as opposed to men's overt manipulation of women) is universal, in the South it is an intricate art form requiring great skill, passed on from mother to daughter, and aided and abetted by doting daddies. As helpful as comeliness is to this time-honored art (hence facelifts and knowing your color palette), *charm* is a girl's most valuable tool. Southern men just *love* thinking southern women feel the world revolves around them. And we do, boys. We truly do.

Charm is rarely direct, always smiles (except when it is prettily but briefly pouty), and never, ever intimidates. Charm minds its manners.

I think it's fair to say that, generally speaking, women are more attracted to smart men than men are to smart women. Tina Turner sings, "I'm a fool for a man with a clever mind." One can hardly imagine Barry White having sung, "I'm a fool for a woman with a clever mind." Although a woman has to be reasonably smart to be

234

charming, if she is *really* smart she'll play it as if she isn't. Intelligent women—most especially *intellectual* women—can be intimidating to the typical male. In the South especially, that's not considered good manners.

***

I feel certain that my friend Annabelle would back me up on the essential link between a southern woman's power and her charm. Annabelle is the Queen of Southern Charm. She is still beautiful, even now in her early eighties, with the best bone structure imaginable and no nips or tucks (to speak of). Born and bred in high-society Nashville, she is highly intelligent, a gifted visual artist, and as willful as they come. Annabelle *owns* the rules and tools of southern womanhood. She was suckled on them at her mother's breast, honing her powers to Olympic-gold-medal level as a young girl on her daddy's knee. Her perspective is informed and informative.

Annabelle's daddy insisted she attend college at Sweet Briar. She insisted on going to Barnard. Up in the Northeast, for the first time in her life she experienced difficulty "man"-euvering: those Columbia boys didn't play by the southern code. She wasn't fluent in theirs, either. Both sexes, you see, must be complicit for the code to work.

Even as she acknowledges the fundamental dishonesty of the arrangement, she readily admits to having grown up regularly using her feminine wiles to wield influence and get her way. "Those were the recognized weapons," she says. "We were brought up using them; we *enjoyed* using them."

Annabelle has tried her best to impart those sacred skills to me, but feels she has largely failed. "You have never listened to me," she says.

"That is patently untrue," I reply every time. (We have had this conversation on several occasions over the course of the past decade.) "I have taken your advice and modified my behavior in many instances. You can be certain it would have been much worse had I not."

At this point in the conversation, she levels her gaze at me and exhales, "Heavens."

I fear she has begun to doubt my educability. She strongly advised me not to write this book.

Annabelle would never take a confrontational stand on politics outside a small gathering of intimate friends. She has probably rarely felt a need to do that, as most of her closest friends are, like her, fairly liberal Democrats (by southern standards, anyway). She would "nevva evva" take a political stand publicly in opposition to her husband.

***

I discovered during the 2004 presidential campaign that simply making a donation to a political candidate of the Democratic persuasion—if you are married to the chancellor of Vanderbilt University—is a newsworthy act of charmless, ill-mannered defiance. Signing a letter protesting your husband's politically inspired choice for a public service award is an act of outright treason. It is treasonous to your husband, to the university, to the president of the United States (and, by extension, the entire country), and, most egregiously, to those who espouse the southern code of acceptable female behavior.

I'll begin with the newsworthy act of defiance.

I very much wanted Howard Dean to win the Democratic nomination for president (when he let loose with his now infamous primary-victory scream, I felt like screaming right along with him). So I did what millions of Americans do—I made a campaign donation. On 22 April, the *Nashville Scene* published an article titled "Deep Pockets."[1] Campaign finance records, the author reported, could be accessed easily on the website Fundrace 2004, an entertaining way to pass the time and find out which presidential candidate your favorite Music Row star is supporting. (My wild guess for most of the denizens of Music Row was George W. Bush.)

The article was graced with a sizable photograph of Gordon and me dressed for a white-tie affair and smiling into the camera. The photo caption read: "An Errant Political Giver—Unlike other prominent Vanderbilt officials who made political donations to W., Constance Gee supported Democrat Howard Dean."

The first bulleted sampling of the article's Fundrace findings noted that: "Vanderbilt is Bush Country. . . . One exception to this rule was Constance Gee, wife of Chancellor Gordon Gee, who

236

gave $800 to Howard Dean." The only other person listed as a Dean supporter was a (now former) school board member who contributed $250 to his campaign. Bush raked in the lion's share of notable Nashville dinero, including $16,000 from eight members of the Frist family, $1,000 from Vice Chancellor Michael Schoenfeld, and $2,000 from a school bus driver. ("There's just got to be more to that story," the author commented.)

Anyone who had any question about my political leanings now had their answer: screaming left.

***

Earlier that spring, Gordon and I had several . . . well, let's say *intense* discussions about his invitation to Condoleezza Rice to be the Senior Day speaker for the upcoming commencement. I had vigorously opposed the Bush administration's "preemptive" strike on Iraq and our entry into an unnecessary war. In fact, I opposed most of the Bush administration's policies—a disposition my husband was well aware of and one that was causing a prickly rash of marital discord.

Since arriving at Vanderbilt, Gordon had become increasingly conservative in his political and social views, and had taken to repeating good-ol'-boy idiocies like "You can tell who wears the pants in that family!" He meant, of course, the person who should be wearing the modest floral print dress. This was not the man I thought I had married.

I was annoyed that he had chosen to provide the Bush administration a forum at the Vanderbilt commencement, but I did not say anything about it to anyone but him. Rice was, after all, National Security Adviser; it is a coup for a university to have the National Security Adviser speak at its commencement, regardless of her political party affiliation. That I clearly understood. I also understood how very pleased most of the Board of Trust must have been that W. and Condi knew Vanderbilt was "Bush Country" and was rewarding the university with a high-profile visit.

I found out several weeks later—not from my husband, but from a fellow faculty member seated next to me at the spring Board of Trust luncheon—that Gordon had just announced that Rice would be awarded Vanderbilt's first-ever Chancellor's Medal for Distinguished Public Service. I was furious about the award and hurt that Gordon had not told me about it himself. He said that he knew what my reaction would be and that he didn't want to hear it.

I felt strongly that Rice was not deserving of such an honor. She had been the provost of Stanford, a private university, prior to joining the Bush administration. What "distinguished" public service had she provided other than helping fabricate the lies that had given Bush an excuse to invade Iraq? Gordon and I exchanged angry words over the issue later that evening en route to a board event. But what was done, was done, so I knew I had to set it aside.

On the first of May, an acquaintance forwarded me a letter, addressed to Chancellor Gordon Gee, protesting the public service award. I joined several hundred others in signing it. The letter read:

> As members of the Vanderbilt community (faculty, staff, and students), we wish to express our dismay over the inappropriate and incomprehensible selection of Dr. Rice for your Public Service award.
>
> We recognize that a university should encourage an open exchange of ideas, and we would have no objection to Dr. Rice participating in a balanced panel discussion of current events. However, the decision to honor her with this award goes far beyond offering her a platform to express her viewpoint. Intentionally or not, it offers the university's good name as an endorsement of her actions at a time when many thoughtful people are questioning the effect of those actions on our nation's security and on the welfare of the people of the world.
>
> This event runs the risk of simply serving as PR for the current administration's efforts to portray their doctrines in a favorable light. Furthermore, we believe that many of Dr. Rice's doctrines and actions are contrary to the principles of Vanderbilt University. We are proud of the number of countries represented in our student body, yet Dr. Rice is contemptuous of international organizations and international law. We expect our university to teach students respect for the truth, yet we offer an honor to

a person who repeatedly misrepresented the truth to tragic effect.

Finally, we wish to express our opinion that there are hundreds of persons more deserving of a Public Service award. Dr. Rice's primary service has been to a narrow ideology that benefits a small segment of society rather than the welfare of all. As members of the university community we have all devoted time and effort to making Vanderbilt a better school. Now we stand ashamed and angry that our goodwill is being abused by the honoring of Dr. Rice. We feel compelled to state: Not in our name!

I showed Gordon the letter and told him I had signed it. I signed Lucy's name to another copy. Several of the residence staff also signed copies. I taped all the copies to the refrigerator door.

When Gordon saw the posted protest letters that evening, instead of being upset with me about it, we had a good laugh. The letter provided me with an outlet. Lucy's conscription to the cause provided some sorely needed levity, allowing the tension between us on this issue to dissipate somewhat. It helps so much when two people can laugh together.

I left to spend the weekend in Monteagle, as Gordon was to be away on business. On Monday Gordon telephoned to tell me that one of the protest organizers had told a news reporter I had signed the letter.

Gordon was now suddenly enraged at my having added my signature, saying that I had allowed myself to be used by unscrupulous people who wanted to gain media attention. "More importantly," he yelled into the phone, "*you have jeopardized my career!*"

He told me that the Vanderbilt board was going to fire him over "this stupidity." I thought he was overreacting terribly, but I could hear the genuine fear in his voice.

"*Fire* you? Why would they fire you?" I asked.

"You have embarrassed the university," he said.

His alarm and his certainty of the board's retribution really frightened me. I apologized for the damage I had caused him professionally and the hurt I had caused him personally. "I'm so sorry, Gordon, I am truly so sorry," I cried.

The chancellor's office public relations team, led by Vice Chancellor Schoenfeld, handled the incident by portraying Gordon as a broad-minded guy who had no problem with differences of political opinion and stood by his wife's right to express hers. He was the chancellor of a great university; universities encourage the exploration and expression of ideas, a value he championed at home as well as on campus—or so the story went.

I spoke to a reporter at the *Tennessean*, backing up the university's public statement and its portrayal of my husband. It was a very different story on the home front. My husband was decidedly *not* happy about his wife's political opinions or her proclivity to express them.

Gordon came out smelling like a rose. He actually gained in popularity, receiving supportive emails, letters, and pats on the back from conservatives and liberals alike. Vanderbilt gained in stature as well, publicly shedding some of its conservative Old South reputation.

On the other hand, I was not treated well in the press, and I received several hate letters and numerous nasty emails. The vitriol genuinely surprised me. Perhaps I had lived too long in the North, where politically errant wives and liberals are not as rare or threatening.

Gordon seemed almost pleased over the uproar once it had subsided and he realized he had come out of it looking good. He had my signed protest letter framed and hung in the upstairs hallway alongside our other family memorabilia.

I was relieved for him and for us, but I knew I had paid a high price for my actions. I was keenly aware that Gordon had chosen to distance himself from me early in the crisis. I was beginning to grasp that under threat he might well jettison me to save himself. That scared me. I hunkered down for a long while after that, keeping my contrary opinions to myself.

19

Down the Rabbit Hole

A THUNDERSTORM CRASHED INTO MONTEAGLE in the early hours of Saturday, 30 October 2004. A bolt of lightning exploded down the cliff just off the back of our house. I jerked upright in bed. Lucy pressed against me, panting heavily. I rubbed my left ear. An uncomfortable feeling of pressure and the sound of static began deep in my ear canal. I moved my jaw side to side, up and down, yawning wide trying to clear my ear. I held my nose and blew. The hissing and pressure would not budge. I finally fell back into an uneasy sleep as the storm moved past the mountain.

Friday had been the perfect Tennessee autumn day, clear and warm. That morning Lucy and I had taken a two-hour hike on a section of the University of the South's Perimeter Trail in nearby Sewanee. The trail follows the bluff line for a twenty-mile loop of spectacular views of forest and farmland, waterfalls and wild-flowers. It had been a particularly lusty hike. All my senses had seemed heightened, and I distinctly remember reveling in the agility of my body as Lucy and I strode surefootedly along an overhang, traipsed through a deep green tunnel of mountain laurel, and scampered over the moss-covered rocks of a pristine stream.

I showered upon our return and hauled an exercise mat onto the back deck to stretch and let the breeze dry my hair. In Downward-Facing Dog pose, with the overturned V my body formed, I dangled my head, looking upside down and backward through my legs across the miles of deep-green ridges and blue sky—now magically transformed into clear blue sea and green sky.

Gordon was at a conference that weekend, so I had invited some friends up to join me for an overnight stay. Cowboy Jack Clement and Aleene Jackson had driven from Nashville, and Walter and Kitty Forbes from Chattanooga. They had arrived in the early afternoon and stayed for supper, and they were now sleeping downstairs. Cowboy had brought his guitar and mandolin; Walter brought his banjo. They had serenaded the ladies out on the deck before supper, and afterward around the fireplace inside the screened porch.

I have a treasured snapshot of that musical afternoon out on the deck. Aleene smiles while gazing dreamily at the mountains. Kitty sings along, eyes closed, resting her head against the back of the rocking chair. Walter's mouth is set just so, concentrating on a complicated banjo passage. Cowboy, wearing one of his signature tropical shirts, smiles at me as he sings. Perfectly coiffed Lucy is stretched out sphinxlike in the midst of it all, effortlessly reigning as best bred and most dignified.

Unable to sleep, I was the first up that morning. My hearing was distorted. The clank of dishes as I placed them in the cupboard reverberated strangely. Lower-range noises seemed muffled, while Lucy's bark to be let outside bounced around uncomfortably inside my left ear.

Kitty and I cut short an after-breakfast hike; I couldn't sort out her words from the crackling of the dry leaves underfoot, which distressed me. Cowboy and Walter were playing music when we returned. The trebly sound of the banjo, which had been such a delight the night before, was painful to me. The hissing static and pressure in my ear did not abate that day or the next or the next.

I made an appointment for that Tuesday, Election Day, at the Vanderbilt Otolaryngology Clinic. Before going in for testing, I drove to the Belle Meade city hall and voted for Senator John Kerry for president of the United States.

***

My ear was tormenting me as I watched the election returns at the home of two close friends, along with ten other fellow Democrats. A little wine and a good supper helped to alleviate my anxiety and elevate my mood. Gordon had stopped in earlier, but he departed after a few minutes, joking that he didn't want to be associated with such blatant liberals on election night. The election appeared to be going in Kerry's favor until about ten o'clock, when George W. Bush began to rapidly pick up votes.

As I drove into our driveway close to midnight, I was more anxious than ever about my ear now that the effects of the wine had worn off. The American flag fluttering in the wind atop the tall flagpole in front of Braeburn caught my attention. I was terribly despondent over the election. I knew Bush was going to take it. Tears came to my eyes as I thought about what four more years of George W. would mean for the world. I opened the car door, walked over to the flagpole, and lowered the flag to half-staff.

Gordon noticed the flag the next day when he went out to get the newspapers. He found the gesture amusing—so much so that he mentioned it to several members of his office staff early that morning. (Gordon generally appreciated my off-kilter humor and was correct in his supposition—my lowering of the flag had been done both in sadness and in satire.) Lauren Brisky, the vice chancellor of finance, promptly telephoned the residence and told the housekeeper to raise the flag.

I soon noticed the flag was back at full-staff and went downstairs to inquire who had done it. House Manager Wife curtly informed me that Brisky had ordered the flag to be raised and that she would call Brisky if I tried to lower it again. Now irritated both at the decree and by the "or else" tone of its delivery, I telephoned Gordon. He did not sound particularly concerned about the matter, but he said Brisky had rushed into his office upon hearing the news (from one of his office staff, he surmised), exclaiming to him that the flag had to be raised *immediately*! "We would not want the press to get hold of that!" she declared.

The entire incident—from Gordon's chuckling about it with a few people in his office to the housekeeper raising the flag—had occurred in the space of an hour. Very soon, the press *would* get hold of it. The *Nashville Scene* deemed it worthy of this snarky, factually incorrect rendering:

> [Constance] Gee ordered her staff to lower the Ameri-
> can flag to half-mast. . . . When the help expressed

unease about complying with this unusual request, [she] simply lowered it herself. Later, sources tell the Scene, a concerned Lauren Brisky, Vanderbilt's vice chancellor for administration and the school's chief financial officer, alerted Chancellor Gee to his wife's bizarre form of political expression. Shortly after, in what had to be a husband and wife conversation for the ages, the chancellor called Constance and told her to raise the flag back to its original height. She did.[1]

This wasn't "the first time the first lady has acted out," *Scene* readers were reminded. "Last May, Constance Gee openly protested her husband's decision to invite national security advisor Condoleezza Rice to speak to Vanderbilt's graduating class."

Wrong again, alert reporter. I did not openly protest my husband's decision to invite Condoleezza Rice to speak at graduation. I protested his decision to give her a medal for distinguished public service and was well within my rights to do so.

I quickly came to understand that it was *not* my right to lower Old Glory—at least not the Old Glory that waved outside the Vanderbilt chancellor's residence. That particular flag was university owned and operated; for me to lower it in personal exasperation was inappropriate. The American flag, I learned, is to be lowered to half-staff only at specifically decreed state occasions, such as Memorial Day or the death of an important government official— not at the death of highly subjective abstract entities such as good government and judicious international policy.

***

I returned to the otolaryngology clinic that Thursday for more testing. By then I was very anxious. The pressure and noise in my ear and the painful hearing distortions were terribly distressing. I had also begun to feel dizzy and nauseated.

The doctors concluded that I most likely had something called Ménière's disease. My symptoms were classic: aural pressure (similar to not being able to clear your ears in a plane during take-off and landing), tinnitus (ringing, roaring, or other noises in the ear), low-frequency hearing loss, and dizziness.

"Why?" I implored. "What causes Ménière's?"

I recounted the night of the electrical storm. Was I somehow indirectly struck by lightning? I had been having a slight, allergy-related sinus problem. Could that have contributed? The otolaryngologist said allergies might have played a role, but he seemed skeptical about my lightning theory.

"Did you have frequent ear infections when you were a child?" he asked.

Yes, I often had earaches when I was young, usually in my left ear. I had severe asthma attacks, which I eventually "outgrew," as they say, and I remember my mother giving me little yellow allergy pills throughout much of elementary school. My father smoked cigarettes, but that was long before anyone gave any thought to the effects of secondhand smoke, especially on young children—not that it would have made any difference. (I still find it amazing that any of us born in the 1950s made it into adulthood healthy and semi-sane, what with all that riding around in smoke-filled cars without seatbelts, and crouching under our little wooden one-armed school desks with our heads between our knees during nuclear bomb drills. Really, what the hell was up with *that*?)

"Do you get motion sickness?"

Yes, all my life, although not as much now as when I was a child. When I was very young, it was not unusual during the fifteen-minute drive to downtown for my mother to have to pull over to the side of the road for me to throw up. I learned early to avoid play-ground equipment that spun around, and friends banned me from joining them on the Tilt-a-Whirl. I once barfed all over my uncle Gene's Cessna four-seater during a flight from Wichita to Salina. He had commanded me to drink a glass of milk at lunch, before the flight. I think my mother was secretly pleased—not at my distress, but because he'd been such a bully about it. That was the last time anyone made me eat or drink anything.

Although I was to learn much more about Ménière's over the next few years, that day I was informed that research indicated it might come about as a result of childhood ear infections caused by allergies, a virus that had found its way into the inner ear, a hereditary predisposition to vestibular imbalance, or a combination thereof. While its underlying cause in most people is unknown, there is general agreement that an excess of endolymph, the fluid contained in the membranous labyrinth of the inner ear, brings on Ménière's symptoms.

The doctor explained that endolymph is normally secreted when one is awake and reabsorbed during sleep, a regular flow and ebb, like the ocean tide. Whether or not my left inner ear was producing too much or absorbing too little endolymph, the result was the same. The excess fluid in my inner ear was making it feel "full," causing the tinnitus and hearing distortion, and making it seem as if the entire world were swaying slightly. There is no cure, I was informed, but the symptoms can usually be managed with a low-sodium diet and oral medications. It is important to avoid emotional stress and fatigue—although Ménière's itself *causes* anxiety, stress, and fatigue.

I was immediately placed on a diuretic to reduce my body fluid volume, and on a kick-ass, three-week dose of the steroid dexamethasone. Steroids are prescribed to Ménière's patients to address any inflammatory reaction a suspected virus may be causing. Decreasing inflammation increases blood flow, which theoretically helps stimulate the absorption and reduce the production of endolymph.

I was told to adhere to a low-salt diet, because salt causes fluid retention. Also, no alcohol or tobacco; nicotine and alcohol reduce the blood supply to the inner ear, and poor circulation reduces the absorption of endolymph. And no caffeinated beverages or chocolate (which contains caffeine), because caffeine may make the tinnitus louder and can induce the constriction of blood vessels in the inner ear, thereby reducing blood flow. Thank goodness I didn't smoke. At least I was doing one thing right.

Switching from regular to decaf coffee and not drinking wine were bad enough, but giving up salty food? Tell me it ain't so! I loved salt. When I was five or six, my mother caught me drinking the dill pickle juice straight from the jar. I preferred green olive juice but had already polished that off. I once joked to a friend of mine, who provided salt licks for the deer that frequented his back acreage, that I had installed my very own lick alongside my kitchen table. Take a bite of food, take a lick of salt—the perfect seasoning for any dish.

I began the prescribed diet and drug regimen, praying for relief, while all the time thinking back over anything and everything I had done or that had happened to me that might have brought on this misery. Surely there was something that had caused it and, if it could be named, then there would be some way to fix it. I had never before had an illness that couldn't be remedied with medicine or a medical procedure, a brief rest, or a change of diet. There *had* to be a reason, and there had to be something a doctor or I could do to fix it.

The previous June I had found a tick attached to my stomach after I had wandered about half lost on some overgrown trails in an isolated section of state forest south of Sewanee. I had also spent July and August in Westport, only a two-hour drive northeast of Lyme, Connecticut. The town of Lyme was where a cluster of cases of the tick-borne infection Lyme disease was first identified in 1975. Everyone in southern New England knows someone who has contracted Lyme.

Could I have Lyme and, if so, might it have caused the Ménière's? I almost wanted to have Lyme, even though it is an awful disease to get. At least then I could point my finger at a culprit.

As it turned out, I tested positive. An infectious-disease specialist at Vanderbilt prescribed a month of daily intravenous antibiotics, which I began immediately. Despite the test results, he seemed to have doubts. But he was dealing with the wife of the chancellor, and both the chancellor and his wife wanted things to *get back to normal*, so he hopped on it. In the meantime he ordered a second test, the more reliable Western blot test, the results of which were deemed inconclusive because the blood sample had been contaminated. A second Western blot test was administered and sent to a Lyme specialist at Massachusetts General Hospital to interpret. The specialist determined that I did not have Lyme disease.

At that point I was twenty-two days into the intravenous treatment. I had refused to have an IV port installed, so I suffered through the daily insertion of the IV needle—often not successful on the first try—rotating from left to right arm, to wrists, to the backs of my hands. In my mind, a port indicated a serious chronic illness. Almost all my fellow patients in the IV clinic had ports. Most of them were being treated for rheumatoid arthritis or some other autoimmune disease. I winced each time I saw one of them draw back her blouse to give the nurse access to the port embedded under her clavicle.

I immediately stopped the IV treatments, grateful that I, unlike the increasingly familiar people around me, had that option. I had Ménière's, not Lyme, and what could be done was being done, I was told.

All the while, the aural pressure and tinnitus intensified. I remember staggering up to our bedroom one evening after hosting a large dinner party at Braeburn. I felt as if my head were going to explode. The tinnitus had dialed up from the sound that accompanied a test pattern on 1950s television to a Niagara Falls roar. I held my head and wailed, *"When will this stop? Will it ever stop?"*

Gordon grabbed me and put his hand over my mouth. "Be quiet! They'll hear you!"

"They," of course, were the university catering waitstaff and residence housekeepers cleaning up on the first floor. A "they" of one composition or another—house manager, chef, caterers, waiters, housekeepers—was almost always somewhere in the residence.

He looked at me as if I were mad, as if it had just dawned on him how out of control and dangerous a crazy wife could be. I saw that assessment in his expression, in the fear in his eyes. For a moment, I saw myself exactly as he did, and it scared me, too. I sank to the floor sobbing. Gordon retreated to his dressing room.

I sat on the floor and cried a while longer, then undressed, washed my face, took a sleeping pill, and went to bed. Unconscious was good.

***

Gordon and I flew to Beaver Creek, Colorado (elevation eight thousand feet), the first weekend of February 2005 to visit some Nashville friends at their vacation home and to celebrate Gordon's sixty-first birthday. I had my first attack of vertigo the first night we were there. It was horrendous. I began hyperventilating in panic. My arms and legs went numb. I thought I was having a heart attack.

The following morning Gordon contacted our family physician, who called in a prescription for Valium and Antivert. I later read that antivertigo medications, including meclizine (Antivert), diazepam (Valium), and alprazolam (Xanax), are used to suppress the inner ear's balance function. Although it seems counterintuitive to suppress vestibular function if one is dizzy, the object is to dull the inner ear's ability to sense motion, thereby slowing down the spiraling vestibular response and blocking messages to the part of the brain that controls nausea and vertigo.

I remained very dizzy throughout the weekend but did not have another all-out vertigo attack. I was relieved to get back home and closer to sea level, where I hoped I would return to normal, or what "normal" had become since October. As maddening as the unrelenting tinnitus and aural pressure were, the vertigo was incapacitating.

I began to feel better soon after our return to Nashville. I found that, after the first vertigo attack, the pressure in my ear leveled off a bit, which also eased the tinnitus. Then everything caved in.

The vertigo overtook me almost daily. Sometimes I awoke in the middle of the night with my ear screaming and everything spinning around and around. It amazed me that the centrifugal force didn't sling Gordon out of bed. The attacks came as I was washing my face or applying makeup in the morning or evening, or when I was working at my computer while reading from several documents on my desk. Those activities require head movement and a shift of eye focus from close up to farther away, up and down and side to side.

I tried doing everything in slow motion, but invariably the room would make a quick zigzag, appearing for a split second like a cubist painting. Within a few minutes, I would be vomiting, face down, on the floor. These wipeouts are known as "drop attacks" in Ménière's parlance. The intensity of the pressure and tinnitus would decrease after the drop attack and then build back up over the next few hours. I came to know when an attack was pending. The tinnitus would reach a teakettle-pitched crescendo several minutes before the chronologically reversed, analytic cubism to post-impressionism art history experience—Georges Braque to "The Starry Nightmare."

On weekdays, I was extremely fortunate to have a residence staff member check on me when people knew I was having an attack. Afterward someone would help me to bed and bring a glass of water and some pharmaceuticals. While I slept, one of the housekeepers would mop the bathroom floor or do damage control on the unlucky carpet. (Making it to one's own bathroom to vomit is the only measure of dignity to which one can aspire during the ferocity of a drop attack. I made it most of the time.) After a few hours of drugged unconsciousness, I would awaken groggy and dehydrated. Nurse Bunny (a.k.a. Chef Bunny) would bring up a bowl of oatmeal and a glass of ginger ale with a straw, so that I wouldn't have to tip my head back to drink it.

***

By late February I was deep into the Ménière's rabbit hole, where most of my time was spent either throwing up on my bathroom floor or lying in bed drugged. I had been scheduled to teach an introductory public policy course that semester. It was a required course for the Human Organization and Development major, a major that was and remains the bread and butter for Vanderbilt's Peabody College. I was fortunate to be team-teaching it with my faculty colleague Leonard Bradley, who had taught it a hundred times before, was bored silly, and wanted to see if we couldn't jazz things up a bit by adding some arts policy and First Amendment issues into the mix. The upshot was that Leonard was miraculously there to cover for me when I couldn't crawl into class, or when I made it but was so nauseated and dizzy that I could barely think, much less read my own lecture notes.

My memory of those months of extreme sickness is hazy, my recollection of Gordon's presence conspicuously so. He traveled as frequently as ever, and while I would have previously accompanied him on some of his "friend-raising" trips, I now remained home in bed as the world turned. Loneliness is one of the worst parts of being seriously ill. It's not just the loneliness that comes with being confined to your bed for hours on end with no company, but the anguishing realization that you are no longer part of the world. It really does go on without you.

When Gordon was in town, he would check in on me for a few minutes before he left in the morning and again in the early evening before he departed for dinner or some other event. I was often asleep by the time he returned. Once or twice a week, he'd arrive home around seven in the evening and we would watch a movie. We'd each have our own bowl of popcorn, a salted his and an unsalted hers. He ceased making physical overtures, rarely touching me as if afraid I would break. Perhaps it was that he was repelled. I couldn't tell and he didn't want to talk about it.

I readily admit to not being the sweetest convalescent. Cheerfulness is a disposition much lauded by the Church of Jesus Christ of Latter-day Saints. I was not cheerful; I was miserable and angry about being miserable. I was not half as brave as Elizabeth during her terrible illness. Gordon and Elizabeth, as Mormons in good standing, had been "sealed" as husband and wife for all eternity in a "celestial marriage." He was fortunate that he would be spending eternity with her rather than me.

As I lay in bed, I thought often of Elizabeth and all that she had related in *The Light around the Dark*. I thought of her aloneness, her descriptions of Gordon's withdrawal, and her frequently expressed wish that they could spend more time together.

Awaiting her first surgery, she described him sitting "curled up for hours on a bedroom chair, one leg hanging over the arm, head pressed to the upholstery, left hand covering half of his face," as he talked on the phone about university business "as though immersion in professional work will carry him to a place where this isn't happening."[2] She found herself thinking frequently about death during her first round of radiation, and about what might come afterward. These were thoughts and questions she tried sharing with Gordon, but she found that he did not "connect much" with what she had to say. "He admits that he never thinks of such things," she wrote. "Sometimes it seems that he could be suffering a kind of denial. . . . This may be a way of affirming his love for me. Still, I wish we could talk."[3]

A year into her illness, Elizabeth wrote, "For the last few years, Gordon has been gone so much that I doubt we have had more than a single twenty-minute conversation." She and Rebekah were so used to "going it alone" that even when he was home, they would "work through [their] routine and leave Gordon sitting by himself in the family room staring at the television."[4]

I tried to remember that Gordon, too, must be lonely. As good as he was at being a university president, he was not so good at dealing with the emotional needs and fears of a dependent loved one who may or may not get better. Few people are. I myself am fortunate not yet to have been tested in dealing with the extended illness of a dependent loved one, for it might be a test at which I, too, would not excel.

I thought about how awful it must be to watch your second wife fall ill, after having witnessed the long dying of your first wife. I felt guilty for putting him through the sickness nightmare once again, and I resented the guilt. I resented feeling needy, *being* needy. *I should be stronger and braver instead of despondent and irritable*, I lectured myself. Then I would throw up again.

I chuckled as I reread the embossed note card Gordon had tucked into *The Light around the Dark* eleven years earlier: "I am enclosing a copy of Elizabeth's book which I hope you will find joyful." Joyful! While there were certainly uplifting descriptions of the precious pleasures of living that only the dying can express, joy was not my takeaway. I began to comprehend that Gordon had been emotionally on Pluto for a very long time.

I also had to acknowledge that Gordon was far more engaged with the university than he was with me. The university was his true love. Or maybe it boiled down to self-love—so completely did Gordon merge his own identity with that of the university he served. Whatever the case, it was I who had become the jealous mistress.

20

Planet Ménière's

AN OLD FRIEND WHO IS a gifted healer and knowledgeable herbalist came to Nashville for an extended visit toward the end of March 2005. I had given Gordon a series of her Rolfing and massage sessions as a birthday present two months earlier. Gordon's posture was disturbingly poor, at times almost fetal. He talked often about wanting to improve it, but he hadn't made any progress. We hoped that an intensive period of Rolfing—the manipulation and unbinding of the body's fascia or soft, connective tissue—coupled with deep-tissue massage might jump-start the process.

My friend found me in deep despair mentally and bad repair physically. I weighed 110 pounds, having lost 17 pounds over the previous few months. "You look awful!" she declared with characteristic bluntness, as she climbed out of her car after the twelve-hour drive from State College, Pennsylvania. She set up her massage table on the third floor of Braeburn and went to work on Gordon, me, and several of my girlfriends who had also signed on for the Rolfing series. She listened intently to my description of the Ménière's cycle of symptoms, trying her best to think of ways to relieve both the physical and emotional distress.

Several days later, the three of us decamped to Monteagle for a quiet weekend. Leaving Gordon at the cabin to watch a basketball game and dictate university correspondence, my friend and I set out to hike some of the Fiery Gizzard Trail. I had bragged to her about "the Gizzard" since I'd first hiked it. She and I had spent many hours together trekking and biking the lush central Pennsylvania state forests during my years as a doctoral student in Happy Valley. I knew she would appreciate the magnificence of the Fiery Gizzard, its towering hemlocks clinging with gnarled root fingers to lichen-painted, house-size boulders; its chimney-rock sentinels; and its glorious waterfalls cascading over striated limestone outcroppings. A state park trail map reports: "Legend has it that the area got its name when Davy Crockett was camping in the gulf and burnt his mouth while taking a bite out of a hot gizzard. Since then, the gorge has been known as Fiery Gizzard."

"Gosh darn! That's one fiery gizzard!" Davy supposedly yelped, as he flung the culprit back into the flames.

We had gotten only half a mile into the hike when I began to get sick to my stomach. My friend and I sat down on the wooden footbridge that crosses Little Fiery Gizzard Creek a couple hundred yards up from where it joins Big Fiery Gizzard Creek, right before it plunges through the slot of Black Canyon toward Gizzard Cove. She took a small, round bonbon tin filled with marijuana and a little wooden pipe out of her backpack. She packed a small amount of the weed into the pipe and handed it to me. I took a couple of draws. The nausea melted away almost immediately. She repacked the pipe, took two hits herself, tapped out the ashes, and handed me the tin and pipe.

"Keep this," she smiled. "It'll help."

"Sure does," I agreed. The effects seemed miraculous. The nausea was gone.

We both laughed as we dangled our legs off the bridge, captivated by the glistening water. It felt so good to laugh.

***

I kept my little stash of marijuana in a Diamond matchbox underneath some mini-pads in the drawer of a small end table next to my toilet. It would have been more readily at hand in the cabinet under the bathroom sink, next to where I did most of my vomiting. But I was afraid the housekeepers would discover it when they cleaned, so I hid it seven feet away beside the toilet, protected by personal hygiene items to discourage the tidying touch.

During an attack, getting to the toilet and, more to the point, remaining upright while keeping my head over the bowl as the room spun around were way beyond my capacity. It was as if an invisible sumo wrestler had me pinned to the ground, his foot on my back. I could barely lift my nose off the floor. I would retch violently onto the back of my hands and into my hair, shivering in a pool of vomit.

First came up any food, liquid, and medication I had managed to ingest earlier. Next came bile, and then convulsive dry heaving. The stages would come in waves, and I would often pass out for a few minutes during the trough before the next mounting crest of nausea. The puking process would last three or four hours, and it came almost every day.

The rest of the day or night, and sometimes both, would be spent in bed drugged up on Valium, Xanax, Zofran, Ativan, or Phenergan—whatever medication various physicians thought would ease the nausea and stop the vertigo.

I had a cabinet full of antinausea drugs. Sometimes they helped; other times they didn't, most specifically when they reappeared, half dissolved, on the bathroom floor. The problem with pills is that they have to remain inside your body long enough to take effect. Another problem is that some of the less potent ones—those that don't knock you sideways—don't do a damn thing for really nasty nausea that is on the verge of morphing into projectile vomiting.

"I got vertigo once," a friend said. "The doctor gave me Antivert, and that really helped."

Oh, puh-leeze. I would like to propose a question for the MCAT verbal reasoning section: Antivert for severe nausea is like (a) baby aspirin for a migraine; (b) a smiley-face Band-Aid for the stump of a severed appendage; (c) a piece of waistband elastic for a bungee cord; or (d) all of the above. (The correct answer is d.)

An additional problem is that the drugs that do keep the vomiting at bay for a few hours, until it's time to take the next one, make for an awfully boring horizontal lifestyle. I began experimenting with my home apothecary, now one medicine richer thanks to my herbalist friend from Pennsylvania.

The introduction of cannabis added a new dimension to Planet Ménière's—a fifth dimension, if you will, for those of you who remember "The Age of Aquarius" or, perhaps more aptly, "Stone Soul Picnic." Vertigo is the first dimension, where the world implodes into a pinpoint and that's all there is. Oral ingestion of diuretics, antihistamines, benzodiazepines, serotonin antagonists, and barbiturates adds a parched, zombified second dimension. The insertion of a couple of these medications in suppository form provides a very special third dimension. The fourth dimension is time: How long will this go on? Is it time to take another pill or suppository? What day is it?

While pot is not perfect for all nauseous occasions (not to be confused with nauseating occasions, such as almost every time Rush Limbaugh opens his mouth), it can be highly helpful in some circumstances. Medical guides on antiemetic drugs cite several side effects of cannabinoids: euphoria, dizziness, dry mouth, and eating too many chocolate chip cookies. Euphoria, I would like to note, is defined as a state of cheerfulness and feeling of well-being. Sign me up! At last, in the throes of my misery, I had found the key to cheerfulness.

When I shared my discovery with my Mormon husband, I thought he would be, well, *cheerful* about my cheerfulness. Apparently there are good kinds of cheerfulness and bad kinds of cheerfulness. I understood by his reaction that, with regard to his wife and regardless of the situation, cheerfulness from illegal substances is very, very bad. "I *do not* want to know about it!" he barked.

Hmmm . . . He hadn't said, "*Don't* do it"—although I probably would have ignored him anyway. He had said he didn't want to *know* about it. Gordon always made a point to follow the *letter* of Latter-day Church law, as opposed to the *spirit* of the law, when it benefited him. This differentiation was most useful with regard to the LDS tenet against drinking coffee or caffeinated tea, and Gordon's habit of imbibing liberally of heavily caffeinated Diet Dr. Pepper throughout the day. After all, nowhere in the Book of Mormon was it decreed, "Thou shalt not drink Diet Dr. Pepper." Thankfully, this legal loophole provided his wife with a cheerfulness-option variance: letter-of-the-law secret cheerfulness.

***

Dizziness, another possible cannabinoid side effect, was not a problem for me because I was *already* dizzy; smoking pot did not make me more so. In fact, it helped to slow the dizziness because it dissipated the anxiety that accompanies dizziness and nausea.

Dizziness, nausea, and anxiety work together like three bad musketeers. Dizziness locks arms with Nausea, who locks arms with Anxiety. Round and round they gyrate, shouting, "All for one and one for all!" Feeding on each other's destructive energy, they get meaner and more indomitable until Dizziness becomes Vertigo, Nausea becomes Vomiting, and Anxiety turns into Panic—at which point their victim is down in the dirt until the bullies get bored with the beating.

I learned that a ten-milligram Valium coupled with a Zofran slowed the spiraling process, as did a couple of puffs of cannabis. Unfortunately, neither the legal drugs nor the illegal drug stopped the eventual onslaught; they just held it off for a few hours. Endolymph was building in my inner ear, and nothing legal or otherwise was going to stop that. The fluid, pressure, and tinnitus would intensify until the rupture (or whatever it was that happened when it released), and then came the vertigo.

The choice, when there was a choice (much of the time it came on so quickly that simply getting to my bathroom and lying, rather than falling, on the floor was the only possible premeditated course of action), was either six hours of pharmaceutically induced oblivion or three or four outlaw hours of being able to walk, talk, eat, and giggle at things that other adults didn't find all that funny.

Finding humor in situations that other adults don't find funny must be, I believe, one of the main reasons marijuana is illegal. Children are always up for a good laugh, especially when they are supposed to be serious. Church services are the prime example, providing the key ingredient for a good, you're-going-to-be-in-big-trouble-when-I-get-you-home case of the giggles: *authority*. The preacher is on his dais (an authority figure) handing down the word of God (an even bigger authority figure) to a sanctuary full of parents (more authority figures), who, back in the 1950s and early '60s, did not negotiate "behavioral expectations" with their progeny. The nonnegotiable expectation was that you were to be still and silent and act as if you were listening—an unnatural state of being that is, in and of itself, hysterically funny to most normal humans from ages three to thirty.

Pot gives one a different perspective on people and situations, sometimes not unlike that of a child in church. It heightens one's sense of irony, exacerbating one's tendency to laugh or make a smart-ass comment when people take themselves oh-so-seriously or act self-important. That is what persons intent on exercising their power and demanding deference call "disrespecting authority." (Of course, any illegal activity is inherently disrespectful of authority.) Another risky side effect of cannabis is irrepressible mirth, which can quickly lead to disrespecting authority to authority's face. That could lead to the collapse of society as we know and cherish it.

Given my fun-filled description of marijuana's effects, it may be reasonable to assume that I always chose the illegal option or, for propriety's sake, "Option B" to combat the Ménière's Musketeers, but I did not. I more often exercised legal Option A, primarily because of exhaustion, depression, and the promised oblivion of unconsciousness—not to mention the fear of getting caught. Also, when you are truly ill, Option B is not exactly a party. I mean, it's not as if you're sharing a joint with a few friends while watching *Saturday Night Live*. Nope, nothing as amusing as I imagine that would be.

Option B simply and compassionately allowed for social interaction with other human beings. I remained dizzy and the tinnitus still buzzed, but I could eat and carry on a conversation (as long as there were no linear differential equations involved)—capabilities I once took for granted but now considered a huge treat. I could take Lucy for a walk, go to a movie with Gordon, or, on a few occasions, do something more ambitious, such as join a dinner party or host a reception at the residence.

***

I remember one very special occasion I was able to attend only because I had the little tin of marijuana on hand. It was late morning, and I was getting dressed for a small luncheon being given at the home of a university trustee in honor of the first woman US Supreme Court justice, Sandra Day O'Connor.

I had not felt well all morning but was determined to get to the luncheon. As the dizziness began to worsen, I knew a vertigo attack was pending. I sat on my bathroom floor with my head in my hands trying to breathe deeply and not cry and ruin my makeup. *Please, don't let this happen*, I beseeched the gods. Then I thought of Option B, tucked under the mini-pads in the little table next to the toilet. Dare I smoke pot before meeting a Supreme Court justice?

It appeared Option B was my only choice if I was going to that luncheon—and *I was going to that luncheon*. I closed the bathroom door, staggered over to retrieve my little stash, leaned against the wall next to the toilet, and lit up, making certain to blow the smoke through the open window. I returned Option B to its little mini-pad lair and sat back down on the floor. After about five minutes, I thought, *OK, you can do this. Just be careful and move s-l-o-w-l-y.*

On the short ride from the residence to the luncheon, I broke the letter-of-the-law rule: I told Gordon what I had done. (Other side effects of pot are truthfulness and talkativeness, a potentially dangerous combination.) He failed to perceive the humorous absurdity of the situation as I was seeing it: meeting a Supreme Court justice while in a Jamaica state of mind.

"Don't be mad," I pleaded. "I want so much to meet Justice O'Connor, and I want to be here with you. Please understand. I am so sick of being sick!"

I held tightly onto his arm as he steered me inside the house, across the marble floor, and into the room where everyone was gathered. After we were introduced to Justice O'Connor, I quickly found a place to sit. I took his arm again as we all walked into the dining room. No one noticed that I wasn't well.

On the drive home I said, "Now that wasn't so terrible, was it? I didn't say or do anything untoward, did I?"

"No, you were fine," he admitted grudgingly.

The moment we got home I undressed, took a Valium, and went to bed. A few hours later I awoke with the room spinning. *Well, at least I got to go to the luncheon*, I thought as I threw up, face down on the bathroom floor.

***

An especially vicious attack confined me to my bed and bathroom for two solid days in mid-April. Finally, I was able to make it to my stash, stuff a small amount into the pipe bowl, and light up. I took one hit, inhaling deeply and exhaling slowly. I set the pipe next to me on the cool white tile floor and relaxed as the nausea receded.

After a few more minutes, I stood up and carefully returned the pipe, pot, and matches to their hiding place. *I'm so hungry*, I thought, *and I need to get the hell out of this bathroom*.

Steadying myself with a hand on the wall and clutching the stair railing, I made it down the stairs. The house manager, seated at her desk, looked up as I staggered into the kitchen and leaned heavily on the counter next to the sink.

"Well, hello!" she said. "You look better."

"I think I could eat a little something," I replied. "Could you please ask Bunny to fix me some oatmeal?"

Then, for no reason in the world other than the pot-induced hypertruthfulness, or perhaps an innate need to connect with another human after being isolated for so many agonizing hours, I said, "I just smoked a little pot and I really do feel better."

I caught some movement behind me and turned to see Bunny frantically waving both arms and mouthing the word "NO!"

A few days later, I returned home one afternoon to be informed that a housekeeper had found a "roach" (the butt of a marijuana cigarette, for readers over eighty or under ten) in a pocket of one of my hiking jackets. House Manager Wife had instructed the housekeepers to check the pockets of all my coats and jackets, purportedly in preparation to send them to the cleaners—a service I had not requested. Unfortunately, the housekeeper who found the roach was not the one who was my ally, but the house manager's whipped-dog minion. House Manager Wife was now in possession of Exhibit A.

21

Ototoxin

SIX MONTHS INTO MÉNIÈRE'S, I had read everything I could get my hands and cursor on about the disease. I had doggedly undergone each and every first- and second-level treatment. I had religiously followed the decreed no-or-low-everything-good diet (cheating occasionally with a half glass of wine) and the regimen of prescribed pharmaceuticals. I had even experimented with the Meniett, a mysterious device that delivers low-pressure pulses to the middle ear through a tube inserted into the outer ear, theoretically causing displacement of inner-ear fluids. An acquaintance of mine found relief with the Meniett. Although I used it faithfully several times a day (while on my knees supplicating to the heavens), my inner-ear fluids were unmoved.

When it was clear that the oral steroids were not doing the trick, my otolaryngologist began a series of steroidal intratympanic perfusions. Dexamethasone was injected into my middle ear so that it would perfuse through the round- and oval-window portals into the labyrinth of the inner ear. A brief summary of the treatment of Ménière's disease provided by the Vanderbilt University Medical Center describes the intratympanic perfusion as "an almost painless procedure."[1]

"Several drops of a topical anesthetic are inserted into the affected ear canal. Then Dexamethasone is gently injected with a needle through the eardrum, into the middle ear space," the summary reads.

I beg to differ about the "almost painless" claim. The anesthetic burned like hell, and even with it, I could still feel the needle "gently" piercing my eardrum.

The dexamethasone injections did nothing except send me into convulsive vertigo right on the examination table. My eternal thanks to Georgette, the wonderful nurse who held a bedpan to my mouth and gently squeezed my hand as I retched and shivered on the cold metal table—until there was a long enough lull in the vomiting for her to bundle me into a wheelchair and get me out of the hospital and into a car to be delivered home, where I could continue throwing up in less clinical environs.

The first- and second-level treatment protocols are generally agreed on among Ménière's specialists as the way to proceed, although there are those who think the entire low-salt theory is hogwash. So if the experts disagree, who really knows? After those treatments, the measures quickly became increasingly invasive, nightmarish, and controversial.

***

Perfusion of the inner ear with an ototoxin, either gentamicin or streptomycin, is frequently offered as the next step. "Ototoxin" literally means *ear poison*. Maybe it's just me, but I think a person has to be damn desperate to agree to have ear poison injected into her ear. This procedure is called a "chemical labyrinthectomy," the goal of which is to selectively destroy the balance organ without destroying the hearing apparatus. That is the *goal* but unfortunately not always the outcome.

If the first round of inner-ear perfusions fails, another round is given. With every additional application, the odds increase that the patient's hearing will be compromised severely or destroyed completely. The destruction-of-the-balance-organ part of this delightful treatment is generally tossed off in a "no big deal" manner, as a consequence for which the brain will eventually compensate to a greater or lesser degree. We'll get to that later.

Other less and more controversial, yet not uncommonly performed, treatments include: endolymphatic sac surgery (described in the literature as a "conservative operation" that infrequently results in "hearing loss, paralysis of the facial nerve, bleeding, infection, and/or leaking of cerebrospinal fluid"[2]); labyrinthectomy (drilling away the balance portion of the inner ear); and vestibular nerve section surgery (severing the eighth cranial nerve, a feat that requires entering the skull through the temple, retracting the brain, and exposing the hearing, balance, and facial nerves).

One of the first physicians I saw gave me a slim, purse-size booklet titled "A Discussion of Meniere's Disease," where I actually read the following: "There have been countless other types of surgical options advocated over the years. These include ultrasonic irradiation and cryogenic freezing of the labyrinth. Approaches to the inner ear through the oval window for destruction and with tacks to rupture the dilated saccule have been reported."[3]

With tacks! Medical science trumps Hollywood horror every time. "Some surgeons still perform these operations," the booklet noted ominously. I'll spare the reader further description of the medieval character of modern medical attempts to deal with intractable cases of Ménière's disease. If you've ever seen the *Twilight Zone* episode "The Earwig," you can well imagine.

With no relief in sight by the end of April, I decided to get a chemical labyrinthectomy. The possibility of losing the hearing in my left ear weighed heavily on me, but I was desperate. During my darkest hours, I had even considered suicide, and it seemed there were more and more of those hours. I had gone as far as ordering a how-to video on suicide, but its gruesomeness served as a deterrent. Perhaps that was its purpose. On one of my better days, I reasoned that it would make more sense to get a labyrinthectomy and take my chances than to proceed directly to one of the options portrayed in the video.

My doctor gave me several published medical studies about the use of intratympanic gentamicin on Ménière's patients. A young but already well-respected otolaryngologist at Johns Hopkins had written the reports. Gordon immediately contacted him; the doctor agreed to see me the following week. He was conducting a study on vestibular-ocular reflexes and wanted to include me in his testing. I quickly agreed to participate. I was ready to have him perfuse my inner ear with gentamicin.

A few days before my appointment at Johns Hopkins, a Vanderbilt board member suggested I speak to an otologic surgeon in Memphis who was renowned internationally for his five decades of work in the field. Since the mid-1980s, his primary research interest

263

had been Ménière's disease. When I spoke with the doctor over the phone, he ordered, "Do not let them put gentamicin in your ear!"

While he very much believed in the benefits of chemical labyrinthectomies for Ménière's patients unresponsive to first- and second-level therapies, he was adamant that streptomycin rather than gentamicin be used for the operation. He faxed me a research paper that he and two colleagues had published in 1994 after concluding a ten-year study comparing the "cochleotoxicity" and "vestibulotoxicity" of the two drugs—that is, the damage done to the hearing and balance functions, respectively, in relation to drug efficacy.

When Gordon and I met with the doctor at Johns Hopkins, I showed him the paper and told him of his much older colleague's condemnation of gentamicin. He was well aware of the work and opinions of the legendary Memphis physician, he said, but the fact remained that almost everyone in the field used gentamicin. He said he did not see much difference between the two drugs, in terms of either toxicity or efficacy.

He then handed me a copy of an email he had received from the Memphis doctor only an hour earlier, while I was undergoing baseline testing for the Johns Hopkins study on vestibular-ocular reflexes. The last-minute missive read:

> Enclosed is a picture of a man whose hearing and balance were destroyed by one perfusion of gentamicin.
>
> Streptomycin is not perfect, but it is more effective than gentamicin in relieving dizzy spells, [and] causes further hearing loss in no more than 1%, and relief from dizzy spells in 90%.
>
> Please give a copy of this email to Constance Gee.

I read the email and studied the photo. The poor man looked as if he had already taken the ferry over the River Styx, having left behind his zombified physical body for further medical experimentation.

"I have two expert opinions here," I pointed out to the doctor and to Gordon, who was also in the room. "One expert is adamant in his belief that streptomycin is far superior to gentamicin. The other sees little difference between the two."

"What do *you* think I should I do?" I implored the young doctor, trying to prod him into offering a firm counterargument. After all, here I was at Johns Hopkins, one of the most respected medical centers in the world. I'd come here to be treated. Everything was set up and ready to go. I needed him to convince me.

"Go with [the Memphis doctor] if you like. He's a good doctor and I respect him," he replied.

"OK, then, I'll go meet with him. I can always come back here if I decide otherwise," I said, still hedging my bet.

Before I left the examination room, I told the doctor I had been smoking marijuana on occasion to help manage the nausea. Did he see any harm in it?

"You're not the first Ménière's patient to tell me that," he said. "I don't see how it would hurt, although I can't officially recommend it."

***

Gordon and I stayed overnight in Baltimore. A hotel room had been booked for us, since the plan had been for me to receive the gentamicin perfusion that afternoon. As it was, we now had a mini-holiday. We decided to go out for a nice dinner. Things had been very tense between us with the progression of my illness, his continued withdrawal, and my anxiety over both.

I remember the evening well; it was our first "date" in over a month. The restaurant was intimate, Italian (our favorite), and candlelit. I allowed myself a glass of wine. We both ordered an arugula salad and pasta pomadora (our favorites). We spoke briefly about my decision to see the doctor in Memphis. Gordon had seemed somewhat embarrassed as we'd said our farewells to the Johns Hopkins physician, effusively thanking him for his time and promising to soon be in touch with him. I wanted Gordon's reassurance that I'd made a wise decision—it was, after all, a big decision to make. "It's fine," he said, a little impatiently.

"Let's talk about something else," I suggested, placing my hand atop his on the table. "Tell me about what's been going on in your world. I feel so out of it."

We talked about the university and several projects he was working on. He apprised me of the latest plans for the upcoming commencement celebration. Gordon had imported several of Brown's commencement traditions to Vanderbilt—one of which was a pops concert/campus dance combo, called "The Party." I'd lobbied hard to ask Little Richard (who lived in Shelbyville, about an hour's drive south of Nashville) to headline this year's party. I was ecstatic to hear that he had accepted. Almost as exciting as the prospect of meeting Little Richard was the news that the 2003 Nobel Peace Prize laureate, Shirin Ebadi, had agreed to be the speaker for Senior Day. Ebadi had received the Nobel for her efforts to further democracy in her native Iran and for her advocacy on behalf of women and children. She was the first Muslim woman and the first Iranian to receive the award. "A *much* better choice than last year!" I noted.

Gordon and I walked arm in arm back to the car. It felt good to get reacquainted with my husband and to reconnect with the world we used to share.

As I sat in bed the next morning, sipping a cup of decaf and reading the paper, the words on the page lurched suddenly side to side. I looked up and the room jerked into the now familiar slanted cubist perspective. I felt the nausea building.

"Oh, Gordon! I'm getting sick," I said.

He looked up from his section of the paper in alarm. We had a return flight to Nashville to catch, which he needed to be on for a scheduled meeting that afternoon.

"I know you need to be on that flight," I said. "You go on and I'll come tomorrow."

"I can't leave you here," he said, even as I could see by the expression on his face that he was considering it.

"Look," I began haltingly, "we might still be able to make the flight. I have some pot with me. But if it's going to work, I have to smoke it *now*." I was fast getting to the tipping point of an all-out attack.

"I don't want to know about it!" he said.

"You need to make this decision with me, Gordon. Do I do it or not?" I pleaded.

"Do it!" he ordered. "But I'm leaving the room."

"Fine, but first, please get it for me. It's tucked into the side of my bag."

He retrieved the slim, quarter-length joint (small enough to quickly chew and swallow if I had to) that I had rolled two nights before and had ferried from Nashville to Baltimore, wrapped in a smidgen of plastic wrap and tucked inside my bra. He handed it to me and quickly pulled on his exercise shorts and a T-shirt.

"I'll be down in the workout room," he said.

The moment he closed the door, I lit up and took two hits. I placed the joint in the coffee cup saucer and waited for the effect. A few moments had passed when I heard a loud knock on the door.

"Security!" a deep voice shouted.

"Um, just a minute," I said, looking around wildly.

"Gotcha!" Gordon laughed as he swung open the door. He lay down on the bed, still chuckling.

"Ha-ha-ha, you think you're so funny," I said.

Then a remarkable thing happened: he stayed and talked with me. For about twenty minutes, we laughed and conversed light-heartedly. It was the most wonderfully gentle connection I'd felt with him in many months.

We made it back to Nashville that day, although I barely managed to get inside the house before going into a full-fledged tail-spin. By the time I emerged from my bedroom the following afternoon, I had made up my mind to undergo the streptomycin treatment in Memphis.

I think I was to the point where I would have had the stuff injected into my ear with a junkie's needle in an alleyway. I just wanted it done. Arrangements were quickly made for us to drive to Memphis the following Monday.

***

Although I'd decided to go with streptomycin over gentamicin, I remained worried about the doctor's standard three-day, three-perfusion protocol. Otolaryngologists at Johns Hopkins and Vanderbilt used a single perfusion of gentamicin. I'd read that it was essential to closely monitor hearing throughout the treatment process to ensure its preservation. I'd also read that it took from two to ten days for the treatment to fully work. Wouldn't it take a minimum of a few days after each perfusion to reliably assess the drug's effect on hearing?

I'd expressed my doubts about the three-day, back-to-back treatment protocol to the Johns Hopkins doctor, who had shrugged off my concerns. I continued to fret about the matter to Gordon, who responded with annoyance, saying that since I had decided to go with the doctor in Memphis, I should follow his protocol. Gordon had wanted me to have the procedure at Johns Hopkins.

The day before we drove to Memphis, I emailed the doctor there:

> I must ask a question and implore you not to get annoyed with me for asking. The only aspect of your treatment that makes me uneasy is the three-day/once per day perfusion protocol. I have chosen strepto-mycin over gentamicin. I am committed to your thinking on this. Undoubtedly you have excellent reasons for your standard dosage application. But I must ask you: Would you consider giving me two doses, waiting two weeks, and then testing me to determine if a third dose is necessary? I have always been very sensitive to medication. Will you please consider this request?[4]

His answer was no, but it was delivered in a manner that convinced me I was in good hands. Everything about this kindly, passionate, surprisingly old but still handsome surgeon was convincing. An evangelical Catholic, he was a crusading healer who to the very fiber of his being believed in his own powers and God-given purpose in life. Crucifixes and printed and framed prayerful passages adorned his office, along with scores of professional commendations, photos of him with famous people, and notes of gratitude from past patients. Every square inch of his office was covered with messages of faith and healing, which were his life's calling and sustenance. Despite my usual suspicion about the highly religious, I was drawn to him. He was reassuring and I wanted to be reassured. He was a healer and I wanted to be healed.

The series of perfusions went well. The tinnitus and aural pressure lessened, and the vertigo stopped. I didn't suffer further hearing loss. I experienced initial unsteadiness but, with daily balancing exercises, recovered within a few weeks. I was elated.

***

Gordon and I went on a wonderful trip to Germany in early June. Although it was a business trip, we arrived a few days early to visit Bonn. We stayed in a small hotel in Bad Godesberg, a lovely district twenty minutes south of the city center, where most of the embassies were located when Bonn had been the capital of West Germany. The hotel overlooked the Rhine and was a fifteen-minute stroll along the river promenade from Haus Steineck, the residence where I had lived and studied during my sophomore year of college. I was thrilled to see it again after so many years—and to have my husband see it too.

"There it is!" I cried, proudly pointing up from the promenade at the imposing white brick, mansard-roofed structure. "But what's that tattered flag on top?"

"Looks like a Saudi Arabian flag," Gordon observed.

We walked up the narrow stone walkway leading from the river to the street in front of the house. Horrors! The spacious front lawn was now walled in behind six-foot-high industrial fencing, blocking even the smallest glimpse of *my* beautiful former abode. Security cameras glared down suspiciously at anyone who dared approach, even though the house appeared to have been abandoned years earlier when the seat of government returned to Berlin. (I do hope someone has bought Haus Steineck from the Saudis and refurbished it by now.)

It was very thoughtful of Gordon to have arranged our side trip to that exquisite and, for me, youthfully sentimental part of the Rhineland. It was also good to have a few consecutive days of private time together. I initiated the first physical intimacy we'd enjoyed in almost six months. We held hands as we walked the promenade. I felt reconnected to him, rejuvenated in spirit and body. I will always remember that trip to Germany with great fondness.

***

The vertigo returned with a vengeance two months later while I was in Westport. As Hurricane Katrina pummeled New Orleans and coastal Mississippi, I vomited and dry-heaved without reprieve for two solid days. I was so sick that I didn't even know what was happening on the Gulf Coast until the day after the storm hit.

Fortunately (at least for me), my former Penn State colleague Anne and her husband, Jerry, were visiting. They cleaned up after me, emptied and rinsed out the plastic wastepaper basket by my bed, brought me water, and helped me back and forth to the bathroom.

Rebekah and Allan (her boyfriend and future husband) were then completing their medical residencies at Harvard. Gordon contacted Allan, who called in a prescription for promethazine suppositories, because I had been unable to keep down oral medication.

"If the suppositories don't stop the vomiting by the evening," Allan instructed Anne over the phone, "you need to get her to the hospital."

I slept, heavily sedated, through the night and into the next day. When I was finally able to get out of bed, I sat dumbly in front of the television, mourning the death and devastation Katrina had wrought. I stared at the victims' dazed expressions and felt keenly as if I had been there with them. It seemed as if the whole world had suffered a spinning, bludgeoning, category-five hurricane.

I didn't remember much of anything I said to Gordon when he called during the Ménière's attack. I barely remembered talking to him at all. Apparently, though, I'd told him, Rebekah, or Allan that I wanted to die, that I wanted to kill myself. I'd not been out of bed for more than an hour when Rebekah called. Jerry handed me the telephone.

"You are ruining my father's and my life!" she screamed point blank.

She said her father was giving me more attention than he had given her mother during her illness with breast cancer. Her mother's illness was terminal, she said; mine was not. How dare I threaten suicide!

"You are so selfish and inconsiderate!" she yelled.

Stunned by her attack and too exhausted to respond, I said, "Rebekah, I am going to hang up now." My friends and I heard her shouting the words "selfish" and "childish," as I pressed the Off button and handed the phone to Jerry.

When I told Gordon about Rebekah's outburst the next evening, he said she had most likely acted that way because she was afraid of losing me as she had lost her mother.

"*Am* I ruining your life?" I ventured, not wanting to hear what I knew to be his real answer.

"Don't be silly," he said in a clipped, slightly annoyed tone of voice. "You always read too much into things."

Yet I knew in my heart that, if I wasn't exactly *ruining* his life, I was making him terribly unhappy. Rebekah's wrath and resentment were devastatingly genuine. There was nothing to "read into" those truths. I wished I could right myself and, in doing so, right us all. But everything was upside down and inside out. I was helpless at the hands of this unpredictable, sadistic force that had come to rule my life, and I hated myself for it. How could Rebekah understand that the blows she dealt were nothing to those I'd inflicted on myself? She and I never spoke of her phone call.

Jerry decided he would grill hamburgers. None of us ate much meat, but Jerry determined I needed some "major nutrition." I also think he'd been hankering for a burger, and my wan visage provided a righteous excuse.

I smoked marijuana for the first time since the hotel room in Baltimore. When Jerry handed me half a burger with a dab of mayo on the bun, I wolfed it down like the piteous, but as yet unsuspecting, Satan-impregnated Rosemary had ripped into that chunk of raw meat while standing over her kitchen sink in *Rosemary's Baby*. Unlike Rosemary, I did not throw up afterward in self-disgust. I just sat on the sofa thinking, *Maybe I'll live after all*.

***

Until then, the dizziness had always subsided between vertigo attacks. But after the "Katrina attack," I stayed staggeringly off balance. I had a second, less severe attack a couple of days later, but I still couldn't shake the terrible dizziness. I remember speaking with my doctor by phone and telling him that if this was to be my life, then I no longer wanted to live.

He told me to return immediately to Memphis for a second operation. I agreed to do so, although I well knew that the odds of losing the hearing in my left ear increased exponentially with every dose of streptomycin. The doctor assured me that would not happen, and because the first operation had gone so well, I believed him. I had to believe him. I felt I had no choice but to submit to the second round of perfusions.

It was clear that I couldn't make the drive from Westport to Nashville; I couldn't perambulate well enough to pack a suitcase. Bunny and another friend offered to drive my car back to Tennessee. Gordon made the necessary arrangements and flew up with them. He hired a private plane to fly me directly to Memphis and to return him and Lucy to Nashville. A car service met me on the tarmac and delivered me to a hotel close to the clinic. I was to begin treatment the next morning, Tuesday, 6 September.

The doctor informed me that he was going to give me four perfusions instead of the standard three. This time around, the anesthesiologist and nurses did not joke with me before rolling me into the operating room as they had done during my first visit. Their faces were set harder; something was different. I think they knew what was going to happen and felt bad about it.

Gordon must have felt a little guilty about leaving me to undergo the perfusion treatment alone. (He'd also left me alone to face the first series of treatments, departing immediately after our initial meeting with the doctor.) He surprised me by flying to Memphis the second evening. We had supper at the hotel and watched a movie in the room. It was a comfort to have him with me, if only for a few hours.

He left early the next morning, before I was to receive the second perfusion of the series. I had a sense of foreboding, as if I were walking into a dark room where something terrible awaited but couldn't turn back.

I could tell that something about me had changed when I awoke after the third perfusion. By the evening, I knew what it was: the hearing in my left ear was decidedly worse. Even so, I reported to the clinic the following morning for the fourth perfusion. As I sat in the waiting room, I became more and more agitated. *What am I doing?* I thought.

I stepped into the back stairwell and telephoned Gordon. When he answered, I began to cry as I told him how frightened I was, and that I knew I had already lost much of my hearing. My voice reverberated shrilly up the stairwell and off the hard metal and cement surfaces. Still he counseled me to follow the doctor's advice and undergo the fourth perfusion.

I started shrieking, "No! No!" I felt completely alone, like an animal in a lab experiment. My cries pained my ears, but I couldn't stop them.

A doctor opened the door, glanced my way with a frown, and rushed past me up the stairs. An hour or so later, I was informed by the office manager that the perfusions would be halted. I flew back to Nashville that afternoon, a day early.

No one had prepared me for what I quickly realized they all knew would happen. I had read that the purpose of perfusing the inner ear with an ototoxin was to selectively destroy the balance organ. I had read that it took up to ten days for the treatment to fully work. I had also read that there was some extended recovery time involved, during which the brain would attempt to compensate for the balance loss. Nothing I read, and not one of the doctors I'd met with, explained how the unilateral destruction of my vestibular system might affect me physically and emotionally. What would happen when the treatment "fully worked" was a mystery to me. I simplemindedly thought it meant that I would not have any more vertigo attacks. Furthermore, no one bothered to tell me what to expect during the period it took for the poison to do its work, the time it would take for my balance organ to *die*—another physiological reality that I failed to comprehend. In my mind, the words "selectively destroy" somehow didn't add up to "die."

My first experience with the streptomycin perfusions had been so benign. I understood (and greatly feared) the risk of hearing loss, but I had no reason to expect an assault on any other front. In short, I was completely unprepared for what was in store for me after the second round of perfusions: a seafaring nightmare and a shipwreck.

For two or three days after the operation I felt progressively off balance. Then it hit me full on. I was immobilized in our bed for the next week and a half, as the room swung insanely from side to side, like a dinghy adrift in raging thirty-foot swells. At some point during my unfortunate maritime experience, I spoke by phone with the Vanderbilt otolaryngologist.

"Oh my God! Everything's swinging from side to side!" I panted.

"It's supposed to," he replied. "I was surprised that didn't happen the first time."

"What? *Why didn't you tell me?!*"

"I thought [the Memphis doctor] would," he said.

Bastards! I thought as I hung up.

***

It was another three weeks before I could move upright down the hallway without leaning against the wall. A mosquito-pitched whining and fluctuating pressure had begun to affect my right ear. I could no longer hear much at all out of my left ear except, of course, the unending hissing.

I was bereft over the loss of my hearing and balance. From the passenger seat of a car, I'd watch two people conversing while they walked along a busy street; I'd ache with envy over their unconscious ability to hear one another over the traffic and walk effortlessly side by side without falling into each other. I'd obsessively place my hand over my right ear, trying to determine what, if anything, I could hear from my left. For the first time in my life, I couldn't tell which direction a car or voice was coming from. I couldn't identify familiar sounds and voices. I couldn't walk in a straight line. I couldn't walk at all in lowly lit environments, such as a movie theater, without holding on to someone or something. *I couldn't, I couldn't.* I was bound up and smothering in grief over all my couldn'ts.

I began seeing a psychologist in October. I finally had to admit to myself that I could not climb out of the grief pit alone. I desperately needed to talk with someone about this disease, my radically altered life, my despair, and my anger. I also recognized that I needed help with my marriage.

Hell, I was a mess. I needed help with *everything*.

22

Busted—and Life on Parole

I HAD BEEN BACK ON my feet (in the most literal sense) for about two weeks when Gordon spit out that Martha Ingram, Denny Bottorff, and David Williams had come to his office to tell him "someone" had informed them that I had used marijuana at Braeburn. Unbeknownst to me, Vice Chancellors David Williams and Lauren Brisky had come to the residence to interview the housekeepers about the marijuana charges while I had been in Westport the previous summer. No one had seen me smoke anything, but of course Exhibit A was on hand and my April confession to House Manager Wife had been duly recorded.

I had been "indiscreet," Gordon charged angrily. I was to report immediately to Williams at the general counsel's office.

I felt like an unruly child being sent to see the principal. It was humiliating. Williams's brusque reception did not help ease my trepidation. He demanded to know if I had used marijuana in the residence. "Yes," I answered truthfully.

I asked him if he knew that I had been terribly ill over the past year. He replied coldly that he had not heard much about it. I tried to relate my experience of Ménière's to him. Hard-eyed and unsympathetic, he said that he was sorry to learn of my problem but that having marijuana on university property was illegal; that was all there was to it.

This was a man I had known since our Ohio State days. I had been thrilled when I learned that he and his family were going to join us at Vanderbilt. His wife and I were friends. She had been up for a girls' weekend at Monteagle the previous spring. The four of us had shared Valentine's Day dinner together at the residence.

His upbraiding stung. I lashed out, saying that I wished he or someone he loved would experience the torment of Ménière's, if only for a few days. Perhaps then he'd find it in himself to show some compassion!

The moment the words spilled out of my mouth and I saw the pained look on his face, I apologized.

"I'm sorry, David, I truly did not mean that. I wouldn't wish that on anybody, most certainly not on you or your family. *Please* forgive me."

He dismissed me from his office.

***

David Williams told Martha Ingram that I was insufficiently repentant for my misdeed; they decided that further action was required. The issue was taken to the executive committee of the Board of Trust, a committee composed of fourteen trustees. Now a dozen more people (and most likely their spouses and a few friends) knew of the incident.

On 30 October 2005, a year to the day of the Monteagle storm and the onset of the Ménière's, I received a formal warning from Martha Ingram on behalf of the board. Her letter charged me with possession of marijuana on university property and mistreatment of staff members. I would be "subject to review and possible discipline." I was instructed to work with Williams to obtain professional assistance to deal with "behavior and drug use issues." The letter concluded: "Failure to accept this help, which could involve enrolling in a University sponsored or approved program for substance abuse and/or anger management will result in a suspension, without pay, for two months. Of course, any future issues involving illegal drugs or behavior could result in harsher penalties, including possible termination."[1]

I replied immediately, apologizing for my behavior. I accepted full responsibility for my actions, pledging never again to have or use marijuana on university premises. (Although my letter did not say as much, I felt that I could not promise in all honesty to never again smoke marijuana. I knew I would resort to using it for its palliative effects in the future if I experienced severe, long-lasting nausea. Also, I refused to rule out the possibility that, at some point in my life, I might just do it again for *fun*.)

Making it clear that I was not trying to "shirk responsibility for the consequences of my actions,"[2] I attempted to relate the nature and intensity of my long illness—an illness of which she, Bottorff, and Williams seemed amazingly unaware or at least had not given much consideration. I wrote that I was already seeing a psychologist and that I would provide David Williams with all necessary information so he might determine whether her professional assistance would meet the conditions set forth by the Board of Trust.

My response was contrite, compliant, and respectful. "I look forward to setting these wrongs right, and thank you for the opportunity to do so," I wrote in closing.

Williams telephoned the psychologist to assess whether or not my work with her would meet the board's requirements. He confirmed that it would. I met regularly with her, and I began weekly physical therapy in mid-December to improve my balance as much as possible. I learned to trust that, even as everything around me always appeared to be slightly swaying or bouncing, if I just placed one foot in front of the other and moved with confidence, I could in fact move confidently for the most part.

I worked hard to make amends with Gordon, the Vanderbilt board, and anyone else I might have offended in the past. I was determined to make things right and to move forward physically and emotionally.

A truce of sorts had been negotiated between Gordon and me. We may not have been hand-holding lovers or even good buddies at that point, but our time together was more pleasant than not. We once again began sharing jokes and asides, which was a fair beginning to something better.

I was keenly aware, however, that my moral and behavioral rehabilitation, as well as any opportunity for redemption, hinged on my walking the straight and narrow on a very short leash. I understood that one more misstep and a shock collar would be clamped around my neck. Worse, I just might be dumped at the pound.

Fear is not the best motivator for teaching a leash-tugging bitch to heel. It may work if reinforced regularly, but at the high price of spirit and affection.

***

277

The new year and new semester would bring the feminist artist Judy Chicago into my life on a regular basis. A prolific artist across multiple media and the author of fourteen books, Chicago remains best known for her iconic installation piece *The Dinner Party*. The work celebrates woman's contributions in all realms of human endeavor, drawing searing attention to the systematic erasure of those achievements from the written history of the Western world. For over four decades, Chicago has focused her art, writing, and political action on issues of power and powerlessness, as exemplified by her works *The Birth Project*, *The Holocaust Project*, and *Powerplay*.

There was a twisted irony in her becoming such an intimate part of my life at that time. The notion of women on short leashes is not simpatico with Chicago's worldview. The double irony was that it was Gordon who brought Chicago and her husband, the photographer Donald Woodman, to Vanderbilt. They were the recipients of the first Chancellor's Artist-in-Residence appointment.

Their residency would constitute a semester-long teaching project in collaboration with twelve Vanderbilt students and twelve local artists. The students and artists were selected from a pool who formally applied to participate in the residency. I, too, would be a part of it. The Cohen Building—slated for complete restoration and rebirth as the Vanderbilt Fine Arts Gallery, but then sitting largely empty—would provide the home for class meetings and the construction of artworks and, ultimately, their public exhibition.

I was informed much later that the dean of Peabody College (who was also my academic dean) had been furious that the residency was held on the Peabody campus. It was a trespass for which she appeared to hold me personally responsible. The dean was correct in assigning me blame: the Chicago-Woodman residency *was* my "fault." I also had a hand in the successful crusade to commandeer Cohen as its base of operations.

I had learned that Chicago and Woodman were coming to visit Vanderbilt in February 2004. They had been invited by the Margaret Cuninggim Women's Center to give a lecture in conjunction with an exhibition of selected work from the *At Home* project. *At Home* was a teaching residency that Chicago and Woodman had conducted at Western Kentucky University in 2001 that probed participants' social and emotional associations with "home."

I invited Chicago and Woodman to stay overnight at Braeburn during their campus visit. Judy and I formed an immediate bond in Braeburn's exercise room through an excited discussion of our views on the ways art is taught in school settings from kindergarten through university. Shortly afterward, we began scheming about a Chicago-Woodman residency at Vanderbilt.

The residency had taken more than two years to realize. The art faculty had been dead set against it in the beginning, but most of them came around after it got under way. As I understood it, their resistance was three-pronged: (1) it wasn't their idea; (2) they didn't much like Chicago's work (too feminist, too literal, too last century); and (3) they didn't much like the person who originally presented the idea to them (me).

On the other hand, Gordon liked the idea. He was fed up with the infighting between the studio art and art history faculties, well understanding the narrow limits of their imaginations in identifying new opportunities and finding ways to collaborate with other humans. He decided to go forward with the residency without the support of the art faculty, devising the Chancellor's Artist-in-Residence program as a classic administrative end run. What's more, he agreed that the Cohen Building would provide the perfect space for it.

I was genuinely surprised to learn of the dean's pique over the residency having been held on the Peabody campus. I had thought she'd be pleased, even proud. I can only surmise that she didn't want to be associated with the physical and ideological untidiness of serious art making or the views on life, politics, and sexuality expressed by the young artists.

I now wish I had made the effort to bring the dean deeper into the project. I think she would have liked Chicago and Woodman more than she might ever have imagined. She and Chicago share an inordinate strength of purpose to educate.

***

Residency participants met as a group twice a week to discuss assigned readings, explore areas of personal and social concern, and collectively develop the content of their individual artwork. Class discussions were always held in a circle, emphasizing the importance of all voices and the highly collaborative and supportive nature of our undertaking. Almost everyone worked on site throughout the day and into the night. This close physical proximity, along with the intense intellectual and emotional engagement of our class meetings, helped create a tightly knit learning community.

Judy Chicago was long practiced and highly skilled at helping her collaborators and students move the personal toward the universal. As a cofounder of the California Institute of the Arts' Feminist Art Program with the artist Miriam Schapiro, Chicago had honed her teaching methodology while working with twenty-six young women on the construction of *Womanhouse* in 1972. Each collaborator was given a room or space, within which to take "to fantasy proportions . . . the daydreams women have as they wash, bake, cook, sew, clean and iron their lives away."[3] Regarded as the first exhibition of feminist art, *Womanhouse* was the art installation and performance piece on which the *At Home* project had been based. She endeavored to help young artists identify and express what was most important to them in a way that also made it meaningful to others. Chicago would ask, "How do you make work that is accessible but not simplistic?"

The goal of our project was to communicate something *worth thinking about* in a way that would allow most people to understand the idea and, with that understanding, contribute to the power of the idea. Even for the most experienced artist, this is no easy task. Its pursuit is profoundly worthwhile, however, and should be at the heart of any good visual arts education program. (Furthermore, good arts programs should be at the heart of K–12 education.)

We spent the first few weeks of class going around the circle, each of us attempting to identify and verbalize our foremost concerns and ideas for their visual expression. Some participants knew early on what they wanted to do. Others came to it more slowly. While most of the participants had moved on from "what" to "how," I was grappling with "who." Who was I in this setting? Was I to function as professor, first lady, art student, or some combination?

Whoever I was, I was afraid. I felt like a little kid, fearful of saying or doing something wrong that would get me into trouble all over again. Whether in the role of professor, first lady, or art student, I had the same overriding, ever-present concerns. I was terribly frustrated over the politics and policies of the Bush administration. I was anxious about taking another misstep in my marriage and at Vanderbilt. I continued to grieve over the effects of Ménière's on my body and my life.

I nervously sidestepped our circle conversations each time my turn came back around. My ragged emotions were painfully obvious, even as I attempted to make light of my situation. Everyone knew about the Condoleezza Rice and flag-lowering incidents, as well as the public lashing I had taken for them.

Finally one afternoon it all came out. I recounted the Rice and flag stories, correcting the untruths that had been perpetuated in the media. I explained the effects of Ménière's, and the emotional and physical difficulties I continued to experience as a result of the disease and its treatment. (My classmates were already aware of my problems with balance and my intermittent dizzy spells.) I read a statement I had written condemning the Bush administration's preemptive attack on Iraq, our violation of the Geneva Conventions in our treatment of Iraqi prisoners, and the government's impotent response to the Katrina disaster.

"*This* is what I want to relate in a work of art," I said, "but I can't. It's too controversial. *I'm* too controversial. I'd be hanged by my thumbs outside Kirkland Hall or 'accidentally' run over on lower Broadway en route to Robert's Western World."

"Yes, you can," they replied, "and you *must!*"

From there, we conceived a work that was to comment straightforwardly on my political concerns while alluding to my trepidation of further censure. To maintain complete anonymity would be cowardly, only heightening my resentment and sense of diminishment.

What if I were to wear a partial disguise—a veil or half mask? Where would the work be displayed? On the second floor, in the most out-of-the-way gallery space, or in the basement? This could not be an in-your-face presentation.

A student told me that she had discovered two small, hidden closets built into the wall of a large classroom space on Cohen's first floor. I could place my work inside the closets, behind doors that would swing shut automatically. The act of entering the closet to see the work would make the viewer complicit.

I painted the interiors of both closets flat black. There was just enough space in each for a video monitor and a black metal chair about three feet away from the screen. In one closet, a short video loop showed a flag flying at half-staff while words of national shame scrolled silently down the left side of the screen:

Iraq Invasion
37,000 Iraqi Civilians Dead
2,500 American Dead
8,000 Americans Severely Wounded
~~Weapons of Mass Destruction~~

Abu Ghraib
Guantánamo Bay
Camp Nama
Bagram
Torture
Unlawful Detainment
Beaten to Death
~~Geneva Conventions~~

FEAR

Domestic Spying
Valerie Plame
Enron
Halliburton

FEMA
Hurricane Katrina
Over 1,300 People Dead
Quarter Million Pets Dead
Hundreds of Thousands Homeless

~~Kyoto Treaty~~
Oil

Perpetual WAR
Perpetual FEAR

Mission Accomplished

The monitor in the second closet ran a video loop of me seated against a black background, "disguised" by a mask covering my eyes and nose. I recited:

I am incensed over the U.S. invasion of Iraq.

I am incensed over the tens of thousands of Iraqi civilian deaths and dismemberments.

I am incensed over the destruction of an entire country's infrastructure, the devastation we have wrought with no intention to amend.

I am incensed over the accompanying murder, torture, humiliation, and unlawful detention of terrorist "suspects."

I am incensed over our country's loss of dignity and credibility around the world because of those atrocities.

I am incensed over the billions and billions of dollars squandered on this, what is to be, endless "war on terror," but which in actuality is a war on the very ideals that once made older generations proud to be American: adherence to the humaneness of the Geneva Conventions; fighting aggression and injustice, rather than being the aggressor and transgressor; and seeking to build rather than to destroy.

I am incensed over the Bush administration's outright lying and manipulation of intelligence data in order to convince Congress and the American people that Saddam Hussein was linked to 9/11, had weapons of mass destruction, and the immediate ability and intent to use them—all as a ruse to engage this country in a Bush family vendetta and to feed corporate greed for oil, power, and money.

I am sickened over the gullibility and intellectual and moral laziness evidenced by Congress and the American people as they were led by the nose and by vengeance to war.

I am incensed over the fact that hundreds of thousands of people and animals were left to die in the wake of Hurricane Katrina.

I am incensed that thousands of Americans, mostly African-Americans, remain refugees in their own country with little hope of returning home.

I am incensed that our federal government chooses to spend massive sums of money on death and destruction, on war without end—money that could have prepared and protected New Orleans from flooding, that could better educate children, and improve primary health care.

I am incensed that those who took us to war do not feel the personal impact of their war—that their families are safe, while tens of thousands of other Americans have lost husbands, wives, children, and grandchildren.

I am incensed that those who failed to act when it was clear Katrina would devastate coastal Louisiana and Mississippi do not suffer the consequences of their inaction and disregard.

I am incensed by the cynicism and arrogance that permeate the White House and Congress, and by the corporate lobbyists who buy their favors and our future.

I am an American, and I am angry, ashamed, and heartsick.

I titled the piece *Half-Mast/Half-Masked*. The title of the residency exhibition was *Evoke/Invoke/Provoke*. Topics were highly personal in nature, ranging from rape to prescription drug addiction to interracial coupling. As grim or preachy as the exhibition might sound, its overall effect was remarkably uplifting for the class in terms of its emotional intrepidness, technical quality, and intellectual sophistication.

The exhibition opened on 21 April and ran through commencement. A single reporter contacted me to ask about my piece in the show. I declined to comment, both in the spirit of the piece itself and because I genuinely did not want to stir things up once more. I knew I had taken a huge risk in making the piece, yet once I determined to proceed, I had to speak the truth of what I believed and how I felt. Brave or stupid, I was still scared.

I also did not want to become the focus of the show. There were better works in it than mine. Those works, and the young artists who had labored so hard on them, should represent the exhibition and residency project. There was no mention of *Half-Mast/Half-Masked* in the local press, which was fine by me.

***

There is one more notable irony in the Chicago-Woodman residency and the resulting exhibition. First Lady Laura Bush had accepted my husband's invitation to speak at Vanderbilt's Senior Day that year, the day prior to the commencement ceremony itself. Like Condoleezza Rice and Shirin Ebadi, she was to receive a medal for distinguished public service. (For the record, I did not learn until well *after* beginning my work on *Half-Mast/Half-Masked* that the wife of President George W. Bush was scheduled to be on campus.)

On 11 May 2006, I found myself in two places at once, in two surreally different postures. In a darkened broom closet on one side of campus, I was publicly denouncing the administration of George W. Bush. On the other side of campus, standing under a small white tent, I was shaking the hand of Laura Bush and intoning the words, "Nice to meet you."

23

Assassination Attempt

A WEEK OR SO BEFORE graduation, Gordon arrived home with the news that a reporter from the *Wall Street Journal* had begun researching a story she planned to write about his financial arrangements with Vanderbilt. She was interested in how universities were responding, if they were responding at all, to the federal Sarbanes-Oxley legislation on the governance of publicly held companies, which was passed in 2002 in the wake of the Enron and WorldCom scandals to protect shareholders and the public from corporate malfeasance. While not legally required to follow its guidelines, university boards felt pressure to incorporate aspects of the law into their governance. Gordon said that he was being targeted because of his high profile and high salary.

This news brought us together for a time. We may have had our political disagreements, but he knew that I thought he was the best university president in the country. He seemed to appreciate my pique on his behalf over the investigation. Things softened between us.

Once again I broached the subject of couples therapy. He finally relented. In mid-May, Gordon joined me for a session with the psychologist I had begun seeing after my second ear operation. We saw her together three or four times before I left for Westport in early July. Our sessions with her were helpful, so we agreed to resume them in September.

The *Journal's* investigation stretched through summer into fall. Two Pulitzer Prize–winning journalists, Joann Lublin and Daniel Golden, had been assigned to the story. Lublin seemed to be calling everyone in Nashville. She even telephoned my friend Reiko to press her about who had paid for the Rolfing sessions I had arranged for Gordon a year and a half earlier. Reiko owned a popular skin care business that I patronized. Several of my girlfriends, including Reiko, had also signed up for the sessions. Lublin told her another source had said that it had all been charged to the university. Reiko was taken aback: "Of course not! *Why* are you doing this to two people who have done so much for this community?" Lublin cut her off in midsentence, hanging up abruptly. She was looking for dirt, not daisies.

Word of the investigation was spreading quickly across campus and throughout Nashville. The three questions everyone was asking were *why*, *who*, and *when*. *Why* was the *Wall Street Journal* spending so much time and so many resources on this story about the Gees and Vanderbilt? Everyone felt that there had to be more to it than Gordon's high profile and salary. *Who* was behind the investigation? More accurately, as the talk-radio busybody Larry Brinton delicately put it, "Who's the snitch? Who went to the *Wall Street Journal* with all the inside information?"[1] Finally, w*hen* was it going to be published? It seemed to be taking forever. Were they purposefully waiting till after classes resumed?

In the meantime, both Vanderbilt's Board of Trust and Gordon had been scrambling to make certain that university financial oversight was above reproach. The entire board had received a letter from Chairman Ingram in late July warning them of the impending *Journal* story.

Gordon became increasingly irritable and withdrawn, often saying he was under enormous pressure. By late August, Kirkland Hall simmered with anticipation.

The new school year began, so I returned from Westport. Gordon was too distracted by the looming article to be coaxed back into our counseling sessions. I resumed seeing the psychologist on my own, anxious about the article and the rapidly escalating tension in our marriage.

***

Gordon had told me in midsummer that Lublin had been informed of my marijuana use. Jim Neal and Aubrey Harwell (founding partners of Neal & Harwell PLC, the high-powered law firm Vanderbilt keeps on retainer) called to tell me not to speak with anyone about the article. Should a reporter find a way to contact me, I should politely but firmly say, "I have no comment." *No comment.* (That and my hourlong session at Ohio State after the announcement of Gordon's and my engagement were the only media advice I ever received as a university first lady.) Of course, we all hoped Lublin would not include my use of marijuana in her story, as it had no bearing on Sarbanes-Oxley fiduciary oversight.

Gordon arrived home one evening in early September to say that he'd been given a reliable heads-up that Lublin fully intended to make the most of that tidbit. He was livid not only at Lublin but also at me all over again for providing the media with something they could use to "get at" him.

He was angry and suspicious at what he perceived to be a growing yet undefined band of conspirators surrounding him. This was an "inside job," he declared. Someone in the upper tier of the administration, along with two or three board members, was feeding Lublin highly confidential information. He said he had known for some time that there was a "leak" in the chancellor's office, but he was not certain who it was.

By then, it was common knowledge among upper-level administrators that several board members were untrustworthy stewards of confidential university business. The grim joke was that the *Tennessean* would know of board decisions in the time it took for someone to walk out of the meeting and speed dial a reporter.

There was another important focus in our lives throughout this tense time: Rebekah was to be married the first weekend of October. The date had been set almost a year in advance. Extensive planning was under way for an exquisite three-day nuptial celebration. At a time when Gordon and I should have been happily absorbed in the upcoming marriage of his only child, we were increasingly on edge over the tone and timing of the coming news story. Here we were, ten days before Rebekah's wedding, and still we waited.

***

The *Wall Street Journal* finally published its front-page story on 26 September 2006:

Golden Touch

Vanderbilt Reins In Lavish Spending by Star Chancellor

———

As Schools Tighten Oversight, A $6 Million Renovation Draws Trustees' Scrutiny

———

Marijuana at the Mansion

Gordon walked into our bedroom, placed a cup of coffee on my nightstand, and held up the paper so I could see the headline.

"How does it read?" I asked, sitting up.

"Not too bad," he said.

"Looks pretty bad from here," I returned, eyeing the last sub-title. "They had to put the marijuana in the headline?"

"That's what sells papers," he said.

With respect to himself, Gordon was right. He not only didn't look bad, he looked downright good. He had the "golden touch": a fundraiser, school booster, and tough but effective manager extraordinaire. So what if he'd spent a lot of money along the way (a reported $700,000 annually for entertaining at the residence)? He'd raised a thousand times more. If anyone on the planet understood the adage "it takes money to make money," it would be *Wall Street Journal* readers.

The six-million-dollar renovation headline might momentarily raise a few eyebrows, but by the second paragraph that would be a big ho-hum as well: "Mr. Gee has dramatically boosted the 133-year-old school's academic standing and overseen fund raising of more than $1 billion."[2] Most university trustees around the country were probably chartreuse with envy.

The Vanderbilt Board of Trust did not fare as well. The opening of the third paragraph sealed the media fate of the

289

Commodore's trustees as a ship of fools, with one of their own characterizing the board's supervision of the chancellor as having been "a little loosey-goosey." The *Journal* article made it seem closer to outright incompetence. The full board had not approved the university's annual budget, most big-ticket spending projects, or debt financing between 2000 and 2006.[3] According to the article, it hadn't known of the residence renovation costs, much less formally approved them.

The *Journal* made it sound as if the board hadn't even known there was going to *be* a renovation: "The university's offer letter [to Gordon in February 2000], reviewed by The Wall Street Journal, didn't mention the remodeling project. It promised Mr. Gee a $504,000 annual salary, annual bonus and two supplemental-retirement plans. Only a few of the nine members of the board's search committee knew the details of the offer letter at the time, according to people familiar with the matter."[4]

I myself had been surprised by the six-million-dollar figure that surfaced at the outset of the *Wall Street Journal*'s investigation. I'd always thought the Braeburn renovation had cost somewhere around four million, but I wasn't certain and didn't ask since the information was never offered up. All I heard (and I heard it on more than one occasion straight from the Vanderbilt Board of Trust chairman herself) was that the renovation of Braeburn "came in on time and on budget." That seemed to be all the first lady needed to know.

"I was told it was done right, it was done well, and it was done on budget," Gordon told the *Journal*. "In hindsight," the article continued, "he [Gordon] agrees he should have learned the amount [of the renovation] and kept the full board apprised."[5] *In hindsight with a gun to his head*, I thought on reading that.

Gordon had made it clear to the board from the beginning that he would not be involved in the renovation budgeting or the project's oversight. When he was informed of the final cost of the renovation many months *after* the project was completed, he still had no reason to believe it had gone over budget, if indeed it had. The *Journal* reported that the original construction cost had been estimated at $2.1 million. Anyone who thought that was a realistic estimate must have been using a substance a lot stronger than marijuana.

It was the quoted figure of $504,000 that most surprised me. One million dollars had been the magic number since Gordon's inaugural tour of Nashville, courtesy of Martha Ingram, Denny Bottorff, and John Hall. I say this as someone "familiar with the matter." They must have promised mammoth hefty annual bonuses if Gordon's base salary was $504,000. I guess that's the way it's handled in corporate America. I was never privileged to know the details of Gordon's compensation package, nor did I feel it was my business to ask. Gordon had always been very private about money matters. I had always been reluctant to inquire. I was inordinately sensitive to Gordon's (and Rebekah's) thinking I cared too much about what money they or we had.

Therefore, it was with great interest that I read the helpful chart featured halfway through the article citing his total compensation from Vanderbilt as $1,326,786 for 2003–2004. This did not include the $400,000 he made that same year by sitting on five corporate boards.

The *Journal*, however, had missed an important detail of the Vanderbilt chancellor's compensation package. Gordon's contract also included a $7,000,000 longevity bonus that he was to receive at the end of his tenth year at Vanderbilt. He told me of that agreement when we first came to the university.

***

I suspect that, like me, more than a few board members also found the university's reported financial arrangement with the chancellor to be of interest. The reported $700,000 annual entertainment tab, however, was old news. The only people who seemed surprised by that expenditure were a few trustees who occasionally radioed in from Alpha Centauri. "We should not be issuing blank checks to university leaders," blustered one extremely emeritus trustee.[6] (I was particularly upset by the suggestion that blank checks were being issued. *Dang, if I'd only known!*)

Until the *Journal* inquiry, the several hundred million dollars rolling into Vanderbilt each year had seemed to nicely offset the $700,000 investment in university profile-raising entertainment and community relations. Until then, it appeared that the Board of Trust could not have been happier with the Braeburn renovation and our extensive use of the residence to showcase the university.

CONSTANCE BUMGARNER GEE

The out-of-town board members and their spouses certainly enjoyed staying at Braeburn when they came to Nashville. Now people were "shocked." At least the Brown University board had waited until *after* we left to act oh-so-shocked about the amount spent on the renovation of 55 Power Street.

The fact is that no one had much to say about renovation or entertainment costs until the *Journal* mysteriously got wind of it. Only then did someone "familiar with the matter" emerge to speak under the condition of anonymity. The Deep Throat, tabloid tone of the article, as well as the Board of Trust's collectively professed ignorance of the renovation budget and other major fiscal decisions, made everyone—with the miraculous exception of the "Star Chancellor" himself—look like the cast of characters in *A Confederacy of Dunces* engaged in a Chinese fire drill. Board members seemed to be either sad little fungi victims of mushroom management (Keep 'em in the dark and feed 'em poop), Rip Van Winkles blinking groggily into a rude flashlight beam, or willing co-conspirators stepping all over one another in the dash toward the *not* mea culpa exit.

The *Journal* reporters conveniently forgot to mention that the money spent on Braeburn's renovation was private funding that was donated and designated specifically for the project. They also chose to overlook other important mitigating details that did not reinforce the sensationalist character of their narrative.

The real savory part—employed here as a bizarre lead into a disjointed litany of university presidential criminal activity from American University to the University of California to Texas Southern University, as well as a *tour d'horizon* of university residential renovations for the Gee family from Colorado to Vanderbilt—was dangled at the close of the third paragraph. The trustees' concern over their chancellor's expenditures, the *Journal* segued wobblingly, "was aroused when they learned that Mrs. Gee was using marijuana at the mansion."[7]

Well, hot dog! Now *here* is something worth plowing through a gazillion gossipy words of "according to this person" malarkey. The story fuzzily unfolded that it was my use of marijuana that led the Vanderbilt board to call for an inquiry into our entertaining expenses: "The marijuana incident troubled some trustees, who were bothered that Mr. Gee never told the full board about it,

292

according to people familiar with the matter. To these trustees, the incident demonstrated that Mr. Gee needed to be more accountable to the board."[8]

The big discovery of the initial inquiry was "an absence of clear records documenting time the chef spent preparing meals for the Gees rather than for university events."[9] We had always been supremely careful not to mix private and business usage of university goods and services. From Columbus to Nashville (and before me, in Morgantown and Boulder), there had always been the Gee refrigerator and the university refrigerator. There was our mayonnaise and the university's mayonnaise, our wine storage and the university's (locked) wine storage. A percentage of the cost of our cars had always been taxed as private income. We reimbursed the university for part of the mileage of Gordon's car and most of the mileage on mine.

Gordon had always paid for a portion of Chef Bunny's $50,000 salary, but he was informed he needed to start paying a flat third of it after the board learned the *Journal* investigation was under way. "When they tell me what needs to be done, I always write the check—but sometimes I get heartburn," Gordon had quipped to a *Journal* reporter.

***

After the first inquiry (or "Bunnygate," as we called it), "restive trustees" had met with Chairman Ingram to insist on a second review of Gordon's expenditures and the board's own governance practices, reported the *Journal*. They said they wanted to make certain that the chancellor and board were in full compliance with Sarbanes-Oxley, citing the American University board's recent dismissal of its president, Dr. Benjamin Ladner, as an example of what might come of lax oversight of a university president.

Ladner and his wife, Nancy, had been charged with making nearly $600,000 worth of questionable expenditures on the university's dime, including first-class airline tickets, swanky hotel accommodations, limousines, and household items such as linens and (for heaven's sake!) vitamins. Spending associated with their chef had also been a point of contention: $219,000 in salary and benefits per year, plus professional development trips to France, Italy, and Britain.[10] (Chef Bunny and I discussed the matter and determined that (1) clearly she was working for the wrong university and (2) sending a chef to England for culinary training is indeed cause for suspicion.)

Mrs. Ladner, the *Wall Street Journal* gossiped, was accused of having stopped in Rome to get her hair styled while they were en route to Dubai on a business trip—an allegation that her husband, more loyal than mine, denied vehemently. (Poor Nancy must have had a House Manager Wife of her own lurking nearby when she made that call, probably on a university-billed phone line, to Biagio's House of Beauty.)

The *New York Times* reported Dr. Ladner as having said that he was "in total shock" that an anonymous letter had been sent to the board urging officials to examine his and his wife's spending. "But instead of sitting down with me, the board brought in a team of investigators, which they didn't tell me about until two months afterwards," Ladner continued. "I was totally caught off guard by [the board's] aggressiveness. They kept me in the dark. It was a bewildering and very surprising episode."[11]

Bewildering and surprising indeed! And Dr. Ladner had never sided with the Securities and Exchange Commission against a university board member, picked a fight with the Daughters of the Confederacy, or eliminated his university's athletic program. One can only surmise it must have been something *Mrs. Ladner* said or did (or smoked) that elicited such a harsh reprisal from the board.

***

In response to the restive Vanderbilt board members' newly excited passion for the Sarbanes-Oxley regulations and their consternation over the American University scandal, Chairman Ingram formed a committee to look into the matter. As reported by the *Journal*, this is when the full board learned it had somehow forgotten to approve the university budget and other major financial items for the past five years.

The committee sagely recommended that trustees pay more attention to the business of the university, particularly in the areas of strategic planning, capital spending, and management compensation. It was also recommended that a special panel be created to monitor all Gordon's business expenditures, including costs associated with maintaining his sizable office staff and the upkeep of

Braeburn. The full committee report and recommendations were duly provided to the *Journal* reporters to assist them in their investigation. An anonymous trustee explained that the tougher oversight measures were intended to make "a chancellor who is performing well [be] more effective."[12]

Following the *Journal*'s smudged, meandering dotted line of causality, one might suppose that it was whispered knowledge of those board-initiated inquiries that launched the paper's own epic investigation into the spending habits of the Vanderbilt chancellor. Alas, so little to show for such a noble journalistic enterprise! The newspaper's publishers must have been ever so grateful for the fragrant whiff of good herb and scandal.

True to the titillating format of yellow journalism, the *Journal* saved the most lip-smacking morsel for the article's end:

> In the fall of 2005, university employees discovered that Constance Gee, a tenured associate professor of public policy and education, kept marijuana at Braeburn and was using it there, according to people familiar with the matter. A few weeks later, several trustees and a senior university official confronted Mr. Gee in his office, telling the chancellor he shared responsibility for allowing marijuana on university property, the person familiar with the situation recalls.
>
> Trembling, the chancellor replied: "I've been worried to death over this," according to this person. Mr. Gee said his wife smoked marijuana to relieve an inner-ear ailment, this person says. The Gees declined to comment on the incident.[13]

An "inner-ear ailment"! With two Pulitzer Prize–winning journalists doing five months of sleuthing, the word "Ménière's" had not been mentioned? Of course, a villainess with a genuinely serious disease might not seem so villainous. Smoking pot on the pretext of a mere "ailment" would better serve sensationalist innuendo.

But wait, *Journal* reader, there's more! Not only is she a pot smoker, she's also a damn *liberal*. (Go figure.) This topic—

intimately germane to our report on the implementation of Sarbanes-Oxley by universities—deserves a subheading all its own: "Causing a Stir."

> Mrs. Gee has caused stirs on campus with her liberal politics. She lowered the American flag outside Braeburn to half-staff after President Bush won re-election in 2004. Mr. Gee says he quickly ordered the flag raised back up. She and others signed a letter of protest to the chancellor when Condoleezza Rice, then Mr. Bush's national security advisor, was invited to address graduating students in 2004. Mr. Schoenfeld says Mrs. Gee posted the letter on the couple's refrigerator door at Braeburn.[14]

One would think that Mr. and Ms. Pulitzer Prize could have at least gotten that part straight. For the umpteenth freakin' time: The letter did not protest the chancellor's invitation to Rice to speak at graduation. The letter protested giving her a medal for distinguished public service.

At least the reporters got the critical piece correct: the letter was in fact posted on the refrigerator. Of course, none other than the university's vice chancellor of public affairs provided them with that important detail. He even allowed his name to be used, brave soul.

***

I had just left a doctor's office the afternoon of the *Journal*'s exposé when my cell phone rang. At that time, only a handful of people had my cell number, so I answered it thinking it was Chef Bunny returning a call to her I had made earlier. (I didn't know that one's cell phone number could be accessed on the Internet.) It was a reporter from the *Tennessean*. When he began to rattle off questions, I did as I had been instructed. "I appreciate your interest, but I have no comment," I said. Then I added, "The 'inner-ear ailment' reported in the *Journal* is Ménière's disease. If you want to find out more about it, go online to Washington University's Ménière's website."

The *Tennessean* published a front-page article the following day with a lengthy description of Ménière's disease.[15] The reporter also wrote that I had confirmed smoking marijuana, something I most certainly had not done during our brief conversation. Perhaps the reporter meant that I had done so in my letter to Martha Ingram a year earlier, but that letter was a confidentially marked reply to a supposedly confidential reprimand.

Gordon marched into our bedroom brandishing the *Tennessean*, his face red and contorted: "I told you not to talk to any reporters!"

I related exactly how the reporter had contacted me and what I had said. He refused to believe me, yelling about my indiscretion and stupidity. I asked him whom he was going to believe, his wife or a reporter. I pointed out the numerous times he had been misinterpreted by the press.

That observation gave him a moment's pause, during which I implored, "Gordon, you saw how terribly ill I was. Would you have rather watched me lie on the floor and vomit, or have had me smoke a little pot for some occasional relief?"

He looked me in the eye and said, "I would rather have seen you sick."

***

The following Sunday, the "Issues" section of the *Tennessean* headlined: "Constance Gee Picks Her Battles: Wife of Vandy Chancellor Keeps Her Counsel after Journal's Story."[16] Although an accompanying editorial reiterated the misinformation that I had confirmed marijuana use "to manage symptoms of [my] illness,"[17] the longer article reported I had "been tight-lipped this past week." It was surmised that I had been "caught up, possibly by accident, in a media bombing originally aimed at [Gordon] and the university he serves as chancellor."

The article was highly favorable, characterizing me as outspoken but courageous, and as showing great loyalty to my husband during the messy Brown exodus. The name "Constance," the article noted, means constant, knowledgeable, steadfast, and loyal. As for the reaction of Vanderbilt students to my having been outed on the front page of the *Wall Street Journal* for using marijuana, the *Tennessean* reported this:

The most important members of the Vanderbilt community don't seem to mind what the chancellor's wife does in her spare time. . . . "Really, students think the whole thing is kind of funny," said Reeve Hamilton, a junior English major from Boston. "I mean, every single person I've heard talk about Mrs. Gee and pot says, 'Big deal, who cares?'"

Even if you don't count the residents of McGill Hall, who proclaimed her an honorary resident after the marijuana allegations, Gee seems to have built a sizable fan base among the student body.

"Legal matters aside, she seems like her own woman," Glenda Pavon, a junior from Atlanta said. "This can be a stuffy place, but she doesn't come across that way. Pot on a college campus, even among faculty, isn't exactly news."[18]

Gordon seemed genuinely pleased with the Sunday press coverage, perhaps even a little proud of me. He said we had "dodged a bullet." I thought to myself, *What do you mean "we," Kimosabe? I took that bullet squarely in the heart.* I was relieved that he seemed to consider the incident largely over, even as I lay bleeding.

I was now "Gordon Gee's pot-smoking wife" and a "drug-addled idiot" on blogs and in other Internet commentary written by the kind of people who enjoy anonymously typing mean-spirited words into their computers. The questions of who had instigated the "media bombing" and why hovered over Vandyland like a toxic mushroom cloud.

***

Rebekah married Allan Moore that same week, on 7 October. I was incensed with the *Journal* for waiting to publish its story so close to her wedding. Its reporters were no doubt fully aware of the upcoming nuptials.

It was the most beautiful wedding I'd ever seen. At the reception, Rebekah spoke at length about her love of her father and her mother, Elizabeth. Gordon spoke proudly of Rebekah and Allan. The three of them stood together on the stage. I stood off to the side of the dance floor, smiling and applauding, and thinking I would die of humiliation. I was not invited to join them, nor was my presence acknowledged.

The following afternoon, shortly before Rebekah and Allan were to leave on their honeymoon to the South Pacific, I asked if I could speak privately with them. I said I knew the *Journal* story had been tough on them as well, and that I was sorry. I told Rebekah that I needed her support in my marriage to her father. "Let us begin fresh as adult couples in support of one another," I pleaded.

She shook her head no, her seething anger erupting as she castigated me for the publicity surrounding my use of marijuana, as well as how my behavior might affect her and her father's careers. Allan stepped in to calm her, gently reiterating my plea that we begin anew as a family.

"Thank you," I said to him, reaching out to grasp their hands. She allowed me to hold her hand for a moment. I gave it a squeeze before she retracted it.

"I have a wedding gift for both of you," I said. "A set of Judy Chicago prints depicting passages from the Song of Songs of Solomon: 'O for your scent' and 'My dove in the clefts of the rocks.' Pretty sexy stuff," I smiled.

I gave Rebekah a jade necklace I had bought for her in New Zealand. The jade was carved in a curved shape depicting a Maori symbol for "safety over water."

***

Gordon and I spent a weekend together in Monteagle soon after Rebekah and Allan's wedding. He hadn't joined Lucy and me for a hike in the woods for several months, so I was delighted when he said he'd like to do so. We'd been walking for about an hour when he said he had something he wanted to tell me.

I gasped, thinking he was going to say he wanted a divorce. Lowering his voice as if, in the middle of the woods, someone would hear him, he said, "The *Wall Street Journal* article was an assassination attempt, and we think we know who instigated it."

"Who is 'we'?" I asked, exhaling in relief that the subject was the *Journal* article rather than divorce.

"Mrs. Ingram, Mike, and David," he explained. "We think Cal, Denny, and Lauren [Brisky] were all involved in some way, but that Cal was the ringleader. We can't prove it, but that's what we think."

He explained that the confidential nature, close accuracy, and detail of information provided to the *Journal* made it clear that the informants were positioned at a very high level within the university hierarchy. What was not clear, he continued, was whether the *Journal* reporters had originally contacted one of the informants with questions about Vanderbilt's compliance with Sarbanes-Oxley, or if Cal Turner (or someone close to him) had called the *Journal*. "We think it's more likely that someone from Vanderbilt called the *Journal*."

"Why would they do that?" I asked.

Gordon reminded me of his role as the chair of the shareholders committee during the Securities and Exchange Commission's investigation of Dollar General, and of his having been sent to inform Cal Turner that he had to step down as CEO of the company his family ran. He also reminded me of his stance with the segment of the board that had demanded that Denny Bottorff, because of his alleged marital infidelities, not be allowed to succeed Martha Ingram as chairman, and how he had encouraged Martha to stay on for another term. Gordon noted that Monroe Carell, the trustee who had alerted him to the situation with Denny, and whom the *Journal* described as "a key Gee supporter on the executive committee," had also taken a hit. (The *Journal* reporters had been informed of "a fuss" in 2002 over a long-held, noncompetitive contract by Central Parking Corporation to manage Vanderbilt's parking facilities.[19] Monroe was the founder and chair of Central Parking.)

"But why Lauren?" I asked. "Why would she have conspired against you?"

"She has long disapproved of the amount of money that was spent on Braeburn, and the way we entertain," Gordon said. (Years later, he would tell me that, in the final months of his chancellorship, it became clear to him that she "hated" me and that she and House Manager Wife "had formed a cabal.")

He also mentioned one other Vanderbilt board member, who was an easily morally affronted, petty old goat whom Gordon had long distrusted for his gossipy and Janus-faced character. This person,

Gordon added, would have been more than willing to tell reporters anything he knew, and then some.

"What are you going to do?" I asked.

He said he was going to watch and wait with regard to the board members, but that he intended "to give Lauren enough rope so she can hang herself." I understood what he meant. But even with all that had happened, I felt sorry for her.

I was grateful he had confided in me. Maybe now he saw me as an ally rather than an enemy. If the *Journal* article was the Fort Sumter of a civil war between the board and Gordon, I wanted and needed him to consider me his aide-de-camp.

Later that weekend, he posed a "theoretical question." Would I prefer to (a) stay at Vanderbilt for a few more years, (b) move on to another university, or (c) return to Ohio State?

"Return to Ohio State?" I asked.

Ohio State was currently looking for a new president, he explained, and his old pals Jack Kessler and Les Wexner (Limited Brands apparel retail magnate and Ohio State alumnus) had given him a call immediately following the publication of the *Journal* article. They, too, saw it as an inside job—a bright red flashing sign, with the words "BOARD TROUBLE." Why didn't he come back to where he was loved?

"But what about the $7,000,000 bonus you're to receive at the end of ten years at Vanderbilt? You'd give that up?"

"I wouldn't go anywhere that didn't make me whole," he answered.

It had been nine years since we'd left Columbus. I didn't see going back as a way forward. I told him I would prefer to remain at Vanderbilt long enough to right ourselves. I wanted to stand together, do a really good job, and prove our enemies wrong so that when we did move on (something I now knew was certain) we wouldn't have to do so *once again* under a dark cloud.

I think that was the wrong answer.

***

We spent the Thanksgiving holiday in New York with the newly-weds. The only time Gordon appeared to enjoy himself was when the four of us were together. He refused to do anything alone with me while Rebekah and Allan were off shopping. He remained in

301

our hotel room much of the day, dictating university correspondence and watching television.

The second week of December, Gordon strode into my home office to announce I was to meet with three members of the board and General Counsel Williams to discuss my university responsibilities. The board had formed a special subcommittee to oversee my work and behavior. Gordon also informed me that they were going to require that I sign a three-year random drug testing agreement. When I protested, he jabbed his finger at me and barked, "You *will* sign it!"

"Now that the board has formed a subcommittee in my honor," I hissed back at him, "I would appreciate it if you would cease serving as their messenger boy. If you won't stand with me, then step aside."

***

I met with the new Constance Gee Oversight Committee the following week, on 18 December 2006. I was handed a contractual letter of agreement signed by Martha Ingram, a copy of which the board member and Atlanta attorney Richard Sinkfield proceeded to read aloud. I would no longer report through the usual academic channel of department chair to college dean to provost. The board had decided that, since the provost reported to the chancellor, the standard faculty reporting line presented "a classic conflict of interest." Henceforth, the board would serve as my "supervisor," determining my annual compensation, pay increases, and travel and research budgets.

I would assume the title of "official university representative" with regard to my duties as first lady. I would be paid $31,000 annually for my faculty position and $55,000 for my work as university representative. The university would continue to provide me with a car but would pay only associated expenses for business use. The business-use stipulation on the car was not a new development, but the contractual detail set forth on each and every university provision was rather surprising:

To the degree there is personal use associated with your use of this automobile, that will constitute additional compensation and will be included in your gross income. This includes cleaning, maintenance, repairs, and gas as well. In addition, the University will provide you with a business assistant from the Chancellor's office staff, whose assignment will be to help you with your business and University activities. Any activities that you may have your business assistant perform that are not University related business or activities, will be deemed personal use and subject to reimbursement for that portion of their salary and benefits. All resident house-staff, office personnel, driver, and others are now required to keep a detailed log of duties and time allocated to such duties. These logs will be reviewed quarterly by the Board of Trust office and their determination of personal and business use will be final.[20]

Seems like a lot of log keeping, but fine by me as long as I'm not the one having to make all the minute-by-minute entries, I thought. Then Sinkfield read a passage that made my blood run cold: "Your term of employment as official University representative will be for one year beginning July 1, 2006. If neither party has indicated a desire to terminate this relationship by May 1, of the following year, then the contract will be continued for the next year."

Say what? The board was stipulating its power to terminate a position I held by virtue of being first lady? Whether or not I was to continue in that position would be decided over the next four months, by 1 May. Did they know something I didn't?

From that point, the contractual language descended into a rehash of Ingram's official reprimand fourteen months earlier, reiterating that there had been past complaints concerning my "treatment" of some of the office and residence staff. While her earlier letter had mandated that I undergo General Counsel–approved drug and behavioral therapy, I was now ordered to sign a "Return to Work Agreement," submitting to three years of random drug testing and whatever other treatment the university deemed necessary along the way. If I did not sign, I would forgo any and all employment at the university.

The letter ended on an inspiringly supportive note: "As an official representative of the University, I am sure you understand and agree that image and perceptions are very important. Any violations of the above obligations or behavior on your behalf that are detrimental to the University or its reputation will constitute cause and can result in termination of this Agreement and dismissal as official University representative, and perhaps even loss of your tenure."

After reading the contract, Mr. Sinkfield lectured extemporaneously about my marijuana use, saying it *could not happen again.* The only other woman present sat with her eyes cast down throughout the reading and lecture. The second male board member glanced furtively at me from time to time; Sinkfield and Williams glowered much like Puritan town fathers in a certain Nathaniel Hawthorne novel, intently watching the scaffold spectacle of humiliation course across my face and into my slumping frame.

I assured my judges that I had not used marijuana for well over a year, not since my second ear operation. I told them I would sign the "Return to Work Agreement" but that I found the scolding tone of the letter to be demeaning. I asked if they could revise it, omitting the punitive language. Such language should not be part of a formal contractual agreement. Williams said he would consider my request.

I also told them I thought I should have an attorney look at the contract, as I felt I had no one in my corner. I could tell this request irritated attorneys Sinkfield and Williams. I did not want to provoke them, so I quickly asked if they knew someone they could recommend. I was later given the name of an attorney with whom I made an appointment. He had been expecting my call.

Two days before Gordon and I were scheduled to leave for Westport, where we were to spend the Christmas holidays with Rebekah and Allan, I received a "revised" letter of agreement. I was greatly disappointed, as much of the punitive language remained. I decided to wait until after Christmas to respond.

***

Gordon and I joined four other couples for a holiday dinner at my friend Laura's home in Providence the evening we arrived. In spite of the tension between us, Gordon and I glanced shyly across the table at one another with genuine affection while laughing at the volley of amusing stories and comments. It was as if being temporarily free of Nashville, surrounded by friends and supported by their good cheer, enabled us to appreciate once more what we had always loved about each other.

By the time Rebekah arrived in Westport the following afternoon, Gordon and I were getting along better than we had in months. The three of us sat talking in our living room before leaving for our favorite local restaurant, where Allan was to join us for supper. Gordon sat with his arm around me on the smaller of the two sofas. Rebekah sat across from us in a rocking chair.

The conversation began amiably, but Rebekah soon launched into one of her diatribes, beginning with a treatise on her admiration for Donald Trump (of all people). This topic got Gordon and me laughing—such was her fervor, the improbability of her announcement, and the silliness of her argument. The more we chuckled, lazily lobbing counterarguments her way while trying to divert the conversation toward something more convivial, the more irate she became. I suspect it was the sight of her father and me *getting along* that most irritated her.

The overarching theme of her treatise was related to money, both getting it and spending it. This was a subject she often interjected into family gatherings, usually in the form of a snide aside about a new article of clothing I was wearing or, most upsetting to her, any jewelry her father gave me.

Unsuccessful in her attempt to get us going on Donald Trump, she switched abruptly to my friend Laura. Laura, you see, was the main supplier of Gordon's gifts of jewelry to me, and, as such, richly deserved Rebekah's savage scrutiny of her lifestyle.

Now this pissed me off. As usual, Gordon offered up nothing—not even a "Now, Rebekah"—in defense of Laura or me (I was the one Rebekah was intent on skewering). So by the time we were to leave for supper, things were back to normal: *tense.*

Over the next two hours, she continued her assault, moving from her father's jewelry expenditures to other matters, including her dissatisfaction with the location of the table, her dissatisfaction with where she was seated at the table (we changed our positions and place settings three times to accommodate her), and her disapproval of the designer label on my jacket. (She noticed the label as I offered it to her when she complained of being cold.) The more upset I became, the further Gordon distanced himself from me and allied himself with Rebekah, and now Allan, who had arrived fifteen minutes late.

Allan looked bewildered and uncomfortable, sensing the hostile vibe as he settled at the table. Rebekah had changed her tune immediately on his arrival. She was now making a dramatic effort to carry on charming Christmas dinner conversation, while the other woman at the table sulked and poured herself another glass of wine.

***

"*You're* the adult! Act like one!" Gordon snapped at me when we finally got into the car. (Rebekah and Allan were driving back to the house in his car.) The evening was ruined, and Gordon was angry with me—which, of course, had been Rebekah's intent all along.

At that point, I simply handed it over to her. There was no way this was ever going to work. I was tired of fighting—fighting Rebekah, fighting Gordon, and fighting the Vanderbilt Board of Trust. *I quit. You win.*

I marched into the house, going straight for a small matchbox that contained the remainder of the joint I had smoked a year and a half earlier—the summer before my second ear operation. I knew precisely where it was. I had run across it the previous summer and hid it inside a purse in the back of my closet, just in case.

I closed the door to our bedroom, went into our bathroom, closed the door, and lit the joint. I took two puffs, quickly putting it out and returning it to its hiding place in my closet, knowing full well that I should flush it, but perversely not doing so. I had just put it away when Gordon knocked on the door and opened it. I knew he smelled it. I hoped it smelled like "*Fuck you.*"

Apparently it did. The remainder of our Christmas was spent with me reading in the sunroom and the three of them huddled together in the kitchen or our bedroom. If I walked into the kitchen, they'd move into the living room. I was utterly demoralized.

For over a month, I had been suffering intense headaches that would awaken me in the middle of the night. I had had an MRI in mid-December and was told that I had an aneurysm in the carotid artery at the base of my brain. Four doctors reviewed the MRI; three of them said they thought it was a bad scan. The fourth maintained that there was indeed something "odd" going on in my artery. I'd decided not to pursue the matter, as I just could not take any more bad medical news or procedures. The nightly headaches now lasted into the day.

***

The day after Gordon and I returned from Westport, he informed me that Rebekah and Allan had searched through my closet and found the roach after he and I had left for the airport. (He didn't use the term "roach." He said "a box of marijuana," but a roach was what they found; that was all there was.) They'd taken a photo of the evidence and returned it to its place.

I telephoned Rebekah on the spot, in front of Gordon and using his cell phone, which I swiftly picked up from the table beside him. She answered immediately, expecting her father.

"Did you enjoy going through my things?" I asked her. "Did it make you feel good?"

She did not reply, except to say she wanted to speak with her father.

I handed him the phone.

"You've burned your bridges with Rebekah," he said, after hanging up the phone. "There's no going back."

24

Rook Takes Queen

ON NEW YEAR'S DAY, 2007, I sat down to compose my response to the second draft of the board contract. I had read the letter many times, trying to parse its implications. I discovered that of the $55,000 I had been paid in 2006 for my services as "official university representative," $26,409 was paid back to the university for personal use of my administrative assistant and the residence chef. "Fringe benefits" of $30,577, taxed at thirty-five percent, had been added to my income, in effect whittling down the remaining $28,591 by nearly another $11,000. One hundred percent of the car had been categorized as a "taxable fringe."

I had not realized the effect of the new expense rules on my salary, primarily because they were being enforced retroactively, but also because Gordon had quietly written the check to cover the $26,409 reimbursement. I had never before questioned the university's generosity, but as the letter's brusquely penned requirements and reprimands sank in intellectually and emotionally, my hackles began to rise. *Mrs. Ingram, Vanderbilt Board of Trust: You may take this job and shove it.*

> This letter is in response to your 20 December 2006 draft Letter of Agreement defining the terms of my employment with Vanderbilt University. I write so as to communicate to you as clearly as possible the terms to which I will and will not agree, and to offer

an explanation of my decisions.

I relinquish all compensation and benefits afforded me as the spouse of the University Chancellor or, as the position is now titled, "University representative." I understand this means I am not entitled to the use of any university staff for personal services. I understand this means the university will no longer provide an automobile for my use. Obviously, it is up to the board to decide whether or not any of my travel expenses will be covered if and when I accompany my husband on domestic or international trips for university business. My relinquishing of above compensation and benefits means that I am under no obligation to the University in any way other than the execution of my work as a faculty member.

I will sign the Return to Work Agreement as requested. I accept and understand the board's position and concern. However, I petition that said agreement be presented as a separate document from the Letter of Agreement outlining my academic duties. Although I understand the continuation of my faculty appointment depends on my submission to the terms of the Return to Work Agreement, an academic Letter of Agreement and a Return To Work Agreement are two distinct agreements.

Now then, I wish to offer an explanation as to my decision not to sign a contractual agreement with the University pertaining to the newly coined position of "University representative" for the work I have done heretofore on behalf of Vanderbilt in my capacity as spouse of the Chancellor. There are two primary reasons, the first being most important and influencing strongly my disposition related to the second rationale.

After being given a brief opportunity to review the first draft of the Letter of Agreement (dated 7 December but not in my receipt until 18 December), I requested the punitive language sprinkled throughout be removed from the text. Unfortunately, much of the same language remained in the second draft. I refer specifically to the second full paragraph of page two. . . . The charges of my "treatment of the office and residence staff" are a reiteration of allegations made in your 28 October 2005 letter to me—a letter to which I responded in a forthright, humble, and compliant manner.

It is diminishing to have old allegations brought up repeatedly. If the charges are more recent, I say they are false. It is no secret that the residence house manager and I do not get along. She is often harsh and overbearing with the housekeeping staff and residence chef, and curt with the gardener who does not report to her. She is snippy with me and imposes her will on us all. She has been rude in the extreme to two of my personal guests.

I daresay that no board member would suffer day in and out such a person in his or her place of residence. I have little doubt that she is the source of much, if not all of the allegations of my "treatment" of residence staff—i.e., herself. I stand my ground that such charges are false and born out of jealousy and spite.

As for my "behavior" of over a year ago during a time of grave and extended illness, I have already apologized for that trespass in my letter of 1 November 2005. I have adhered to all demands the board made of me at that time. I have acted in good faith; I have upheld my end of the bargain. But now, fourteen months later, the board demands more from me on that single count—i.e., submission to a three-year term of random drug testing backed by the threat that, if I do not sign the Return to Work form, I will lose my tenured faculty position. Could not the board exhibit discretion in this situation and refrain from ongoing censuring language in its official correspondence to me? I hope we all will be able to proceed with dignity.

This brings me to my second reason for declining the contractual obligations of "University representative." With the realization of [the financial outcome per personal use and fringe benefit tabulation], the proffered agreement does not seem much to my advantage. Consequently, I will forgo that employment opportunity.

I do want you to know that I will continue to host fundraising and social events with the Chancellor, attend University celebrations, welcome University guests into the residence, maintain University-related correspondence, and give loving attention to the aesthetics and atmosphere of the residence and its grounds. Henceforth, those efforts should be considered a gift to the University. I sincerely hope the board, in appreciation of this gift, will allow me peace in my private life.[1]

I showed Ingram's second draft and my response to my attorney. He registered no concern over anything in Ingram's letter, but he raised his eyebrows over the tone of mine. I walked him through Ingram's letter, pointing out the passages I felt should be removed from the main text and, if need be, placed in an appendix. In short, I basically wrote my attorney's response to General Counsel Williams—a reiteration of my initial concerns that had not been addressed—and paid him to send it. He added some collegial, attorney-to-attorney niceties.

I then requested to meet with Williams in the presence of my attorney to discuss the contract and explain my position on its wording and tone. I felt that if we could all sit down together and discuss the matter civilly, we could come to agreement and be done with it. Williams insisted we meet in the offices of Jim Neal and Aubrey Harwell and that they be present for the meeting.

When I entered the expansive reception area of Neal & Harwell on the twentieth floor of the US Bank building, I understood the intimidation factor of the setting. It was three big-boy lawyers—Neal and Harwell being among the top corporate litigators in the country—to one kindly, seventy-five-year-old, semi-retired estate planning specialist.

Williams informed me that the terms of my academic appointment needed to be reconsidered. He pointedly questioned whether the provost would allow me to retain my position as a tenured faculty member. This was an issue that had not previously been raised.

The intimidation ploy was working brilliantly. I was clearly out of my league, and as I glanced at my attorney, I saw that he was out of his. I grew increasingly agitated, telling Williams how hurt I was by his and the board's rough treatment. I said that a little empathy on his part at our initial meeting in October 2005 would have helped immensely. My attorney said very little.

Although Williams remained detached and unsympathetic during the meeting, by its end he was in a cold fury. I knew I had done myself further damage. Williams was Gordon's henchman and a dangerous enemy. I could hear the chink of the toppling dominoes coming ever closer.

***

Several days later, still extremely unnerved, I decided to pursue my last hope to stave off pending disaster: I telephoned Martha Ingram and requested an audience. She agreed to see me at her home.

Once again, I tried to explain how hurt I was by the tone of the contract and the harsh treatment I'd received. I implored her to reconsider the language used in the contract. I did not want my employment agreement to read as an indictment. Otherwise, I was willing to sign off on everything the board demanded of me.

"I'm not trying to be difficult, but please, can't the board allow me this small measure of dignity?"

Then I continued to plead in a ridiculously undignified manner: "Martha, we're friends. *Please* help me with this."

Chairman Ingram let me know in no uncertain terms that (1) her first loyalty was to Vanderbilt and (2) she did not view us as being particularly good friends. She curtly informed me that the university had suffered great damage from the report of my marijuana use, and that there were those who had voiced the opinion that *both* Gordon and I should be fired. Parents and alumni had threatened to stop donating money to the university, she claimed, if I specifically was not fired. I should consider myself fortunate.

She then recounted a news story about the CEO of a major corporation who had used cocaine in the presence of others on a tropical vacation in another country. He had been dismissed (rightly so, she added). The fact that the board had not fired Gordon and me should be seen as a sign that we were being supported as much as possible. I reminded her that I had used marijuana, not cocaine, for medicinal purposes in the privacy of my bathroom, not for fun on a tropical vacation. She saw little difference.

"I'm afraid I'm going to lose my husband over this," I told her. "The board doesn't want to see us divorce, do they?"

Her eyes widened slightly as if I'd surprised her by articulating the truth. She said that the board comprised many individuals, but she did not think that was what was wanted.

She then stood, indicating my audience with her was over. I remember feeling something like the stunned little silverside that had just had its insides expelled from its rear by a very efficient kingfisher.

The next day I telephoned my lawyer to tell him I was capitulating completely and would sign the original contract letter. My marriage was more important to me than saving face, I said.

I called Williams and told him the same thing, asking him to send me the original agreement, or, better yet, I would come to his office that very day to sign it. He said he needed to work through my lawyer and would send him the letter of agreement as soon as possible.

A week later, having not heard from Williams, I released my attorney. I immediately telephoned Williams and told him that, as I no longer had legal representation, he could deal directly with me. He said he had been traveling and busy with other matters, but he would get the contract to me "soon." It was now mid-January.

***

After our decidedly unholy Christmas, I managed to persuade Gordon to return to counseling with me. We set up three appointments: the first in early January, the second two weeks later, the third in early February.

I had voiced my fear that Gordon would divorce me. I even told a close girlfriend, with angry bravado, that I thought it might be best if he did. That was *not*, however, what I wanted. I wanted my husband to love me again, and I wanted to love him again, as we once had before the Brown bruising, before the Ménière's insanity, before the *Journal* uproar, before the Christmas idiocy—before all the bad things happened.

At the first meeting, our therapist told Gordon that mending our marriage would take time and energy on his part as well as mine. She said we needed to spend more private time together, some of it *away* from Vanderbilt and Nashville. I said that I would like nothing more than that. Gordon sat sullenly, not saying much.

Gordon began our second session with the announcement that he had thought "long and hard about it" and had decided that he did not want to spend the time and energy on repairing the marriage.

"I want a divorce," he said. "I cannot stay married to you and remain chancellor of Vanderbilt."

My breath left me. I felt as if he had punched me hard in the stomach.

I followed him out to his car, begging him to reconsider. I gave him every reason I could think of to stay with me. I told him that I would do anything he wanted, *anything*, to keep our marriage together. He said he would think about it, most likely to get me out of his car so he could be on his way.

Throughout the next week and a half, I tried every means I could think of to make him change his mind. At one point, I even got on my knees and begged him. He would say "no" one day, and "I'll think about it" the next.

He kept our third meeting with the therapist to angrily inform me that he had not changed his mind, and to berate me for having "jeopardized" his career and "alienated" Rebekah.

Gordon is ruthless when he makes the decision to fire someone. I had witnessed the sentencing and beheading of two provosts and several upper-level administrators over the course of our marriage. It was chilling to observe.

I remembered that he had just completed a gruesomely efficient decapitation at Ohio State when, during one of our early postnuptial Sunday afternoon drives through the country, he first explained his technique to me. He would give the intended victim some rope—allowing him the illusions of free will and Gordon's continued confidence—while at the same time cutting off the intended's access to sensitive internal operations. He would then step back and watch as the person began to falter with the realization that doors were shutting around him. With growing panic, the person would make more and larger missteps, until he found himself trapped and flailing in a corner. Gordon would wait just a bit longer, watching and gathering the most damning evidence, and then summon the person to his office for a cool kill.

"I hope you don't fire me," I'd said with a shudder.

"I would never fire you," he'd replied. "You're my wife."

I flashed back to that conversation. *I've been fired.* Why hadn't I recognized the familiar pattern? When he had confided in me during our walk in the woods three months ago, when he said he was giving Lauren "enough rope to hang herself"—had he also meant that for me? If so, for how long had this sting operation been going on?

At the time, I thought the kill had been made. He'd said he wanted a divorce. I'd been fired. What I didn't understand until later was that the game was entering into its most ferocious stage. I desperately needed to believe that Gordon didn't fully understand it either.

***

Gordon and I convened with Aubrey Harwell and Jim Neal at their offices on 15 February. I had not felt that it was in my best interest to meet with them, since Neal & Harwell represented Vanderbilt. It seemed to me like a gorilla-size conflict of interest—once again, a big gang of them versus a diminutive gang of me, myself, and I. Gordon dangled the hope that, if I met with them, he might change his mind about the divorce. He said that Harwell had agreed to serve as arbitrator. I asked why we needed an arbitrator if there was the possibility we might not get a divorce. That question did not please my husband, so I backed down and agreed to the meeting. After all, I *had* told Gordon that I would do "anything" to save our marriage.

Gordon began the meeting with the declaration that he wanted a divorce. Three lawyers looked at me for my reaction.

"I don't," I said.

"You can't deny him a divorce," one of the partners replied.

"Yes, I can," I said.

I was so numb with grief and fatigue that I don't remember much of the conversation, except that at one point I was sitting in silence for several minutes with all of them staring at me. One of them had just asked me for the third or fourth time if I would agree to a divorce. I turned in my chair to look at the city of Nashville stretched out below, the Cumberland River dividing it like a giant brown serpent. *I should just get up and leave*, I thought, but I was so tired.

"OK," I mumbled finally.

"Good," someone said.

I think it was about then that Neal pulled a chair up close to mine and asked in a condescendingly, pseudo-fatherly manner if I "trusted" him.

"No," I replied.

My consent having been achieved, the topic turned immediately to how to go about it. Gordon insisted that Harwell would arbitrate a settlement, even though Harwell had advised us early in the meeting that we should each hire a lawyer.

"We don't want to go to court," Gordon said, presumably for the both of us. I didn't say much because what I had to say didn't matter much. I sat quietly crying as Gordon made plans. The meeting lasted for two miserable hours.

Harwell walked me to the elevator. As I stepped in, he said, "Get your own lawyer. Be selfish. Think of yourself."

***

General Counsel Williams had the third contract draft hand-delivered to my former attorney the very next day. Williams had not forgotten that I'd telephoned him a month earlier to tell him I had released my attorney. He hadn't forgotten that I'd said I would come to his office to sign the original letter of agreement.

The general counsel, in representing the Board of Trust, had now shut off direct communications with me. I no longer existed except as a third party. From my perspective, this bypass looked like an extended middle finger thrust in the face of the tortured by the torturer as he tightened the screws.

Williams asked the man who was no longer my attorney to review the draft copy and "let me know what you think." "As I mentioned," the cover letter continued, "I still need to run these by our Board committee before they are presented to Dr. Gee for signing."[2] My former attorney had himself told Williams that he no longer represented me, but Williams forwarded the document to him anyway.

The only aspect of the letter that had changed was the section regarding my "term of employment as official university representative." The language describing the termination process was now much more detailed—even though I had already formally declined the position in my letter to Martha Ingram six weeks earlier. The board was covering its bases.

My former attorney forwarded me a copy of the letter the same day he received it, Friday, 16 February. I signed it and handed it to Williams at a basketball game the following evening. I wanted this awful mess to be over. I still held out the slim hope that with my complete and documented surrender, Gordon would see that I was sorry for everything and find it in his heart to give me another chance.

When I told Gordon I had signed and returned the contract, agreeing to everything, he replied, "Well, if you'd done that in the beginning, we might not be where we are today." Until then, he'd maintained that he hadn't shared his divorce plans with anyone, but he now announced that Williams, along with "several others," had known for some time he'd been "thinking about" divorcing me.

Four days later, my former attorney received another letter from Williams, which read:

> As I mentioned to you on the telephone on Monday, I received a signed copy of the <u>draft</u> Letter of Agreement for Dr. Constance Gee that I forwarded to you on February 16. At the end of Vanderbilt's basketball game with Florida on Saturday, Dr. Gee gave me a sealed envelope with my name on it. Inside I found a signed copy (by her) of the draft I had forwarded to you. In addition, there was a handwritten note from Dr. Gee stating that she wanted to cease the "back and forth" and "sign the original." As I informed you on Friday, this draft was not for presentation for signing purpose until I could clear the letter with my Board of Trust members.
>
> In addition, Dr. Gee's note indicated that she had released you and instructed me to deal directly with

her. As you can imagine, this is very confusing since I am not sure if I should deal with you or Dr. Gee. Furthermore, I am sure you understand that the draft Dr. Gee has signed has no legal effect for a number of reasons, i.e., (i) it was a draft, (ii) it was not signed by Mrs. Ingram, and (iii) it was not presented for signature but rather for comment.
Please advise.[3]

Dear General Counsel Williams, as they say in Rhode Island: *fugetaboutit!* I decided to take Harwell's advice to hire a divorce attorney.

***

Gordon announced that he wanted to have a "talk" with me, scheduling it for that Saturday afternoon. He began the meeting by telling me that he intended to proceed with the divorce, but he might change his mind at any time up until its finalization. Whether he changed his mind would "depend on how well the arbitration goes." That is, if everything goes smoothly and doesn't get litigious or hostile, he could, up until the moment of signing the divorce papers, stop the proceedings. Even if he decided not to divorce me, he would ask me to sign a financial postnuptial.

At that point in his monologue, I asked if I could recount his points to be certain that I accurately understood each one. I quickly went to my office to fetch a pad of legal paper and pen, returning to my chair, which was facing his. I could see that he was uncomfortable with this turn of events.

I began, "As I understand it, you want to:

1. Proceed with the divorce?"
   "Yes."
2. "Might change your mind up to the last moment of negotiations?"
   "Possibly."
3. "The condition of your possibly changing your mind is that everything goes smoothly between us during the arbitration process?"

318

As I recorded that item on my legal pad, he looked alarmed and began to backpedal. He said he was not giving me a "condition" per se. It was just that he was "determined we be fair with each other and that we determine we are going to remain friends." "One should always be open to the possibility of changing my mind," he explained ungrammatically.

What he meant, he continued, was that "keeping open the possibility of not getting a divorce would depend on how we move ahead." That is not a "condition," he reiterated, "but a matter of civility." That is, if things became contentious, he "certainly wouldn't feel like getting back together."

Obviously flustered and growing angrier and more agitated, he added, "But I'm willing to take that [the possibility of reconciliation] off the table!"

I have to admit that by then I was feeling rather smug about my newfound lawyering ability. It was much more comfortable being the cross-examiner than the cross-examined. I steadily recounted the final point:

4. "If there were to be a last-minute reconciliation, the continuation of our marriage would rely on my signing a postnuptial?"
    "Yes."

He said he required "a financial agreement so that everything would be made clear in the future." He then added that not only would there be no possibility of reconciliation without a financial postnuptial, but he would also want a "behavioral postnuptial" stating that I would (1) never again smoke marijuana; (2) never again exhibit anger toward other people, specifically university staff; and (3) undergo anger management counseling.

He then said he wanted us to agree on a formal statement to the board that would also serve as a press announcement. He planned to tell the board at its meeting on Wednesday that "we are considering divorce." He handed me a paper on which he had written: "Constance and I have been confronting serious difficulty in our personal life. As we continue to review our options we remain supportive of each other and committed to our responsibilities to Vanderbilt and the community."

"Why does the board deserve to know we are *considering* divorce?" I asked. Perhaps a few of *them* are considering divorce. Does that mean they owe *us* an explanation?

Why in the world would the university want to release a press statement to that effect? If he and the board issued a statement, it should speak only for him. "Remember, it's you, not me, who want a divorce," I said.

Furthermore, I was not going to sign any statement attesting to our personal difficulties and continued "commitment" to Vanderbilt and the community.

I then told him that I had hired a lawyer and that from here on he would need to have his lawyer speak with mine. He became very angry, saying that I was *not* to have hired a lawyer until *after* the arbitration process, and only then "to review the facilitated agreement."

Gordon claimed that he had not yet hired a lawyer—something that might have been true according to the letter, but not the spirit, of the law. I had heard it, well, let's say, from "a person close to the matter" that the most renowned divorce attorney in Nashville had been "reserved," if not actually contracted, on Gordon's behalf.

"*Do you know why I'm divorcing you?* Have you *thought* about it?!" he snarled.

"I've done nothing but think about it," I said. "Have *you* truly thought about it?" I asked.

Incredibly, we went out to dinner and a movie later that evening. During dinner, he asked if I would go out with him on occasion after we were divorced.

"Go out with you?" I asked.

"Not on a date," he sputtered, "but for lunch and sometimes a movie."

"You know I don't do lunch," I said.

He laughed and said he knew that. He didn't like lunch engagements much either. "But I'd still like to see some movies with you. I love to talk with you about movies."

"You sound confused," I said.

"I am," he replied.

He admitted rather apologetically that he really hadn't thought this all through. I believed him on that point, but I also wondered if he was trying to keep me off balance. I had maintained my composure through our afternoon "talk," but it was harder at a table for two in a candlelit restaurant.

I did believe he was unnerved about what he had unleashed, but I knew he felt he could not back down. It broke my heart.

The next day, as if to shake off the tenderness of the night before and rev up his own resolution, Gordon reiterated that he still intended to make the formal board announcement about our "considering" a divorce. *And then what?* I thought wearily. *Another month or two of playing Cat Smacks Around Half-Dead Mouse until . . . until what?*

I telephoned my lawyer Monday morning and told her I was ready to file for divorce. *Maybe seeing the end of our marriage in writing will jolt him into reconsidering*, I thought halfheartedly. She agreed that we should do so prior to Gordon's announcement to the board. I told Gordon the following morning that I had filed, and that he needed to be home by six o'clock that evening to receive the papers. "Why did you do that?" he asked. He seemed genuinely surprised.

The twenty-something guy hired to serve the divorce petition stood with me in the back hall of the residence, waiting. As the time approached, the tears began to spill over; I didn't want him to see me brushing them away. Gordon was a few minutes late.

He swung open the door, entering suddenly like an actor whose cue had taken him by surprise. "So sorry to keep you waiting!" he chimed to the process server, as if the young fellow were a dinner party guest. Gordon chatted breezily with him as he scanned and signed his acknowledgment of receipt, asking him where he was from and where he had gone to college.

Gordon's complete lack of empathy did me in. I was crying and he was smiling. The contrast was too much to comprehend. I thought about a fairy-tale February thirteen years before in a raspberry-hued dining room, when all the world had seemed to fade away as we conversed urgently, hungrily. I thought about falling in love on a revolving dance floor high above Fifth Avenue. The sweet beginnings and an entire marriage, now eclipsed. My heart squeezed tight, hurting. *Why are we doing this? This is a terrible mistake. Please do not sign those papers!*

Gordon finished and neatly saw the young man to the front door with a warm "Thank you, goodbye!" He barely looked my way as he walked past me out the back door and left for a dinner engagement.

By ten o'clock the following morning, Wednesday, 28 February, the word was out and online with a prepared statement from the Vanderbilt chancellor: "Constance and I have agreed to seek divorce. While this is a difficult decision, we remain committed to each other's happiness and success. I ask that you respect our privacy regarding this issue."[4]

Vanderbilt's online student news, InsideVandy.com, reported:

> Vanderbilt spokesperson Michael Schoenfeld is confident the divorce will not have an effect on the chancellor's career at Vanderbilt.
>
> "It is, of course, a difficult personal decision for him, but Chancellor Gee is deeply committed to Vanderbilt's success and is eager to continue building on the extraordinary progress that has occurred over the past six years in every part of our mission," Schoenfeld said.
>
> Some people speculate if Constance Gee will continue to teach at Vanderbilt once the divorce is finalized.
>
> Five calls and detailed messages to her university phone number went unanswered.
>
> The split comes five months after a report in The Wall Street Journal addressed Constance Gee's use of marijuana in the chancellor's university-owned residence, Braeburn.[5]

All reports on the divorce, from the beginning of the process to its end, cited the *Wall Street Journal* article and my marijuana use. Most media commentators relished using the descriptor "dope smoking," or something equally derogatory, over the less sensationalistic phrase "use of marijuana." Vanderbilt student reporters writing about the subject were much more professional in their tone and wording than many of their "adult" counterparts.

Several days later, a faculty friend telephoned to tell me what her husband (also a Vanderbilt professor) had said on hearing the news of our divorce: "Gordon will have to leave Vanderbilt. He has allowed himself to be publicly castrated by the board."

***

Over the course of the previous month, I'd received several terse email reprimands from Gordon's office manager about a variety of matters, the most hurtful being Lucy. Office Manager Wife had decreed that Lucy was "not to attend any food events at Braeburn" and was no longer permitted in the catering kitchen. Lucy had always been allowed to wander through parties large and small at all the residences where we'd lived. She was often with aunt Bunny in the catering kitchen, just as any household pet likes hanging around the warmth and good smells of a kitchen, and the hum of activity that goes on there. Lucy was a regular Braeburn personality; our guests asked for her all the time and would go from room to room looking for her. She'd always been perfectly behaved, but recently she had become a little more intent on dispatching any meaty tidbits left unguarded at coffee-table level. Guests insisted on sneaking her hors d'oeuvres, finally managing to undo her years of training not to beg or eye people's food. (I once caught a man trying to give her a lump of sugar. "She's not a horse!" I told him.)

Perhaps one of the reasons guests had begun feeding her more often was that she was becoming noticeably thinner. Lucy had been diagnosed with liver cancer the previous summer and had begun to lose weight, despite our efforts to get her to eat. (She'd usually make an exception, however, for a chunk of grilled lamb proffered by a kindhearted but misdirected guest.) We now had to watch her more closely. When she'd start sniffing at the hors d'oeuvres table, we had to shut her in the family kitchen. I hated doing that, especially because I knew how much she wanted to be a part of things, but I knew it was best for all concerned.

When it became clear that the ax was coming down on my head, Office Manager Wife apparently felt the need to pile on. I suppose she figured that writing harshly worded emails about Lucy would be an effective way to do so. Lucy was to be kept locked in my "private living quarters" from here on during any university events. Lucy and I were now two bitches banished on the same boat. Frankly, I couldn't have begged for better company.

***

A glimmer of happiness came my way soon after the divorce announcement. The administration finally agreed to get House Manager Wife out of Braeburn. For the duration of the "transition" (the time it took for me to vacate the premises), my domestic nemesis would work out of an office in Kirkland Hall. She would continue to perform her duties at the residence during scheduled events (when I was confined to the attic) and oversee the house staff through off-site meetings and by telephone, but she would not be in the house on a daily basis. Hurrah! The chef, gardener, and housekeepers were elated by the news. Even with the heaviness of the divorce hanging smoglike over lovely Braeburn, and my abrupt change in status from first lady to first persona non grata, things were significantly more pleasant without her.

25

Endgames and New Beginnings

IT WAS AGREED THAT I would leave early for Westport that summer and move out of Braeburn the following fall. Gordon told me that I should move into the Monteagle house in the interim, but, as unsettling as it was living as a ghost at Braeburn, I didn't want to be so far away from the handful of friends in Nashville who were standing by me. I was also trying to write a research paper and needed reliable Internet access.

The complete truth of it was that I still harbored the fantasy that Gordon would come to his senses, profess his undying love, and whisk me away to Paris for a romantic reunion, after which we would ride out of town together to the University of Happily Ever After.

This, unfortunately, was not to be. Instead, he repeatedly told me, "I already consider us divorced."

When I brightly pointed out that although we were in the process of getting a divorce, we were, by law, as married as ever, he snapped, "I don't care. We're divorced! I'm through with this marriage!" (Leave it to a lawyer to think he is exempt from the law.)

"I've moved on to a new life and I'm very happy about it," he said unhappily.

He could now attend more university events since he no longer felt "compelled" to come home.

"Even more university events? Well, that *does* sound like fun," I retorted.

As annoyed as he was that I was hanging around, he still wanted to have dinner and watch a video together on the nights he wasn't out enjoying his new life of more university events. We'd eaten dinner and watched a video together for the past twelve years of our lives. The routine was a comfort to us both.

It was as if we were watching ourselves in a movie. Surely this was happening to two other hapless nitwits. Then some barbed zinger would fissure our mostly cordial formality, and it would all get personal again.

"You're just not cut out for this," he pronounced one evening. ("This" meaning the role of a university president's wife.)

"Do you think it's too late to learn? Perhaps I could sign up for a little remedial course in presidential spousing," I countered. "Or maybe it's that I'm not cut out to be the *Vanderbilt* chancellor's wife—although, to be fair, you have to admit I deserve an A in southern hostess-ship. I think it was the 'keep your mouth shut' part of the job that destroyed my GPA."

"This is all your fault," he said. ("This" meaning the divorce and the entire mess surrounding it.)

I offered to take seventy percent of the blame, if he'd assume the other thirty percent. No? "OK, what about I take eighty percent?" No dice.

"All right," I continued to bargain, "I'll take 97.6 percent. Will you take 2.4 percent?"

"*No!* It's *all* your fault!" he shouted.

Then, noticing my bemused smirk, he chuckled grimly at himself and at the inanity of the exchange.

"OK, you're right," I conceded. "It *is* all my fault. Now will you forgive me?"

***

I'd wept when I said my Westport farewell-to-the-river prayer the year before. Even as I'd said the words—*Please protect this house and let Lucy and me come back safely next summer*—I knew it would be the last time she'd stand with me on the dock. She was failing fast now, even as everyone at Braeburn pampered her. It's amazing we kept her alive as long as we did. She didn't seem to be in any pain, so as long as we could entice her to eat and to stalk a squirrel or two, we willed her to live. Or maybe it was that she willed herself to live—*for me*, I believe. By spring, my beautiful dog was skin and bones.

I let her go on 25 May 2007. The vet came to the residence. I'd given her a Valium, as he'd instructed, so she'd be relaxed. I didn't need to; she was already relaxed. She knew what was going to happen and was ready. I lay beside her on our bed, stroking her as the doctor inserted the catheter into her hind leg and gave her an intravenous sedative. He left the bedroom for several minutes while it took effect. I thought she would lose consciousness, but she didn't. Her eyes showed that she heard me when I whispered, "Lucy, Mommy loves you. Thank you for being with me. You're such a good girl." The doctor returned to inject the euthanasia solution. I placed my hand over her heart and, a second after he injected the drug, felt its final beat.

Bunny helped me to gently wrap her body in a blanket and place it in the backseat of my car. I had arranged to have her cremated and planned to remain at the pet crematorium while it was being done. It takes a surprisingly long time for a body to turn into bits of bone and ash. The walls outside the small waiting room were covered floor to ceiling with messages of love from humans to their animal companions. That was where I first read the words to the poem "The Rainbow Bridge." Please let it be so, for that would be my heaven.

Gordon was the only person at Braeburn who didn't join in the communal grieving over her death. (Even House Manager Wife cried for Lucy, for as much as she disliked me, she loved Lucy.) I think Gordon could not allow himself to express any emotion, other than anger, for fear of losing momentum in his and his team's drive toward divorce. The university had already expended a lot of public relations capital on the affair, as well as weeks of the general counsel office's time in gathering and organizing Gordon's financial information for his lawyers. Vanderbilt had much invested in a speedy resolution to this unattractively distracting aspect of the chancellor's life.

I left for Westport with Lucy's ashes in a small cherry-wood box on the seat next to me.

***

Not long after I arrived in Westport, a friend sent me an issue of a Nashville weekly with a cover photograph of Gordon and Martha Ingram dancing at "Swan Ball 2007."[1] Martha is facing the camera with a big yahoo smile, one arm wrapped around Gordon, the other flung gleefully skyward. "Like a Dallas Cowboy cheerleader riding a mechanical bull," read a Post-it note attached to the paper. (No disrespect intended to Dallas Cowboy cheerleaders.)

Ingram was riding tall in the saddle astride her bull a week later after the news broke that he had turned down an offer by Ohio State for a sequel as its president. Echoing a press statement in which the chancellor promised to remain at Vanderbilt for "a long time to come," she told the *Tennessean*, "I expect Chancellor Gee will be at Vanderbilt University for a long, long time."[2]

"My commitment to Vanderbilt is unwavering and unshakable," said the chancellor.[3]

Two weeks later, the bull bolted for "Cowlumbus," leaving the cheerleader sprawled unladylike on the ground.

The news that Gordon had jumped ship for Ohio State was all over the Internet by the time I found out about it. It was a good thing that Gordon thought to telephone me, because a reporter from the *Tennessean* called five minutes after we hung up. The title of the resulting article, "Departure Catches Gee's Wife by Surprise, Too," pretty much summed it up.

Well, that's that, I thought. The tenuous hopes I'd harbored of patching things up after a couple of months' separation vaporized in the glare of the early-afternoon sunlight on the water. My married life passed before my eyes—so much of it good, *really* good, but some of it not so good, and in fact truly painful. We met and fell in love at Ohio State, moved to Brown, then on to Vanderbilt. Now he was returning to Ohio State, and I was being left on the roadside like a greasy taco wrapper. What if we'd simply stayed put at Ohio State? It might have all turned out so differently.

A new fellow came into my life in early August, from the same bloodline as sweet Lucy. I looked into his black-brown eyes and said, "It's you and me, babe."

He fastened onto my gaze with a Bob Marley look that said, "Everything's gonna be all right."

His name is "Rastafari Mon" because he is a black, handsome, laid-back, dready dude.

Rasta and I played on the beach for three weeks and then reluctantly began the drive south and inland. "This is going to be a real bummer," I warned him, but he just wagged his tail. He was cool with whatever awaited as long as it was with me, there was a ball, and he had a way to get wet, mon. I love dogs.

***

For the final time, the life Gordon and I built was being dismantled. This time around, he and I would place our belongings in separate piles. His boxes, labeled "EGG," were traveling six hours north. My boxes—labeled "CBG's personal effects" by House Manager Wife, as if I were deceased—were traveling ten minutes east to a house with a year's lease. My boxes were sad.

Missing from my boxes was a small cache of minicassette tapes and pocket-sized notebooks. Soon after the publication of the *Journal* article, while Lucy and I walked in the woods or drove to and from Monteagle, I began recording my thoughts about the downward spiraling of my marriage and my conversations with Gordon, House Manager Wife, and others. I had stowed the tapes and notebooks in a cabinet in my home office before leaving for Westport. Most of the contents of my office had been packed and itemized for storage by the time I'd returned to Braeburn in early September. I never found my tapes and notebooks.

After Gordon's departure for Ohio State, one of the first edicts sent from the succeeding chancellor's office was that Braeburn should henceforth be called by its street address: 211 Deer Park. Referring to the house by its given name was deemed too grandiose by an administration trying to jettison any remnants of the previous administration's reputation for "lavishness." The new chancellor announced that he and his family would not reside at 211 Deer Park.

***

November 2007 brought a flurry of news stories about highly paid college presidents, in which the new Ohio State president always figured most prominently. The *Chronicle of Higher Education* (or "The Barnacle," as fun-loving faculty call it) dedicated an entire issue to executive compensation: "What Leaders Make." Gordon received his very own special section, "The View from the Top: E. Gordon Gee Goes Public."[4]

A *New York Times* article, "More College Presidents in Million-Dollar Club," cited E. Gordon's pre-bonus pay package as "probably the highest of any public institution."[5] NashvillePost.com trumpeted "Annual College Heads' Comp Poll Has Gee in 4th Place."[6] The *Tennessean* followed with "Presidents Earn Degree in Ka-Ching."[7]

This was smack dab in the middle of the discovery phase of the divorce. I hoped he had a bad case of heartburn.

***

I decided to remain in Nashville and continue teaching at Vanderbilt until I could figure things out a bit. I was terribly confused about what to do and, still smarting from all my losses, couldn't bear to make another big mistake.

Gordon's abrupt departure made that decision easier in some ways and more difficult in others. It was easier in that I didn't have to see him around town and read about him, day in and out, in the local news. I was spared watching him living the large life as I crept along the periphery of the life we once shared. His leaving made it more difficult because much of the Vanderbilt community (like the Brown community beforehand) blamed me for his defection. I could count on the three-fingered hand of a blind sawyer the number of Vanderbilt faculty who offered me a single kind word the semester following his disappearing act.

I accept a modest percentage of blame for Gordon's quitting Nashville. But I can tell those who continue to bemoan his departure—and there are many who still do—that he would never have remained at a place where he could not trust the people with whom he had to work closely. The *Wall Street Journal* article was stark material evidence of what his intuition had long whispered.

Then there was that small matter of the $7 million longevity bonus, which would have been counted as part of our marital assets should he have remained at Vanderbilt until June 2010. He had told me in no uncertain terms that he would "never go anywhere that didn't make [him] whole." That type of compensation needn't be spelled out in a contract if a wealthy donor is underwriting it. Better to have an undocumented than documented wholeness during a divorce.

Amid our divorce proceedings, my department chairman summoned me to his office "to talk about your future." When I told him I intended to remain at Vanderbilt, he advised me "as a friend," in a most *unfriendly* tone of voice, "If I were you, I'd get the hell out of Dodge!" He (and many others, he intimated) clearly resented my having tenure. "You were forced down our throats," he said.

I used to think that, had I been braver, I would have packed my bags and gotten out of Dodge as advised. I have now come to think that it takes a heap more courage to face the music than to flee it. This is not to say that remaining on the battlefield is a *wiser* course of action. As conventional wisdom has it, you've got to know when to walk away and know when to get on your horse and ride. Gordon knew when, and he rode like the wind.

I wanted to prove myself to Nashville (a city whose musical soul I had come to love) and to myself. I needed to prove that I was not the horrible person that a failed marriage (not to mention a humiliating public scandal) makes you feel you are. I decided I would stay in Nashville, do penance, and walk away, not run, when the time seemed right.

I was also reluctant to leave for financial reasons. Gordon had told me repeatedly during the divorce proceedings that I would be foolish to give up my tenured position at Vanderbilt. I would need the income, it was pointed out. I doubted seriously that I would be able to find a comparable position at another university. Not after I'd been teaching and publishing sporadically for the past nine years, having set aside much of my academic work for the time and effort required to fulfill the role of first lady. Not after I'd been outed on the front page of the *Wall Street Journal* for smoking pot. Not after I'd been through a very public divorce from one of the most admired university presidents in the country. Academically I felt adrift farther south than Cape Horn. Safe harbor at Tierra del Fuego Community College was not even an option.

Vanderbilt was stuck with me and I was stuck to Vanderbilt, like a piece of spat-out gum on the sole of the Commodore's big black boot. I adhered, and I put all that hadn't been flattened out of me into teaching.

***

Gordon didn't bother showing up for our 18 March court date. His lawyer sent his own second-in-command to answer the obligatory questions.

I took the stand. The judge asked me several questions, including whether I wanted to change my name. I declined, thinking "Gee" might be a bit more useful than "Bumgarner" for local restaurant reservations. It would be infinitely more useful should I write a sleazy tell-all.

Our thirteen-year marriage was over in a matter of minutes.

A week later we spoke on the telephone:

"Sorry about all that," he said.

"Yeah, me too."

Gordon and I met for dinner two months later, when he was in town for a Gaylord Entertainment board meeting. The fact was that, in spite of all that had happened, we missed each other's company. The fact was that I was still in love with him.

Shortly afterward, Gordon sent me a two-page puff piece from the *Columbus Dispatch*, "It Starts with Me"[8] (*me, me!*), and a recent issue of the periodical *At Home in Columbus*.[9] "I do want you to see that what I told you privately, I confess to publicly," he wrote in an enclosed note.

The cover shot of *At Home* sported the highest-paid public university president in the country, wearing a wide grin and pink polka-dot bowtie strategically askew, opening the front door to his stately, newly renovated presidential manse. *See how easily you can be replaced by an interior designer?* his smiling visage seemed to say. A six-page, full-color spread chronicled the gorgeousness of the residence and his delight at how perfectly it turned out. Remnants of our married life hung on walls and perched in corners.

I was still living in complete disarray, with most of my belongings stacked to the ceiling or stored in cardboard boxes in the garage. Rolling my eyes at his obliviousness in blithely sharing his luxurious housing circumstances with me, I began reading the *Dispatch* story:

> Ohio State President E. Gordon Gee likes to joke he
> is married to Carmen Ohio. He sort of is, just as he's
> been devoted to the four other universities he's led.

But that dedication has cost him. Gee believes that his commitment to his work helped cause his recent divorce from his second wife, whom he had met and married during his first term at Ohio State University.

"I loved my wife and didn't want to get divorced," said Gee. . . .

"Yes, I want time for my family, myself, my friends; but I just love the university. It is my one and only priority right now. It is my life."[10]

I loved my wife and didn't want to get a divorce. The "I loved my wife" part was probably true. Whenever we spoke over the telephone and during our recent dinner, he told me repeatedly that he still loved me. But the "didn't want to get a divorce" part? Was he implying that *I* was the one who wanted the divorce, or was he saying that some outside entity imposed it on him? Were his trousers alight, dangling in the night, or had he let himself be bullied into divorcing a woman he "loved"?

He was now admitting to the world (or at least to readers of the *Dispatch*) that his obsessive work habits had contributed to the demise of our marriage—a big *aha* he had also shared with me during our dinner date. He was finally ready to accept part of the fault I had offered him fifteen months earlier (maybe even more than 2.4 percent). My cynical self couldn't help but note the safety factor in doing so *after*, rather than prior to or during, the hardball divorce negotiations.

Ever the public relations strategist, Gordon the workaholic (ex-)husband made a vulnerable confession that must have appealed to all the ignored wives of central Ohio. Certainly, Buckeyes far and wide would feel more kindly toward a man who loved his wife and didn't want to get a divorce than one who didn't love his wife (at least not as much as his job) and initiated a divorce. Here is a fellow who sacrificed his marriage for love of the university—his one and only priority, *his life*.

Elwood Gordon Gee. That's my husband emeritus—student body president, best actor, Eagle Scout, and one of the greatest university presidents in the country.

***

Douglas Adams's *The Hitchhiker's Guide to the Galaxy* was one of the more memorable reads of my happily, hazily misspent midtwenties. Printed on its cover were the words "DON'T PANIC." The science fiction writer Arthur C. Clarke once observed that "don't panic" is "perhaps the best advice that could be given to humanity."

I had told Gordon as we navigated the dark rapids of the crocodile-haunted Pasión River in Guatemala that, should we capsize: *Don't panic. Do not thrash about. Stay calm and I will pull you to shore.* Luckily, we were not put to the test that night—but we later were and we both failed. Our marital boat became ever more unstable as we thrashed about, each subsumed by our own panic, until we capsized into a black river of crocodiles.

The Good Ship Ohio State plucked Gordon out of the water. He barely even got wet. I was relieved for him because I knew he couldn't swim emotional depths, even though he could move powerfully through political currents. I felt relief for myself because his rescue meant that I had not shipwrecked his career— the consequence he most feared and the source of his panic.

Another good piece of advice offered by the *Hitchhiker's Guide* is to keep track of your towel. A towel "is about the most massively useful thing an interstellar hitchhiker can have."[11] Wrapped around you, it offers warmth. It is something to lie on or sleep beneath. It can serve as a sail on a small raft or be waved in emergencies as a distress signal. And, of course, "you can dry yourself off with it if it still seems to be clean enough." Yet, even more important than its undeniably great practical value is a towel's "immense psychological value."

> For some reason, if a strag (strag: non-hitchhiker) discovers that a hitchhiker has his towel with him, he will automatically assume that he is also in possession of a toothbrush, face flannel, soap, tin of biscuits, flask, compass, map, ball of string, gnat spray, wet weather gear, space suit, etc., etc. Furthermore, the strag will then happily lend the hitchhiker any of these or a dozen other items that the hitchhiker might

accidentally have "lost." What the strag will think is
that any man who can hitch the length and breadth of
the galaxy, rough it, slum it, struggle against terrible
odds, win through, and still knows where his towel is,
is clearly a man to be reckoned with.[12]

It took me another four years to make it to shore. Kind people
buoyed me up as I dogpaddled frantically in one direction and then
another—until I finally caught sight of land. Little by little the
panic subsided and my swimming strokes became stronger and
smoother. Then my toes touched bottom and I walked calmly onto
the beach where, lo and behold, there was a nice blue-and-white-
striped towel, folded and waiting for me. My towel assumes various forms: the peace I find when Rasta and I walk in the woods, the
pleasure of sharing a meal with a small group of friends, and the
satisfaction that writing gives me.

My father stated in his diaries that he had to write his way to
understanding and acceptance: "I have to write in order to face it,
so I can move on." I remain my father's daughter in many ways, but
I am also my mother's. I now better understand her material inse-
curities, her lack of self-respect, and the circumstances of her self-
imprisonment. No longer do I have contempt for women who
subjugate themselves to men out of fear and dependency; I
empathize with them. While I had no cause to fear for my physical
safety, as my mother did, there were times when I feared Vanderbilt's control of my husband and his power over me. I'd become
dependent on Gordon for continued access to a prestigious
lifestyle, for financial security, and, most disturbingly, for my concept of who I was and what I was worth.

When I married Gordon I liked to think that, other than a law
degree and a high IQ, he had nothing in common with my father. It
took me many years to recognize that Gordon used his work like
my father used alcohol—to barricade himself from other people.
Although he came into daily contact with hundreds of people,
Gordon could define (and confine) his interactions with them
through his persona of a very friendly but extremely busy university president. The vast majority were thrilled to have the busy university president speak a few words in passing (and remember their
names!). By the time he made it home to the sofa and television,

Gordon wanted nothing more than to *disengage* from other humans—especially those inclined to make emotional demands. I understood and generally respected that, yet the feeling of always being the last in line for a measured dollop of male attention carried a particularly powerful punch for me, as an adult child of an alcoholic father. I was already highly susceptible to that family dynamic, and I picked just the right man to help me re-create it in a more socially acceptable manner. That dashing man who my mother thought would take care of her, give her more than she had, and make her more than she was? I married him, too.

Gordon and I spoke frequently over the course of my writing this book. Our remembrances of various events and our discussions of our years together served in some ways as the couples therapy we should have pursued at difficult times in our marriage. Many times after our divorce, when he and I belatedly tried to sort through what had happened, what we *had allowed* to happen, he would say: "You never had a chance; you walked into the middle of a movie set. I was blind to your struggles." His blindness, he said, applied both in terms of the university and in terms of the other focus of his life, Rebekah. Elizabeth and he had grown up and into the presidency and parenthood together. I was, he said, "a stranger to both roles"—in the first, a novice actor who'd been tossed onto center stage without a script; in the second, an interloper.

He is partly right, but not completely so. I had many chances and choices. But coulda, woulda, shoulda will only make you crazy.

***

Rebekah's husband, Allan, died in July 2008 from a head injury he sustained in a moped accident. She was riding with him and was also seriously injured. The last time I saw her was in the receiving line at Allan's funeral. Her blue eyes were slate gray and blank. She has since recovered, has become an obstetrician-gynecologist on the faculty of Louisiana State University, and is remarried with three small stepchildren.

I received a note from Rebekah last December. With the exception of Allan's funeral, it was our first contact in over five years—since the awful Christmas of 2006. Rebekah wrote that she had "a new sense of the difficult side" of being a stepmom, and "a new perspective on how you must have also felt at times." She also said that she "would love to reconnect sometime." I immediately wrote her back. Perhaps, one day, we can rebuild that bridge we set aflame.

***

Tinnitus and aural pressure are always with me, and they can change in intensity from moment to moment. My Ménière's symptoms come and go, but they have lessened markedly in intensity and duration. When I have a bad bout, I take a toke and lie down until I feel better. I'm learning not to be so hard on myself—and with that life lesson, not to be so hard on others. I make a point to inhabit the "can" rather than the "can't" with regard to my hearing and balance. I give thanks everyday for what I can hear out of my right ear, as opposed to lamenting what I cannot hear out of my left. When my balance is steady, I do a little Snoopy dance. I am fortunate to get to do lots of Snoopy dances these days—most defiantly, around my living room in my skivvies to high-volume rock 'n' roll. There is a definite upside to *not* having a house staff.

***

I resigned from Vanderbilt at the close of the 2010 fall semester, finally emerged from the water, and found my towel. That's when I decided to begin making preparations to move to Westport, back into what is now my house.

My dog, Rasta, and I will leave for Westport this fall. A friend of mine says, "We'll all go under eventually. The measure of a person is how far you are from the shore." I'm ready to wade back into the water.

I will miss Nashville because I now have many true friends here. I've got my towel in my knapsack, along with my toothbrush, laptop, a tin of dog biscuits, a rubber ball, my favorite cowboy boots, and all of Cowboy Jack Clement's CDs. If we need anything else, I'm hoping a kindhearted strag will lend it to us.

Afterword

PEOPLE OFTEN ASK ME WHY I didn't speak up on behalf of medical marijuana when the *Wall Street Journal* article came out. The truth is, when I was married to Gordon I didn't want to do anything that might further harm our relationship. I understood that in order to make a strong case for the support of medical marijuana, I would have to take a very public and very controversial stance. That was something I simply couldn't justify at the time. Setting the record straight would ultimately have been about saving my face, not saving Gordon's. Even though I was hurting, my marriage was far more important to me than the public's opinion of my "recreational habit."

There were also, of course, the legal ramifications. One Vanderbilt official had threatened a front-page-news exposé featuring me being led out of Braeburn in handcuffs for all to see. Not exactly a scenario I wanted to court.

Even within the pro-legalization community, there were people who questioned my exemption from prosecution. I had been spared from more dire measures, it was rightly pointed out, because of my social position. A single, inch-long roach was the only physical evidence of my crime—evidence that defense attorneys could have challenged with regard to the means by which it had been obtained. Of course, I had straight-out told the residence manager that I had "smoked a little pot," and then later I had readily admitted my use of marijuana to the university's general counsel. Both were stupid mistakes. If I'd had my corporate wits about me, I should have had "no comment" or, smarter yet, flat-out denied the "allegation." That is what 99.9 percent of our politicians and industry leaders would have done.

While all of that still stands true, part of me really regrets not having taken a public stand for the legalization of medical marijuana at the time. It has taken me six years to find the confidence and nerve to speak out. In April 2012 I testified before the Tennessee House of Representatives in support of House Bill 294, the Safe Access to Medical Cannabis Act. I did so alongside John Donovan, a very brave young man who was diagnosed with juvenile rheumatoid arthritis when he was sixteen. Within a few months of his diagnosis, John could barely walk and spent most of his time in bed or languishing on the sofa in excruciating pain. He credits marijuana with his ability to walk (although he does so with a pronounced limp) and with keeping the pain manageable. Medical studies have shown that cannabidiol (CBD) and tetrahydrocannabinol (THC)—the psychoactive ingredient of cannabis—are potent anti-inflammatory agents and that CBD actually blocks the progression of rheumatoid arthritis and lessens its symptoms.[1] (CBD also inhibits cancer cell growth.)

Cannabis is enormously useful for a wide variety of medical conditions. For those afflicted with severe and ongoing nausea, it can be a godsend. It was for me. Thousands of Americans have been arrested and prosecuted for availing themselves of marijuana's soothing effects while suffering with cancer, multiple sclerosis, rheumatoid arthritis, HIV, and numerous other chronic and fatal diseases—diseases made at least a little, sometimes a lot, less devastating by the simple act of smoking cannabis.

***

Amid all the slander being thrown around town and campus, in the news, and over the Internet, very few people bothered to look into the nature of my "inner-ear ailment." It was to the *Tennessean*'s credit that it ran the lengthy and informative article about Ménière's disease, even if the opinion of the only physician quoted probably did me more harm than good. When I was contacted by the *Tennessean* reporter after the publication of the *Wall Street Journal* article, I directed him to Washington University's Ménière's website to learn more about the disease. Unfortunately his contact, Dr. Timothy Hullar, an assistant professor at the Washington University School of Medicine in St. Louis, said he "never heard of anyone using medical marijuana to treat symptoms of Ménière's." He went on to say, "There are a whole lot of other ways to treat it, lowering salt intake, taking water pills, many other things—I can't imagine going to the extreme of marijuana."[2]

The *Tennessean* article also noted that "a handful of pro-marijuana Internet sites do link medical marijuana to Ménière's." The fact remains that Dr. Hullar wasn't the only physician to balk at marijuana's value to Ménière's treatment—many others did and still do.

I emailed Dr. Hullar in August 2010 to inquire whether, in the four years since making his statement to the *Tennessean*, he had heard of any Ménière's patients "going to the extreme" of using cannabis for relief from nausea. He responded promptly, making the point that he had not meant "to indicate that marijuana isn't useful for Ménière's-related nausea." His concern, he elaborated, was that

> it probably acts solely on the symptoms of nausea and not on the underlying cause of the dizziness. . . . With MM [medical marijuana] taking care of the symptoms, a patient may take the (drastic?) step of giving up on other treatments that address the underlying problem. . . . I also worry about the possibility of a dizzy patient who self-diagnoses with Meniere's and uses MM until his or her face is paralyzed from the growing vestibular schwannoma that had been causing the symptoms in the first place.[3]

During a telephone conversation following our email exchange, Hullar explained that he had originally used the word "extreme" because he considered resorting to an illegal drug to be an extreme act. He continued to maintain, however, that he had never had a patient tell him that he or she had used marijuana. He also did not know of any physicians who prescribed it for relief from Ménière's-related nausea. "It is not part of the standard repertoire," he said.

O'Shaughnessy's, a journal published by the California Cannabis Research Medical Group, had specifically addressed Hullar's remarks in its Winter/Spring 2007 issue. I read him the following passage:

> Knowledgeable California doctors routinely approve the use of cannabis by Meniere's patients who say that it helps ease their symptoms. "Meniere's causes dizziness, dizziness causes nausea, cannabis relieves nausea," says David Bearman, MD. "I wouldn't be surprised if the symptoms caused Mrs. Gee to be a little depressed—and of course cannabis helps that, too."
>
> Robert Sullivan, MD, corroborates: "I've issued many [cannabis] recommendations for Meniere's, as well as tinnitus [ringing in the ears]. It works well enough to make a significant improvement in patient's lives, i.e., symptoms not gone but much abated so they can function and carry on their daily activities, instead of sitting and suffering."
>
> R. Stephen Ellis, MD, of San Francisco, has given some thought to how cannabis might help in the treatment of Meniere's. "Three possible mechanisms come to mind," he says. "Number one, the anti-anxiety effect of cannabis would be very useful to a Meniere's patient. These people are as anxious as can be when they hit the ER. When they get an attack, it's as if they are wired—that's why Ativan is one of the treatments, to bring them down. Two would be the anti-nausea effect. The third is slowing down the vertigo itself—the sensation of spinning caused by the inner ear problem."[4]

"What do you think about these remarks?" I asked Dr. Hullar. He was unmoved in his opinion.

A "vestibular schwannoma," by the way, is a rare, slow-growing, benign tumor that can cause facial paralysis and deafness if left unchecked. The vast majority of Ménière's sufferers are *not* inflicted with vestibular schwannomas. It would seem that Dr.

Hullar's concerns over the use of "MM" to fight nausea are based primarily on the "drastic" step of a patient ceasing other prescribed Ménière's treatments and on the highly unlikely possibility of a vestibular schwannoma. This extreme way of thinking about marijuana—medical and recreational—characterizes our nation's patchwork of related legislation, not to mention the stubbornly self-imposed ignorance and, frankly, cowardice of much of the medical community.

Hundreds of thousands of people die each year in the United States from alcohol poisoning and diseases related directly to alcohol and tobacco use. The Centers for Disease Control and Prevention (CDC) has reported an enormous rise in the nonmedical use of prescription and over-the-counter drugs. According to CDC statistics, emergency room visits for overdoses of opioid painkillers jumped from 144,600 in 2004 to 305,900 in 2008. Overdoses of benzodiazepines—antianxiety drugs, including Xanax and Valium, both of which I had multiple prescriptions for—rose from 143,500 to 271,700 in the same time period.[5] The Substance Abuse and Mental Health Service Administration (SAMHSA) reported 1.2 million emergency room visits involving overdoses of pharmaceutical drugs in 2009. The CDC estimated that twelve million Americans used prescription painkillers nonmedically in 2010.[6] Kevin A. Sabet, a former senior adviser in the White House Office of National Drug Control Policy, reports: "Drug overdoses have increased almost six-fold in the last 30 years. They now represent the leading cause of accidental death in the United States, having overtaken motor vehicle accidents for the first time on record."[7]

It is almost impossible to find any information on emergency room visits certifying marijuana overdose. I spent days searching the Internet. I emailed the CDC and SAMHSA numerous times requesting assistance in locating information on confirmed overdoses of marijuana. I downloaded and combed through scores of pages of statistical data suggested by the CDC and SAMHSA website inquiry departments.

It is important to note that just because I have been unable to locate this information does not mean it does not exist. Its scarcity and inaccessibility do suggest, however, that marijuana overdose among Americans is not a grave governmental or medical concern. On the other hand, statistical data and annotated reports on certified alcohol poisoning, prescription drug overdose, and overdose from illegal drugs such as cocaine, heroin, and methamphetamine are easy to come by.

I should note that I was not searching for emergency room visits where THC was found in a person's system *along with* large quantities of alcohol or other drugs. My search was for reliable data on how many people have been admitted to emergency rooms for overconsumption of marijuana *alone*. I have no doubt that there must be those who smoke or ingest too much cannabis and end up in an emergency room, more likely than not, from cannabis that has been laced with another, more dangerous, drug. This is—or at least ought to be—a significant public concern when a widely used substance is unregulated and provided largely through a wildly profitable and violently dangerous black market. More than ten thousand people died from drinking denatured alcohol during this country's thirteen-year, spectacularly unsuccessful experiment with alcohol prohibition.

While any substance can be abused, cannabis is far less likely to cause real harm than tobacco, alcohol, and prescription drugs. A World Health Organization study on the health implications of cannabis states: "The acute toxicity of cannabis is very low. *There are no confirmed cases of human deaths from cannabis poisoning in the world medical literature*" (italics mine).[8] Although the report cautions that one should not be complacent with regard to heavy daily use of cannabis, it concludes, "On patterns of existing use, cannabis poses a much less serious public health problem than is currently posed by alcohol and tobacco in Western societies."

The fact is that a person who has smoked a lot of marijuana would as likely die of choking on her "munchies"-induced tenth chocolate chip cookie as from an overdose of untainted cannabis itself. This is not to say that a person can't feel as if she has inadvertently consumed more cannabis than she ought to have. This has only happened to me, however, on the rare occasions when I have *ingested* marijuana. At two different times in my life I ate what I thought was a very small amount only to realize an hour later that I was uncomfortable with the effect. This not uncommon reaction to ingested cannabis is why many medical and recreational marijuana users much prefer to smoke it. The effects are almost immediate when you inhale it, which makes it far easier to gauge the proper dosage.

I wasn't looking for a party when I used marijuana to tamp down nausea and anxiety. I was doing my best to *approximate normal*. I simply wanted to feel well enough to do the things most of us usually take for granted, such as eat and get a little exercise and fresh air. I think I can speak for most medical cannabis patients when I say that we would welcome having the guesswork taken out of our dosage calculations through quality and potency controls and regulation.

Over $40 billion was spent in 2010 alone by federal, state, and local governments on America's "War on Drugs"—otherwise known across the land as our *spectacularly unsuccessful experiment with drug prohibition*. The FBI reported 1,663,582 arrests for drug law offenses in 2009—858,408 of which were for cannabis violations. Of those arrested for cannabis violations, 89 percent were charged with simple possession only, and almost always for having less than one ounce.[9] A recent study conducted by the Harvard University economist Jeffery A. Miron reported that US citizens spend $113 billion annually on black market marijuana. Legalizing marijuana would save approximately $8.7 billion annually in prohibition enforcement expenditures, while generating about the same amount in tax revenue.[10]

The Safe Access to Medical Cannabis Act failed to make it out of committee in the Republican-dominated Tennessee Legislature—just as it had the year before and the year before that. It may fail again next year, but we will not give up. One day this country will look back in disgust at the barbarism of denying those in pain and misery this simple, effective, and inexpensive medicine. It's time to legalize, regulate, and tax marijuana for medical and recreational purposes.

Notes

Chapter 1

1. Roy Blount Jr., "Bringing in the Sheaves," in *Long Time Leaving: Dispatches from Up South* (New York: Alfred A. Knopf, 2007), 3.

Chapter 2

1. Jim Lasley, "Black Students Seek Answers," *Daily Times-News* (Burlington, NC), 16 May 1969.
2. "Thirty-Three Years Ago," *Alamance News (Graham, NC)*, 23 May 2002.
3. Jim Lasley, "Black Youth Killed in Night of Violence," *Daily Times-News* (Burlington, NC), 17 May 1969.
4. Charlie Frago, "Violence of 1969 Still Haunts Victim's Family," *News & Record* (Greensboro, NC), 20 May 2001.
5. *Burlington: A City Divided*, dir. Daniel Koehler, Elon University, 2010.
6. "Who Killed Leon Mebane?," *Alamance News* (Graham, NC), 30 May 2002.

Chapter 5

1. Margaret Atwood, *Oryx and Crake* (New York: Doubleday, 2003), 119–20.

Chapter 8

1. Amy Wallace, "Panel Said to Back Outsider for Top UC Post," *Los Angeles Times*, 18 June 1995.

2. Amy Wallace, "Regents, Nominee Face Hard Choice," *Los Angeles Times*, 20 June 1995.
3. Ibid.
4. Herb Caen, "His Royal Dottiness," *San Francisco Chronicle*, 21 June 1995.
5. Pamela Burdman, "UC Nominee Gave Secret Bonuses; Controversial Deals While in Colorado," *San Francisco Chronicle*, 21 June 1995.
6. Ibid.
7. Ibid.
8. Pamela Burdman, "Lawmakers Troubled by UC Choice; They Want Probe of Deals by Presidential Candidate," *San Francisco Chronicle*, 22 June 1995.
9. Amy Wallace, "Top Choice to Lead UC System Declines Post," *Los Angeles Times*, 23 June 1995.
10. Ibid.

Chapter 12
1. "A Week in February," Editorial, *Brown Alumni Monthly*, March 2000.
2. Ibid.
3. Jerry E. Patterson, *The Vanderbilts* (New York: Harry N. Abrams, 1989), 16, 53.
4. Burton I. Samors, "Bilt, as in Gilt," Letter to the Editor, *Providence Journal*, 21 February 2000.
5. Jodi Wilgoren, "President Stuns Brown U. by Leaving to Be Vanderbilt Chancellor, *New York Times*, 8 February 2000.
6. D. Morgan McVicar, "Brown: Gee Broke 'Commitment,'" *Providence Journal*, 9 February 2000.
7. Ibid.
8. Ibid.
9. "A Week in February."
10. McVicar, "Brown: Gee Broke 'Commitment.'"
11. "Carrying the Mail," Letter to the Editor, *Brown Alumni Monthly*, April 2000.
12. Richard Walton, "Good Riddance to E. Gordon Gee," Letter to the Editor, *Providence Journal*, 19 February 2000.

Chapter 13
1. Margaret Mitchell, *Gone with the Wind* (New York: Macmillan, 1936), 175.

Chapter 14
1. "Art Not for Sale," Editorial, *Vanderbilt Hustler*, 7 April 2000.
2. Edward Stoner, "VU Art to Be Showcased in Gee Home," *Vanderbilt Hustler*, 7 April 2000.

Chapter 15
1. John Noble Wilford, "Splendid Maya Palace Is Found Hidden in Jungle," *New York Times*, 8 September 2000.
2. David F. Salisbury, "Lost Kingdom Rediscovered," *Vanderbilt Magazine*, Winter/Spring 2001, 24.
3. Ibid., 25.

Chapter 16
1. Thomas Jones (1892–1969).
2. Daniel Golden, "In Effort to Lift Their Rankings, Colleges Recruit Jewish Students," *Wall Street Journal*, 6 May 2002.
3. Ibid.
4. Ibid.
5. Jeff Woodhead, "Vandy's Name Changing Spree," *The Slant*, 9 October 2002, 5. Reprinted by permission.
6. Scott Jaschik, "Confederates Defeat Vanderbilt," *Inside Higher Education*, 5 May 2005, *www.insidehighered.com*.
7. *Yale Herald*, "Residential Colleges: Not Just Dorms, but Microcosms of Yale's Community," *www.yaleherald.com*.
8. Mark Bechtel, "The Vanderbilt Experiment," *Sports Illustrated*, 22 September 2003, 17.
9. Ibid.

Chapter 17
1. "SEC Sues Dollar General Corporation and Five Individuals for Accounting Fraud," *SEC News Digest*, 7 April 2005, *www.sec. gov*.
2. William Hinton, "Company Man," *Nashville Scene*, 6 October 2005, *www.nashvillescene.com*.

3. Ibid.
4. Ibid.
5. David A. Fox, "Cal Turner Jr. Awarded $800,000 Cash Bonus for Scandal-Plagued 2001," *nashvillepost.com*, 3 May 2002.
6. Dollar General Corporation Quarterly Report, 30 June 2002, 10.
7. Fox, "Cal Turner Jr. Awarded $800,000."
8. Author interview with Gordon Gee, 10 February 2010 and 25 April 2011.

Chapter 18
1. Roger Abramson, "Deep Pockets," *Nashville Scene*, 22 April 2004.

Chapter 19
1. Matt Pulle, "Flag Down on Play," *Nashville Scene*, 25 November 2004.
2. Elizabeth D. Gee, *The Light around the Dark* (New York: National League for Nursing Press, 1992), 1–2.
3. Ibid., 53.
4. Ibid., 80.

Chapter 21
1. David S. Haynes, Robert F. Labadie, and Kenneth E. Watford, "Meniere's Disease," patient bulletin, Vanderbilt University Medical Center, 20 November 2003, 3.
2. Ibid.
3. The Otology Group, "A Discussion of Meniere's Disease," *The Meniere's Network* (1989), 23.
4. Email from author, 8 May 2005.

Chapter 22
1. Letter from Vanderbilt Board of Trust to author, 28 October 2005.
2. Letter from author to Vanderbilt Board of Trust, 1 November 2005.
3. Faith Wilding, from *By Our Own Hands* (1977), *womanhouse.refugia.net*.

Chapter 23

1. Larry Brinton, "Wall Street Journal Questions Vandy's Spending," *Word on the Street* commentary, *wsmv.com*, 31 July 2006.
2. Joann S. Lublin and Daniel Golden, "Vanderbilt Reins In Lavish Spending by Star Chancellor," *Wall Street Journal*, 26 September 2006.
3. Ibid.
4. Ibid.
5. Ibid.
6. Ibid.
7. Ibid.
8. Ibid.
9. Ibid.
10. Michael Janofsky, "American University Chief Is Investigated over Spending," *New York Times*, 23 September 2005.
11. Ibid.
12. Lublin and Golden, "Vanderbilt Reins In Lavish Spending."
13. Ibid.
14. Ibid.
15. Ralph Loos, "Vandy Shrugs Off Gee Revelations," *Tennessean* (Nashville), 27 September 2006.
16. Ralph Loos, "Constance Gee Picks Her Battles," *Tennessean* (Nashville), 1 October 2006.
17. "Marijuana Issue Hits Home," Editorial, *Tennessean* (Nashville), 1 October 2006.
18. Loos, "Constance Gee Picks Her Battles."
19. Lublin and Golden, "Vanderbilt Reins In Lavish Spending."
20. Letter from Vanderbilt Board of Trust to author, 7 December 2006.

Chapter 24

1. Letter from author to Vanderbilt Board of Trust, 1 January 2007.
2. Letter from David Williams, on behalf of Vanderbilt Board of Trust, to author's attorney, 16 February 2007.
3. Letter from David Williams, on behalf of Vanderbilt Board of Trust, to author's attorney, 21 February 2007.

4. E. Thomas Wood and Walker Duncan, "Vanderbilt Chancellor Gee and Wife Agree on Divorce," *nashvillepost.com*, 28 February 2007.

5. Allison Smith, "Students Begin to Respond to Gees' Divorce Announcement," *insidevandy.com*, 1 March 2007. Reprinted by permission.

Chapter 25

1. *Nashville Today*, 14 June 2007.

2. Ralph Loos, "Gee Says No to Ohio State Offer," *Tennessean* (Nashville), 26 June 2007.

3. Corey Spring, "Livin' in Cowtown," *Tennessean* (Nashville), 11 July 2007, *uweekly.com*.

4. Paul Fain, "The View from the Top: E. Gordon Gee Goes Public," *Chronicle of Higher Education*, 16 November 2007.

5. Jonathan D. Glater, "More College Presidents in Million-Dollar Club," *New York Times*, 12 November 2007.

6. E. Thomas Wood, "Annual College Heads' Comp Poll Has Gee in 4th Place," 12 November 2007, *nashvillepost.com*.

7. "Presidents Earn Degree in Ka-Ching," *Tennessean* (Nashville), 13 November 2007.

8. Encarnacion Pyle, "It Starts with Me," *Columbus Dispatch*, 8 June 2008.

9. Katherine Harben, "Fundraising and Friend Raising," *At Home in Columbus*, June/July 2008, 14–20.

10. Pyle, "It Starts with Me."

11. Douglas Adams, *The Hitchhiker's Guide to the Galaxy* (New York: Harmony Books, 1979), 27.

12. Ibid., 28.

Afterword

1. Anita Gonzales, "Rheumatoid Arthritis, Cannabis Based Medicine Eases Pain and Suppresses Disease," Medical News Today, MediLexicon Intl., 11 November 2005, *www.medicalnewstoday.com*.

2. Ralph Loos, "Vandy Shrugs Off Gee Revelations," *Tennessean* (Nashville), 27 September 2006.

3. Timothy Hullar, personal correspondence, 28 August 2010.
4. Fred Gardner, "Note from the Managing Editor," Commentary, *O'Shaughnessy's*, Winter/Spring 2007, 2, 22. Reprinted by permission.
5. Roni Caryn Rabin, "Sharp Rise in Abuse of Legal Drugs," *New York Times*, 22 June 2010.
6. Centers for Disease Control and Prevention, "Policy Impact: Prescription Painkiller Overdoses," 19 December 2011, *www.cdc.gov*.
7. Kevin A. Sabet, "Overdosing on Extremism," *New York Times*, Sunday Review, 1 January 2012.
8. Wayne Hall et al., "World Health Organization Project on Health Implications of Cannabis Use: A Comparative Appraisal of the Health and Psychological Consequences of Alcohol, Cannabis, Nicotine and Opiate Use," 28 August 1995, *www.drug library.org*.
9. Available at *www.drugsense.org*.
10. Jeffrey A. Miron and Katherine Waldock, "The Budgetary Impact of Ending Drug Prohibition," Cato Institute, 27 September 2010.

CPSIA information can be obtained at www.ICGtesting.com
Printed in the USA
LVOW131404150513

333949LV00001B/8/P

9 781457 513657